Academic Transformation

THE ROAD TO COLLEGE SUCCESS

De Sellers
Cerridwen, Inc.

Carol W. Dochen
Texas State University–San Marcos

Russ Hodges
Texas State University–San Marcos

PEARSON
Prentice Hall

Upper Saddle River, New Jersey
Columbus, Ohio

Library of Congress Cataloging-in-Publication Data

Sellers, De.
   Academic transformation: the road to college success / De Sellers, Carol W. Dochen, Russ
Hodges.
      p. cm.
   Includes bibliographical references and index.
   ISBN 0-13-048615-9
   1. Study skills. 2. Learning, Psychology of. 3. Academic achievement. 4. College student
orientation. I. Dochen, Carol. II. Hodges, Russ. III. Title.

   LB2395.S45 2005
   378.1'7028'1--dc22   2004016712

Vice President and Publisher: Jeffery W. Johnston
Senior Acquisitions Editor: Sande Johnson
Assistant Editor: Erin Anderson
Production Editor: Holcomb Hathaway
Design Coordinator: Diane C. Lorenzo
Cover Designer: Ali Mohrman
Cover Photo: Getty One
Production Manager: Pamela D. Bennett
Director of Marketing: Ann Castel Davis
Marketing Manager: Amy Judd
Compositor: Carlisle Communications, Ltd.
Cover Printer: Phoenix Color Corp.
Printer/Binder: Phoenix Book Tech

> *We dedicate this book to our past,
> present, and future students.*

Pearson Prentice Hall™ is a trademark of Pearson Education, Inc.
Pearson® is a registered trademark of Pearson plc
Prentice Hall® is a registered trademark of Pearson Education, Inc.

Pearson Education Ltd.   Pearson Education Canada, Ltd.
Pearson Education Australia Pty. Limited   Pearson Educación de Mexico, S.A. de C.V.
Pearson Education Singapore Pte. Ltd.   Pearson Education Japan
Pearson Education North Asia Ltd.   Pearson Education Malaysia Pte. Ltd.

10 9 8 7 6 5 4 3 2 1
ISBN 0-13-048615-9

Contents

3   Loading Up on Strategies for Learning Excellence   45

A Call to Arms!

4   Learning, Knowledge, and Intellectual Performance   81

I Think, Ergo I Learn.

5   Investing in Our College Lives   105
I'm Trying Not to Overdraft.

8 Establishing Direction in Your Life   193
The Promised Land.

9 Making Behaviors Work for You   223
Walking the Academic Tightrope.

10   Appropriate Stress Reduction Techniques   263

AAUUUGH *%^$#&!@ (I Feel Much Better Now.)

11 Neural Development, Attending, and Understanding   291

My, What Nice Frontal Lobes You Have.

12   **Storing, Retrieving, and Achieving Maximum Performance   319**

Lights, Camera, Action!

Preface

More than three decades ago, I walked to the other side of the desk and began teaching. The classroom had always been my arena of competition, and I was routinely successful as a student. If I ever gave any thought to other students who were not as successful as I, I just assumed they were lazy. It was not until I began to teach that I noticed many of my students tried to learn but failed nonetheless.

Suddenly, teaching was not as easy as I had assumed it would be. It was not simply a matter of presenting content. Each day during that first year of teaching brought questions. Was I teaching if they did not learn? Why was learning difficult for some students? Why was it so easy for me? The questions continued to pour in. Clearly, many of my students were intelligent, and I could witness their effort, but why did they often struggle to learn? What was the cause? It would have been simple to retreat to the ivory tower and proclaim that their high school preparation was poor, that they just didn't try hard enough, that not everyone could benefit from a higher education.

Instead, I started to ask real questions. How do we learn academically? Could anyone learn more effectively? The journey that started so long ago led me back to graduate school, then on to decades of teaching, and now to this text. Along the way, I have been blessed with dynamic and innovative colleagues, challenging and adventurous students, honest teachers, and administrators who knew when to turn a blind eye to daringly experimental programs.

My seemingly simple questions came to have complicated answers. My colleagues and I searched in numerous fields, unearthing both theoretical and research answers. Over the decades, we have been part of this new field of developmental education. Developmental education has emerged in response to the needs of thousands of American students who want to be more successful academically and to the desires of institutions that want these students to succeed.

This text is the amalgamation of our experiences. These are the concepts and practices based in theory and research that help our students reach their academic goals. These concepts and practices are rooted in the ideal of an autonomous student, a person fully equipped to meet the learning challenges in academics as well as the work world.

De Sellers

IN THIS EDITION

We begin this book by introducing the concept of academic transformation and seven principles for becoming an autonomous learner. Chapter 2 focuses on academic motivation, and we propose our own theoretical model along with strategies for increasing and maintaining motivation. Chapter 3 covers practical study strategies to help students get organized, learn and apply different methods of taking notes, and comprehend college-level reading assignments. In Chapter 4, we explore the concept of academic learning through types of knowledge (i.e., declarative, procedural, metacognitive) and levels of intellectual performance using the recently revised Bloom's Taxonomy (cognitive domain). Chapter 5 completes our general review and application of academic success research, focusing on expert and novice learning and levels of commitment and involvement. In Chapters 6 and 7, we take a more introspective approach to learning as we explore the stages of development (i.e., personal and intellectual) that humans share, followed by research and discussion on talents, will, and preferences that make us unique individuals. Our bias about the important impact of self-regulation on student success is reflected in our devoting three chapters to this topic. We cover attaining achievable goals, reducing procrastination, and increasing timeliness in Chapter 8; we discuss our stage model of self-regulatory ability, key routines, time management, and balancing our lives in Chapter 9; and we conclude with stress management and reducing academic anxieties in Chapter 10. The last two chapters of the book are dedicated to achieving academic goals through successful performance. Chapter 11 focuses on neural development, different approaches to learning (i.e., surface, deep, achievement), and strategies for improving attending and understanding. In Chapter 12, we explore the role of critical thinking in study, learning through storage and retrieval, and conclude with a review of techniques to improve test-taking and other academic performance.

ACKNOWLEDGMENTS

We have relied on many people to help us through the lengthy, complicated process of publishing our first book:

- Steve Beebe, our colleague at Texas State, who mentored us while we outlined our ideas and drafted a proposal that would appeal to prestigious publishers, and continued to cheer us on month after month as we wrote

- Tobin Quereau, our colleague at Austin Community College, who provided us with the community college perspective as well as comments on initial drafts of the first several chapters

- Ron Brown, dean of University College at Texas State, for understanding and supporting the need to maintain a regular off-campus writing schedule until project completion

- Kathryn Lee, a valued colleague at Texas State, for generously sharing her learning framework course materials and creative ideas

- Graduate students Rich Parsells, for providing exercise ideas and end-of-chapter materials for the entire book, and Chris Costello, for providing examples of student work in Chapter 3

- The Student Learning Assistance Center staff at Texas State, for providing edited examples of student work for Chapter 12 (Audrie Cruz, Lesley Lawrence, Zhongling Liu, Cecilia Reyes, Elizabeth Sebald, Brandon Silberman); designing figures and visual/graphic organizers and providing extensive technical support (Lisa Whittaker and Kevin Dunaway); editing and formatting (Rene LeBlanc); proofing (Harry Zambrana); and keeping the learning center running smoothly while their director was coauthoring this book (James Mathews, Donna Joy)

- Our friends and family members: John McVey, for his creativity with the table of contents and the postscript, and his willingness and talent to help us clarify our thoughts when we got lost (more than once) in the writing process; Drew Johnson, for his illustration in Chapter 11; Kerrie and Daniel Dochen, for providing years of inspiration and keeping us in touch with today's teenagers and college students; and Bob Patterson, for continuous support of this project by graciously housing our entire operation in his and De's home and keeping us well fed during the last 18 months

- Patty Knox, administrative assistant extraordinaire, whose impeccable organizational skills, attention to detail, unwavering patience, and sense of humor in the face of several unforeseen obstacles and challenges ensured that this book actually became a reality

- Our reviewers, who offered constructive suggestions: Diane Eisenberg, California State University, Long Beach City College; Jeanne L. Higbee, University of Minnesota; Jo Ann Lewis, University of Louisiana at Monroe; Joel McGee, Texas A&M University; Susan M. Perlis, Marywood University; Tobin Quereau, Austin Community College; and Gretchen Starks-Martin, St. Cloud State University

De Sellers
Carol Dochen
Russ Hodges

About the Authors

 **Dr. De Sellers** began one of the earliest cognitive-based learning skills course for college students in the U.S. in 1973 at Texas State University–San Marcos, incorporating both the emerging theory and the research-based practice from subdisciplines in psychology and educational psychology into the course. She continued to teach the course for more than 25 years before retiring. Some of her administrative posts included Dean of the College of General Studies, Director of the Student Learning Assistance Center, and Director of the International Office. She holds both an M.A. and a Ph.D. from the University of Texas at Austin, where she focused her studies on adult learners. De is now the president of Cerridwen, Inc., a consulting company for educational and psychological services.

 **Dr. Carol W. Dochen,** employed at Texas State University–San Marcos since 1979, is currently the Director of the Student Learning Assistance Center. She also teaches undergraduate courses in both the Department of Educational Administration and Psychological Services and in University College. Carol earned her Ph.D. in Higher Education Administration, with a minor in Educational Psychology, from the University of Texas at Austin. She is actively involved in state and national developmental education organizations and was a founding member of the annual statewide College Academic Support Programs conference. Carol is a frequent presenter at state and national conferences and received a College Academic Support Programs award for Outstanding Conference Institute. She has published in a variety of journals and books and has obtained grants to establish model Supplemental Instruction (SI) and Online Tutoring programs at Texas State.

 **Dr. Russ Hodges** has worked at Texas State University–San Marcos since 1986 and coordinates the university's learning framework course, EDP 1350, Effective Learning. Russ also teaches graduate courses in Developmental and Adult Education and in Education. Russ earned his Doctorate of Education, specializing in Developmental Education, from Grambling State University in Louisiana. He is currently president-elect of the College Reading and Learning Association (CRLA). He is a frequent presenter at state and national conferences and received the Award for Outstanding Article from the *Journal of Developmental Education* (Vol. 24) in 2002. He also received a College Academic Support Programs award for Outstanding Conference Institute.

1

The Road to Autonomous Learning

*I don't know where I'm going,
but I'm making good time.*

As twenty-first century Americans, we are experiencing an increasingly complex and challenging world. Each year more than 15 million of us choose higher education as a way to prepare ourselves for this ever-changing world. Yet many of us have conflicted emotions about our studies.

"Is it all about grades? I have to do well; a degree is my ticket to a good life."

"I try so hard, but then I blow it on the test."

"I do really well in a class if the teacher is interesting."

"I am always excited at the beginning of the term, but by the end I am just trying to survive."

"I know my future is on the line, but I just can't get motivated."

"My family has such high aspirations for me; I have to do well."

The American higher education system is the most accessible in the Western world, and many students are successful, but many drift away from college without finishing. This book is a guide to show you how to become the collegiate student you wish to become—how to academically transform yourself. If you are not quite the student you wish to be (or not nearly the student you wish to become), then open your mind and your heart to the messages herein. We are learners, too, both as students and as teachers, and we have walked these roads before. Come with us and we will show you what college learning is all about and how you can master it.

---

exercise 1.1

SELF-ASSESSMENT: My Openness to Academic Transformation

The first step in becoming an autonomous learner is to begin to assess your openness to the demands of college. With 5 being "Almost Always" and 1 being "Almost Never," assess your readiness for academic transformation. Rate each of the following statements honestly by circling the appropriate number. Completing this exercise will help you determine your readiness for beginning the transformation process.

	Almost Always		Sometimes		Almost Never
1. I am confident about my abilities to succeed in college.	5	4	3	2	1
2. I am open to change some of my academic behaviors and study habits.	5	4	3	2	1
3. I set realistic academic goals for myself.	5	4	3	2	1
4. I get personal satisfaction from completing my goals.	5	4	3	2	1
5. I am able to identify my academic strengths and weaknesses.	5	4	3	2	1
6. I seek help when I need it.	5	4	3	2	1
7. I accept suggestions from others.	5	4	3	2	1
8. I monitor my progress in my classes.	5	4	3	2	1
9. I have the self-discipline to manage my time wisely.	5	4	3	2	1

10.	I engage in difficult academic tasks without giving up too easily.	5	4	3	2	1
11.	I will do my best in all of my classes.	5	4	3	2	1
12.	I enjoy learning.	5	4	3	2	1

Add up the numbers circled. Your total score will be between 12 and 60. The higher your score, the more likely you are to be open to academic transformation. For total scores below 36, write or reflect on items for which you have concerns. Also, consider talking with a trusted friend, a family member, a teacher, or an advisor.

INTRODUCTION

What a joy to be human! We have harnessed the physical world; we can reflect on our feelings. We can understand important aspects of this world, including ourselves. We can change what we do and how we feel. We can achieve what we wish. The opposites are also true. Our humanness can be a burden. We can be ignorant of the world and ourselves. We can stay stuck in old ways of being and feeling. We can fail ourselves and others.

What makes the difference between these two possibilities? It is our basic nature to survive and to invent and to achieve and to change. It is the nature of humans to learn, but fear and laziness get in the way. Although learning is a basic skill, it must also be developed.

At the heart of the learning process is a mystery. Scientists are just beginning to know how our brains work. For tens of thousands of years, this extraordinary ability has been hidden from us. Now technology is opening a vision of mental functioning. Each day we are discovering more about how humans learn and change. We know we have learned something when we experience a change in our thoughts, feelings, or actions. Those changes are evidence that we have learned from experiencing new information or circumstances (Lefrançois, 2000). Thus, learning happens continually as we interact with all that is our environment.

One fact about being human is not a mystery—we can direct our thoughts and feelings and choose our actions. In other words, we have free will. We exercise that will within a societal framework of laws and cultural expectations. You may not feel very free at all, but in a real sense, you are. As authors and teachers, we believe your abilities to choose goals and behaviors are foundational to becoming a successful student. Certainly as a college student you have made the choice to pursue a program/profession. In every class you are free to learn or not. You choose what receives your attention and effort. You choose what you value.

The purpose and strategies of this text rest on your ability to choose (and to control) your thoughts and behaviors to reach carefully selected goals. We will share how you can increase your ability to evaluate your individual academic situation and plan and execute appropriate action. Becoming a competent student is an individual journey; each of us is a unique learner. Our term for this journey is *academic transformation.*

ACADEMIC TRANSFORMATION

Often we contemplate what it would be like to be different. Our fantasy lives are filled with images of success and acclaim, attractiveness and competence, pleasure and joy—all without effort or cost. The no-man's-land between fantasy and reality is a hard, barren place, but we want to share with you an oasis in that desert. It is possible for humans to transform themselves, in their thoughts, behaviors, and feelings. It is possible for us as students and teachers to transform ourselves, but we must choose carefully exactly how we want to change and what we want to become.

This text focuses on academic transformation, how to become the college student you wish to become, but the principles and strategies herein will be easily transferable to other areas of life. Our conviction is that truly successful college students are those who do more than make a good grade point average (GPA); they also have fulfilling personal and social lives, have a clear view of their future professions, develop their physical and spiritual lives, and participate in their communities. **Academic transformation** is *the process whereby college students carefully assess their current status as students, determine specific short- and long-term academic goals, chart changes necessary to reach those goals, and then make those changes.* Along the way, they must continually evaluate their progress and make the appropriate adjustments; even their long-term goals may change.

> ## THE SIX STEPS TO ACADEMIC TRANSFORMATION
>
> 1. Assess your current academic situation.
>
> 2. Set short- and long-term academic goals.
>
> 3. Create a plan of action to meet your goals.
>
> 4. Work to accomplish your goals.
>
> 5. Evaluate your progress.
>
> 6. Make adjustments as needed.

Throughout this text we will introduce you to the research, theories, and practices that form the foundation for the steps of academic transformation. This six-step process will become habitual because you will do it again and again.

You may already have strengths in certain areas, such as goal setting, and want to improve your ability in creating action plans. Conversely, you may have the motivation to work hard but have difficulty knowing the best methods of working to meet your goals. The exercises at the end of this chapter will help you begin to master this process. As you read each chapter and complete the exercises, you will increase your mastery.

---

exercise 1.2

Strengthening the Transformation

As a beginning exercise in using the six-step process of academic transformation, do the following:

1. Brainstorm a list of at least three outcomes you would like to accomplish within the next six months.

2. Give a very brief reason next to each item on your list.

3. From this list create one goal that you could accomplish within the next few months.

4. Set a plan of action (at least three strategies/specific behaviors) to help you complete this goal.

5. Design a method to track the chosen behaviors you are doing.

6. Evaluate your progress weekly for your goal.

7. Make changes and adjustments as needed after you evaluate your progress.

GETTING THE MOST FROM THIS BOOK

In this text, we focus primarily on one aspect of learning—collegiate learning. As teachers and students, we have come to understand that competency as a college student can be learned. We hope this text will support your work in college. Many of you may be enrolled in courses that foster your development as a college learner. These academic success courses have a long history in American higher education. They have many names, emerge from differing academic disciplines, and help diverse students. They foster students' abilities to monitor and regulate their own learning through the development of a perspective about themselves as learners. Theories from cognitive and behavioral psychology are deeply rooted in the course curriculum. This text flows from the traditions of this field, although we incorporate theories and strategies from other disciplines, such as personality theory, business, and philosophy.

We also use stories representative of the many students we have worked with over the years. Their stories explain and illustrate critical theories and strategies that can help you achieve academic success. The exercises scattered within each chapter and the journal questions at the end of each chapter give you specific opportunities to adapt the concepts to your own life.

How we begin a new enterprise matters, so we have thought deeply about how we should introduce you to the concepts and skills you need to accomplish your goals as a college student. As a result of our reflection, we begin with the exploration of values, goals, and motivation in the first two chapters. Then Chapter 3 gives essential strategies for classroom learning, including note-taking skills, and out-of-class learning, especially text-reading skills. Chapter 4 presents some basic theories about human and academic learning, and Chapter 5 provides evidence for a method of becoming a committed, successful student. In each chapter, we share the reasons underlying our choices. With each concept we provide specific, realistic suggestions that you can put into immediate use.

The next section, Chapters 6 and 7, investigates the two primary methods of understanding ourselves: how humans are alike and how humans are different. The more we understand ourselves, the better we can pursue transforming our thoughts, feelings, and actions to reach our goals. In the third section, "Self-Regulation," Chapters 8–10 build on those concepts to help us manage our behaviors so that we do not procrastinate, so that we minimize stress, and so that we are efficient. Then Chapters 11 and 12 explore numerous learning theories and strategies to help you build an array of skills to use in diverse academic settings.

One important skill in reading a collegiate text is to preview the territory before you read. We strongly suggest that you look over each chapter carefully and note the headings and the structure. Each chapter begins with topic headings, and at the end you will find a summary and reflection questions. After you read a section of the text, go back and mark the most important ideas, and then write your own ideas in the margins.

BECOMING AN AUTONOMOUS LEARNER

An important goal of any determined and ambitious college student is to become an autonomous learner. *Autonomous* is a word with rich connotations of independence, self-reliance, freedom, competence, and self-governance. Thus, when we become an autonomous or self-directed learner, we are competent in a wide variety of academic tasks. If we become autonomous learners in our undergraduate years, then we have an opportunity to move toward collaborative learning in our graduate studies and careers. We believe that there are seven characteristic competencies of an autonomous learner. As you read the following, evaluate how much of each competency you have already acquired.

Autonomous learners have a healthy view of themselves and their academic abilities. Separating fact from fantasy, reality from wishful thinking, about ourselves is a major psychological task as we move from adolescence to adulthood. An emotionally healthy and realistic self-esteem is foundational to the effort of reflection, evaluation, and acceptance of our own academic abilities.

Autonomous learners are ethical. A healthy self-awareness leads to a clear understanding of our own values and ethics. Simply believing in a principle is insufficient; living by our values and beliefs is essential to healthy self-esteem. When we are students, academics is our work. Academic honesty and integrity are important components of a successful college career, and they are the method by which we develop our system of professional ethics. If we cheat on college tests or papers, then we are likely to cheat at work.

Autonomous learners set realistic and appropriate goals for academic achievement. Few abilities are as crucial as that of setting realistic and appropriate goals for any endeavor, and academics is no exception to that premise. A goal can be as large as graduation or a semester GPA, or it can be as immediate as planning to study history for one hour tonight. To set realistic academic goals when you have other legitimate goals in your personal, family, social, work, and physical life is a difficult skill for some college students to master. Balance is the elusive goal for which we strive; the closer you get to balance, the closer you will come to the good life.

Autonomous learners understand their own learning strengths and weaknesses. To set realistic and effective academic goals, we must know our own learning strengths and weaknesses. For example, if I am a slow reader, then I have to allocate more uninterrupted time to my assignments than my roommate who is a skilled reader. Through accurate academic self-assessment, we can choose the best major, the best semester schedule, and the best learning strategies.

AUTONOMOUS LEARNER COMPETENCIES

- Holding healthy views of themselves and their academic abilities

- Behaving ethically

- Setting realistic and appropriate goals for academic achievement

- Understanding their learning strengths and weaknesses

- Using effective learning strategies and adapting those strategies to new situations

- Managing their behaviors to reach their goals

- Using appropriate resources

Autonomous learners use effective learning strategies and adapt those strategies to new situations. Hundreds of learning strategies are available for use, but choosing the most effective way to study a particular subject at a particular time is a skill acquired by reflection and practice. The common metaphor for this skill is a *toolbox,* a reference to the idea that a competent student creates a collection of strategies that she uses appropriately in different situations, depending on her goals, situation, and abilities. You can enhance and expand your current collection of strategies through the various ideas and examples in this textbook.

Autonomous learners manage their behaviors to reach their goals. Having appropriate goals and knowing the best strategies are meaningless unless we do the behaviors to learn. In other words, we have to work at being a student in a timely way. Procrastination and avoidance can destroy academic achievement, so we must learn how to control our own actions.

Autonomous learners use appropriate resources. Teachers, study groups, tutoring programs, library resources, other students, and many other resources exist for any course. Accessing those resources promptly is an important skill.

---

exercise 1.3

Are You an Autonomous Learner?

Answer each of the following questions and then write at least two specific examples to support each of your answers. This exercise will help you identify autonomous learner competencies and help you gain insight into competencies that you can work toward.

1. Do you hold positive views of yourself and your academic abilities?

   _____ Yes _____ No _____ Sometimes

   Examples:

2. Do you behave ethically when completing academic tasks?

   _____ Yes _____ No _____ Sometimes

   Examples:

3. Do you set realistic and appropriate goals for academic achievement?

   _____ Yes _____ No _____ Sometimes

   Examples:

4. Do you understand your learning strengths and weaknesses?

_____ Yes _____ No _____ Sometimes

Examples:

5. Do you use effective learning strategies?

_____ Yes _____ No _____ Sometimes

Examples:

6. Do you manage your behaviors to reach your academic goals?

_____ Yes _____ No _____ Sometimes

Examples:

7. Do you use appropriate academic resources?

_____ Yes _____ No _____ Sometimes

Examples:

A QUALITY WORLD

Humans are the only creatures who can imagine perfection but not attain it. Bookstores and magazine racks illustrate our yearning for perfection and for the control to attain it, but we are inherently imperfect. Are we ever smart enough, beautiful enough, good enough, fast enough, lovable enough, successful enough? The no-man's-land we all live in is in between our concept of perfection and our own state of imperfection. While "trying to be perfect is the most tragic human mistake" (Kurtz & Ketcham, 1992, p. 5), we are loathe to relinquish our ambitions and slide into inaction. Finding the balance between the ideal and the real is the focus of the remainder of this chapter.

As humans, we dream of the lives we want—relationships, accomplishments, values, and possessions. That vision is one we begin to create from birth. Glasser (1998) calls it our **quality world,** and each is unique to the individual. Each of us has mental pictures of "(1) the *people* we most want to be with, (2) the *things* we most want to own or experience, and (3) the *ideas* or systems of *belief* that govern much of our behavior" (p. 45). It holds our deepest values and feelings. It holds our

• • • ANNA • • •
A student finding her way in her quality world

Anna is beginning her second semester of college. Although she has had her share of surprises and disappointments about roommates, assignments, and professors, generally she is faring well. She is comfortable on campus and has begun to make genuine friendships, she goes home to see her parents only every five weeks or so, and she seems to have gracefully relinquished the relationships that had so dominated her last two years of high school. Academically, she has found her footing. She has had to change her study habits; now she studies every day. Her grades have stabilized at the C+ to B level, and she has begun serious inquiries about different majors. She plays intramural soccer and has started working 10 hours a week for the student center. She regularly participates in the student organization of her religious denomination. Anna's friends often verbalize that they envy how easily Anna seems to balance academics, friends, family, and other activities. When she hears her friends' comments, Anna feels puzzled, for she is just doing what seems comfortable and right to her. Why do her friends seem to struggle so? They are all talented; they have the same opportunities. Yet they fall prey to procrastination; their decisions often seem like reactions to immediate situations.

Anna and her friends do have much in common—they share background and abilities—but a closer look reveals a dramatic difference. Although she has her parents' support, Anna made a deliberate choice, on her own, to attend college. She has long had a goal of college graduation and professional status in the community. She does not know yet what that work will be, but she is very clear that she wants the knowledge and the credentials that are possible with a college degree. Early in her life, Anna understood that her concerted efforts were necessary if she wanted to achieve. In simple terms, she learned to work hard for what she wanted. She learned how to be a good friend, a competent student, a reliable worker. She had setbacks and bad times, as everyone does, but she persisted. Anna has carefully created a picture of who she wants to be, and she has tried diligently to match that picture. Anna's internal picture is much clearer and more realistic than those of her friends; thus, she can balance the complicated life of a student with greater ease. The internal pictures we create of the lives we want have powerful influences on how we live our lives.

hopes for the way we would like to live. Our quality world holds the best ways to satisfy one or more of our basic psychological needs—love/belonging, power, freedom, fun. It is the place where we would feel completely loved and protected. These are the concepts about which we care passionately. We look upon each new experience—person, thing, or idea—from the perspective of whether it contributes or detracts from our quality world. Does it move us closer to that world, or farther away?

Even though we move back and forth between the everyday external world and our quality world numerous times each day, it is rare when we conceptualize, or imagine, our quality world as a *world,* a place that holds the summation of our hopes and beliefs. Every time we think about the perfect mate, the grades we want, the job we desire, or any one of the dozens of attractive images that come to mind during the day, we are thinking about our quality world. When we experience hope about a relationship, excitement about an idea, or longing for a possession, we are shaping and reshaping our quality world.

Are our quality worlds healthy and good? Unfortunately, not always. An addict yearns for the next rush; the power hungry fantasize about exerting their control over others; the selfish long for love without having to love in return; the lazy look for accomplishment without effort; the greedy want more than their share; the cruel enjoy the pain of others. As we mature, self-reflection can help us ascertain how healthy and ethical our quality worlds are. However, self-reflection in isolation rarely works. We desperately need feedback from the people and systems we respect. We have to use that feedback, not simply accept it unconditionally. Our parents cannot design our quality world; neither can our teachers, preachers, politicians, or peers. It is our job, our responsibility, to build our quality world; it is, according to Glasser (1998), the core of our life, no one else's.

> ### ELEMENTS OF OUR QUALITY WORLD
>
> *Our deepest values and feelings.*
> *Hope for the way we would like to live.*
>
> | The people we most want to be with | The things we most want to own or experience | The ideas or systems of belief that govern much of our behavior |
> | --- | --- | --- |

Ironically, no one specifically tells us that we must build our own quality world; in fact, far too many people try to build it for us. College can be a brutal experience if our quality world is not congruent with, or does not match, the reality of that life. For example, one of Anna's friends, Jesse, goes to college at his parents' insistence.

· · · JESSE · · ·
A student searching for his place in his quality world

Jesse earned a football scholarship, an accomplishment that fulfilled his parents' dreams. They were excited that he was going to college, but even more thrilled that he would play football at the collegiate level. He accepted their vision without question and dreamed of athletic success. However, reality was shocking. He was no longer the star. As a freshman, he was not even a starter. Classes were more difficult than in high school, and he felt he had no time for himself. Academics were forced to a backseat as he strived to succeed on the team. Jesse grudgingly kept the vision of athletic success through two seasons, but he grew to understand that the quality world he wanted included academic as well as athletic achievement. Finally, at the end of his sophomore year, Jesse told his parents the truth. He was uncomfortable in the conflict between athletics and academics and ashamed of his grades. Jesse withdrew into himself the next summer and painfully pondered what he wanted in his life, now and in the future. Gradually, he came to the conclusion that he wanted a sense of freedom to explore new ideas and different types of people. His competitive spirit was still alive, but now it turned to the classroom. He wanted the ability to choose his own priorities, his own actions, his own direction. His quality world was forming as he thought about the college life he wanted to build. He chose to leave athletics and his scholarship, knowing that he would have to find a part-time job for financial support and take student loans to finish school. However, that choice gave him more study time and more energy to focus on academics.

Since our quality world drives so many of our fantasies, dreams, goals, and actions, a crucial decision that we make is whether we will ground it with a value system that is ethical, balanced, and wise. In this postmodern age in which diverse traditions and systems are honored, such a decision is complicated and difficult. One example is knowing where our rights end and the rights of others begin. For some of us, that boundary of self-esteem is treacherous. We either take advantage of others or allow them to take advantage of us. We may do too much for others and not expect them to do for us. Ethical, balanced, and wise quality worlds are the greatest guarantee that we have to build a good life.

Improving Our Quality World

As teachers for many years, we believe an important life skill is our ability to discern and improve our quality worlds. How should such discernment occur? What follows is one method, a series of reflective questions in four major arenas of life—relationships, work, faith, and service (see Figure 1.1).

FIGURE 1.1   The Four Major Arenas of Life

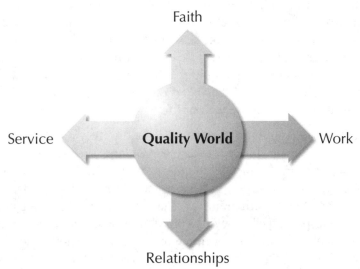

Faith

Service   **Quality World**   Work

Relationships

Relationships.   As humans, we are social creatures. Most of us place relationships at the core of our lives. A significant other, family members, friends, colleagues, roommates—these are the people with whom we share our lives. We laugh with them, fight with them, cry with them, celebrate with them, dream with them. There is a tie, a bond, among us. These are the people who know the truth about us, and they love and care for us. We know and do the same for them. Trust and safety are at the center of our quality relationships. What are the quality relationships in your life? How closely does the reality meet the dreams and hopes you have for relationships? Where are the differences? Are your visions of quality relationships healthy and hopeful? How do relationships give meaning and purpose to your life?

Work.   Across all cultures and all times, people work most of their lives. Work is a major avenue of deriving feelings of productiveness, a basic requirement of a healthy self-view. As a young child, you began working by going to school and learning. That was your job in your family, although you probably also had chores to do as well. School may still be your primary work, even if now you work at a part-time job that earns you a paycheck. On the other hand, school may take second or third place after family and your job. At this time in your life, you probably have several visions of work in your quality world. One is the vision of how you wish to be as a college student; in other words, what collegiate experiences do you wish to have? How will you perform collegiate work and what feelings will ensue from your efforts? What subsidiary role does other work play? Another vision is the one you hold of the work you are currently doing. A vision most of you carry is the work you will do after graduation. Remember Anna's clear vision of herself in a professional career. What is your vision of your working career? Where will it occur? What responsibilities will you have? What do you wish to achieve? How does work give meaning and purpose to your life?

Faith. All of us have faith; that is, we believe in something. Whether we believe in the sacred or the secular, order or chaos, atheism or religion, we all believe. It is our human nature to try to make sense of our existence. We rely on our families and our culture to help us find those explanations that fill our quality world. As we move from stage to stage in life, it is healthy to question those explanations. What are your beliefs? What values do you think are important? What beliefs give meaning and purpose to your life?

Service. A basic tenet of human behavior is that we rely on others as they rely on us. We are individuals, but we are also part of larger groups. Thus, some people are willing to work for the common good by participating in service activities. Obviously, volunteer work is a service activity, but there are many others as well. Voting, paying taxes, helping a neighbor or a stranger, contributing to a charity, showing patriotism, obeying community laws—all are service behaviors. Circumstances at particular times in our lives dictate how much or how often we are willing to serve. However, service is one of the core components of a healthy life, so determining a variety of service behaviors gives us many more opportunities. What role does service play in your quality world? How does service give meaning and purpose to your life?

The concept of a quality world may be new to you. We hope you will give it careful consideration, for we believe that if you carefully and thoughtfully adjust the images and feelings that constitute your quality world to a greater congruence with the life you realistically desire to lead, then your motivation to achieve that life will become easier.

---

exercise 1.4

Your Top Three Life Factors

Create a list of the 10 most important factors in your life. Be as specific as you can. Rank the list in order of importance. Select three of the most important items on the list. Explore the benefits of college and any relationship that college might have on supporting or changing your top three factors.

CONCLUSION

In this chapter, we have asked you to carefully consider three concepts: academic transformation, autonomous learner, and quality world. We hope that you will engage in a serious reflection of these concepts as they apply to you through your completion of the guided journal questions following the chapter summary and key concepts. Simply reading an idea has little or no effect on us unless we make the effort to relate that idea to us and our own thoughts, feelings, and behaviors. Here's your chance to make these concepts meaningful.

Table 1.1 gives some recent data on postsecondary enrollment and retention. There have been some dramatic shifts since 1990, and those shifts seem to be continuing. You will notice that considerably more students attend American postsecondary institutions than in the past, and those numbers continue to rise.

TABLE 1.1   Overview of Postsecondary Enrollment and Retention

A. Student Enrollment in Degree-Granting Institutions

	1990	2000	Change (%)
Total	13,818,637	15,312,289	10.8
Full-time	7,820,985	9,009,600	15.2
Part-time	5,997,650	6,302,689	5.0
Male	6,283,909	6,721,769	7
Female	7,534,728	8,590,520	14

B. Student Enrollment in Degree-Granting Institutions by Ethnicity

	1996 (%)	2000 (%)	Change (%)
White	71.4	68.3	4.3
African American	25.3	28.2	11.5
Hispanic	10.5	11.3	7.6
Asian	8.1	9.5	17.3
American Indian	5.8	9.5	63.8

C. Student Enrollment as a Percentage of all 18- to 24-Year-Olds by Gender and Ethnicity

	1990 (%)	2000 (%)	Change (%)
Total	22.5	35.5	58
Male	32.3	32.6	1
Female	31.8	38.4	20.7
White	35.1	38.7	10.3
Black	25.4	30.5	20
Hispanic	15.8	21.7	37.3

(continued)

TABLE 1.1 *(Continued)*

D. Retention Rates by Type of Institution and by Enrollment Status for 1998

Type of Institution	2-Year (%)	4-Year (%)
All students	56.4	81.6
Full-time	77	87.6
Part-time	53.8	75.7

E. Total Number of Full-Time and Part-Time Students Enrolled in the Fall in Degree-Granting Institutions by Age

Age	1990	2000	Change (%)
18–24	7,855,000	9,193,000	17
25 and older	5,788,000	5,975,000	3.2

Note: Degree-granting institutions are defined as 2- and 4-year degree-granting higher education institutions that participated in Title IV federal financial aid programs. Retention rates are based on students who leave a 2-year college with no credentials after 2 years, and students enrolled in a 4-year institution who leave with no credentials within 3 years.

Source: National Center for Education Statistics. http://nces.ed.gov/.

SUMMARY

- Academic transformation is about making choices—the choices you can make as a collegiate learner.

- There are six steps to academic transformation: assessing your current academic situation, setting short- and long-term academic goals, creating a plan of action, doing the work, evaluating your progress, and making needed adjustments.

- Our goal is to foster your ability to monitor your learning through the development of a perspective about yourself as a learner.

- We suggest that you preview each chapter before you read, noting the headings, topics, applications exercises, summary, and journal questions. After you read each section, mark the most important ideas and write your own ideas in the margin.

- The word *autonomous* denotes concepts such as independence, self-reliance, freedom, competence, and self-governance.

- Autonomous learners have a healthy view of themselves and their academic abilities, are ethical, set realistic and appropriate goals for academic achievement, understand their own learning strengths and weaknesses, use effective learning strategies and adapt those strategies to new situations, manage their behaviors to reach their goals, and use appropriate resources.

- Our quality world begins with the people we want to be with, the things we most want to own, and the ideas or systems of belief that govern much of our behavior. Our quality world holds our deepest values and feelings. It holds our hopes for the way we wish to live. It is a place where we feel loved and protected.

- Our quality world should be steeped in our value system—one that is ethical, balanced, and wise.

- When we experience hope about a relationship, excitement about an idea, or longing for a possession, we are reshaping our quality world. Self-reflection is the basic tool we use to evaluate and reshape our quality world. We also use the feedback from others we trust.

- Four major arenas of life—relationships, work, faith, and service—are used to foster, evaluate, and reshape our quality world.

- There continues to be a significant increase in student enrollment in American postsecondary institutions.

KEY CONCEPTS

Academic transformation

Autonomous learner

Collegiate learning

Discernment

Faith

Getting the most from this book

Quality world

Relationships

Service

Work

GUIDED JOURNAL QUESTIONS

1. Describe your academic strengths and weaknesses as a learner, particularly in relation to reading, writing, mathematics, and critical thinking. Be as specific as possible by citing previous experiences, courses, and grades. What concerns do you have about beginning this semester?

2. Define "transformation" in your own words. What types of transformation would you consider important for yourself during this period in your academic pursuits?

3. Review the list of seven competencies of an autonomous learner. Which competencies have you successfully achieved? Which are you willing to work toward achieving? Explain.

4. In this chapter, you were introduced to a student named Anna. Consider this line from her story: *Anna has carefully created a picture of who she wants to be, and she has tried diligently to match that picture.* Do you believe, as the authors do, that the internal pictures we create of the lives we want have powerful influences on how we live our lives? Why or why not? What internal pictures have you created for the life you wish to lead?

5. In this chapter, you also met Jesse, a student searching for a place in his own quality world. Considering his circumstances, did he make the right choice to leave athletics and give up his scholarship? What would you have done if you were Jesse?

6. What do you envision to be your life's work? Is it different from what you may currently be experiencing? How does (or will) work give meaning and purpose to your quality world?

7. Select two trends from Table 1.1. How could they be important to you during your professional career?

The Last Word

This book began 30 years ago when I walked into a classroom of 20 unsuspecting freshmen who wanted to be successful in college. I had always been a successful student, but at that moment I realized I didn't know how to teach anyone how to do it. Thanks to all those students who went with me down paths of discovery as I figured things out.

—De Sellers

2

Stoking the Motivational Coals

I know I can, I know I can.

If only I were motivated! Then . . .

Most of us long to feel eager about the tasks we have chosen. The energy and happiness seem automatic when we are eager to do something. It is so simple; all we need is an eagerness pill. If only it were that easy. Becoming and remaining motivated seems elusive to many people, including students. Few aspects of human behavior intrigue psychologists as much as why motivation varies among humans. Each of us is motivated in different ways by different things for different reasons. No one explanation exists; instead there are numerous theoretical attempts to understand how and why humans do what they do.

Over the years we have searched for a comprehensive explanation that would help our students increase and maintain their academic motivation. In the past century, some of the giants in psychological theory turned their gaze on this issue. Just a few of those whose theoretical and research investigations form the foundation of this field are Skinner, Maslow, Bandura, and Weiner. Their contributions, as well as the contributions of many lesser-known thinkers, form separate directions in learning theory. All have important concepts to contribute to the topic of motivation.

However, in spite of hundreds of studies, there is no consensus among theorists on any single model to enhance motivation. What has emerged is how complex motivation is for each individual. Students can be highly motivated in one class and grand procrastinators in another. They can work diligently at a part-time job and delay studying. They can pursue every social invitation and conveniently forget to pay bills. They can have the best intentions and then disappoint themselves by not taking action.

This text highlights those concepts that we believe to be most directly influential for college students' academic success, with the full realization that we are omitting much of the rich material in the field. Our work reflects the general shift in the field to a recognition of the importance of beliefs, values, and attitudes in addition to observable behaviors. Since this text represents an attempt to bring pragmatic, relevant, and useful information directly to students, we have created a simple model of motivation and a direct strategy to increase and maintain academic motivation.

---

exercise 2.1

SELF-ASSESSMENT: Your Motivation for a Course

Select the course you expect to be most challenging this term. With 5 being "Almost Always" and 1 being "Almost Never," assess your academic motivation for the course. Rate each of the following statements honestly by circling the appropriate number. Completing this exercise will help you identify realistic motivational concerns you may be experiencing.

	Almost Always		Sometimes		Almost Never
1. I am interested in learning the material for this course.	5	4	3	2	1
2. I am allowed to express my opinions during class.	5	4	3	2	1
3. I feel appropriately challenged by this course.	5	4	3	2	1
4. I am willing to put forth high levels of effort to complete this course with a good grade.	5	4	3	2	1

5. I feel confident I will receive a good grade in this course.

    5   4   3   2   1

6. I have a clear understanding of what is expected to succeed in this course.

    5   4   3   2   1

7. The amount of outside work I must complete is appropriate (class assignments, readings, exams, etc.).

    5   4   3   2   1

8. I feel confident I am able to complete the assignments and outside readings on time.

    5   4   3   2   1

9. I expect to receive timely feedback on assignments or exams.

    5   4   3   2   1

10. My instructor is enthusiastic about the course material.

    5   4   3   2   1

11. I use the support of other classmates to help me learn.

    5   4   3   2   1

12. Out-of-class academic support options such as tutoring, supplemental instruction, test review sessions, and help from the instructor or teaching assistant are available.

    5   4   3   2   1

Add up the numbers circled. Your total score will be between 12 and 60. The higher your score, the more likely you are to be academically motivated for the course. For total scores below 36, write or reflect on items for which you have concerns. Also, consider talking with a trusted friend, a family member, a teacher, or an advisor.

MOTIVATION

A working definition of **motivation** is *those thoughts and feelings that initiate, direct, and sustain action.* Obviously, there are many factors that affect academic motivation, both internal (intrinsic) and external (extrinsic), and we will consider the most important factors a little later in this chapter. We first want to look at five issues that researchers investigate in the motivation of college students (Woolfolk, 2004):

- **Choices.** What do we choose to do? Some students attend class regularly whereas others miss class to catch up on sleep, errands, and so forth.

- **Initiation.** How rapidly do we begin the behavior? Some students study before they go out with friends whereas others delay studying until the next day.

- **Intensity.** How hard do we try? Some students are actively engaged in the lecture/discussion in classes whereas others go through the motions of taking notes.

- **Persistence.** How long do we try? Some students are determined to understand study material and seek help when necessary whereas others give up when learning is difficult.

- **Thoughts/feelings.** What do we think and feel while we are engaged? Some students feel confident that they can successfully complete an assignment whereas others worry that they will fail.

Research evidence and common sense tell us that these five factors are important in determining level of motivation. If we direct our attention to our own behaviors, thoughts, and feelings through the lens of these issues, we can determine our own motivation level, and we urge our students to do just that. Take a few moments to reflect on your current level of academic motivation. Does it vary across courses? How much does procrastination impede your work? Are you a strong starter, a strong finisher, or consistent throughout the semester? Is your attitude about academics helpful to your efforts?

exercise 2.2

A Lower Grade Than Expected

Select a course you have completed (in high school or college) and conduct this motivational analysis. This exercise works best for a course in which you earned a lower grade than you would have expected based on your knowledge of yourself and your ability. Completing this analysis will help you consider areas for self-improvement in future courses. Be sure to explain each of your answers.

1. **Choices.** What were two or three in-class or out-of-class choices you made that negatively influenced your performance? What are two or three choices that might have proved successful?

2. **Initiation.** How may you have been slow to initiate appropriate behaviors? What are two or more behaviors that you should have begun at the onset of the course?

3. **Intensity.** How hard did you try? In other words, how intense were your efforts? What are one or two actions you could have done that you chose not to do?

4. **Persistence.** How long did you try? In other words, did you give up too easily? What are two actions that you should have engaged in longer?

5. **Thoughts/feelings.** What negative thoughts and feelings do you remember having about the course? What two or three thoughts could you have expressed to yourself that would have had a more positive effect on your thinking?

MODEL OF ACADEMIC MOTIVATION

If we can understand and control the factors of choices, initiation, intensity, persistence, and thoughts/feelings, then we have a much greater opportunity to increase academic motivation. What influences these factors? Researchers have identified many psychological elements that seem to affect these factors. We have organized the most important into three groups: values, needs, and expectations. In Figure 2.1, the Model of Academic Motivation, you will notice that we have placed opportunity in the first position. In academic settings, opportunities abound; they occur with every assignment and every lecture. Each semester you begin with hundreds of academic opportunities. Attending an outside lecture, conducting research with a professor, engaging in serious conversation with fellow students, studying, seeking help from tutors, participating in test review sessions, writing, teaching a lab—all these and more are available.

When we consider an opportunity, we have three types of psychological elements that impact our level of motivation to reach the desired behavior or outcome. *Why do I want to accomplish this task?* represents both internal and external values. Internal reasons include interest, utility, and goals. External reasons include incentives and expectations of others. *What drives me?* is the key question for those elements of need that include our need for achievement, competence, self-worth, and creativity. *Can I accomplish this task?* encompasses our expectations based on previous experience, observation of others' success, and feedback about

FIGURE 2.1   Model of Academic Motivation

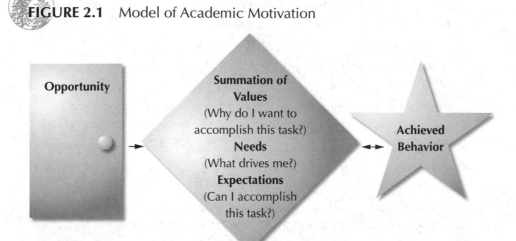

our own performance. Two other important expectations are the belief we hold about our ability to perform the particular behavior (self-efficacy) and how we explain our success or failure (attribution) (McMillan & Forsyth, 1991; VanderStoep & Pintrich, 2003). Both self-efficacy and attributions are explored later in this chapter.

When the psychological elements are added together, they impact our motivation to achieve the desired behavior. Each time we achieve the desired behavior, that success impacts certain psychological elements and our motivation usually increases. If we do not achieve the behavior, our motivation can decrease. However, sometimes an unexpected failure grabs our attention and shows us that our motivation and our behaviors need to change.

Values

Values are the reasons why we prize or disregard the completion of a task (VanderStoep & Pintrich, 2003). Internal reasons are those personal ideas and beliefs that we hold inside, such as how interested we are in a task, how personally useful we think the task is, and how much we want to accomplish the task. External reasons are the rewards we will receive and how important people in our lives will view us.

Internal.   The internal, or intrinsic, reasons include the following:

- **Interest.** I will/will not enjoy accomplishing this task solely for the experience of the activity (note that sometimes interest is temporary and therefore termed *situational interest*).

- **Utility.** I believe completing this task will be useful/useless to me.
- **Goals.** This task is/is not something I want to achieve.

External. The external, or extrinsic, reasons include the following:

- **Incentives.** I will/will not be externally rewarded for completing this task.
- **Expectations of others.** My [family, friends, boss, coach, . . .] expect/do not expect me to accomplish this task.

· · · **TAMARA** · · ·

She has the right combination of motivational factors working for her

Tamara is a sophomore taking her first course in communications. She is a traditional-age, first-generation student who entered college on a probationary contract. She knows that she must pass all her courses this term in order to remain in school, and she is determined to do well from the beginning of the semester.

Her assignment is to create and deliver a persuasive speech, and she chooses the topic of free campus parking for students. All five value components will be positive for Tamara. She believes learning how to do a persuasive speech will be a useful skill in her chosen profession (utility); she will be rewarded with a grade (incentive); she will feel good about finishing the assignment (goal); she is interested in the parking issue because she had to pay more than $50 for a parking permit this term (situational interest); and her teacher expects her to complete this assignment (expectations of others).

Needs

The second set of components for motivated behavior is needs (What drives me?). "Needs tend to motivate students to behave so as to attain satisfaction and rewards. They are innate feelings and beliefs that direct attention and energy toward determining priorities and goals" (McMillan & Forsyth, 1991, p. 42). The needs most relevant to academic motivation are achievement, competence, self-worth, and creativity:

- **Achievement.** I will risk in order to be successful/I am afraid of risk because I might fail (Atkinson & Feather, 1966; McClelland, 1961).

- **Competence.** It is/is not important to me to accomplish my goals and control my surroundings (Deci, 1975).

- **Self-worth.** I want/do not want to have a positive opinion of my abilities (Covington, 1984).

- **Creativity.** I enjoy/do not enjoy thinking and expressing my own ideas.

Tamara has many need elements that will enhance her motivation for her speech assignment. She sees herself as a good student (self-worth) who wants a collegiate education to further her skills and opportunities (competence). She is excited about researching the topic and creating her own arguments (creativity). Most important, she is willing to risk choosing an interesting topic because she believes it enhances her chance of success (achievement).

The achievement needs of college students are a rich field of study. "Depending on childhood environment (especially parenting) and other experiences, some people develop a strong need to achieve success, while others develop a need to avoid failure" (McMillan & Forsyth, 1991, p. 44). If we have a strong need for academic achievement, then we tend to work diligently at tasks and use feedback to improve. While we enjoy external rewards, internal rewards of feelings of pride and self-worth are highly motivating. If we fail at an academic task, we usually have the ability to use the feedback from that failure to improve our next attempt, even if we are temporarily embarrassed by our performance. If we perceive a task as realistically achievable, then we are motivated to attempt it.

The need to avoid failure is a serious danger to collegiate learning. If we

are afraid to fail because we believe failure is shameful and humiliating, then we will avoid challenging tasks, opting for the easy way or the outrageously difficult way. In other words, our success is certain or impossible. We may also suffer from intense anxiety about academics and deliberately avoid attending class and studying. Occasionally, a student will exhibit this psychological characteristic of fear of failure in only one subject, such as math. If the academic anxiety is moderate, then the specific suggestions given in Chapter 10 for managing stress should help. If the academic anxiety is intense, then a counselor or tutor can provide a calmly structured environment with ample positive feedback. In that setting, students can overcome their fear of failure (McMillan & Forsyth, 1991).

Expectations

Can I accomplish this task? is the question that encompasses our judgment about our competence to achieve the task and our ability to control our behavior. The primary expectations relevant to academic tasks are as follows:

- **Previous experience.** In the past I have done well/poorly in similar situations.

- **Success of others.** I compare favorably/unfavorably with other people in this category.

- **Feedback.** I pay attention to evaluation according to how much I trust the source (Deci, 1975).

- **Self-efficacy.** I feel/do not feel confident in my own ability to meet the challenge of . . . (Bandura, 1986; Branden, 1994).

- **Attribution.** I did well/poorly because . . . (Weiner, 1986).

Tamara is confident that she can make a competent speech because she did well on the debate team in high school (previous experience, self-efficacy); however, college seems so much more competitive than high school, and she is surprised at the rigor of the professor's critiques (success of others). Therefore, she wants to rehearse her speech with the teaching assistant because she believes he can give her good information about improvement (feedback). She believes her past successes in high school speech have come from careful research and rehearsal, so she is using the same strategies for this speech (attribution). She wants to earn a B or better on this assignment because she considers that grade a reasonable goal given her experience, her preparation, and her practice.

Our academic **self-efficacy,** *the confidence that we can meet whatever performance standards the situation requires,* has a profound impact on our expectations. If we have high self-efficacy, then we are more likely to engage actively in learning, even if the tasks are difficult and complex, because we will persist (McMillan & Forsyth, 1991). Clearly, this characteristic is interwoven with our achievement needs. The combination of high academic self-efficacy and high academic achievement needs provides powerful motivation for academic behaviors. Conversely, low academic self-efficacy and low academic achievement needs can lead to a sense of helplessness and a lack of academic motivation.

Throughout our academic experiences, we explain our success or failure in many ways. Such explanation is termed **attribution.** *Our beliefs about the causes of our academic success or failure influence our emotional reactions.* Lefrançois (2000) says

The cognitive view of motivation is based on the assumption that people continually evaluate their behaviors, look for reasons behind their successes and failures, anticipate the probable future outcomes of intended behaviors, and react emotionally to success and failure. It is not the attribution of behavior to one cause or the other that motivates behavior, says Weiner (1980); it is the emotions that occur as responses to specific attributions. The outcomes of attribution, he suggests, might be anger, guilt, gratefulness, or a variety of other emotions. (p. 303)

If we believe we are responsible for our own success, that our ability and effort help us become more competent, then our self-efficacy (confidence) improves. We believe we can control outcomes. Even if we fail at a particular task, we are willing to try again, changing strategies and increasing effort. We may take responsibility for not trying hard enough, or even feel some guilt, but we believe we can be successful.

On the other hand, if we believe our success or failure is controlled by external factors, then we tend to attribute our performance results to luck, difficulty of the task, or outside circumstances. Even a successful outcome does not increase our confidence, because we do not believe we have caused the success. Sometimes, feelings of hopelessness occur if we believe we do not possess either the ability or the will to complete a task. Attributions, either positive or negative, are important factors in motivation, and the strategy for increasing academic motivation in the next section uses helpful attributions as well as other components of the model.

Figure 2.2 illustrates the combined components that affect academic motivation.

---

exercise 2.3

Motivation for a Task

Select a major undertaking that you are about to begin. For example, list a possible major area of study that you are considering, or perhaps an upcoming major class assignment. Any important academic opportunity will suffice. Then answer each of the following questions. This exercise will help you assess your academic motivation for a task using the Model of Academic Motivation.

Describe in detail the academic opportunity you wish to accomplish.

VALUES: WHY DO I WISH TO ACCOMPLISH THIS TASK?

Internal Reasons

1. Do I have a genuine interest in this task?

_____ Yes _____ No _____ Unsure

FIGURE 2.2   Three Psychological Elements Impacting Our Motivation

Values
Why do I want to
accomplish this task?

Internal
Interest, Utility, Goals

External
Incentives, Expectations
of Others

Needs
What drives me?

Achievement
Competence
Self-worth
Creativity

Expectations
Can I accomplish this
task?

Previous Experience
Success of Others
Feedback
Self-efficacy
Attribution

2. Will completing this task be useful to me?

_____ Yes _____ No _____ Unsure

3. Have I set a realistic goal(s) to complete this task?

_____ Yes _____ No _____ Unsure

External Reasons

4. Will someone reward me when I complete this task?

_____ Yes _____ No _____ Unsure

5. Do others expect me to complete this task?

_____ Yes _____ No _____ Unsure

6. Are my expectations realistic?

_____ Yes _____ No _____ Unsure

NEEDS: WHAT DRIVES ME?

7. Is it important for me to gain competence in the task?

_____ Yes _____ No _____ Unsure

8. Will I feel good about myself as I try to accomplish this task—even if the task is difficult?

_____ Yes _____ No _____ Unsure

9. Can I express my own ideas and creativity as I complete this task?

_____ Yes _____ No _____ Unsure

EXPECTATIONS: CAN I ACCOMPLISH THIS TASK?

10. Have I had previous experience accomplishing this or a similar task?

_____ Yes _____ No _____ Unsure

11. Do I compare favorably with others who are also completing this task?

_____ Yes _____ No _____ Unsure

12. Will I use the feedback I receive from others while I am trying to accomplish this task?

_____ Yes _____ No _____ Unsure

13. Do I have a strong belief in my ability to accomplish this task?

_____ Yes _____ No _____ Unsure

14. Have I attributed my completion of a similar task to my own ability and effort?

_____ Yes _____ No _____ Unsure

Answering No or Unsure on at least two questions within each of the three categories (values, needs, expectations) may indicate a possible motivation deficit in that area. Read the next section to further your understanding of how your motivation may be affected by values, needs, and expectations. Consider talking with a trusted friend, a family member, a teacher, or an advisor if you have concerns about your motivation.

• • • COLIN • • •

He has high ability but demands little from himself

One student we remember fondly is Colin. As a sophomore, Colin was a talented but extremely lazy student. He had drifted through high school, mastering the art of doing the least amount possible to get by. He had a dozen excuses for every result, and he had a high opinion of himself in high school because he was smart and popular. He cruised into college with those same behaviors and attitudes, but that cruising turned into a crash after his first round of exams. He was shocked and decided to try a little harder, but the seductions available on a college campus were stronger than his will. He made friends and enjoyed parties, but he continued to use the old, casual behaviors, such as not taking notes in class, skimming the readings instead of seriously studying them, and waiting until the night before to study. Inside Colin's mind, all his troubles occurred because of other people. It was all their fault! His roommate kept the TV on late at night so Colin overslept and missed his classes; his girlfriend expected him to spend time with her so he rarely opened his books; his classes seemed boring so he would daydream or sleep. His friends expected him to play hoops in the afternoon. There was never any time to study. Often he had good intentions, but distractions interfered.

Not surprisingly, his first semester ended with a pitiful GPA. For the first time in his life, Colin had publicly failed. His confidence was badly shaken, and he hated carrying the news home to his parents. They kept telling him how much they believed in him, but Colin had begun the dangerous slide downward into self-doubt. Returning in the spring, he felt more apprehension about his performance than he had ever felt before; in fact, sometimes he did not believe he was "college material." Maybe he should just leave and join the military or get a civilian job. Some of the friends he had made the first semester had already left campus. He worried about his studies and tried to apply himself, but he had no organized study behaviors. Soon, he felt anxious every time he picked up his textbooks, but he did not give up. He managed to complete the second semester with marginal grades, but his belief in his own abilities was still shaken by his collegiate performance. At the beginning of his second year, Colin came to see us.

A REALISTIC STRATEGY FOR INCREASING MOTIVATION

We are now going to demonstrate a beginning method of becoming more motivated—it is neither simple nor easy, but it can work. We use the work of three modern theorists from psychiatry and psychotherapy—Glasser (1998), Branden (1994), and Peck (1978)—to build the steps of this approach.

If we define **motivation** as "the processes that initiate and sustain behavior" (McMillan & Forsyth, 1991, p. 39) and **academic motivation** as "a process in which students value learning and involve themselves in classroom assignments and activities" (pp. 39–40), then it is obvious that Colin does not have academic motivation and does not know how to achieve it. Hundreds of Colins have come to us and asked us for the magic pill of motivation. What we have to offer is not magic; instead, it is a series of specific decisions and actions.

STRATEGY FOR INCREASING MOTIVATION

- Accept responsibility.
- Believe in myself.
- Set appropriate goals.
- Choose to approach.
- Balance my life.
- Maintain my motivation.

Accept Responsibility

We confronted Colin with a shocking truth. He is an adult and responsible for his own actions. *No one else is responsible; only he is responsible.* Colin argued with us—blaming his roommate, his girlfriend, his teachers, and the boring textbooks for his lack of success. We challenged every statement he made. It is his responsibility to go to class; it does not matter how late his roommate stays up. Colin can ask his roommate to turn down the TV. It is his responsibility to stay awake and focused in class; moving to the front of the lecture hall can help focus attention. Colin has acquired a dangerous habit: He blames other people and other circumstances for his own failures; he thinks of himself as a victim, and that is simply untrue.

Accepting full responsibility for our own actions and thoughts is the first step to acquire enduring motivation. Such acceptance rests on the foundation of consciousness. We must be aware of the exact nature of our behaviors and thoughts. One place to begin is to examine how we spend our time—exactly how we spend our time, not a romanticized notion of *I really studied for this history test* but, instead, the accuracy of *I studied for four hours for this test after I had finished all the assigned reading. During that four hours I reviewed all my class notes and my highlighting in the text. Then I outlined answers to possible essay questions.* We have to be aware and we have to be honest to accept full responsibility. Such dedication to the truth is central to our acceptance of responsibility.

Glasser (1998), Branden (1994), and Peck (1978) all place ruthless and truthful acceptance of responsibility at the core of their respective theories of personal freedom, self-esteem, and discipline. We agree that acceptance of responsibility is the essential first step to motivation; through it we take the power we need to create a purposeful life that is congruent with our quality world.

> **WE RECOMMEND**
>
> *Choice Theory* by William Glasser
>
> *The Six Pillars of Self-Esteem* by Nathaniel Branden
>
> *The Road Less Traveled* by Scott Peck

As we mentioned earlier, educational psychologists who have studied student motivation use the word *attribution* to *describe how students explain their successes and their failures.* Students who believe that they can control the outcomes of their endeavors, that is, that they are responsible for their academic performance, are more motivated than students who attribute their performance to factors outside themselves—luck, teachers, events, and so forth (Weiner, 1986). If we believe that our actions do not matter, then we become resigned and feel helpless. Claiming responsibility is a crucial first step in managing and increasing our motivation.

Although academic ability varies across students, most college students who are consistently motivated, and thus have consistent learning behaviors, can competently perform in most courses. An important corollary to claiming responsibility is having the courage, and perhaps some confidence, that you will act to reach your desires. That confidence is often called self-esteem.

Believe in Yourself

From our earliest moments, we are aware of ourselves. Throughout the days and years that follow, we create a system of ideas, beliefs, and feelings about ourselves. Our parents, siblings, and friends can powerfully influence our thoughts and feelings about ourselves. That influence can be loving and positive, or it can be cruel and negative. When we have a distorted view of ourselves, when we believe we are bad or stupid or worthless or, conversely, when we believe we are wonderful, brilliant, or entitled, we do ourselves a great injustice. Having an accurate view of ourselves grounded in a sense of our own worth is an essential foundation for a good life. This topic is the subject of endless movies and books; many people seek counseling because their self-view or self-concept is distorted.

How can we know if our view of ourselves is a healthy one? The primary indicator is something called self-esteem. *How we accept ourselves and the value and worth we place on ourselves* is called **self-esteem.** "Self-esteem is the reputation we acquire with ourselves" (Branden, 1994, p. 69). Branden is the primary authority in this field, and his works give specific directions on

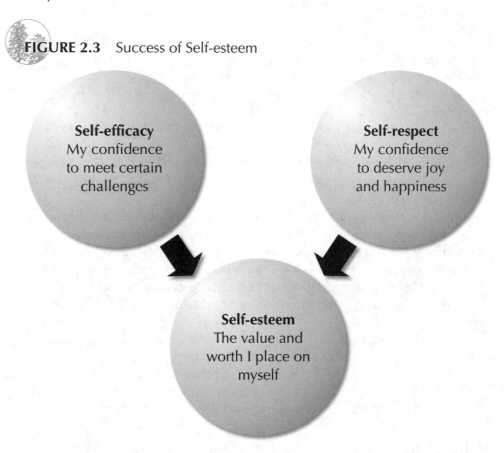

FIGURE 2.3   Success of Self-esteem

determining our level of self-esteem and, if necessary, moving it toward health. Our self-esteem is constructed from two sets of thoughts/feelings. *When we feel confident in our own abilities to meet whatever challenges life brings,* that confidence is called **self-efficacy.** *When we also feel confident that we deserve joy and happiness,* that confidence is called **self-respect** (see Figure 2.3). When we have both sets of thoughts/feelings in a realistic manner, then we know that we have healthy self-esteem (Branden, 1994). Throughout Branden's writing, he emphasizes our responsibility to choose how we use our consciousness. He agrees with Glasser's (1998) contention that we are responsible for our choices.

Branden (1994) advocates six practices for creating and maintaining healthy self-esteem; in so doing, we are guaranteeing that our self-concept is healthy as well. These six practices have a reciprocal relationship with the status and formation of self-esteem and self-concept. The practices are how we create and maintain a healthy and vital self-esteem.

When Colin entered college, his self-concept was healthy because he had come from a loving family who encouraged and supported him and because he competently fulfilled the expectations that his family and his friends had of his childhood and adolescence. In this new environment, Colin was not competent, and his academic failure damaged his self-concept. He became uncertain and anxious as he struggled to master the new situation. When we explained Branden's ideas of self-efficacy and self-respect, Colin immediately realized that both aspects of his self-concept had been damaged by his careless behaviors. He had not thought seriously about college as professional preparation; therefore, he did not choose friends who valued academic success. As he studied Branden's six practices, Colin realized that he would benefit from concentrating on two of them—living consciously and purposefully. He chose to pay attention to how he spent his time and energy toward academics. To do that, Colin needed to carefully set specific goals, both short term and long term. This realization led him to the next step.

BRANDEN'S PRACTICES FOR BUILDING SELF-ESTEEM

To live consciously means to attend to and understand what is really going on, both within ourselves and within our world. When we live consciously, we are in harmony with what we see and know.

To practice self-acceptance is to be my own friend. It is to claim the totality of who I am and what I do.

To take responsibility for myself means that I am responsible for my goals, my behaviors, my feelings, my happiness.

To practice self-assertiveness means to speak for myself, to be who I am openly; to treat myself with respect.

To live purposefully is to work to achieve my goals.

To have integrity is to behave in ways true to my values.

---

exercise 2.4

Building Self-Esteem

Quickly read and respond to each phrase. Then revisit this exercise and add to or revise your responses until you are satisfied. Candor is essential. This exercise will provide you with an action plan to enhance your self-esteem.

1. To live more consciously, I will _____

2. To practice more self-acceptance, I will _____

3. To take more responsibility for myself, I will _____

4. To practice more self-assertiveness, I will _____

5. To live more purposefully, I will _____

6. To have more integrity, I will _____

Set Appropriate Goals

By our nature, we are purposeful creatures; that is, we set goals and try to achieve them. When we are children, we have some goals of our own, but our families and our society push many goals on us. So an understandable reaction is resentment. Children and adolescents struggle with the resentment of imposed goals, even if they acknowledge the merit of them. As we move into adulthood, we have the opportunity to set our own goals—goals that are congruent with our quality world and with our values. Goal setting is a learned skill, and many college students have little practice in carefully creating an integrated set of realistic goals. Note that word *realistic;* it is difficult to restrain ourselves to goals that are achievable. We will explore goal setting in greater detail in Chapter 8, but for now the following questions give a quick overview of the types of issues appropriate for college students.

Academic. As college students, academic goals should be a priority (if they are not, then why are you here?). Academic goals have two dimensions: mastery and performance (Dembo, 2000). What do you want to learn from your academic program? From each course you are taking this term? As you examine the requirements in each course, ponder what skills and prior knowledge you already bring to that study. How much are you willing to work in this course? What is the best grade you believe you could achieve in this course? What is the lowest acceptable grade? What GPA would you get if you receive the best possible grades in all your courses? The lowest acceptable grades? What do you believe is a realistic GPA goal for this term? Will that GPA be sufficient to meet other requirements, such as ambitions, scholarships, financial aid, athletics, or ROTC?

Social. Social goals encompass the relationships we want to nurture or begin, our participation in organizations or events, and our experiences within the college context. Do your college relationships reflect the quality world you desire? Are you developing a high caliber of friendships with people of diverse backgrounds and values? Are you participating in several organizations? How much of your time and energy is spent pursuing social goals?

Personal. An integral part of the collegiate experience is the desire to develop our sense of ourselves, that is, our own identity, apart from our family and our peers. Personal goals often involve serious reflection about values and exploration of our deepest feelings. What is your ethical code? What do you believe in? What role does spirituality or religion have in your life? What are your prejudices? Your habits? How is your physical health? Do you have any dangerous habits, such as eating disorders or smoking or drug/alcohol abuse? How well do you handle money? What role do economic pressures play?

The composite picture of our combined academic, social, and personal goals becomes essential to the vision of our quality world. Realism and balance are critical to this picture; our goals must be achievable. Can we accomplish them?

Colin got excited when he began to answer these questions. He began to construct a set of goals—academic, social, personal. After reflection, he calculated that his semester GPA goal would be 2.5; he would not cut a class; and he would study at least 10 hours per week. Colin also realized that he needed to make some new friends, friends who also wanted to succeed in school. He decided that intramural basketball and a service fraternity would give him some healthy social outlets. When he honestly looked at the last year, he realized that his partying had extended over three or four nights a week. While he wanted to continue his social life, he chose to go out only on Friday and Saturday nights. His plan was realistic and achievable, so he was ready for the fourth step to increase motivation, choosing approach behaviors.

exercise 2.5

Beginning Goal Setting

Complete the following goal exercise by creating three goals you are willing to accomplish by the end of this term, one personal, one social, and one academic. Be sure your goals can be measured easily for success and have a completion date. The best way to create a goal statement is to explicitly state a behavior to accomplish. Know that you can increase, decrease, maintain, start, or stop a behavior. For example: *I will quit smoking cigarettes by the very last day of this month.* Completing this exercise will give you direction and purpose for making positive changes for yourself.

1. Personal Goal Statement

   What is your rationale for creating this goal?

   Is this goal challenging?

   Is it realistic?

   Strategy 1:

   Strategy 2:

   Strategy 3:

2. Social Goal Statement

   What is your rationale for creating this goal?

   Is this goal challenging?

   Is it realistic?

   Strategy 1:

Strategy 2:

Strategy 3:

3. Academic Goal Statement

What is your rationale for creating this goal?

Is this goal challenging?

Is it realistic?

Strategy 1:

Strategy 2:

Strategy 3:

Choose to Approach

In countless moments each day we choose actions that either lead us closer to our goals or farther away from them. Motivation simply means *our ability to consistently choose those behaviors that will help us reach our goals,* in other words, **approach** behaviors. We all know these behaviors; it does not require a genius IQ. It means we simply do what we know we should do to achieve a goal. We attend class; we study; we exercise; we spend time with friends; we get enough sleep; we play; we tell the truth; we pay our bills; we honor our promises. If only it were as easy as it sounds, but each approach behavior has its underside, the avoidance behavior. We cut class, we procrastinate studying, we delay exercise, we watch hours of TV, we stay up late socializing, and so forth. Many of us develop the habit of avoidance—we do not balance our checkbook so that we do not have to face what we have spent; we "forget" an assignment; we spend time with people who do not fit our quality world. Many of us are continually pulled between approach and avoidance behaviors.

Sometimes college students exhibit extreme avoidance behaviors. They may spend much of their time socializing or working. They go through the motions of being a student by attending class sporadically, but they do not turn in papers on time and sometimes they do not even bother to take exams. Usually, they do not withdraw or drop courses. Whatever they do, they avoid the reality of what they are doing. They pretend to themselves and their families that they are really trying. Such extreme behaviors can have a variety of causes, including rebellion, addiction, perfectionism, fear of success or failure, depression, and lack of goals. It is usually hard, if not impossible, to rescue yourself from any of these conditions without professional help. Luckily, most college campuses have counseling centers with professional staff expert in helping students recover. If you know someone (including yourself) who seems to fit this pattern, see a counselor soon and ask for help.

Colin was typical of many college students in his lackadaisical attitude toward approach behaviors until he understood their power. When he studied the six practices to increase self-esteem, he began to realize how few approach behaviors he had been using. Each of the practices is active; thus, each time we approach a task, the next task is easier. Colin realized that his biggest avoidance behavior was procrastinating studying. He decided to study each day in the library after classes before he went back to his room. He also joined study groups in two courses and signed up for a tutor in math. Colin has already begun to consider the fifth step, balancing.

Balance Your Life

One of the hardest truths in life is that we have only 168 hours in a week. There is simply not enough time to do all that we want and need to do. A fine art that adults must master if they are to have a successful and healthy life is the art of balancing. Peck (1978) defines balancing as "a complex task requiring both judgment and wisdom" (p. 64). Balancing is our ability to wisely allocate our time and energy to meet various goals while maintaining our flexible response to the present moment. What do we do now and what later? How do we respond to a last-minute invitation? Where is the reasonable point between chaos and rigidity? College is a wonderful opportunity to develop this ability because college life is simultaneously more complex and less structured than high school.

Colin's choice to live consciously and purposefully means he chose to continually review his priorities as he moved through each day. His priorities were not all academic; he had social and personal goals as well. Each day he had to choose how he would balance his time and energy across several goals. He had to be flexible enough to incorporate the unexpected—friends coming in from out of town, the flu, a flat tire, no clean clothes. As his sophomore year progressed, Colin learned how to juggle his actions gracefully. With each approach behavior he took, he found that he felt more in control and less anxious. His self-efficacy and self-respect grew accordingly, and the better grades he was receiving helped increase his willingness to stay on track. In other words, his motivation increased.

Maintain Your Motivation

Increasing motivation is not simple or direct because we are not simple or direct. We get excited and then discouraged, move forward then backslide, encounter little resistance then massive roadblocks. Once you have moved through the first five steps, you begin the journey of maintenance. How do you remain consistent? How do you regain consistency when you let it slide? First, it is important to acknowledge that the strength of our motivation can diminish, but the best strategy is to respond to such feelings immediately. As soon as we begin to avoid and have elaborate excuses for doing so, we know we have begun to backslide. At that moment, do an approach behavior, even if it is only for 5 or 10 minutes. Yes, at that moment, open a text and read two pages if you have fallen behind your study schedule. Or work the first two problems of your homework. Set two alarms so you will make your 8 A.M. class tomorrow. Whatever you have done or left undone, accept the responsibility for where you are (Step 1) and reassess what you need to do and where you want to go. Then start over. Ask for help from friends, family, campus professionals.

Colin had several setbacks throughout his sophomore year, both academic and personal. Each time he felt his motivation ebb, he redoubled his efforts, asking for help and encouragement from his family and friends. The first setback was scary because he felt he had lost all his progress, but each time he regained his momentum, his confidence strengthened.

CONCLUSION

As we stated earlier, human motivation is complex. If we want to change, direct, and sustain our academic motivation, then we need to understand our deepest desires in our quality world, what external and internal beliefs affect us (values, needs, expectations), and which strategies might be useful to us. Our paths differ dramatically because we differ from each other, but all of us can manage our behaviors by utilizing motivational principles.

SUMMARY

- Motivation can be defined as those thoughts and feelings that initiate, direct, and sustain action.

- Five factors determine our level of motivation: the choices we make, how rapidly we initiate the chosen behavior, the intensity of our efforts, our persistence, and our thoughts and feelings as we are engaged in the chosen behavior.

- The Model of Academic Motivation indicates that when we consider an opportunity to take an action, there are three types of psychological elements that impact our level of motivation to reach the desired behavior: values, needs, and expectations.

- Values are the reasons we prize or disregard a task. They can be internal (intrinsic) and/or external (extrinsic). Internal reasons can be categorized as interest, utility, and goals. External reasons can be categorized as incentives and expectations of others.

- Needs are those factors that drive us to take on and sustain actions. The needs most relevant to academic motivation are achievement, competence, self-worth, and creativity.

- Expectations are the judgments we make regarding how competent we are to achieve a task and our ability to control our behavior. These judgments are based on the following factors: our previous experience in similar situations, how we compare with the success of others, feedback that we have received, our self-efficacy, and our attribution of our level of performance.

- Academic self-efficacy is our individual confidence in being able to meet the challenge being asked of us. The higher our level of self-efficacy to meet the challenge, the more likely we are to be actively engaged in the learning experience.

- Attribution is how we explain our successes and failures. These explanations can be internal, our ability and efforts, or external, outside factors that control the outcomes.

- Academic motivation is a process in which students value learning and involve themselves in classroom assignments and activities.

- Steps to increase motivation involve accepting responsibility, believing in yourself, setting appropriate goals, choosing to approach, balancing your life, and maintaining your motivation.

- Accepting responsibility is related to the attributions you assign to an outcome of a given task. Students who believe they control the outcomes of their endeavors are more motivated than students who attribute their performance to external factors.

- To believe in yourself is to have an accurate view of yourself and your own worth. Self-esteem is how you accept yourself and the worth you place on yourself. Self-esteem comprises two sets of thoughts/feelings: self-efficacy and self-respect.

- Branden's practices for building self-esteem are to live consciously, to practice self-acceptance, to take responsibility, to practice self-assertiveness, to live purposefully, and to have integrity.

- Academic, social, and personal goals must be set realistically to enhance your success.

- An approach behavior is choosing behaviors (strategies) that will help you reach your goals. These behaviors are usually easy to identify. The opposite of approach behaviors are avoidance behaviors.

- To balance your life is to wisely allocate time and energy to meet your various goals while maintaining flexibility to respond to the present moment.

- Consistency is essential to maintain your motivation. Respond to a reversal of motivation by immediately engaging in an approach behavior, accept responsibility, and reassess the strategies to meet your goal.

KEY CONCEPTS

Approach and avoidance behaviors

Branden's practices for building self-esteem

Choices

Expectations: previous experience, success of others, feedback, self-efficacy, attributions

Goals: academic, social, personal

Initiation

Intensity

Model of Academic Motivation

Motivation

Needs: achievement, competence, self-worth, creativity

Persistence

Self-esteem, self-efficacy, self-respect

Strategy for increasing motivation

Thoughts/feelings

Values: interest, utility, goals, incentives, expectations of others

GUIDED JOURNAL QUESTIONS

1. Reflect back to a time in your life when you were highly motivated to accomplish a goal. What made you so successful? What thoughts and feelings do you remember? Were you mostly internally or externally motivated?

2. If you had to select only one, which would contribute more to your academic motivation—your values, needs, or expectations? Why?

3. How satisfied are you with your current academic motivation? Explain.

4. We believe "the need to avoid failure is a serious danger to collegiate learning. If we are afraid to fail because we believe failure is shameful and humiliating, then we will avoid challenging tasks, opting for the easy way or the outrageously difficult way. In other words, our success is certain or impossible." Do you agree or disagree with this statement? Why?

5. Self-efficacy is your confidence in your ability to complete a task. For which of your current classes do you have high self-efficacy? Why? For which do you have low self-efficacy? Why?

6. Compare two academic incidences: one when you accepted responsibility for causing a negative action or outcome with one when you did not. How did you feel in each case?

7. How "balanced" is your life? What changes, if any, should you make for a well-balanced life?

8. Remember Colin? Many of his friends left college after their first semester, but he managed to turn things around for himself. Why is it that some individuals make it in college and others drop out quickly? Can you think of several characteristics that successful students might share?

9. After having read this chapter, what questions can you ask or suggestions can you offer to a friend who says to you, "I am no longer motivated to attend my history class"?

The Last Word

When I'm truly motivated to complete a difficult task, the challenge is exhilarating. When I complete it successfully, my soul smiles to reward me.

—*Russ Hodges*

3

Loading Up on Strategies for Learning Excellence

A call to arms!

By the time you get to college, you have been a student for at least 12 years. You made each transition between levels: preschool to kindergarten, kindergarten to elementary . . . but the shift to college is often the hardest. One of the reasons is that you are simply expected to be an independent and competent learner. Easier said than done, even if you worked hard in high school.

This chapter contains most of the crucial study strategies you need to implement early in the semester. We have used student voices to give realistic and pragmatic advice. Be prepared to sit up and take notice.

CHAPTER HIGHLIGHTS

- Getting Organized

- How to Learn in Class: Lecture, Problem-Solving, Discussion, and Distance Classes

- How to Learn Outside Class: Text, Homework Problems, and Groups

exercise 3.1

SELF-ASSESSMENT: Skills for Success

Organizing yourself, taking good notes, and being a competent reader are essential skills for college success. With 5 being "Almost Always" and 1 being "Almost Never," assess your skills for success. Rate each of the following statements honestly by circling the appropriate number. Completing this exercise will help you identify concerns you may be experiencing about these skills.

	Almost Always		Sometimes		Almost Never
Organization					
1. I use a calendar (or planner) to organize myself.	5	4	3	2	1
2. I plan appropriate amounts of time to study.	5	4	3	2	1
3. I use a regular study place.	5	4	3	2	1
4. I can easily find all my notes, handouts, syllabi, etc. for each class.	5	4	3	2	1
Note Taking					
5. I take organized and legible notes.	5	4	3	2	1
6. I review my lecture notes before the next class session.	5	4	3	2	1
7. I vary my note taking to fit different types of classes.	5	4	3	2	1
8. I use a partner to help me fill in missing gaps in my notes.	5	4	3	2	1
Reading					
9. I am a competent textbook reader.	5	4	3	2	1
10. I am able to concentrate while I read.	5	4	3	2	1

11. I monitor my comprehension   5   4   3   2   1
    while I read.

12. I easily learn new   5   4   3   2   1
    vocabulary.

Add up the numbers circled. Your total score will be between 12 and 60. The higher your score, the more likely you are to be skilled in organizing, note taking, and reading. For total scores below 36, write or reflect on items for which you have concerns. Also, consider talking with a trusted friend, a family member, a teacher, or an adviser.

GETTING ORGANIZED

For many years we have begun our learning framework courses by inviting some experienced and successful juniors and seniors to advise our students about the realistic practices of academic survival. What follows is a version of that session. Here, and in the classroom, as teachers we reserve the right to comment and add other explanations.

Our students are Tanya, a business major with a specialization in marketing; Paul, a biology major heading toward medical school; and Kim, an elementary education major. All have completed a learning framework course. Tanya initiates the session by sharing her memories of a freshman year fraught with stress and disorganization. She learned quickly that she had to become organized. She has brought her own notebooks to demonstrate how she now organizes each semester.

Tanya *My starting point is the syllabus I get in every class. They are much more complicated and specific than any I had in high school. Once profs have given us the information, they expect us to remember everything! Assignments, projects, tests, everything. They also have to give us, in writing, all the departmental and school policies, as well as their own policies about attendance and grading. It's really a contract; it tells me the professor's expectations of my work and how I*

TYPICAL CONTENTS OF A SYLLABUS

- Course title and number
- Instructor's name and contact information
- Office hours
- Instructor's philosophy of teaching
- Purpose of the course
- Course goals/objectives
- Textbooks and required materials
- Suggested textbooks and learning resources
- Web-based course components
- Required learning activities
- Exam and assignment due dates
- Grading criteria
- Attendance policy
- Disability statement
- Course calendar/outline

will earn my grade. Last term, one of my professors never passed out a syllabus. She just put it on the course website. I had to print a copy for myself.

exercise 3.2

Syllabi Matrix

Complete the syllabi matrix in Figure 3.1 by filling in the information requested. This exercise will help you organize important class information into one graphic for future reference.

Paul   *I pay particular attention to the purpose, goals, and structure of the course. It's the best way for me to figure out what's important to the professor and when it'll be covered.*

Kim   *Me too. I put all the important due dates on my master calendar. I have one academic calendar that has all the due dates for all my courses. That way, I can easily see where the conflicts are. My tests always seem to happen in the same week.*

Paul   *I finally started carrying a planner so that I could write down appointments, meetings, and my work schedule. I use it as a master academic calendar as well. I realized that I was much less stressed when I put all my obligations—academic, personal, social—in one place. When my dad saw it, he said I was only a step away from an electronic planner, but I don't want to try that yet.*

Here are suggestions for creating an academic calendar:

- Identify your committed times (classes, work, meals, commuting, etc.). List these activities during the appropriate times on your schedule.

- Identify your best times to study. Do you read better during the early evening hours? Are you a better writer during the early morning hours? Complete your academic tasks when you are most alert and able to concentrate.

- Determine how much study time you need. Some students use the rule of two hours of study time for every hour of class time. We do not believe there is any one formula that ensures success. You must decide how much time you need to stay engaged in learning. Remember that studying is a behavior—you will be reading, writing, creating, practicing, teaching, and thinking. Be as specific as you can on your academic planner about the behavior you intend to complete.

FIGURE 3.1 Syllabi Matrix

Course Title & Number	Course Title & Number	Course Title & Number	Course Title & Number	Course Title & Number
Instructor's Name	Instructor's Name	Instructor's Name	Instructor's Name	Instructor's Name
Office Hours	Office Hours	Office Hours	Office Hours	Office Hours
Absence Policy	Absence Policy	Absence Policy	Absence Policy	Absence Policy
Assignment Due Dates	Assignment Due Dates	Assignment Due Dates	Assignment Due Dates	Assignment Due Dates
Test Due Dates	Test Due Dates	Test Due Dates	Test Due Dates	Test Due Dates

exercise 3.3

Academic Calendar

Fill in the calendar in Figure 3.2 using the following guidelines:

1. Identify your committed times (classes, work, meals, commuting, etc.) and list these activities during the appropriate times on the calendar.

2. Identify your best times to study and then determine how much study time you need. Schedule academic tasks when you are most alert and able to concentrate.

3. Be as specific as you can about the behavior you intend to complete (reading, writing, creating, practicing, teaching, and reviewing).

Completing this exercise will help you organize your time for the semester.

Kim   *Let's talk about the comprehensive notebook we learned how to construct in this class. I've taught all my friends how to make one. It's a notebook that holds everything I need for one class, and its lab if there is one. That's where I put the syllabus, all my class notes, handouts, printouts from the course website, assignments, test review questions, everything! I like using loose-leaf notebooks for each course. I carry a small hole punch and a stapler in my backpack so that I can put handouts in right away. That way, I never lose anything.*

Paul   *I'm not organized enough to use loose-leaf notebooks; I really like spiral notebooks with pockets. I get the really thick ones so that I have one for my Monday-Wednesday-Friday classes and another for my Tuesday-Thursday classes. I put a zippered bag in my backpack with a stapler, pens, highlighters, blue books, answer sheets, etc. I just staple handouts next to the lecture notes I take. You're right about the syllabus; I put it in the pocket so that I always have it with me. However, my classes are getting so complicated and difficult, a preview for med school I think, that I may have to start using a different spiral for each class. This term I have had to use a separate notebook for genetics because the lab work is so extensive.*

Tanya   *There's something else to do to get organized. My desk is the only part of my room I make sure is neat. It's only for study. I set it up so that I have room for my laptop and printer, but also I have a dictionary, a thesaurus, and all my supplies. I bought a good*

FIGURE 3.2 Academic Calendar

	Mon	Tues	Wed	Thur	Fri	Sat	Sun
6:00–7:00							
7:00–8:00							
8:00–9:00							
9:00–10:00							
10:00–11:00							
11:00–12:00							
12:00–1:00							
1:00–2:00							
2:00–3:00							
3:00–4:00							
4:00–5:00							
5:00–6:00							
6:00–7:00							
7:00–8:00							
8:00–9:00							
9:00–10:00							
10:00–11:00							
11:00–12:00							
12:00–1:00							

BEGINNING CONSIDERATIONS FOR AN ORGANIZED STUDY SYSTEM

- Where should I keep my academic calendar?

- Should I use loose-leaf or spiral notebooks?

- Should I use separate notebooks for each course or multisubject?

- What kind of notepaper should I use?

- Where should I put the syllabus?

- How should I carry all the other stuff—pens, highlighters, etc.?

- Where should I place handouts?

- How should I carry test materials—blue books, answer sheets?

- How and where should I set up a study place?

- What are the necessary equipment, supplies, and materials for an efficient study place?

study light too. The small bulletin board above my desk is just for academics—no pictures or other distractions. That's where I put a copy of the academic calendar plus reminders about assignments and study sessions.

For learning to occur, information must be organized and meaningful. Your individual preference for learning is your own natural ability to organize and make meaning of the material. As you attempt to master college-level material, you may find that your individual preferences for learning do not always match your instructor's style of teaching. You may learn best by seeing information and can easily recall printed information in the form of words, phrases, or sentences. Or you might be more inclined to recall information presented in pictures, charts, or diagrams. Perhaps you learn best by listening, whereby information that you hear becomes easily remembered. Maybe you learn best by doing, as you create and manipulate objects. For many of us, using a combination of these techniques is extremely helpful.

Constructing an organized, comprehensive notebook will enhance your ability to learn college material on your terms. The notebook is more than simply a place to record notes; you can integrate note taking, visual aids, test preparation, and reviewing systems into the notebook. It is also a place to reflect on the course content through journaling and guided questions. Think of the possibilities as you adopt ways to organize, associate, expand, apply, analyze, visualize, synthesize, and evaluate course content. Creating maps, networks, hierarchies, comparison charts, time lines, sample test questions, and many other learning techniques will become second nature to you. As we introduce you to new learning strategies, we want you to experiment and explore new ways of learning that enhance your individual preferences through the integrative notebook.

Your notebook should allow for flexibility so you can find, add, and move materials easily. To do this, organization is paramount. If you decide to use a loose-leaf notebook, we suggest that you begin by dividing it (using labeled dividers) into sections:

COMPREHENSIVE NOTEBOOK SECTIONS

- course syllabus
- semester calendar

- lecture notes
- handouts
- textbook notes
- supplemental resources from the library or the Internet
- assignments/exercises
- review materials
- test preparations/sample test questions

exercise 3.4

Comprehensive Notebook

Set up a comprehensive notebook for one or more of your courses. You will need to purchase one or more loose-leaf notebooks, loose-leaf paper, and section dividers. Divide the notebook(s) into the following categories and begin to place items in the notebook(s).

- Course syllabus
- Semester calendar
- Lecture notes
- Handouts
- Textbook notes
- Supplemental resources from the library or the Internet
- Assignments/exercises
- Review materials
- Test preparations/sample test questions

This exercise will assist you in organizing class material and facilitate your ability to review.

HOW TO LEARN IN CLASS

In four years of college you will spend almost 2,000 hours in classrooms listening to lectures and participating in class discussions. If you master the skill of learning in class, not only will you be more successful academically, but your college experience will be much less stressful because studying out of class will be more effective.

It is easy to spot students who know how to learn in class and those who clearly do not. Pretend you are from another century or planet and watch a typical American undergraduate class. How many students arrive well before the instructor or wander in 10 or 15 minutes late? Head toward the back of the room or insist on sitting in the first two rows? Sink gratefully into a seat and are immediately asleep or take notes attentively? Participate in class discussion or daydream through most of the class period?

Make no mistake. The purpose of a college class is to advance your learning in that course. The ideas that are presented, explained, and developed are often not duplicated in the text. When you learn what you should in class, your study time can then focus on the outside readings and exercises instead of on the material you should have already mastered in class.

Tanya   *I remember being so scared in my first college class. It was so different from high school. My teacher lectured so fast that I could hardly keep up. I learned that I had to read the chapters before the class; that way, I knew immediately what was new information and could be sure to write that down. Since I knew the topics and had seen the vocabulary, I could take notes faster.*

Kim   *Right. I learned to print the notes posted on the course website and take them to class. I always sit in the front of the room, at least in the first three rows. It's so much easier to concentrate there.*

Paul   *Oh yes, I remember sitting in the back row when I was a beginning freshman. I was so tired most days because the guys on my hall never went to sleep before 2 A.M. I bet I slept through the first three weeks of class before I realized that I wasn't learning anything. I knew if I was going to survive here, my social life had to slow down. It was hard, but I did it. My roommate didn't survive academically; he partied every night and was hung over most days. Even if he got to a class, he couldn't concentrate. I had to convince myself that going to class was my job; I had to show up ready and able to work.*

Kim   *Yes, we've all had to learn that. And lots more. You really have to learn to adjust to all different kinds of teachers. This term I have an instructor who lectures from the text; I've learned to take my notes directly in the book.*

Tanya   *Another strategy I use frequently now is a two- or three-minute review. Between the time I get to class and the beginning of the lecture, I look back over the notes I took last time and try to remember the last class. I remember my educational psychology teacher calling this technique the academic warm-up. Even though it takes just a couple of minutes, it helps me remember the ideas and facts I learned last time.*

There are few learning activities that are more cognitively demanding than taking notes during a college lecture. "Students must listen to the lecture, select important ideas, hold and manipulate these ideas in working memory, interpret the information, decide what to record, and then write it down" (Armbruster, 2000, p. 176). Educational research clearly shows that the completeness of lecture notes is positively related to academic achievement (Armbruster, 2000); in other words, the more complete our notes are, the more likely we are to be successful in that course. "The bottom line is that the real value of taking notes is to have them for review" (Armbruster, 2000, p. 179). Curiously, another person's notes are usually not very helpful. What seems to matter is that we do the work to listen, select, hold, interpret, decide, and write. Succinctly, the task is difficult but important for academic success in order for you to have the materials you need to study for tests.

Passivity is your greatest enemy when you sit in class. You must find a way to engage in what is happening in the classroom. Class learning is more than simply transcribing the instructor's notes into your notebook. It is more than remembering the stories and jokes the instructor uses as illustrations and forgetting the main ideas. It is more than watching slides or computer displays. Becoming competent in note taking takes most college students one or two semesters. Your learning strategies should vary in lecture, problem-solving, discussion, and distance education classes. What follows is a brief description of these types of classes and an introduction to several of the respected note-taking techniques.

Lecture Classes

In lecture classes, you create study notes that when combined with your outside sources should constitute your learning resources. Those notes should not replicate the book, but, instead, they should comprise a record of the main points of the lecture (there are usually five or six), relevant facts to support those points, examples that illustrate those points, and explanations of difficult ideas. Listen for concepts and facts you did not find in the readings.

Tanya   *When I begin to take lecture notes, I think about what I am trying to accomplish. What do I want to learn? How will I be tested? How much do I already know about the subject? How easy is it for me to learn in this subject? I search for the main ideas of the lecture by carefully watching my professor and the materials displayed on the board or the screen. She or he may present an outline for the lecture, make introductory comments during the first moments of class, repeat an idea several times, raise her or his voice, use words such as* the main point, most important, in summary. *When I hear any of these, I know a main point is coming.*

Paul   *Usually I will capture a main point in a sentence or phrase. Writing the concepts in my own words helps me understand them. I found out the hard way that if I simply copy the professor's words without understanding them, they are useless. Putting the key ideas in my own words increases the likelihood that I will understand them. When I understand the material, I remember it better.*

Kim   *I record definitions, facts, and opinions that seem relevant. I had to learn not to write down everything the professor says; instead, I carefully select what I write. Here is where reading or skimming the text before class helps. I cannot spend all my time rewriting material that is in the text, but I always write down new material.*

Tanya   *I leave space between topics and number or organize whenever I can. A friend taught me to put a question mark whenever I get lost or confused and leave blank space so I can ask for help after class. I mark with an asterisk [*] things I believe will be on the test. I don't recopy anymore because it takes too long, so I try to make my notes readable.*

Paul   *My key to creating a useful set of lecture notes is thinking. I think about what is important in this material; I think about what I need to learn; I think about whether I am writing down the main points and supporting details.*

Cornell Notes

Created over 40 years ago at Cornell University by Walter Pauk (1997), this system requires dividing note pages into three sections: the note-taking section, the cue column, and the summary area. This method works well for mostly lecture-based classes (especially those with facts, details, and examples). It is an organized method for recording, revising, and reviewing notes.

To create a page for Cornell notes, draw a vertical line two and one-half inches from the left edge of the paper; end the line two inches from the bottom of the sheet. Then, draw a horizontal line two inches up from the bottom of the page. Also include your name, date, and the page number at the very top, on the left or right side. Paper in this format is available from most college bookstores in loose-leaf, spiral, and tablet form.

Once you have taken your notes, read over them and fill in any gaps to make your notes more legible. Then, determine the main ideas from the notes and write questions in the cue column. Using a plain sheet of paper, cover up the notes in the right-hand column. Read the questions you created and then recite aloud the answer. Check your answer by removing the plain sheet of paper. Repeat the sequence until you have mastered the material. After your initial review, write a summary statement (a couple of sentences) for each full page of notes in the summary area. See Figure 3.3 for an example of notes taken using the Cornell system.

Tanya   *The Cornell system really works for me in all my lecture classes. I take notes in the wide column to the right. I try to leave space in between sections and I make sure I don't let everything get crowded. Since I don't recopy my notes, I print because my handwriting is terrible. I've learned that the 10 minutes right after class are the most important for me. That's when I do a rapid mental review of what I just learned. If I can, I skim my notes quickly, fill in any gaps, and write questions in the cue column on the main ideas. Then I cover*

FIGURE 3.3   An Example of Cornell Notes

Jared Schultz 9–30 p. 13	Karl Marx - (pg. 1)
What is Marx's reasoning?	- Constant drive for new markets. - Creation of new and insatiable needs.
What makes one's life his own?	- The recognition of one's morality as the necessary condition of authentic living.
What is authenticity?	- Authenticity is morality. - The creation of the culture of fantasy, the eclipse of time.
When was Freud's synthesis?	- Freud's synthesis was between enlightenment and romanticism.
What is the importance of the shift?	- Shift to psychogenic from organic understanding of mental disease to understanding of psychogenic. - Discovery of the unconscious. - Expansion of the sexual. - The future of illusion.

Marx's reasoning is the constant drive for new markets & the creation of new & insatiable needs.

According to Marx authenticity is morality.

the notes part of the page and answer the questions I created. Such a simple technique and it really works. Later, when I'm studying, I do the same thing again. I cover my notes, read the questions I created, and then recite aloud the answer. I repeat the sequence until I have mastered the material. Then I write a summary statement (a couple of sentences) for each full page of notes.

Pauk believes that it is important to review notes as soon as possible, at least before going to sleep. He stresses the importance of getting a global view of the notes while trying to retain the details. To do this he encourages students to reflect by asking, "What's the significance of these facts or ideas? What principles are they based on? How can I apply them to what I already know? How do they fit? What's beyond these facts and ideas?" (Pauk, 1997, p. 209).

In an extensive review of research on lecture note taking, Armbruster (2000) reported that students typically record fewer than 40 percent of lecture ideas (one study reported as little as 20 percent) and that students tend to record fewer notes during the latter part of a lecture. The research is also adamant that the quality and quantity of notes are both important; the more complete the notes are for review, the greater the potential for learning. How students prefer to learn can also influence learning. Some students tend to learn more from the actual note-taking process (as they organize and find relationships while writing the notes), whereas others tend to learn more while they review the notes. Thus, the pressure on college students is to be active and involved learners in the classroom as well as to become expert and flexible in the skill of reviewing their notes outside of class.

---

exercise 3.5

Cornell Notes

Practice taking notes in the Cornell format from a lecture class for at least two class sessions using the following guidelines:

Before class:

- Draw a vertical line two and one-half inches from the left edge of a sheet of paper; end the line two inches from the bottom of the sheet (look for preprinted wide-margin paper at your college bookstore).

- Draw a horizontal line two inches up from the bottom of the page.

During class:

- Take notes in the right-hand column as you would normally.

- Leave the cue column on the left blank except for brief notations to emphasize potential test questions, key terms, significant facts, etc.

After class (as soon as possible):

- Fill in any gaps to make your notes more legible.

- Determine main ideas from the notes and write questions in the cue column.

Before the next class session:

- Cover up the notes in the right-hand column using a plain sheet of paper.

- Read the questions you created and then recite the answers aloud.

- Check your answers by removing the plain sheet of paper.

- Repeat the sequence until you have mastered the material.

- After your initial review, write a summary statement (a couple of sentences) for each full page of notes in the summary area at the bottom of the page.

Invite another student (one who is familiar with this note-taking system) to read over your notes and give you feedback. This exercise will strengthen your note-taking skills and aid you in learning lecture material.

Problem-Solving Classes

The purpose of problem-solving classes is simple: class time is used to solve problems and to discuss the process of doing so. The strategy for taking good notes in such a class is to write down not only the problem but also the verbalization of the steps. In other words, write down each step and then explain what was done in your own words. The sequence of steps is crucial. Math, accounting, economics, finance, computer programming, statistics, logic, and case study–based courses are all examples of problem-solving classes.

T-Notes

Introduced in 1983 to assist college students, T-notes, created by Davis and Clark (1996), are a way to organize and learn different types of lecture information. Similar to the Cornell method, the T-notes system is also a method to record, revise, and review notes.

To use this system, begin by dividing a page of paper by drawing a large "T." Extend the top of the T from the left margin to the right margin, leaving a space of one and one-half inches across the top of the paper. Extend the leg of the T down the center of the page beginning from the top line to the bottom of the page. Above the T, center the title of the lecture or major topic. Also include your name, date, and page number at the very top of the left or right side.

As you encounter lecture information, divide the information between the two columns. For example if you are given a term to learn, place the term on the left side of the T and the definition and examples on the right side. Or, if you are to learn a visual such as a diagram, draw the diagram to the left of the T and the explanation to the right. See Figure 3.4 for an example of T-notes.

T-notes are especially useful for learning procedures such as those common in mathematics or statistics. For example, if you are learning an algebra equation, place the formula on top of the T. Then write the steps to solving the

FIGURE 3.4 An Example of T-Notes for Learning Terminology

Bibiana Alvarado
   1–23
   p. 6 Add and Multi Principle	

- Variable	Represents a value; x, y, c
- Equation	Problem x + 3 = 6, $a^2 + b^2 = c^2$
- Expression	$x + 3, c^2, a^2 + b^2$
- How do we determine value of variable	Solve for the variable
- Evaluate	Substitute / "plug-in"
- Like terms	2x, 5x; 15zy, .05zy
- Unlike terms	2x + 5xy 3xy + 7zy
- Distributive property	a(b +c) = ab + ac

- Addition principle	For any real #s a, b, c
	a = b =) a + c = b + c

- Multi principle	For any real #s a, b, c
	a = b =) ac = bc

- Using both +/– principles together	ID variable +/– terms as needed simplify/combine like terms –/÷ to isolate variable simplify answer

equation to the left of thc T and examples that correlate with the steps on the right of the T (see Figure 3.5 for an example).

T-notes are designed to be used as a self-test system similar to 3×5 index cards; however, the advantage is that you do not have to rewrite the information but simply cover any part of the T to self-test.

Paul   *Since I take so many science and math courses, I use T-notes. Across the top I write the lecture topic, the formula, and the subject of the process. If there are a lot of terms, I put them on the left side and the definitions/examples on the right. If it's a diagram or a flow chart, I draw it on the left and put the explanation on the right. T-notes really help me learn procedures, especially in math. I write the steps of the problem on the left side and the explanation on the right. I can test myself by simply covering any part of the T.*

---

exercise 3.6

T-Notes

Practice taking notes in the T-note format for a problem-solving class (math, accounting, science lab) for at least two class sessions using the following guidelines.

Before class:

- Divide a page of paper by drawing a large "T." Extend the top of the "T" from the left margin to the right margin, leaving a space of one and one-half inches across the top of the paper. Extend the leg of the "T" down the center of the page.

During class:

- Above the "T," write the name of the procedure or topic.

- As you encounter lecture information, divide the information between the two columns. List the steps used to complete the procedure to the left of the "T" and examples to the right.

After class (as soon as possible):

- Fill in any gaps to make your notes more legible.

Before the next class session:

- Cover up the notes on either side of the "T" using a plain sheet of paper.

- Recite aloud the answers.

- Check your answers by removing the paper.

- Repeat the sequence until you have mastered the material.

FIGURE 3.5 An Example of T-Notes for Learning an Equation

Rod Hill
2–11
p. 25

The Quadratic Formula

$$x = \frac{-b \pm \sqrt{b^2 - 4ac}}{2a}$$

X represents the solutions of:
$$ax^2 + bx + c = 0$$

Steps:

1. First must find standard form of equation

2. Then should try and factor—if it is not possible, then use the quad formula

3. Determine values for a, b, c and substitute into formula:
$$x = \frac{-b \pm \sqrt{b^2 - 4ac}}{2a}$$

4. The solutions of any quadratic equation can be found by using the quad formula (ALWAYS!)

Ex 1: Solve $5x^2 - 8x + 3 = 0$

(Already in stand. form)
$a = 5, b = -8, c = 3$

Using quad form:

$$x = \frac{-(-8) \pm \sqrt{(-8)^2 - (4)(5)(3)}}{2(5)}$$

$$x = \frac{8 \pm \sqrt{64 - 60}}{10} = \frac{8 \pm \sqrt{4}}{10}$$

$$x = \frac{8 \pm 2}{10}$$

So,

$$x = \frac{8 - 2}{10} \quad or \quad x = \frac{8 + 2}{10}$$

$$x = \frac{10}{10} \quad or \quad x = \frac{6}{10}$$

So,

$$x = 1 \quad or \quad x = \frac{3}{5}$$

Thus, the solutions are 1 & 3/5

Invite another student (one who is familiar with this note-taking system) to read over your notes and give you feedback. This exercise will strengthen your note-taking skills and aid in learning problem-solving material.

Discussion Classes

Discussion classes are often great fun, but students frequently leave class without any notes. That behavior is dangerous because we rarely remember concepts unless we write them down and go over them, even if we have been interested in the discussion. In this type of class, the professor usually summarizes a main point when the discussion ends. Listen for those summaries and record them. Discussion notes tend to be shorter, and they usually do not follow any particular structure. Ideas are important here, not details. Sometimes a good strategy is to meet quickly with another class member after class and compare notes. Before exams brainstorm possible test questions in a study group. See Figure 3.6 for an example of discussion notes and possible test questions.

Good note-taking strategies develop with time and practice. The criteria are always whether the strategies help you learn what you need to learn. Obviously, strategies should vary from class to class and from student to student. Here are some general strategies that we recommend:

GOOD NOTE-TAKING STRATEGIES

- Get enough sleep the night before classes.
- Attend all lectures.
- Arrive early with the right materials.
- Sit toward the front of the room.
- Date the first page of your notes each day.
- Use a heading to label the notes.
- Write in pen on one side of the paper (pencil fades).
- Use phrases, not sentences.
- Create your own symbols and abbreviations.
- Write down the main ideas, supporting details, and examples.
- Gently bring your mind back to the subject (when it wanders).

- Write down what the instructor emphasizes through pauses, repetition, summarization, and energy.

- Look for and mark relationships between the concepts.

- Review the material before the next class session and continue the review process several times each week.

FIGURE 3.6   Example of Discussion Notes and Possible Test Questions

Sandy Chang
11–28
p. 89

Discussion on Social Stratification

- Social Stratification?

    System by which a society ranks categories of people in a hierarchy.

- 4 principles of Social Strat:
  1. Char. of society–not simply a function of individual diff.
  2. Persists over generations.
  3. Varies in form.
  4. Rests on widely held beliefs.

- Davis-Moore Thesis:
  - Positions that are most important (for society) and that require talent and/or training must be the most highly rewarded.
  - Most highly rewarded positions should be those that are functionally unique & on which other positions rely.

- Social Strat (An explanation by Weber)
  - Model of Class Structure.

POSSIBLE TEST QUESTIONS:

1. Describe social stratification. Be sure to include the 4 principles of Social Strat.
2. According to Weber, what are the 6 social classes?

Frequently Asked Questions

What should I do if my instructor lectures from an outline?

Kim *If your instructor displays the outline, copy it quickly on a left page in your notes and then incorporate it into your notes as the primary organization. I don't use Roman numerals, just simple numbers if they help.*

See Figure 3.7 for an example of outline notes.

What should I do if my instructor uses PowerPoint slides and gives us the handouts for them?

Tanya *By all means, use the handouts as structure but be sure to add details and examples to them during the lecture. The information on the slides alone is not sufficient.*

See Figure 3.8 for an example of notes using a PowerPoint handout.

What should I do when my instructor gives a disorganized lecture?

Paul *If a lecture seems completely disorganized, take the time to reorganize your notes during review. I prefer to take notes without any system and then rewrite using a Cornell, a T-note, or an informal outline format.*

What should I do when my instructor talks too fast?

Tanya *Get the main concepts (the primary purpose of note taking). If you can, ask questions or ask the instructor to slow down. Work in tandem with another student and combine notes. If you read the material before class, the topics may be more familiar. Check to see if the course website has extra materials. You're responsible for the material no matter how fast the teacher lectures.*

What should I do when the material is confusing and overwhelming?

Kim *I know how to answer this question because I had this experience my freshman year. The first step is to read the text again (assuming you have already read it before class). If you still have problems understanding the material, then ask for help immediately from the instructor, the teaching assistant, or the campus learning center. Check with a campus librarian for other explanations of the subject that might be easier to understand. A friend of mine used the extreme strategy of taping the lecture (with the instructor's agreement) and listening to it while she commuted or did chores. Although it takes a long time to listen to the recording and create study notes, it may be worth your time for a complicated and demanding course.*

FIGURE 3.7 An Example of Outline Notes

Chantal Washington
     10–3   Perry's Theory of Cognitive Development
     p. 19

- Cognitive Theory – intellectual & ethical development of college students

I. Students' developmental tasks are to:
- become academically competent
- learn to develop satisfying friendships + relationships
- become ind. of parents + authorities
- choose career + lifestyles
- examine values + beliefs

II. William Perry (1970)
- worked in Harvard U's Bureau of Study Counsel
- encountered personality differences
- became aware that what were thought to be personality differences were developmental patterns

III. Perry's Theory
- identified 9 stages through which individuals progress in becoming more cognitively complex
- these strategies are sequential
- to simplify the 9 stages they are presented in 4 categories:

- Commit w/ relativism
- relativism
- multiplicity
- dualism

Distance Classes

A significant change in higher education has taken place in the past 20 years. Distance education has evolved through four generations of structure, although all four are still used. Distance education provides instruction when students and instructors are separated by physical distance but connected by technology.

FIGURE 3.8   An Example of Notes Using a PowerPoint Handout

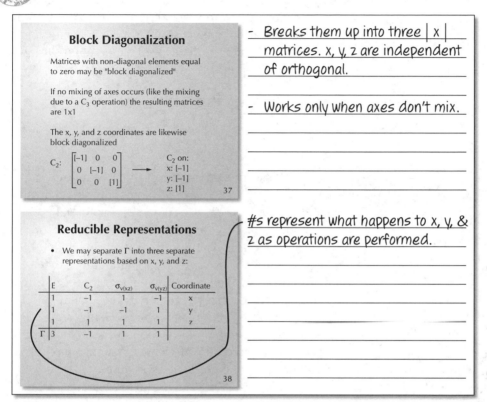

The simplest distance education programs are correspondence courses in which students study independently and send their lessons and tests by mail. The next level in complexity are those courses with video and/or audiotapes and, perhaps, some audio broadcasts during which students can ask questions. The third generation uses the Internet for one- and two-way videoconferencing, email, chat rooms, and so forth. Some schools have recently begun to offer fourth-generation multimedia (multiple forms of communication such as audio and video) and hypermedia in which students participate in teleconferencing over the Internet; have access to a multitude of online sources such as tutorials, course materials, and online databases; and "collaborate over e-mail and within chat rooms" (Caverly & Peterson, 2000, p. 306). An important characteristic of both the third- and fourth-generation distance education programs is whether the students interact with each other in real time (synchronous) or in delayed time (asynchronous).

To learn successfully in such situations, students must analyze the circumstances and create the appropriate notes for study. Although there are arguable advantages of flexibility for the individual's circumstances, the disadvantages of solitude and ample opportunity for procrastination may make distance education

ONLINE LEARNING ENVIRONMENTS

- **Course Web pages.** Usually include syllabus, course information, lecture notes, reminders, assignments, test reviews, and sample tests.

- **E-mail.** Messages that can be sent or received from instructors or classmates at any time. Documents can be attached.

- **Virtual chats (live chat).** Participants type messages back and forth or even speak to each other in synchronous (real) time over the Internet.

- **Discussion boards (threaded discussions).** Participants post virtual messages and responses to each other.

- **Listservs.** Participants, using a special e-mail program, connect to each other for online discussions.

- **Whiteboards.** A window that appears on the computer screen allowing participants to write on the screen much like a chalkboard.

- **Online courses.** Contain downloadable course material, interactive tutorials, streaming audio/video media pieces, virtual libraries, and Web links. Online office hours and examinations are common. Streaming audio/video feeds stream files into your computer so they play immediately from the beginning while downloading the next parts in sequence.

- **Hybrid courses.** Mixes components of the traditional lecture course and the online course.

Source: Adapted from Winograd, K., & Moore, G. S. (2003). *You Can Learn Online.* Boston: McGraw-Hill.

coursework more difficult than traditional classroom study. Dropout rates are 15–20 percent higher for online courses than for traditional courses (Winograd & Moore, 2003). In distance education, students need to have strong time management and online research skills as well as the ability to self-direct learning.

HOW TO LEARN OUTSIDE CLASS

Most freshmen think about studying often. They talk about it, complain about it, procrastinate about it. They religiously take their books home on the weekend, or to the park, or to a friend's place. They promise themselves that they will study after the party or after the movie. Do they study? Well, sometimes, but rarely is it effective, because most freshmen believe that memorizing by itself is enough. Memorizing at the last minute (or cramming) is the most popular form of freshman studying. No wonder so many are disappointed with their test performance.

Understanding, not memory, is the foundation of college learning. The trick is to study to understand, then memorize what is important. Studying is different from reading. We read the newspaper, a recipe, a novel. The purpose is usually to acquire information or to be entertained. To **study** is to *apply the mind so as to acquire understanding and knowledge*. We tend to understand something by being active in the learning process. Simply listening to a lecture or reading a chapter in a textbook may not be enough. Yet, if we begin to demonstrate, discuss, manipulate, or teach the information, our comprehension and learning increase dramatically.

Learning from Text

Kim *I remember when I started college. I couldn't believe how many books and articles my profes-*

sors assigned. Since I never read much in high school, I realized that I had to change in college, but I really didn't know how to handle my assignments. I got so much conflicting advice: read before class, read after class, don't read at all, or just read the summaries.

Tanya   *Oh, yeah, it took some time for me to figure out when and what to study. Some instructors don't emphasize the text, but most take questions from the readings. I found I could often make a C if I took good class notes and studied those, but to make a strong B or an A, I had to study the readings. Cs just don't help the transcript.*

Paul   *That's right. I cannot afford many Cs. In my classes, I know I have to read, but I often read the text after the lecture, not before.*

Kim   *In my toughest classes, I have to skim the material before the lecture so I know what's coming; then I study it afterward. At the beginning of the semester, I look at how the chapters are organized. Are they grouped into units with introductions? What is the structure of each chapter? Do they contain case studies, summaries, introductory outlines, boxed inserts, graphs and charts, problems, questions? What appendices exist? Is there a glossary (a dictionary of terms used in the book), an index, background information (science books often contain an explanation of the scientific method, and government books contain the Constitution, and so on)? I learned if a study guide exists for the text, buy it; it is worth every dollar.*

Paul   *You are thorough!*

Kim   *I have to be. I realized quickly that all those years avoiding reading had made me into a poor reader. So I've learned to use all the help the author gives me. If you're like me, it's hard to know what to study. I began by marking so much in the material that the entire page was yellow. When I realized that I could not even find the main ideas, I went to the learning center and learned some reading comprehension strategies. When I could understand the main ideas in the text, then I knew what to mark.*

Tanya   *I had to learn to view each chapter as a whole, even if it takes me several days to read it. My first step is to look over the entire chapter. Then I read the main headings and the summary if there is one. I try to think about the two or three main ideas that the chapter is about and say them aloud or write them down. When I can, I try to make those ideas into questions because that's how I will remember the right information.*

Most modern textbooks are partitioned into sections and subsections. This deliberate structure helps you learn, for as you create meaning from new ideas and information, you need to store those understandings in your memory. Research tells us that if we understand the concepts of the material we study, then we are better able to remember and use that information in other ways (Bransford,

Brown, & Cocking, 1999). Thus, focus first on understanding the material; then work to remember it. As you read each section of a textbook, follow these steps:

STEPS IN READING A TEXTBOOK

1. Preview.
2. Use the headings.
3. Identify the primary idea(s).
4. Read before marking.
5. Continue the process.
6. Review.

Preview. You have many possibilities: Look over the table of contents, title, chapter objectives, introduction, headings and subheadings, italicized or bold-faced words, charts, diagrams and illustrations, summary, chapter questions, and so on. The purpose is to begin to relate what you are reading to your prior knowledge of similar information.

Use the headings. Use the headings to help formulate questions about the material as you read. The purpose is to make you less passive and more active in the reading process. Questions will provide you with a purpose for reading as you search for answers.

Identify the primary idea(s). The primary idea or ideas will begin to emerge as you preview and use the headings and ask and answer questions while reading a subsection. Usually the primary idea occurs within the first or second paragraph of a subsection of text. When you find a primary idea, mark it by underlining or highlighting, or annotate key words and phrases in the margin.

Read before marking. Read the first subsection without marking anything. Stop and think. What in that subsection is important about the primary idea? You may find one or two or three items to mark or annotate, but be selective, for if you mark or annotate too much, the process becomes useless.

Continue the process. Work your way through each subsection, back and forth, reading . . . thinking . . . marking or annotating. As you work, be sure to look over any charts, graphs, or boxed inserts. These graphic aids will help you understand the ideas, as will completing any of the exercises that are included within the chapter. Work for 15 to 20 minutes and then get up and take a 5-minute break. Then go back to work.

Review. Review as soon as possible—we recommend within the first day or so of reading the material. You may want to create review strategies, such as chapter review cards, mapping, study guides, or test preps to aid your review (see Chapters 11 and 12). Continue to review the material several times each week until test time.

The end result of a productive study session is twofold: you have an understanding of the main ideas of the text reading, and you have a marked or annotated text that will help you prepare for exams. The markings are yours, your choices; that is why it is useful to buy unmarked texts. What other people have marked will not help you.

Improving Concentration, Comprehension, and Vocabulary

Three kinds of reading difficulties are much more serious and require direct intervention. The first is poor concentration. When you pick up a textbook do you get sleepy immediately? Kim's comments in the previous dialogue illustrate the second difficulty, poor reading comprehension. If you are seriously concerned that you have problems in reading and comprehending college-level texts, go to your campus learning center and take a reading diagnostic test. The results will tell you if you need special help through a reading skills class or tutor. The third reading difficulty is a lack of expertise in vocabulary. What follows are some techniques you can implement to overcome these difficulties.

Sharpening concentration. If you have poor concentration or are a gifted daydreamer, if your mind wanders each time you pick up a textbook, the cure is ruthless. Study in 10-minute sessions. Read the chapter one subsection at a time. Turn the heading into a question and when you find the answer, write it down. Hold yourself accountable for every minute you are looking at the page. If you have to stand up and hold the book, do so. After each 10-minute session, test yourself on the material (note how many paragraphs you read while concentrating). Look over those paragraphs and quickly recall the most important points. Continue with this procedure and finish reading the first subsection.

Daydreaming is a habit; so is concentration. Get in the habit of concentrating when you are looking at a text. Each time you realize that you are daydreaming, pull your mind back to the information on the page.

Several sensible strategies to improve reading concentration are to set specific goals (*I will read and understand the first 10 pages of Chapter 7 in the next hour*), to read purposefully to meet those goals, and to choose the best time of day to read. Take a 5-minute break every 20 minutes. These actions help develop a positive attitude.

Two types of distractions can impinge on concentration when we study: external and internal. External distractions concern the place you study: Is it orderly or chaotic? Quiet or noisy? Comfortable or crowded? Look at your environment for study. What changes do you need to make to support your study concentration? Internal distractions include boredom or active dislike for the subject matter, personal problems or worry, and feelings of fatigue and being overwhelmed. Using goals and self-talk may help you to overcome such distractions, but if serious personal problems exist, we recommend that you speak with a campus counselor.

exercise 3.7

Internal and External Distractions

Complete the grid in Figure 3.9. This exercise will aid you in identifying and eliminating distractions that interfere with your learning.

Monitoring comprehension. Good readers are aware when they understand the material. They routinely reread when necessary, locate primary ideas, and infer implied primary ideas. They identify supporting details, recognize patterns of organization, rephrase ideas into their own words, reread difficult sections, and create sample questions. If you are lucky enough to have a study guide for the text (a call to your college bookstore will tell you if one is in print), use it to organize your efforts by going back and forth between the guide and the text. Instructional CDs and online study guides can also help.

exercise 3.8

Comprehension-Monitoring Exercise

To learn to monitor and increase your comprehension, select a reading assignment in one of your textbooks for a lecture-based class (this exercise is unsuitable for math, literature, or philosophy texts). As you do this exercise, use your most powerful concentration strategies, trying to control both external and internal distractions.

1. In two or three minutes, look over the chapter title, the main headings within the chapter, and any introductory or summarizing material. Answer the following questions: What is the author's main purpose in this chapter? What are the main ideas? What is the structure of the information presented?

2. Divide the chapter into sections; it is usually a good idea to use the primary or secondary headings as the dividers. Read/study each section using the following strategies:

   • Look at the section heading and turn it into a question. You will be reading to answer that question.

   • Look for the general definition or primary idea of the section's topic in the first two or three paragraphs and mark it by underlining, highlighting, or bracketing.

FIGURE 3.9 Self-Analysis of Internal and External Distractions

Internal Distractions	Check all that apply	Describe the problem	Plan to correct the problem
Negative reactions to noise (your feelings and self-talk)			
Daydreaming			
Personal problems and worries			
Boredom			
Anxiety/dislike for subject			
Awesomeness of study task			
Fatigue			
Other			
External Distractions			
Study area			
Auditory distractions			
Visual distractions			
Furniture/work space			
Lighting			
Temperature			
Other			

- Read/study each paragraph. What information is the author giving? Why is he or she giving it? Place a check mark beside the paragraph if you can answer both questions and an "X" if you cannot.

- At the end of the section, stop, reflect, and attempt to relate the information to the section title and the main idea. Look at any paragraphs you marked with an "X." Do they make sense now? If so, cross out the "X." If not, write down questions to ask your instructor.

- Mark one to four important ideas, facts, or conclusions you believe you should remember.

- As you finish each section, on your own paper write a short summary statement of what you believe to be the most important ideas of the section.

Developing vocabulary. Another type of reading difficulty is lack of a collegiate vocabulary. If every tenth word in your freshman English reader is unfamiliar, you need to do specific vocabulary development. The fastest method is to go to the campus learning center and study Greek and Latin roots and prefixes. Another is to keep a dictionary with you at all times *and use it.* Make vocabulary cards, write sentences using new words, and become a wordsmith, a craftsman with language. Reading will greatly aid your vocabulary development. Persistence is the key; if you can truly learn one new word each day, your vocabulary will grow as your intellectual abilities grow.

If there is new vocabulary to learn, make flash cards (à la grade school) with the word on one side and the definition on the other. Some students find it extremely helpful to add an image to each flash card—especially those students who learn visually. To use this method, think of an image that represents the information and then draw the image using stick figures or symbols. The actual process of thinking about an appropriate image will facilitate your memory. Flash cards also work for identifications and grouped items (types, characteristics). Carry them in your backpack or pocket and practice them several times a day.

Learning from Solving Homework Problems

Paul *We need to talk about problem-solving courses like math, statistics, accounting, and physics. These courses require some really different strategies for homework studying.*

Tanya *Absolutely. Accounting was a nightmare for me until I learned how to study for it. The hardest lesson for me was the realization that I needed a lot of time to learn these topics. Practice, practice, practice. I attempted the* *homework right after class because that is when I remember more from class; in fact, I scheduled these classes with free time afterward. I made sure to buy all the workbooks; they really helped.*

Paul *When I did math problems, I talked aloud about what I was doing and why I was doing it, as if I were teaching it to someone else. I had to learn to take short breaks when I got stuck, then go back and try again. I'm glad I'm persistent. Sometimes when I got really stuck, I went to the tutoring center or found a classmate who could help.*

Tanya *Persistence is the key to success. Whenever I hear myself say that, I sound just like my dad.*

Paul *Problem-solving courses are about learning processes, that is, how to do something. A good way to ensure that I understand, rather than just remember, the process is to explain it to someone else. Trust me—don't ever settle for memorization; that's not enough for college tests. Do whatever you have to do to understand the material—tutors, study groups, labs—and do it fast. There's lots of help, if you don't delay. Cramming just does not work in these courses.*

Learning from homework problems is much more than simply getting the answer. We have to learn the process so well that we are able to use it in other situations. Since we tend to learn better in one mode over another, we learn better either through words or through quantitative symbols such as numbers and letters. It is wise to use our strongest mode of learning as the primary way we approach a problem, then translate solving that problem into the other mode. Paul is doing that when he talks his way through problems. T-notes can be quite helpful in using both modes to solve problems.

GOOD READING STRATEGIES

- Make sure you have all the assigned print materials, in either paper copy or electronic version.

- Set aside time to read when you are alert. Decide whether you need to read the material before or after the lecture.

- Choose what you are going to read and how long and make a deliberate intention to learn.

- Find a place that supports your concentration, that is, minimal distractions.

- Preview the material to be read to help assess your memory.

- Read to understand the material; then mark the primary points or take notes on them.

- Practice rehearsing and explaining what you understand.

- Reread sections that are confusing or ask for help.

- Set aside time in your schedule to review your reading material for each class.

Learning from Groups

Kim *A third type of study is the study group. Groups can be either opportunities or dangers. The dangers are obvious: you may visit instead of learn; your partners may give you wrong information; you may spend all your time teaching them and not learning anything new; your group may contain a leech who cannot contribute but clings to others. However, the opportunities* *are equally great. As a freshman, I joined study groups for history and psychology. When they worked well, we combined our skills and knowledge as well as motivated each other to greater accomplishments. Now, in the courses in my major, I use study groups about half the time. It's a good way for me to learn and meet people who share my interests.*

If you want to establish an effective study group, choose two other students who share your desire for success (three is the magic number for a group). Set a specific time, place, and topic. A good place is a study room in the library. Expect everyone to have completed the initial study of the material and to bring questions to the group. Compare notes from the lecture across the group. Focus the discussion on two points: the unanswered questions about the material from the lecture and assigned readings, and the predicted questions for the next test.

A lively, competitive interaction in a group will help everyone's learning. Debate the issues or quiz each other. Assign topics and let each person "teach" for five minutes. If you have been unwise enough to choose a lazy person or a leech, eject him or her from the group. Older, returning students are good additions to a group because they are usually highly motivated and willing to work hard.

CONCLUSION

Studying is not just reading and memorizing, although it encompasses both. Remember that studying is applying the mind so as to acquire understanding and knowledge. It is the work of a student. Most study skills books tell students to study 2 hours for every hour of class. Not a bad average, but it is an average. Some courses will require 4 hours for every hour of class and some will require 30 minutes. The two-for-one average will usually yield average grades. Yes, unlike high school, it takes effort even to make Cs; As and Bs come much harder still.

Studying is like any job. With time and effort and attention, you can learn to do it well. By practicing studying, you will be able to master the most powerful skill in the human arsenal: the ability to understand.

SUMMARY

- A class syllabus is like a learning contract. Once you have the syllabus in hand, you are responsible for all of the details contained in it.

- Organization is key to success in college. A well-organized notebook; an organized place for study; and a calendar that details academic, personal, and social commitments are tools that aid in getting organized.

- Learning in class will allow you to use your time outside of class to deepen your understanding of the material through reading and studying.

Some methods to assist with learning in class are to come prepared for class by reading the assigned material ahead of time, sit in the front of the classroom, review notes from the last class before class begins, and actively take notes during class.

- A comprehensive notebook includes the course syllabus, semester calendar, lecture notes, handouts, textbook notes, supplemental resources, assignments and exercises, review material, and test preparations and sample test questions.

- According to research, the more complete your notes, the more likely you will be successful in a course.

- Taking notes can vary depending on whether the class is a lecture class, a problem-solving class, or a discussion class.

- The Cornell note-taking method works well for lecture classes; this system consists of a note-taking section, a cue column, and a summary area.

- Cornell notes should be reviewed as soon as possible to aid your memory.

- T-notes work well for problem-solving classes because you divide a page of notes into a "T" to create three separate areas: the name of the procedure, the steps used to complete the procedure, and examples correlating with the steps of the procedure.

- In discussion classes, listen for your instructor to summarize the main points at the end of the discussion and then record them.

- Special strategies must be implemented when instructors lecture from PowerPoint slides or outlines. Integrate these instructional techniques into your note-taking format.

- Four generations of distance education have emerged: (1) correspondence courses: (2) video/audiotapes (or broadcasts); (3) Internet venues such as videoconferencing, email, and chat rooms; and (4) multimedia and hypermedia teleconferencing.

- Dropout rates are 15–20 percent higher for online courses than traditional courses.

- To study is to apply the mind so as to acquire understanding and knowledge. Focus on understanding the material before you try to memorize it.

- Steps in reading a textbook include previewing, using the headings, identifying the primary idea(s), reading before marking, continuing the process, and reviewing.

- To sharpen your concentration set specific goals, read purposefully, choose the best time of day to read, and take breaks.

- Two types of distractions can impinge on concentration when we study: external and internal.

- To improve comprehension you should reread when necessary, locate primary ideas, identify supporting details, recognize patterns of organization, rephrase ideas into your own words, reread difficult sections, and create sample questions.

- To increase your vocabulary, study Greek and Latin roots and prefixes and keep a dictionary with you at all times. Remember, the more you read the more your vocabulary will develop. Creating visual vocabulary note cards is an effective strategy.

- Solving problems is a good way to learn procedural knowledge. Working problems at the end of each chapter and resources such as study guides, labs, study groups, and tutors are all useful.

- A study group is a good resource for most classes. Three is the magic number of participants, yet the key is the people who form the group. Look to study with others who are motivated, come prepared, and are at or slightly above your level of comprehension.

- Studying is not just reading and memorizing. It is applying the mind to the material so you are able to comprehend and use the knowledge.

KEY CONCEPTS

Academic calendar

Comprehensive notebook

Cornell notes

Course syllabus

Developing vocabulary

Discussion classes

Disorganized lecture

Distance education

Getting organized

Good reading strategies

How to learn in class

How to learn outside of class

Learning from groups

Learning from print

Learning from problem solving

Lecture classes

Monitoring comprehension

Organized study system

Outlines

PowerPoint slides

Problem-solving classes

Sharpening concentration

Steps in reading a textbook

T-notes

Too much information

GUIDED JOURNAL QUESTIONS

1. What is your favorite type of class—lecture, discussion, or problem solving? Explain and use examples.

2. What method(s) do you currently use to manage your time? Are these methods currently working? How many hours per week do you study? At what times do you complete the majority of your studying? Are these your peak learning times? Explain.

3. Think about the classes you are best able to take notes in and those you find the most difficult for note taking. What are the differences in these classes? What can you determine from these differences?

4. Describe your current methods of taking notes from lectures and studying from lectures. Now that you have read this chapter, how do you think the Cornell and T-note systems will be useful to you?

5. Describe your current methods of reading and learning from your textbooks. Now that you have read this chapter, how do you think the reading suggestions will be useful to you?

6. Reflect on when you are able to concentrate the most on your reading. Is there a pattern for the time of day, surroundings you are in, subject matter? What can you determine from the results of this reflection? Explain and give examples.

7. What approaches have you used in the past (or will begin to use) to monitor your comprehension as you read difficult college textbooks? Explain.

8. College classes require more intensive and in-depth study strategies. What techniques will you implement to achieve success in your current courses?

The Last Word

The information in this chapter alone would have saved me countless hours of ineffective and even wasted study time my freshman year. My grades were good, but I paid a high price to earn them.

—Carol Dochen

4

Learning, Knowledge, and Intellectual Performance

I think, ergo I learn.

As we delve into the world of college thinking, we discover complex and challenging theories to guide our development. Becoming expert learners, autonomous learners, means developing within ourselves the capacity to learn and demonstrate our knowledge in widely diverse situations. Many of your college experiences simulate the work life you desire. As a professional, you will have to learn throughout your entire career, often independently. Understanding and using your collegiate academic experiences successfully will develop your ability as an autonomous learner.

CHAPTER HIGHLIGHTS

- Definitions of Human and Academic Learning
- Types of Knowledge
- Levels of Intellectual Performance
- Range of Difficulty of Material

SELF-ASSESSMENT: Thinking About Learning

College requires you to think and learn at very different levels of complexity. With 5 being "Almost Always" and 1 being "Almost Never," assess your assumptions and feelings about your thinking and learning at different intellectual levels. Rate each of the following statements honestly by circling the appropriate number. Completing this exercise will help you identify areas of concern you may have as you begin to contemplate more complex learning activities.

	Almost Always		Sometimes		Almost Never
1. I enjoy learning facts, dates, names, and events in courses such as history.	5	4	3	2	1
2. I enjoy learning how to work through a procedure in a math or accounting problem.	5	4	3	2	1
3. I am good at deciding when to use a particular learning strategy as I move from course to course.	5	4	3	2	1
4. I can easily recognize what level of learning will be required of me for each of my courses.	5	4	3	2	1
5. I am comfortable with both objective and essay exams.	5	4	3	2	1
6. I often paraphrase information when I am learning something to test my comprehension.	5	4	3	2	1
7. I prefer to apply (demonstrate, compute, construct, solve) what I am learning when possible.	5	4	3	2	1

8. I am comfortable comparing and contrasting ideas such as two or more theories or historical events.	5	4	3	2	1
9. I find it easy to critique my own work such as a research paper I have written.	5	4	3	2	1
10. I find it easy to critique my peers' work.	5	4	3	2	1
11. I enjoy creating (devising or developing) new ideas based on what I have learned in class.	5	4	3	2	1
12. The more complex the material, the more dedicated to and resolved I am about learning it.	5	4	3	2	1

Add up the numbers circled. Your total score will be between 12 and 60. The higher your score, the more likely you are to be open to thinking and learning at higher levels well beyond memorization. For total scores below 36, write or reflect on items for which you have concerns. Also, consider talking with a trusted friend, a family member, a teacher, or an advisor.

DEFINITIONS OF HUMAN AND ACADEMIC LEARNING

Human learning means *a difference occurs within the learner.* We think differently, behave differently, and/or feel differently as a result of mental activity. Thousands of scholars since ancient times have struggled with **epistemology,** "the philosophical term for the theory of knowledge. It attempts to understand how knowing occurs and to discover its ground, its limitation, its validity and trustworthiness and its relation to truth" (Hosinki, 1992, p. 150). One of the goals of this text is for you to develop a comprehensive understanding of the many ways in which learning can be discussed. As philosophers and psychologists try to describe human learning, they usually resort to comparisons. Here are several typical comparisons for human learning used in the last 25 years:

Describing mental processes as if the brain were a computer.

Describing human memory as a filing cabinet.

Describing study skills as if they were tools in a toolbox.

Each of these metaphors has its advantages and limitations. As you read this text, you may create your own comparisons to help you understand concepts.

Academic learning is *that set of knowledge and skills that our society expects as a result of school experience.* Although this definition applies through all education, from kindergarten to graduate school to continuing education, we focus our attention on adult learners.

> ### • • • JENNIFER • • •
> #### *She is just beginning her college experience*
>
> *Jennifer, a beginning freshman at a local community college, is excited about being in college. During orientation she worked with an advisor and registered for 16 credit hours: English Composition, College Algebra, World History, General Biology (with a lab), and Educational Psychology. Jennifer was a B+ student in a large, urban high school, and she is a little apprehensive about this first semester. She is living in an apartment near campus, but her parents are not far away. In high school she was a competent student, but she rarely felt challenged. She successfully balanced academics and extracurricular activities. Jennifer is eager to do well in college, for she wants a professional career like her parents have.*

In the following sections, we use Jennifer's course schedule to show three important characteristics of college learning: types of knowledge, levels of intellectual performance, and range of difficulty of material.

TYPES OF KNOWLEDGE

An extremely useful metaphor for categorizing a dimension of academic learning is the recent investigations into types of knowledge. Three types—declarative, procedural, and metacognitive—seem to be especially helpful for collegiate learning because each type varies from the other in three important ways: how we acquire (or learn) that knowledge, how we store that knowledge in our memories, and how we retrieve and use that knowledge.

TYPES OF KNOWLEDGE		
Declarative	**Procedural**	**Metacognitive**
Knowing specific information about something	*Knowing how to do something*	*Knowing when and why to use a particular strategy based on understanding the task and ourselves*

Declarative Knowledge

Declarative knowledge is *possessing specific information about something.* Examples of such knowledge are remembering and understanding our name, our social security number, the quadratic formula, four proposed causes of the Civil War, the chemical symbol for sodium, or Einstein's Theory of Relativity. Declarative knowledge is usually facts or theories, but it can also be personal experiences, such as knowing which classes you are taking this semester. For the purpose of academic learning, we focus on declarative knowledge as factual (terminology, specific details) and conceptual (categories, principles, theories, models). In collegiate learning, **factual knowledge** consists of "the basic elements students must know to be acquainted with a discipline or solve problems in it." **Conceptual knowledge** is "the interrelationships among the basic elements within a larger structure that enable them to function together" (Anderson & Krathwohl, 2001, p. 46). Several of Jennifer's classes rely heavily on declarative knowledge: World History and Educational Psychology and the lecture section of her General Biology class. All are full of definitions, data, and concepts, that is, declarative knowledge.

Propositions

Some of the most interesting research in learning has been the investigation of the nature of declarative knowledge and how it is believed we store it in our memories. Researchers have labeled the basic unit of declarative knowledge as the **proposition,** *one thought or one idea* (Gagné, 1985). For example, the sentence *The courageous student asks a question in class* has three ideas or propositions: the student is courageous, the student is in class, and the student asks a question. As we are reading a textbook or listening in class, we do not consciously think of the single, small ideas that flow and combine into larger and larger units, but psychologists believe that our brains recognize individual propositions and store them as discrete units (schemata) that are linked by meaning. **Schemata** are defined as *mental networks of related facts and concepts that influence the acquisition of new information* (Slavin, 2003).

Many study strategies for declarative knowledge use structured and deliberate memory storage and retrieval practice as the primary model for mastery.

These strategies attempt to mimic the way in which we believe our brains store and retrieve this type of knowledge. Such strategies help us deeply process our learning to make connections to what we already know. Later chapters describe in detail many of these techniques such as summarizing, visualizing, mapping, networking, diagramming, and creating compare and contrast grids. One other helpful characteristic of declarative knowledge is that college students seem able to acquire and store this type of knowledge quickly, and the more time they allow themselves, the more likely they are to master it at deeper levels.

Although Jennifer is a good reader and has an excellent vocabulary, she is quickly stunned by the amount of reading her instructors expect her to complete in the declarative knowledge classes. In high school, she simply paid attention in class and looked over the material the night before the test and remembered enough to answer the questions the next day in class. However, college texts seem different; she finds that they tend to have much more information and that the information seems far more complicated. Upon reflection, she begins to understand that she can remember the factual knowledge, but she is having trouble with the complexity of the concepts. She slowly begins to change her study techniques to pay special attention to the conceptual knowledge her teachers stress. She also chooses to participate in several study groups with other students who have similar learning goals.

Since our understanding of an idea mandates how our brains store and later access and retrieve that idea for use on a test or on the job, an important study strategy for declarative knowledge is to stop and test ourselves on what we have just been studying. Can we explain it in our own words? Can we give examples from our own experiences? A further strategy is to integrate this knowledge into something we already know. How does our prior knowledge relate to the ideas just presented? Can we link this knowledge to something we learned in another class? Does it contradict something the teacher said? The more connections we can make between this new piece of knowledge and other pieces already stored in our brains, the more likely we will remember it when we need it and the more likely we will really understand it. (See Figure 4.1 for an example of learning declarative knowledge.) No one had taught Jennifer to read/study in these ways, so she struggles during her first semester.

Most declarative knowledge presented to college students is in words, through either lecture or printed text. Yes, effective teachers and writers also use graphs, charts, and tables, but the major message is in words. So the task of the student is to take the words and do something with them to achieve meaning.

FIGURE 4.1   An Example of Learning Declarative Knowledge

One method the Roman leaders used to pacify the populace during the first and second centuries, C.E., was large-scale entertainment.	
Strategy	**Example**
Explain it in your own words.	Roman emperors used street festivals, executions, and games (gladiators) to pacify the populace in Rome.
Create examples from your own experience.	Professional sports provide a vicarious experience to release aggression and experience competitiveness.
Think about similar ideas or concepts.	Present-day government programs give services or tax cuts to specific parts of the American public.
Link to prior knowledge.	The movie *Gladiator* shows how the government pacified the general public.
Create questions to test yourself.	Compare methods of how governments influence and control their constituents, with special attention to the Roman government of the first and second centuries, C.E.

Procedural Knowledge

To know how to do something is different from knowing about something. When we *know how to do something,* such as read, add fractions, create an income statement, or write a marketing case study, we have **procedural knowledge.** When we use procedural knowledge, either physically or mentally, we are actively creating a result. Generally, acquiring procedural knowledge means learning a skill. An example would be the ability to add fractions. A simplistic overview of the steps of that ability contains the determination whether like denominators exist; if not, the conversion of all denominators to one common term; then the conversion of numerators to the appropriate units; then the adding of the numerators (but not the denominators); and, finally, the reduction of the resulting fraction.

Productions

Psychologists have labeled the *process of knowing how* as **productions** (Gagné, 1985). A production flows in a logical, systematic sequence, something like a flow chart that is often used in designing computer programs. When we are first learning a production, each step comes slowly. We may make errors in the sequence—omitting, inserting, or transposing steps. Our work is conscious and slow. But something happens as we practice the task. We become faster and more accurate, and, most important, we do not have to devote much of our conscious minds to the task. Doing the task becomes automatic.

Understanding or meaning plays as important a role in learning procedural knowledge as it does in learning declarative knowledge. If we only memorize a production, a rule, or a procedure without understanding it, we are unable to adjust to a slightly changed situation or problem. We just follow rules blindly and are helpless when we are confronted with changes. However, if we understand the production and why it is structured the way it is, then we can often apply the production to new situations.

Jennifer is taking two primarily procedural knowledge courses this term: English Composition and College Algebra. The lab section of General Biology is also somewhat procedural. In high school, Jennifer did fairly well in mathematics because there were frequent homework assignments, quizzes, and exams. She had many opportunities to practice problems, and most of the high school quizzes relied heavily on memory. Her first College Algebra test was a shock, for the instructor combined several procedures into one problem. Sheer memory no longer worked; she had to understand the procedures in order to make the necessary changes.

Procedural knowledge cannot exist without the appropriate declarative knowledge. For example, our knowledge of what a fraction is and what properties it has (declarative) pairs with knowledge of how to reduce a fraction (procedural). Psychologists believe that the two types of knowledge are stored closely to each other in our brains, again hypothesizing that meaning is the link.

For Jennifer, learning (acquiring) procedural knowledge is quite different from learning declarative knowledge. Since she has difficulty understanding the concepts of procedural knowledge classes such as math or accounting, the key to success is ongoing effort. Excellent class attendance and participation, supported by a large quantity of homework exercises, are the beginning steps. Teachers rarely give (and students rarely do) enough homework exercises to truly master a production; therefore, successful students usually work extra problems until the process (production) seems easy, automatic, and fast. (See Figure 4.2 for an example of learning procedural knowledge.) Since acquiring a production is most likely to happen by practicing over a long period of time, procrastination and the resultant cramming are deadly for this type of learning. It is almost impossible to learn procedural knowledge at the last minute. Jennifer quickly adjusted her study techniques in College Algebra by working more problems every day and attending tutoring sessions, so her performance on the second test improved. Procedural knowledge requires time and practice to acquire. It is an active process that yields a product. Although it is slow in the beginning, it becomes rapid, accurate, and automatic. If we understand the process, we will be able to apply it in new situations.

FIGURE 4.2   An Example of Learning Procedural Knowledge

Learning how to write a persuasive essay	
Strategy	**Example**
Participate as much as possible when learning the new procedure.	When reading/studying sample essays, mark the structure of the persuasive argument.
Work extra problems and exercises to "overlearn" the material.	Choose three possible topics about which you have strong feelings and brainstorm a rough outline for each.
Practice over periods of time (work a little every day).	Brainstorm on one day, search the Web on the second day, choose a topic and create an outline on the third day, write a rough draft on the fourth day, and edit the final copy on the fifth day.

Metacognitive Knowledge

Metacognitive knowledge—knowing when and why to use particular strategies—is a third type of knowledge directly related to academic learning. When we understand the nature and the requirements of an academic task such as a test or project, we are using metacognitive knowledge. When we are aware of our own learning strengths and weaknesses and adjust our studying accordingly, we are using metacognitive knowledge (Anderson & Krathwohl, 2001). (See Figure 4.3 for an example of using metacognitive knowledge.) Much of this text is about acquiring the most appropriate strategies for collegiate learning. Students with highly developed metacognitive strategies are expert learners; they are both efficient and effective. They are able to thoughtfully maximize their abilities, whether they are in the classroom, a study group, or private study. Expert learners know what memory techniques are most suitable for a science class; they use the appropriate note-taking techniques for a lecture class that uses objective testing; they use specific types of strategies to prepare for an essay exam; they organize their study time to competently master accounting procedures; they control external distracters to their concentration by manipulating their study environment. We believe that metacognitive strategies involve more than just the knowledge of when and why to use certain strategies; they also involve the knowledge of how to understand and control our own behavior. It is not enough to know what to do to reach our goals; we must be able to regulate our behavior so that we do what we should do when and how we should do it. That cluster of skills is difficult to master, but we have been helping students like Jennifer accomplish that task for many years.

FIGURE 4.3   An Example of Using Metacognitive Knowledge

Selecting note-taking systems for different classes	
Strategy	**Example**
Know different strategies for different academic tasks.	The Cornell note-taking system can be used for World History and the T-note system for College Algebra.
Understand why you should use certain strategies.	Cornell note-taking works best for declarative knowledge-based courses such as World History, whereas T-notes work best for procedural knowledge-based courses such as College Algebra.
Know how to regulate your study.	Since Jennifer is a good reader, she plans to review her history notes twice a week, which should be sufficient given her level of comprehension. Jennifer realizes that she is an average math student and needs extra practice in solving problems. She schedules extra study time and attends review sessions.

Jennifer continues to expand her understanding of the many ways in which college academics differ from high school learning. She has increased her cognitive strategies (metacognitive knowledge) by utilizing different approaches to her declarative and procedural courses. She is coming to understand both her strengths and her shortcomings as a college learner. Now she needs a clearer understanding of both the levels of intellectual performance she must master in college and the range of difficulty of the material in collegiate courses.

exercise 4.2

Using Declarative, Procedural, and Metacognitive Knowledge

Match the type of knowledge to the correct activity. Completing this activity will facilitate your understanding of the three types of knowledge.

A. Declarative knowledge

B. Procedural knowledge

C. Metacognitive knowledge

1. _____ Practicing a problem using the Pythagorean theorem

2. _____ Explaining the law of supply and demand

3. _____ Memorizing musical symbols

4. _____ Selecting a note-taking format for sociology class

5. _____ Comparing behavioral psychology with cognitive psychology

6. _____ Giving a persuasive speech

7. _____ Creating sample test questions to study for a biology exam

8. _____ Memorizing the state capitals of the United States

LEVELS OF INTELLECTUAL PERFORMANCE

There are several levels of intellectual performance—not different subjects or even different kinds of learning tasks, but different levels of mastery of one concept or one set of data. The primary contributor to this approach was Bloom (1956). He posited six levels, each with direct applicability to the academic setting. Bloom envisioned a stair-step model, with each successive level dependent on the one(s) below, and that model is still taught today to people entering the teaching profession. Recent scholars (Anderson & Krathwohl, 2001) have revised Bloom's model to include a more intensive reflection of recent theoretical models of learning. In this text, we use the revised model so that we can investigate more closely the center point of collegiate learning—the necessity of understanding the meaning of academic material if we wish to retain and use it. Figure 4.4, on the next page, provides a matrix using the revised Bloom's Taxonomy.

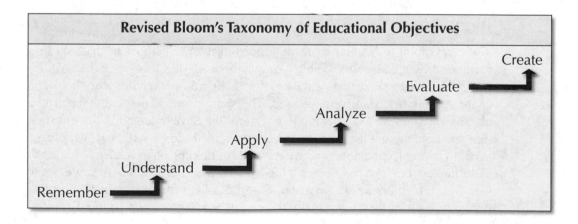

Revised Bloom's Taxonomy of Educational Objectives

FIGURE 4.4   Matrix Using the Revised Model of Bloom's Taxonomy

Level	Definition	Sample Verbs	Examples
Remember	The ability to recognize or recall an idea, a fact, or an occurrence in a form similar to the original presentation	Define, describe, identify, label, list, match, name, state	Reciting "The Raven" by Edgar Allen Poe
Understand	The ability to construct meaning from the literal message in a communication	Classify, describe, discuss, explain, give, interpret, paraphrase, summarize	Explaining the meaning of Poe's "The Raven"
Apply	The ability to use understanding of ideas correctly and appropriately in a new situation	Apply, demonstrate, determine, compute, construct, solve	Labeling the differing rhyme schemes in Poe's "The Raven"
Analyze	The ability to break the material into its constituent parts and detect the relationships and organization of those parts	Analyze, categorize, compare, contrast, diagram, discriminate, distinguish, infer, outline, separate, subdivide	Comparing and contrasting Poe's "The Raven" with "Serenade"
Evaluate	The ability to render a value judgment based on criteria and standards	Appraise, conclude, critique, decide, defend, interpret, judge, justify, recommend	Writing a critical analysis of Poe's "The Raven"
Create	The ability to create a new product from the ideas or materials understood	Compile, compose, create, design, develop, devise, hypothesize, invent	Creating a poem with meter and rhyme scheme similar to Poe's "The Raven"

Remember

The entry point to learning academic material is to remember it, that is, to re-member it long enough to be able to think about it. Most of us take this skill for granted until we realize that we have just spent 30 minutes reading a textbook and cannot remember what we have read. The same phenomenon can happen in a classroom when we are listening to a lecture. We have to attend to the informa-tion and hold on to it if it is going to become something we will keep. Marking a text and taking lecture notes are two methods of holding on to academic material. The chapters on cognitive learning theory and strategies give many strategies to help you remember academic material. Most college students remember infor-mation for a test; this is especially the case when they use the simplest form of memory, that is, recognizing that they have seen something before. Multiple-choice tests often require that kind of memory. When we memorize a fact or a definition for a test but do not understand what that piece of information means or how it could be applied to another situation, we are remembering. The definition we use here for **remember** is *the ability to recognize or recall an idea, a fact, or an occurrence in a form similar to the original presentation* (Bloom, 1956).

Understand

Students frequently resort to memorizing without understanding and are then lost when professors ask them to use or evaluate the information. Although memory is necessary, it is insufficient for collegiate learning. The foundation of collegiate learning is to **understand,** *the ability to construct meaning from the literal message in a communication.* Understanding is a complex phenomenon; when we comprehend/understand we are able to translate, interpret, and extrapolate the information remembered (Bloom, 1956). In this text, we use *comprehend* and *understand* interchangeably.

To acquire comprehension may take much more attention and effort than simple remembering requires. We begin to examine this complex level of knowledge by using an example from Jennifer's course in educational psychology, the concept of multicultural education. Understanding usually begins with a concept or idea that is worded in either abstract or concrete terms. Most textbooks present a concept in abstract terms, such as the following example of a definition of multicultural education: "all students, regardless of the groups to which they belong, groups such as those related to gender, ethnicity, race, culture, social class, religion, or exceptionality, should experience educational equality in the schools" (Banks, 1993a, p. 24, as cited in Woolfolk, 1998, p. 163).

> **UNDERSTAND**
>
> **Step 1** Translate a concept into specific examples.
>
> **Step 2** Explain in your own words the relationship between the concept and the examples.
>
> **Step 3** See connections and make predictions.

The first step to understanding is to *translate an abstract idea into specific examples.* When Jennifer reads the assignment, she creates several specific examples of what would constitute educational equality for people of different groups; then she reflects on the definition of exceptionality and thinks of an example of that idea. Often the most powerful method of translating an abstract concept into a specific example is to use a personal memory that exemplifies the concept, so she reflects about an incident that had happened in her middle school science class when some of the students were gifted in science and others were not. Another example of translation occurs during the lecture when her college instructor presents a concept in concrete form first, then expects his students to move from that example to the abstract idea. His lecture begins with a story of a specific child's experience in a fifth-grade classroom. Jennifer's ability to translate that specific incident into an abstract statement of the concept imbedded in the example demonstrates her mastery of the first step of understanding.

The next step to understanding is the ability to **interpret** or **explain,** *to articulate the difference between the concept and a specific example, to tell about the idea in your own words* (Bloom, 1956). In our example, Jennifer would explain the core concept of educational equality. How would she explain this idea to someone from another country? Or another century? Does this concept mean that all children should have the same educational experience? Grappling with a concept is not an easy matter, so she begins to ask herself many questions. Her competency in explaining a concept lies in her ability to communicate the idea in her own words, without simply repeating the words used by the text or the professor.

The third step to comprehending is to **extrapolate,** *the ability to see connections between two or more identified ideas or to make predictions based on the understanding of the ideas* (Bloom, 1956). In many circumstances, our ability to simply ask *What if . . . ?* may help us extrapolate the information. In the case of our example of multicultural education, some simple questions would help us understand this concept, such as *What if funds are limited?* or *What textbooks would we need?* or *What if teachers do not have sufficient knowledge to . . . ?* It is not necessary, or practical, to examine all possible questions; usually one or two forays of extrapolation are sufficient to understand the concept solidly.

Apply

When we understand a concept or idea, then we can begin to use it in a variety of intellectual activities. To **apply** is *the ability to use understanding of ideas correctly and appropriately in a new situation* (Bloom, 1956). The most obvious example of application would be a case study. If Jennifer were given a description of a specific school curriculum, would she be able to recognize whether it followed the principles of multicultural education or not? Although our example is declarative knowledge, many application levels of college learning occur with procedural knowledge classes such as mathematics, accounting, and statistics. In understanding, "the emphasis is on the grasp of the meaning and intent of the material. In application it is on remembering and bringing to bear upon given material the appropriate generalizations or principles" (Bloom, 1956, p. 144).

Analyze

Another level of knowledge, **analyze,** is the focus of much college testing. It is *the ability to break the material into its constituent parts and detect the relationships and organization of those parts* (Bloom, 1956). Our example of multicultural education lends itself to many variants of analysis. An obvious analysis would focus on the different components that would have to exist for such education to occur, such as curriculum, materials, and teacher training. However, many other kinds of analysis are also possible. If you can analyze, then you can compare and/or contrast both within and outside the concept. Jennifer could describe the similarities (comparison) and the differences (contrast) between two different curricular proposals or three different texts with reference to this definition of multicultural education. She could trace the development of a multicultural education program in a school district.

Evaluate

The next level of knowledge is **evaluate,** *the ability to render a value judgment based on criteria and standards* (Bloom, 1956). An important aspect of evaluation is a critical reflection on both the internal logical consistency of a process or product and the external validity of that same product or process.

Evaluation assignments are quite common in the advanced courses in your major. Sometimes they involve group work and group presentations. In our example from educational psychology, Jennifer could be asked to review a middle school curriculum by the criteria presented for multicultural education and rate that curriculum with her rationale. She might be asked to defend the school's decision to create an honors program for gifted students or a tutorial program for athletes during a school budget crisis.

Create

The highest level of knowledge, **create,** is often the most exciting of all the levels. Originally titled *synthesis,* it is *the ability to create a new product from the ideas or materials understood* (Bloom, 1956). One of the most common creative assignments is to design a new example of a concept or an idea. An assignment might require that Jennifer write a fifth-grade history curriculum unit that would meet the premise of this concept. She could also be asked to infer three problems that could occur when such a curriculum would be proposed to a school board.

Using the Taxonomy

An important skill of expert learners is that they know the level of knowledge expected in different classes by different professors because the desired performance mandates the study strategies required for that level of mastery. In simple terms, you use different study strategies for an essay test at the analysis level than you do for a problem-solving test on the application level. Expert students vary their class notes, their study notes, their study times, and their test preparation according to the level at which they will be tested.

---

exercise 4.3

How Do You Learn at Each Level?

For practice using the revised Bloom's Taxonomy, use any chapter you have already read from this textbook to complete this exercise. After reviewing the chapter, provide an example of how you could use each level of the taxonomy in learning a portion of the chapter's content. We have given you an example for the first level. Completing this exercise will help you understand how to use the taxonomy as a study tool.

The chapter I have selected is Chapter _____.

Remember	<u>I could create note cards to help me memorize the important terms.</u>
Understand	_____
Apply	_____
Analyze	_____
Evaluate	_____
Create	_____

---

exercise 4.4

Determining Levels for Test Questions

Review an old test (preferably a college exam—especially one from a declarative knowledge–based course). For each question, determine the level of intellectual performance required according to the revised Bloom's Taxonomy. This exercise can be completed on most any type of exam (multiple choice, true/false, essay, etc.). Completing this exercise will help you see how different questions can test you at very different levels of thinking.

RANGE OF DIFFICULTY OF MATERIAL

Why are some topics easy to learn and others difficult? The difficulty of academic content varies dramatically in college across three dimensions: the inherent difficulty level of the content; the manner and method of presentation; and the skills, learning preferences, and prior knowledge of the learner. Expert learners assess the difficulty level of their courses and vary their study strategies accordingly.

Content Difficulty

The first dimension—the inherent difficulty level of the content—is important to acknowledge. Some subject areas are simply more complex than others; they require a more formal intellectual process.

> **RANGE OF DIFFICULTY**
>
> • **Content difficulty:** How difficult is the material?
>
> • **Quality of presentation:** How well is the material presented?
>
> • **Skills, learning preferences, and prior knowledge:** How intuitive or formal is the material for me?

Higher levels of thinking require more complex vocabulary. An example is differential calculus, which is more difficult than algebra. Assignments in research methods in psychology tend to be more complex than social psychology. Anatomy and physiology are more difficult than botany. Organic chemistry is more difficult than inorganic chemistry. Tax accounting is more difficult than general accounting. And so on. Collegiate courses are not equal in their content difficulty. Expert students carefully schedule such difficult courses; they try to take them in long semesters and often try to enroll in only one or two such difficult courses in a term. Even if students are interested and talented in the courses, these difficult courses tax them.

Quality of Presentation

The second dimension of difficulty is the manner and method of presentation. A good writer or a good lecturer can present material in an understandable format. The reverse is also true; poor writing or lecture skills can muddle a presentation and make the content difficult to learn. Many textbooks are badly written; they give the reader little help in discerning which ideas/facts are most important. On the other hand, some textbooks have a plethora of learning aids—introductions, graphs, definitions, summaries, questions, illustrations, and the like. And some teachers use visual displays, outlines, and handouts. Now the Internet is often used to provide extra study material for a course.

College students realize that some of their instructors are knowledgeable in the content field but may not be expert teachers for beginning students. Poor or inappropriate teaching styles can include inarticulate speech, lack of clear examples, disorganized lectures, too rapid delivery of information, and reluctance to entertain questions/alternate points of view. When such a mismatch occurs, the responsibility for learning is on the student. If the information for a course is poorly presented, then expert students initiate efforts to secure outside sources, such as tutors, supplemental readings, and study groups.

Another difficulty is if the material was created in a different time or culture. Art from another time or place can be difficult to understand. Translations are harder to read than originals; you are reading the ideas once removed. If the writing occurred in another century or culture, you have to make an imaginative leap to read as if you were from that time and place. Primary sources (those writings in which the author is the originator of the thought) are more exciting, and often more difficult, to read than secondary sources (those writings in which the author writes about the thoughts of others). Almost all textbooks are secondary sources. You are more likely to read primary sources in literature and philosophy courses.

Skills, Learning Preferences, and Prior Knowledge

We learn all the time, but academic learning is different from other learning. The difference between learning the plot of a movie and learning the political philosophy of Machiavelli is vast. The content may be inherently more difficult, and the presentation challenging or clumsy, but an individual learner's skills, preferences, and prior knowledge can also dramatically affect how difficult a particular course may be for that student. We call this dimension of the range of difficulty the **intuitive–formal continuum.** The easier and more natural a learning situation is for us, the more intuitive it is. The situation may seem easy because we bring life experiences that relate to the topic, because we have already learned many things that are related to the new material, or because we have a talent for that type of mental process. Whatever the reason, we can just go with it. The teacher's explanations seem clear, and we frequently think about the material outside of class. There is little or no anxiety, and we are often eager to learn. The readings seem easy, and we believe that they are easy because we are interested. The truth is probably the opposite; we become interested because it seems easy, natural, intuitive. We will study the material, trying to remember certain definitions or facts, but night-before cramming seems to be sufficient. Generally, in intuitive learning situations, we do not have to make any specific effort to understand; understanding just seems to happen naturally.

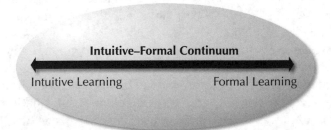

By contrast, in a formal learning situation, the material seems so difficult and confusing that it is easy for our minds to wander from the lecture or the text, and we become bored. The boredom is often rooted in how hard it is for us to achieve understanding. Formal learning situations demand energetic, purposeful strategies and formal reasoning processes to make understanding easier. It is as if we are swimming upstream against a strong current. We may have to read the book before class (and again afterward), sit close to the front of the classroom, use a formal note-taking system, and ask questions. We may have to study that subject every day, preread and outline the chapters, use a study guide, and find other students with whom to form a study group. The deliberate activity level is high, for the result of our efforts should be understanding. If we cannot understand the material, what we may memorize does us no good, now or in the future. One encouraging note is the more successful we are in a formal learning situation, the more likely the subject will gradually move to the left on the continuum and become easier to us.

Jennifer quickly realized that World History was an intuitive course for her. She had liked history in high school and read many extra biographies; she often watched the History Channel. Her college history teacher was a good lecturer and the required readings were long, but interesting. Jennifer had to learn how to take college notes quickly and how to answer complicated analysis test questions, but generally her study skills of reading and class attendance adjusted to the college level rapidly. On the other hand, General Biology was instantly intimidating. The professor lectured rapidly, and the numerous terms and concepts seemed unfamiliar and confusing. The textbook was worse. Within three weeks, Jennifer knew she was in trouble. She went to the campus tutoring program several times a week, joined a study group, and spent long hours going over the text and her notes. Her efforts helped her barely pass the first test, but she knew that this formal learning situation would be her biggest challenge in the term.

The more formal and difficult a learning situation is for us, the more deliberate our learning strategies need to be in order for us to be successful. Many students fear one course or another because they have struggled in that subject before. Their own anxiety and worry can sabotage a new effort. We are convinced that if students carefully plan how they will approach the subject, they can be successful.

---

exercise 4.5

Range of Difficulty of Your Classes

Choose the two most difficult courses you are taking this semester and answer the questions by marking an "X" on the continuum. Then complete the statement listed below. This exercise will help you assess the range of difficulty of two of your courses. It will also help you brainstorm strategies to help you become successful in these courses.

Course #1 _____

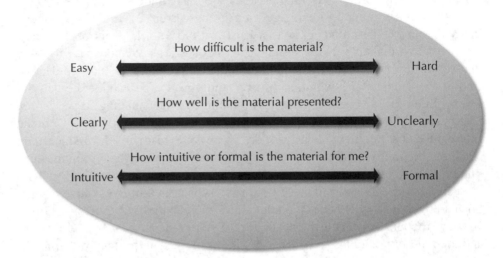

Based on my ratings, I predict I will need to use the following learning strategies:

_____   _____

_____   _____

_____   _____

Course #2 _____

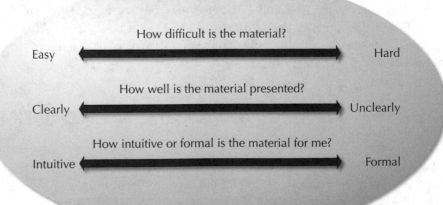

Based on my ratings, I predict I will need to use the following learning strategies:

_____   _____

_____   _____

_____   _____

---

exercise 4.6

Creating Test Questions

Pretend you are a teaching assistant for your class and are asked by the instructor to develop six questions, one for each level of Bloom's Taxonomy, to test students on the material from this chapter. Completing this exercise will give you additional insight into how college test questions may be written from lower to higher levels of required thinking.

CONCLUSION

In this chapter, we have given you some complex and important concepts that undergird successful academic performance. We will use these concepts repeatedly to demonstrate which study strategies will lead to the best performance in differing courses, assignments, and so forth. In this chapter and throughout the text, we will encourage you to develop your metacognitive skills to understand yourself as a learner and to strategically use your time and talents to achieve your academic goals.

SUMMARY

- Human learning means that a difference occurs within the learner. Academic learning is that set of knowledge and skills that our society expects as a result of school experience.

- There are three types of knowledge: declarative, procedural, and metacognitive.

- *Declarative knowledge* is possessing specific information about something. The basic unit of declarative knowledge is the proposition, one thought or one idea.

- Schemata help us recognize individual propositions, and the use of these mental networks helps us connect new information with prior knowledge.

- Strategies for learning declarative knowledge include explaining in your own words, creating examples from personal experiences, thinking about similar ideas or concepts, linking to prior knowledge, and creating practice test questions.

- *Procedural knowledge* is knowing how to do something, and a production is the process of knowing how. Productions flow in a logical, systematic sequence.

- Strategies for learning procedural knowledge include participating as much as possible when learning the new procedure, working extra problems and exercises to "overlearn" the material, and practicing over periods of time.

- *Metacognitive knowledge* is knowing when and why to use particular strategies based on understanding the task and ourselves.

- The use of metacognitive knowledge involves knowing different strategies for different academic tasks, knowing why to use certain strategies, and knowing how to regulate study behaviors based on personal learning strengths and weaknesses.

- According to the taxonomy, there are six levels of intellectual performance, each successive level being more complex and dependent on the one(s) below.

  - *Remember* is the ability to recognize or recall an idea, a fact, or an occurrence in a form similar to the original presentation.

  - *Understand* is the ability to construct meaning from the literal message in a communication.

  - *Apply* is the ability to use understanding of ideas correctly and appropriately in a new situation.

  - *Analyze* is the ability to break the material into its constituent parts and detect the relationships and organization of those parts—the ability to compare and contrast.

  - *Evaluate* is the ability to render a value judgment based on criteria and standards.

  - *Create* is the ability to create a new product from the ideas or materials understood.

- College classes range in difficulty based on the content; the quality of presentation from lecture and text; and the skills, learning preferences, and prior knowledge of the learner.

KEY CONCEPTS

Academic learning

Bloom's Taxonomy (Revised) of educational objectives: remember, understand, apply, analyze, evaluate, create

Content difficulty

Declarative knowledge

Formal learning

Human learning

Intuitive learning

Learning preferences

Metacognitive knowledge

Procedural knowledge

Productions

Propositions

Quality of presentation

Range of difficulty

Schemata

Skills and prior knowledge

GUIDED JOURNAL QUESTIONS

1. Of the courses you are currently enrolled in, which are the most and least enjoyable? Analyze your answers based on the type of knowledge each class primarily involves (declarative, procedural, metacognitive). Many classes may be a combination of the three. Do you see a trend in which type of knowledge-based course you are most comfortable with taking? Explain.

2. As you learned in this chapter, your college instructors will require different levels of intellectual performance. Using the taxonomy, list each of your courses. What do you predict to be the highest level of intellectual performance required for each class? Support your answers with concrete examples.

3. How do you learn material for a course that requires you to understand material such as sociology or psychology? Include in your answer several examples of learning strategies.

4. How do you learn material for a class that requires you to apply material such as accounting or mathematics? Include in your answer several examples of learning strategies.

5. How do you learn material for a class that requires you to analyze material such as world history or philosophy? Include in your answer several examples of learning strategies.

6. List a course from high school or college that has required you to evaluate or create material. What type of activity was required of you?

7. How do you prefer your instructors to present the material (lecture, class discussion, PowerPoint slides, computer-assisted instruction, group work, etc.) in a declarative knowledge–based course? In a procedural knowledge–based course? Why are these your preferences?

8. List three activities (such as hobbies) in which you feel you have intuitive skills and background knowledge. How do you believe you acquired such intuition for each of these activities? List three academic courses in which you feel you have intuitive skills and background knowledge. How do you believe you acquired such intuition for each of these courses?

The Last Word

Learning something new is always an exciting ride for me. In that way, I am perpetually childlike. I invite you to this perspective—just for today—get excited about learning.

—De Sellers

5

Investing in Our College Lives

I'm trying not to overdraft.

A college education is more than just a diploma documenting that you have completed a collection of courses, that you have acquired a particular set of skills. College is not a legal requirement in our culture; it is a choice. You have chosen to invest at least two to four years in this enterprise. Whether you are 18 or 68, or anywhere in between, these years can and should be formative. That is, you should become a different person from who you are now. The experience of college—the ideas you study and debate, the people you encounter and with whom you enter into relationships, the events that capture your heart and mind, the subject that becomes your passion—all these and more influence the remainder of your life.

This chapter explores three powerful concepts that can deepen and enrich your collegiate experience—academically, socially, and personally. We hope that these ideas help you appreciate the unique opportunity of your college years so that you will make the best possible use of them.

SELF-ASSESSMENT: My Commitment and Involvement

How committed and involved are you in meeting your college goals? With 5 being "Almost Always" and 1 being "Almost Never," assess your assumptions and feelings about your commitment and involvement. Rate each of the following statements honestly by circling the appropriate number. Completing this assessment will help you reflect on your current dedication to college success.

	Almost Always		Sometimes		Almost Never
1. I tend to keep promises I make to myself.	5	4	3	2	1
2. I tend to keep promises I make to others.	5	4	3	2	1
3. I do not need others to make me honor my commitments.	5	4	3	2	1
4. I like setting realistic academic goals for the semester.	5	4	3	2	1
5. I look at difficult college courses as a challenge and growth opportunity.	5	4	3	2	1
6. I feel a strong sense of commitment to my college institution.	5	4	3	2	1
7. I attend all my classes regularly.	5	4	3	2	1
8. I meet with my instructors on a regular basis outside of class.	5	4	3	2	1
9. I study regularly and enough to be successful in college.	5	4	3	2	1
10. I seek out others who can help me to be successful in college.	5	4	3	2	1

11. I am appropriately involved in collegiate extracurricular activities (not too little and not too much).   5   4   3   2   1

12. I like being a college student.   5   4   3   2   1

Add up the numbers circled. Your total score will be between 12 and 60. The higher your score, the more likely you are to be committed to and involved in college. For total scores below 36, write or reflect on items for which you have concerns. Also, consider talking with a trusted friend, a family member, a teacher, or an advisor.

INTRODUCTION

Three concepts rooted in both educational research and common sense give specific pathways into examining our current status as learners and plotting a new journey. We examine these three concepts—expert versus novice learners, commitment, and involvement—through a story of one student, Robert.

$\cdots$ **ROBERT** $\cdots$
Returning to college as a sophomore
after a difficult first year

Robert is a first-semester sophomore at a medium-size university, and he made the decision to attend college when he was in the tenth grade. That year he began to study, and he made good enough scores to gain acceptance at a nearby state university. Initially, his dream was to be a doctor, so he enrolled in calculus and chemistry his first semester. He was simply overwhelmed by the amount and difficulty of the work; his first semester GPA was disastrously low, 1.7, and he abandoned premed and chose business as his major. The next semester was difficult in another way; his high school girlfriend ended their relationship and his grandmother was diagnosed with cancer. In spite of those personal worries, he struggled to stay focused on school and his new college friends, and he lifted himself out of probation to a GPA of 2.1. That next summer he went home to work and save money; he saw his friends who had chosen not to attend college and a few who were dropping out. He thought for a long while and had conversations with his dad, who encouraged him to return to college and give it another try. Robert sat down and wrote some goals for the next year. Although he did not have specific long-term goals, he knew he wanted to enjoy a professional career, and he was embarrassed by his low academic performance in college. He made the trek to campus in late July and met with a career counselor and an academic adviser. After taking several career interest inventories, he tentatively chose marketing or management as possible majors within the general field of business. He and his academic adviser consulted and planned a fall schedule that included a learning strategies course. Since he had failed calculus the year before, he would also have to take business calculus, in addition to economics, two notoriously tough courses on his campus. Robert knew that his high school study strategies were insufficient for college; all he had to do was look at his transcript from last year. So he begins his second college year with a combination of excitement and trepidation. He knows this is his opportunity, and he is willing to try harder, but he is still confused about how to become a good student.

EXPERT VS. NOVICE LEARNING

What Robert desires is to become a competent learner, instead of a beginning college learner. Contemporary researchers use the paradigm *expert and novice* to differentiate between two dramatically different levels of skill in collegiate learning. While most research on this concept has focused on the narrow task of problem solving (Glaser & Chi, 1988), we believe that the terms can expand to include a broader view of a student's academic life, even though the evidence is more subtle (Woolfolk, 2004). Our definition of **expert learners** are *those individuals who have attained a higher level of competence in a wide variety of academic tasks; in other words, they can learn what they need to learn and then perform it.* Expert learners use appropriate strategies and behaviors to perform at the necessary level of the revised Bloom's Taxonomy. College learning demands a different level of expertise from grades 1–12. **Novice learners** are *those individuals whose learning is often insufficient or halting.* They still learn, but they may devote large amounts of time to little avail, they are frequently unaware of what is required of them, and their performances are usually disappointing. The key differences (Schunk, 2000, p. 205) between the two groups are as follows:

Expert learners spend more time planning and analyzing than novice learners. An expert learner is thoughtful and does not leap immediately into a task without having a clear strategy. If Robert were an expert learner, when he receives the syllabus for his economics course this fall, he would look first at the overall structure and schedule. How will he earn his grade? How many tests or quizzes or exams are there? When are they? Does homework count directly or indirectly toward his grade? Are there attendance rules? What are the resources, such as texts, workbooks, labs, tutors, and review sessions? Who is his instructor, where is his or her office, and what hours is it open? Robert would put the major due dates on his calendar/planner and purchase all the required materials. He would choose new books, rather than used ones, for he will want to put his own markings in the text. Then Robert would reflect about the nature of the course and reach the conclusion that the most important taxonomy level for this course will be application. He will have to memorize terms and formulas and comprehend basic principles, but primarily he will have to apply those concepts to new problems and situations. When Robert reflects about his own abilities, he realizes that he has been competent in quantitative subjects when he studied the subject daily and asked questions when he was confused. He had done those behaviors in high school math, but the college calculus class last year had intimidated him. He had procrastinated studying and then been too embarrassed to ask for help. By the time he realized that he was in trouble, it was too late to salvage a passing grade. This year, he resolves to study and do the homework problems every day, and he decides to make an exploratory trip to the campus tutoring center to determine its hours for help in economics. While Robert makes this initial analysis and plan, he realizes that he will have to continue these behaviors as the course progresses. He will use some of the same skills to prepare for tests.

Expert learners have a different knowledge base than novice learners. As we introduced in the previous chapter, knowledge has the dimensions of type and level, and expert learners differ from novice learners in specific and important ways. The first type of knowledge, declarative knowledge, is possessing specific information about something. Expert learners simply have more information, and that information is relevant and helpful for future learning. Robert will take a required course in political science this fall, and he has a generalized, shallow understanding of the subject. Although he passed the required courses in high school, he has never been particularly interested in politics. He does not read the newspaper regularly nor watch television news. He has never voted, and the concepts of government are foreign to him. Robert is clearly a novice learner in this subject; he has heard of some of the technical terms before, but he has little understanding of them. Compare Robert's knowledge base with that of another student, Sally, who has been fascinated with state and national politics for years. That student regularly reads newspapers and magazines about elections and current political issues. She even volunteered for a local campaign. These two students begin a political science course from entirely different starting points. In this example, the other student has a definitive advantage in declarative knowledge. Another aspect of declarative knowledge is the hierarchical manner in which that knowledge is organized and can be remembered. It is important to note here that Robert, as a novice learner, will have to work hard to learn the basic declarative knowledge for this political science course and then decide how to organize that knowledge. Study techniques such as flash cards for vocabulary acquisition, outlining, and summary sheets would be helpful for Robert in this circumstance.

The second type of knowledge is procedural, knowing how to do something. Expert learners have more powerful procedural knowledge; in other words, they can do the procedures quickly and accurately. Robert will use procedural knowledge in business calculus this term, and many of the basic procedures he will use are derived from algebra. Robert's basic quantitative skills are good; he worked hard in high school to acquire those skills at an application, not just memory, level. Although he is not an expert in this field, his skill level is more than that of a novice. Robert will have to be careful about practicing the new procedural knowledge in business calculus, and a good strategy for that goal is to do extra homework problems two or three days a week in addition to his regular homework. Another option is for Robert to join a problem-solving session in math (a math study group). A crucial part of procedural knowledge is the ability to solve problems. Much of the research between expert and novice learners focuses on this skill. Expert learners "recognize problem formats more easily . . . and represent [those] problems at a deeper level" (Schunk, 2000, p. 205). Some basic techniques that Robert can employ to improve his problem-solving ability in business calculus are to verbalize the problem, write down every step, and create diagrams or models.

Metacognitive knowledge, the third type of knowledge, is knowing when and why to use particular strategies based on understanding the tasks and ourselves. Expert learners are better in this ability than novices. Robert's abilities in this area resemble those of a novice, rather than an expert. Last year, he was overwhelmed and confused by the new expectations of college professors, and he tried to learn and study the way he had in high school. The learning framework course will be the source of much of Robert's improvement. For example, he can realize that he reads with greater concentration in the mornings and thus needs to organize his study time to read his most difficult subjects then. To get the main ideas from a text, Robert needs to read the chapter summary and the main headings first and then create an outline of the main points. In preparation for the first political science exam, Robert realizes that he should begin by organizing all his notes and materials five days before the exam. He makes sure that he attends the review session and has questions written down before he goes. Robert also begins to understand what strategies to use in his primarily procedural courses like math and economics. That realization of what strategies and when to use them is the heart of metacognitive knowledge. This ability to transfer, or use appropriate strategies across different disciplines, is another characteristic of an expert learner. Thus, Robert is careful to practice linking the appropriate formula to each type of problem. He understands that procedural courses usually take more time and practice to master, so he adjusts his schedule accordingly.

For the sake of discussion, we have separated declarative, procedural, and metacognitive knowledge into three discrete categories. In reality, those knowledge bases intertwine and interrelate continually, shifting and moving through the learning process. However, this categorical distinction can help us to understand and improve our learning processes because we are able to grasp one view at a time, a process that gets its power from breaking a complex task into several simpler ones.

---

exercise 5.2

Your Expertise

Each of us has developed talents and abilities in academic pursuits, hobbies, sports, music, etc. Your expertise in those areas may have come from natural intuition or years of exposure and practice. List several areas in which you have developed such talents/abilities. For each, describe how you discovered your unique talents/abilities. What have you done to enhance and build upon these? Completing this exercise will help you focus on how you have already become an expert in a number of areas of your life.

Expert learners routinely monitor their comprehension and adjust their learning strategies accordingly more than novice learners. Such monitoring, or checking that we understand the concepts and information that we are seeing or hearing, is a routine, automatic function of expert learners. All of us use comprehension monitoring in simple situations; for example, if someone says something and we do not understand a word, we usually ask that person to repeat the information. However, in complex academic situations such as reading a difficult textbook or listening to a lecture, novice students often never stop and consider if they

BECOMING AN EXPERT LEARNER

- Set goals to complete your academic tasks.

- Create a time plan to accomplish your tasks.

- Implement learning strategies appropriate for the tasks.

- Use your background knowledge to connect new information to what you already know.

- Monitor your comprehension.

- If necessary, adjust your learning strategies.

- Evaluate the success of your learning.

understand the message. Frequently, they just skip that sentence or simply write down the verbatim statements from the lecturer. On the other hand, expert learners are instantly aware when they do not understand something from a text or a lecture. They stop, reread, or ask a question. They know they must understand the information if they are to learn it at a higher level. Comprehension monitoring is considered metacognitive knowledge in the research literature because it involves the ability to step away from the learning process and reflect objectively.

The paradigm of expert/novice learner can be useful as a reflective tool for students. In what ways are we novice learners? Are we gaining expertise in particular skills and knowledge? Does our level of expertise vary across different subjects? What specific strategies can we use to move toward expertise as a college learner?

exercise 5.3

Complete a Goal to Gain Expertise

Begin the process of learning how to gain mastery over a task by completing this goal-setting and monitoring exercise. This exercise will give you a step-by-step method to successfully complete an academic goal, thus building your expertise for your chosen task.

1. Set a challenging but realistic academic goal (task) to complete within the next few weeks. Consider something like studying for a major exam or writing a paper. Make sure the goal is a behavior—some type of academic task for which you can keep track of your actual success.

2. Create a realistic and effective time line to accomplish the goal.

3. What learning strategies will you use to complete the goal? If this is indeed a realistic and challenging goal, think of several strategies to help you achieve success.

4. What do you already know about the task at hand (the goal)? What have you done similarly that proved successful? Make a list or write several paragraphs to help you think about connecting what you already know to the task at hand.

5. Throughout the next few weeks, monitor your progress by keeping a goal diary of your activities connected to completing the goal.

6. If necessary, make changes by adjusting or trying new strategies to help you become more successful. Write about the changes you make in your diary.

7. In your diary, evaluate your success at the end of your time line. Address what you could have done differently to have ensured even more success.

COMMITMENT

When Robert returned to college for his second year, he renewed his commitment to a college education and a professional career. Researchers who study the reasons why some students are successful and others are not find that students who have a strong commitment to a college education and the acquisition of a degree are more likely to graduate than those students who do not (Astin, 1993; Tinto, 1987). **Commitment** is a powerful word that reflects *a promise we make to an idea, a group, another person, or ourselves.* The strength of our commitment rests on our determination to fulfill that promise. One of the most important tasks of childhood and adolescence is learning how to choose commitments and honor them. Most of us have had the experience of joining a group or activity and then wanting to quit halfway through. Do we quit? Or do we honor the promise we made to the other participants of the group? Usually, we begin to learn quickly that we need to choose carefully, even when what we are choosing is a friend or a romantic relationship. A hard life lesson is the realization that life does not just happen to us; we choose it. Choosing our commitments carefully and honoring them is a characteristic of successful students. Honoring our commitments supports good self-esteem and self-discipline.

When Robert was in high school, he decided he wanted to attend college, but he had little knowledge of the level of effort and skills necessary for success there. After his disappointing freshman year, he realized that both his behaviors and his skills would have to change. However, his commitment level was strengthened by his decision to return and try college again. Although Robert has taken an important step in thoughtfully choosing a career path in business, he still has many decisions before him about the specific major he will choose. He knows the learning strategies course he is taking will help him determine how he needs to change his study behaviors and academic skills, so he is willing to attempt the suggestions and strategies he learns in that course. He has promised himself that he will attend all of his classes and be prepared for class lecture and discussion.

Life without serious commitments can be a life filled with a sense of purposelessness. What makes the difference is whether we are thoughtfully searching for those commitments that form the foundation of a good life or whether we are simply wandering from one casual interest to another. Such a search permeates every facet of life as we look to those ideas, groups, and individuals to which we commit our beliefs and our actions. Although this discussion focuses on the academic commitments we have, it is noteworthy that college life (at whatever age) is usually a time of exploration of all categories of commitments—intellectual, spiritual, social, personal, occupational, physical. We may retain some of our commitments from earlier times, but even these are shaped by the crucible of college.

Personal and Institutional Commitments

There are two types of academic commitments: *personal* and *institutional* (Tinto, 1987). Robert has intensified his personal commitment to academics in three ways: first, he wants a college degree and the professional life that can result; second, he has chosen a general career area, business; third, he has promised himself he will become a better student in order to make better grades. More intense personal academic commitments may occur for him later in his college years; for example, he may commit to achieving a specific GPA in order to go to graduate school, or he may develop a passion for a particular subspecialty in his major. Robert has already begun to realize that these commitments must come from him. If he were to return to college just because his father wants him to return, he would have little or no motivation to succeed because the commitment would be his father's, not his.

Robert is minimally committed to the college he attends; he has made some friends, but he does not yet seem to be especially committed to the institution. It is normal for humans to desire a sense of belonging and loyalty to the institution where they study, just as it is normal for people to commit to workplaces, clubs, religious groups, etc. Sometimes students attend the same colleges as their parents or older siblings and their loyalty starts years before they enroll. It is helpful for students to attend orientation programs and learn the history of the campus. In any case, the old ties to former schools are broken, and new ties need to be built. Students can become so attached to a particular institution that they frequently turn down opportunities to transfer, even if they had originally planned to transfer after one or two years at the college. A strong commitment to the institution helps students persist and succeed in college.

In general, research on the retention of college students over the past 25 years indicates that both types of academic commitment increase the likelihood of academic success and graduation (Dochen, 1993). The institutional commitment seems to play a greater role in the initial years of college, whereas the personal commitment becomes much more important as students move deeply into their majors and begin to set specific career goals. Most institutions make serious efforts to attract and acclimate new students to the campus and its traditions. Commitment often begins with a student's initial choice of the college if that choice has been carefully made. For example, Robert simply chose the closest state institution to attend; he did not carefully consider all the choices he had. He made what might be considered a choice by default. Thus, he arrived on campus with moderate feelings; he had not considered the implications of his choice. The second year was different, however, because Robert intentionally chose to return to the campus, thereby intensifying his commitment to his goals and to the institution.

Strategies for Assessing Our Commitments

Reflecting and *journaling* are the two most powerful tools to help us understand our own levels of commitment. What are your thoughts and feelings about the institution you attend? Are you proud to be a student there? Is it important that your degree come from this institution? Do you feel a sense of belonging; in other words, is this institution a *good fit* for you? Are you comfortable in your dealings with the faculty, the staff, and other students? Have you relinquished your bonds to your former school and transferred your loyalties to this one? These and other reflective questions can help you evaluate your sense of commitment to your institution.

Another set of reflective questions will focus your attention on your commitment to *personal academic goals.* How important is it to you to have a college degree and the resulting professional career? Have you made a clear choice of a major? What are your academic ambitions, including GPA and honor societies? Have you investigated graduate/professional programs? Have you completed internships or volunteered or worked part-time in the field?

Of course, commitments occur in other areas of our lives: spiritual, physical, social, family. Early in their college years, students often seriously commit their time and talent to social or family relationships, to religious ideals or organizations, to athletics, to work. At times such commitments enhance our academic commitments, but it is easy to get unbalanced and allow other commitments to devour all of our time and attention. The balance of commitments is especially difficult for freshmen. Robert's first year is a typical example. In the first semester, he underestimated what he needed to do and he did not seek help in a timely way. He kept going home to see his girlfriend, who was attending the local community college. On campus, he struggled in this totally new, less-structured environment to make friends and find his way. In the spring semester, his girlfriend ended their relationship, and Robert felt lonely. Then, his grandmother was diagnosed with cancer. Robert had to choose between being on campus and being at home with his family. He decided that being with his family was more important. He would take books home with the intention of studying, but he would not study.

The college years are a time during which we should learn how to develop, deepen, and balance our commitments. The first step is self-awareness, and that is achieved by persistent reflection, both in conversation with people we trust and in journal writing. Taking an inventory of what we really value, not what others tell us we should value, is sometimes painful. The key is to look at our behaviors. What do we do? Not what do we say we should do, but *what do we do?* How do we spend

KEEPING A COMMITMENT

- State your commitment by putting it in writing.

- Reflect on the importance of keeping your commitment. Answer the question: "Why is this commitment important to me?" Write about your thoughts and feelings as they relate to the commitment.

- Monitor and assess your progress.

- Reward yourself for progress.

- Evaluate your success.

our time, our money? Do we say that academic achievement is important to us and then cut class several times a week? Do we say that we are committed to our friends and then gossip about them? Do we say that we value physical health and then avoid exercise and eat junk food? Do we say that we do not have serious problems and then get drunk three times a week or make ourselves vomit once or twice a day because we believe we ate too much?

A *realistic inventory* pushes us to consider what we really value and what we want as our life commitments. Any list of commitments should include the behaviors that would demonstrate our willingness to choose each commitment. The list should also reveal priorities—Which commitments are most important? Least important? One method is to deliberately create an intention statement. At the beginning of his second year, Robert wrote the following statement: *I intend to work diligently to achieve a 2.5 GPA, to visit my family at least once a month, to participate in two campus organizations in order to make friends, to exercise at least twice a week.* Such an intention statement lists and prioritizes Robert's commitments by specifying the behaviors he will do. Now his task is to manage his time and efforts to achieve this intention statement. Many of the chapters in this book illuminate the techniques necessary to turn intention statements into specific goal statements into specific behaviors.

---

exercise 5.4

Are You Committed?

How strongly are you committed to college? Answering the following questions will help you clarify and reflect on your current experiences and commitment to college.

1. Your thoughts and feelings about the institution you attend:

    a. Are you proud to be a student there?

    b. Is it important that your degree come from this institution?

    c. Do you feel a sense of belonging; in other words, is this institution a *good fit* for you?

    d. Have you relinquished your bonds to your former school and transferred your loyalties to this one?

    e. Are you comfortable in your dealings with the faculty, the staff, and other students?

2. Your goals for attending college:

   a. What is your main goal for attending college?

   b. Have you made a clear choice of a major or selected a program of study?

   c. Is it important for you to have a college degree or to get certified in a particular program?

   d. Will attending college result in a better job or change in career?

   e. Have you investigated graduate/professional programs?

   f. Have you completed any internships or volunteered or worked part-time in a field related to your academic goal?

   g. What are your academic ambitions, including GPA and honor societies?

3. Support from family members:

   a. Does your family support your desire to attend college?

   b. If you live at home, do they make it possible for you to study?

   c. Do they help you financially?

---

exercise 5.5

Creating Commitment Intention Statements

Make a list of at least three academic and three personal commitments. Turn each commitment into an intention statement. Remember to write your commitments in terms of behaviors you will accomplish. The list should also reveal priorities—Which commitments are most important? Least important? Creating a list of intention statements will help you clarify your priorities and set and meet your goals for the semester.

INVOLVEMENT

Robert's involvement in the academic enterprise is deepening his second year on campus because he is spending more time and attention and feelings on all parts of his college life. Involvement is closely related to commitment, but **involvement** is *the true amount of time, attention, and feelings that*

we dedicate to an activity, an idea, or a relationship. Involvement is what we really do. The more absorbed we are in an activity, an idea, or a relationship, the
more involved we are (Astin, 1993; Tinto, 1987).

Psychological health is marked by an appropriate level of involvement in
those activities, ideas, and relationships that are related to our commitments. The
tricky word in that sentence is *appropriate.* All of us have witnessed the disas-
ters that happen when a person becomes overly involved in something, obsessed
with a particular thing. The furthest extreme is called *addiction,* such as the TV,
alcohol, the Internet, exercise, or work. The opposite end of the continuum is
passivity or nonaction. Passivity is related to depression, fear of success, or fear
of failure. None of these extremes works well. What does work for most people
is a balance of effort in those behaviors that are directly related to their goals.
That statement, although easy to say, is difficult to live by for many beginning
college students, and Robert was no exception.

Robert's first year reflects his struggles with involvement. First, he seriously
underestimated the amount of study time college courses require. He procrastinated in his reading assignments, did not review his class notes until the night
before tests, and did not participate in organized study groups. Although he attended class most of the time, he often daydreamed and had incomplete notes.
He spent more time worrying and talking to his friends about studying than actually studying. Thus, his *time on task*—the actual amount of time spent studying and learning—was inadequate.

Many types of involvement lead us away from academic involvement, and
Robert's first year reflected some of those conflicts. At the beginning of the year,
he was in a relationship with his high school girlfriend, so he went back home
most weekends. As a result, he never got involved in campus organizations or
weekend activities such as sports events, concerts, or parties. His grandmother's
illness in the spring also drew him away from campus since he went to see her
many times. Robert's involvement with his family during that crisis was most
appropriate, but the cost was that he felt even more disconnected from his
classes and the campus. He did not tell his professors what was happening and
just tried to catch up on his own. A better strategy would have been to speak to
each professor and made arrangements to make up missed work, find other students who would make copies of their notes, and try to stay connected to his
courses by using his professors' websites.

Other types of involvement that can compete with academic success did
not affect Robert in his first year, but they are often powerful factors in the
lives of other students. It is easy to feel isolated from campus if you commute
and only come to campus to attend your classes. An antidote is to spend more
hours on campus, studying in the library, going to the student center, attending
campus events, joining campus organizations. Trying to maintain close relationships with friends who attend other schools can drain your time and en-

ergy. It is painful to realize that many relationships change when you come to college, so you must choose carefully which relationships are worth retaining. Email is cheaper than long distance telephone calls; driving is cheaper than flying. If you work a job for more than 20 hours per week, it is difficult to have enough time and energy for a full-time load of academics. Managing your money is often the best strategy to maintain your work hours at a reasonable level. On-campus jobs are especially desirable because many have flexible hours, and there is no commute time. Also, most on-campus employers will respect that you are a student and will try to accommodate your schedule.

The educational research, primarily done by Astin (1993), indicates that two types of involvement help a college student's academic performance, such us GPA and graduation. Those types are referred to as *academic involvement* and *social involvement*.

Academic Involvement: Seeking Help

The primary characteristics of academic involvement are time on task, time spent talking with faculty outside class, and relational connection to other students (Astin, 1993). Other helpful activities include participating in group projects, study sessions, tutoring, or a mentoring program; thoughtfully choosing an academic major; and taking a part-time job on campus.

BECOMING ACADEMICALLY INVOLVED

- Schedule time to study and complete assignments for each of your classes. Avoid cramming and waiting until the day before an assignment is due to begin your academic tasks.

- Meet with your instructors on a regular basis. Most instructors schedule weekly office hours and want you to discuss your work with them outside of class.

- Set up weekly study partnerships or study groups. Ideally, study groups should be small, with three to four students.

- Attend weekly supplemental instruction sessions that are offered for your classes.

- Attend test review sessions.

- Attend special lecture series that supplement your courses.

---

exercise 5.6

Find a Study Partner for Each Class

Get to know at least one student in each of your classes this week. Exchange phone numbers and email addresses and discuss the possibility of reviewing course material together throughout the semester. Make at least one contact (phone, email, personal visit) with each student during the week. Write one or two paragraphs to reflect on the experience. This exercise will help you meet new people and find support from your peers.

A critical element in academic involvement is a student's willingness to seek help in learning. Ironically, research indicates that most college students report that they could have used help with course content or study skills, but few seek help (Karabenick & Knapp, 1991). Robert was typical of many freshmen in that he did not seek help from his professors, his fellow students, or any tutoring programs. Robert is intelligent and he knew he was in trouble, but he did not ask for help. What could explain this behavior? After years of working with undergraduate students, we believe the answer is simple and sad: Robert believed that he should be able to successfully learn in college without help. If he asked for help, then other people (professors, students) might think he was dumb or lazy. Often, he did not even know what to ask! His procrastination just intensified the problem because he was embarrassed that he was not doing the work. These thoughts were directly related to Robert's self-esteem. As many freshmen, Robert had experienced a precipitous drop in his academic self-esteem when he moved from the towering heights of being a senior in high school to the lowly depths of his freshman status. Another contributing factor is the style of collegiate courses. Professors rarely initiate help-seeking involvement; they expect the student to initiate.

Nelson-Le Gall (1985) postulated a practical model for seeking academic help. It includes self-awareness, deciding where to get help, and self-evaluation.

Self-awareness. The first step to seeking academic help is to be aware that you may not be learning the academic content at the level the professor expects or you desire. You may feel confused or intimidated by the complexity of the ideas. You may not understand how the examples relate to the ideas. Testing yourself on the material by explaining it to someone else or by answering study questions at the end of the chapter or in study manuals is a good method of determining whether you need help. Ideally, you will make a timely decision. How long will you persist before you give up trying to learn the material on your own? It is important to try on your own and then to try again if your first attempt is unsuccessful, but more than two unsuccessful tries is usually unproductive and frustrating.

Deciding where to get help. Once you have made the decision to ask for help, whom do you ask? Who or what is the most likely source of the information you need? Learning how to choose the appropriate resource is a skill that expert learners have developed, but how can a novice learner know what to do?

Academic help comes in assorted formats. Does the professor have a website with lecture outlines or

SOURCES OF ACADEMIC HELP

- Instructors
- Teaching assistants
- Other students
- Tutoring (one-to-one, group, online)
- Supplemental instruction, review sessions
- Supplemental materials (Web-based materials, library, supplemental reading)

extra study materials? Are the professor's office hours at times you can go? Does the course have a teaching assistant or grader who is available to answer questions? Are peer-led study sessions, supplemental instruction sessions, or tutors available? Is there online tutoring support for this course?

Self-evaluation. Once you have sought academic help, it is imperative that you evaluate its usefulness. Has your understanding of the academic material increased? Are you performing competently on exams? Most important, are you reaching your academic goals? While you are trying to use effective academic involvement, you will also be determining your social involvement.

---

exercise 5.7

Visit the Learning Center

Visit the learning center (tutoring center) on your campus. During your visit write down the hours of operation. If possible, meet with a tutor to review the process for receiving help and be sure to discuss any academic concerns you may be experiencing. Indicate to the tutor the current classes in which you are committed to seeking assistance. Write one or two paragraphs to reflect on the experience. This exercise will help you become comfortable with using the campus learning center as an academic resource.

Social Involvement

The second type of involvement that helps a student's academic performance is social. Realistically, social life involvements are especially important for most beginning college students because students are creating a new life in college. They have left their old lives behind, whether high school, another institution, the military, or work. Finding their way into a new web of social connections requires intent, focus, and time. Often, activities that help students connect with others detract from their academic studies. The tension between meeting both academic goals and social goals is usually intense, difficult, and fraught with guilt. Two realizations help students live in that tension. First, what is your primary goal? If it is academics, then a full-time load requires the same attention and effort that a full-time job does. Second, there are two types of social involvements: those that help a student's academic success and those that hurt it. A list of the latter is easy to hypothesize. Excessive partying, drinking, and hanging out results in little sleep and lack of preparation for classes.

Social involvements that help a student's academic success include belonging to campus organizations to which the student seeks membership, athletic and

intramural sports teams, theatre and music performance groups, religious organizations, and student government. (See Figure 5.1 for examples of different types of organizations.) For this type of social involvement to be helpful, a student must have enough time to participate in activities and make close connections with other students. If you belong to too many organizations, then your participation in any single organization will be too shallow. Not only must you be careful about the number of organizations to which you belong, but you must seek to find those that truly appeal to your interests and in which you can establish meaningful relationships. There was so much turmoil during Robert's freshman year that he did not join any campus groups nor attend church and he did not work at a campus job. Robert has promised himself that he will participate in two campus organizations in order to make friends. One method of shaping that commitment so that it could benefit his academic goals is for him to choose one organization that relates to his major, business. Joining a study group for one of his classes might also help him meet both social and academic goals.

---

exercise 5.8

Your Level of Involvement

How involved are you with college? An appropriate level of involvement will help you obtain college success. Answering the following questions will help you clarify and reflect on your current involvements.

1. What is your level (high, average, low, none) of academic/social involvement on your campus? Explain.

2. Do you attend (or plan on attending) campus events? Explain.

3. Do you belong to any campus organizations? If so, which ones? If not, do you plan on joining at least one? Why or why not?

4. How much time do you spend on campus?

5. How many new friends have you made on campus?

6. Do you work? If so, where and how many hours a week do you work?

7. Is your job on or off campus?

8. What is your level of involvement with your courses (high, average, low, none)? Explain.

9. What is your level of involvement with your major field of study (high, average, low, none)? Explain.

10. How much time on task do you devote to studying?

11. How would you describe your connection to your institution?

12. Which types of involvement do you currently have that support your academic goals?

13. Which involvements detract from your goals?

FIGURE 5.1   Examples of Campus Organizations

Type	Examples
Chartered	Student Government Association, Student Association for Campus Activities
Department	Chemistry Club, Psychology Club, Society of Student Journalists
Honors	Alpha Chi (Academics), Alpha Kappa Delta (Sociology), Kappa Delta Phi (Education), Sigma Delta Pi (Spanish)
Multicultural	Asian Student Association, Black Student Alliance, German Culture Club, Native American Association
Political	College Democrats, College Libertarians, College Republicans, Students for Social & Political Awareness
Professional	American Sign Language Association, National Art Education Association, Student Economics Association
Recreational	Outdoor Adventure Club, Scuba Diving Club, Yoga Club, intramural sports teams
Religious	Bahai College Club, Campus Christian Community, Muslim Student Association, Organization for Alternative Spirituality
Residence hall	Residence Hall Council, Resident Assistant Council
Social	Various Greek organizations (e.g., fraternities and sororities)

CONCLUSION

This chapter has presented several powerful factors that can increase your success in college. You have the opportunity to become an expert learner, to make an intentional commitment both to your own goals and to your school, and to deliberately become involved in your own academic goals as well as your social goals. These characteristics do not happen by chance; they occur only when you pursue them.

SUMMARY

- The terms *expert* and *novice* differentiate between two dramatically different levels of skill in collegiate learning.

- Expert learners plan and analyze their learning tasks; have more sophisticated use of declarative, procedural, and conditional knowledge; and routinely monitor their comprehension and adjust their learning strategies accordingly.

- Commitment is a promise we make to an idea, a group, another person, or ourselves; it is the determination to fulfill that promise.

- Two types of academic commitments are necessary for academic success: personal and institutional. Research indicates that institutional commitment plays a greater role in the initial years of college; personal commitment becomes much more important for students in the latter years.

- Reflecting, journaling, setting personal academic goals, and creating a realistic self-analysis inventory are powerful tools to help students understand and achieve commitments.

- Involvement is the true amount of time, attention, and feelings that a student dedicates to an activity, an idea, or a relationship. Appropriate levels of involvement are determined by a student's commitment.

- Too many involvements can interfere with academic success.

- One important aspect of academic involvement is a student's willingness to seek help. However, many students do not seek help on their own volition.

- Social involvements help students create a campus life within the college community. Belonging to campus organizations, athletic and intramural sports teams, theatre and music performance groups, religious organizations, and student government are positive examples of activities.

- Social involvements can be beneficial if they lead to close connections with other students and support rather than hinder successful academic performance.

KEY CONCEPTS

Campus organizations

Commitment: institutional and personal

Declarative knowledge

Expert learning

Intention statements

Involvement: academic and social

Metacognitive knowledge

Novice learning

Procedural knowledge

Seeking help

GUIDED JOURNAL QUESTIONS

1. Colleges and universities usually require students to obtain a broad educational background by completing a core set of college classes selected from many academic disciplines. What are the core requirements at your institution? Do you agree or disagree with this practice? Which classes do you feel will be most advantageous for you to complete and why? Which will be least advantageous and why?

2. Intense study in a major academic discipline begins your transformation from novice to expert. Your institution may also require you to select a major field of study and to take many courses from that field. Have you selected a major yet? If so, how many courses are required? Which courses are required? Which courses will you consider taking as electives?

3. Commitment reflects a promise we make to an idea, a group, another person, or ourselves. List two major commitments you have made in your life that you have kept. What helped you honor these commitments? How did it make you feel to keep these commitments?

4. List two major commitments you have made in your life that you did not keep. What prevented you from honoring these commitments? How did it make you feel to break these commitments?

5. A commitment to regular class attendance is essential for college success. What are the advantages of attending each and every class session? Justify reasons when it would be appropriate to miss class.

6. How committed are you to completing this semester of college? This year? Your degree?

7. How important is it for you to become actively involved in extracurricular activities on your campus? List several organizations offered on your

campus that you might be interested in joining. How much time are you willing to devote to these activities each week?

8. Some students become overinvolved in extracurricular activities that interfere with their academic performance. What would cause students to fall prey to this occurrence? Predict your tendency for overinvolvement.

9. How many of your classes offer supplemental instruction (sometimes referred to as SI) or out-of-class review sessions? What are the advantages of attending? Are there any disadvantages? How committed are you to attending these sessions? Explain.

10. Many students must work while they attend college. How many hours of classes would be appropriate to schedule each semester if you are working at least 10 hours a week? Twenty hours? Thirty hours? How much would these different amounts of work hours interfere with your academic success? Explain.

11. In this chapter you were introduced to Robert, a first-semester sophomore returning to college after a difficult freshman year. From the new choices that Robert has made, what do you predict will be his likelihood for success this year? Explain.

The Last Word

My involvement in campus organizations was as valuable in learning life skills as any lesson I learned in class.

—*Russ Hodges*

6

Patterns in Human Development

All these people are like me?

. . . the development [of humans] resembles what used to be called an adventure of the spirit.
—*William Perry*

Almost always, we see ourselves through three lenses. I am an individual, unique in this world, a product of all I was born with and all I have experienced. I am a member of a group (or groups) of humans with whom I share some idea or circumstance (my family, my friends, my country). I am human, like all other humans—I was born in this world and will die in this world. I laugh, love, think, work, play, worship. Each of these lenses has a name: the individual, the group (culture), the universal. We can deepen our self-awareness by examining ourselves through each of these three lenses.

In this chapter, we look carefully at a primary concept called developmentalism. It is the story of how we are alike as all humans (universal) and how we are like some humans (culture). In the next chapter, we look at several personality theories that describe how our uniqueness arises from the interaction of our personality and the specific circumstances of our lives. By combining both worldviews, we can come to a rich understanding of ourselves and how to live our lives well and wisely.

SELF-ASSESSMENT: My Independence and Autonomy

Striving for personal independence is a major goal of many college students. With independence comes a move toward autonomy (making your own decisions and working for your own approval). With 5 being "Almost Always" and 1 being "Almost Never," assess your level of independence and autonomy. Rate each of the following statements honestly by circling the appropriate number. Completing this assessment will allow you to begin to examine your movement toward a new stage of psychological development.

	Almost Always		Sometimes		Almost Never
1. I feel comfortable appropriately challenging someone's beliefs or opinions when I disagree with their views.	5	4	3	2	1
2. I take full responsibility for the decisions and choices I make.	5	4	3	2	1
3. I am okay with being viewed as different or having different beliefs from my peers.	5	4	3	2	1
4. I am psychologically less dependent on my parents for emotional support.	5	4	3	2	1
5. I am not afraid to voice my own opinions to others—even to my parents, spouse, and teachers.	5	4	3	2	1
6. I respect others' points of view even if I do not agree with them.	5	4	3	2	1
7. I like to find personal relevance in what I am studying.	5	4	3	2	1

8. I see making mistakes as a learning opportunity and not as personal failure.	5	4	3	2	1
9. I tend to be a more self-directed learner as opposed to a teacher-directed learner.	5	4	3	2	1
10. I tend to closely examine many alternatives before I make a major commitment.	5	4	3	2	1
11. I do not have to depend on others for my happiness.	5	4	3	2	1
12. I am more independent than dependent on others.	5	4	3	2	1
13. I am beginning to seek out the meaning and purpose of my own life.	5	4	3	2	1

Add up the numbers circled. Your total score will be between 13 and 65. The higher your score, the more likely you are to be moving into independence and autonomy. For total scores below 39, write or reflect on items for which you have concerns. Also, consider talking with a trusted friend, a family member, a teacher, or an advisor.

THE UNIVERSAL

From conception to death, the one constant in human life is change. The amount and the rate of change may vary over our life span, but its relentless roll occurs, whether we welcome it or shrink from it. Across every dimension of life—physical, mental, emotional, spiritual—we change in predictable patterns and timing. These commonalities are some of the universal dimension of humanity. Augsberger (1986) says,

> Five dimensions are universally present among humans: *biologically* we are a common species; *socially* we have common relational prerequisites; *ecologically* we must adjust to a common atmosphere and a limited number of climates; *spiritually* we invariably seek to touch the numinous, the transcendent, the meaning of our existence; and *psychologically* we have an intraspecies sameness of processes. (p. 52)

The Life Cycle

Prenatal

[BIRTH]

Childhood

[PUBERTY]

Youth

[INDEPENDENCE]

Adulthood

[MIDLIFE]

Maturity

[RETIREMENT]

Old Age

[DEATH]

In addition, Augsberger (1986) refers to the human psychological processes as "the psychic unity of humankind" (p. 55), which include the cognitive abilities to perceive, memorize, and reason; the ability to feel (emotion); and the ability to exercise free will or volition.

The arc of life begins with the helpless dependence of infancy, throws off limitations as adulthood brings independence, rises to interdependence in maturity, and subsides again to dependence in later years. Our movement through the life span occurs in alternating periods of rapid, irreversible change (transitions) and periods of stable consolidation (stages). Although writers from earlier times and places have described these life stages, Erikson (1963, 1982) was the one who conceptualized the Western worldview in his famous Eight Stages of Psychosocial Development. Each stage has a crisis that must be resolved for the individual to move forward in a healthy manner. Recently, other scholars have elaborated on Erikson's work by adding other stages (Newman & Newman, 1995).

For our purposes in this book, we present the Life Cycle, an adaptation of stage theory that emphasizes six crucial transition periods, each with its subsequent stable stage. From this model, we focus on two transition periods that seem to be the most relevant for college students: independence and midlife.

To begin, the stages are prenatal, childhood, youth, adulthood, maturity, and old age. The transition period from prenatal to childhood is birth, from childhood to youth is puberty. The next two transition periods—independence and midlife—capture our attention because they are remarkably parallel. Each lasts 7 to 10 years, and together they constitute the periods of greatest change in adult lives. Retirement and death are the last transitions. When we place the stages and transitions in sequential order, the pattern in the accompanying box emerges.

---

exercise 6.2

Where Are You in the Life Cycle?

Developmental psychologists believe that major transitions take place throughout our lifetime and that we move from one developmental stage to the next during these transition periods. Answer the following questions to determine where you and those closest to you fall in the life cycle.

1. As you look over the life cycle, what stage or transition do you believe most characterizes your life right now? Is your developmental age congruent with your chronological age?

2. What are the developmental ages of the people closest to you, such as your partner, parents, children, close friends?

INDEPENDENCE

The transition time between youth and adulthood has greatly expanded for much of American society during the past century as higher education has become more available. That time, called independence, is the gradual movement from the security and protection of our families to the acceptance of responsibility for our own lives—psychologically, financially, and emotionally. For many people, especially college students, it is a time of fits and starts, a time of striving for independence and rushing back to the security of family. The entire transition usually takes seven to ten years, and sometimes even longer. There is an awkwardness to the transition to independence for most people; it is rarely graceful or smooth. Parents and older siblings sometimes interfere with unwanted advice. A large part of this transition time is the trying on of ideas, roles, language, and beliefs different from those of our families. Becoming independent is a crucial step toward becoming a healthy adult.

> ### · · · JASON · · ·
> #### *In the midst of the transition period independence . . .*
>
> *Jason, a 20-year-old junior business major, feels he is finally finding his way through college and into adult life. A popular and athletic teenager, he entered college as an engineering major and quickly found that he was bored in his classes and unmotivated to study. His grades were marginal; his attention wandered in class and when he tried to read. Jason watched his friends make decisions about majors and life paths, but he held back. His twentieth birthday was not a happy time because he felt frightened that he was directionless. He felt like he was wandering without any goals. His parents voiced increasing dismay, and he thought about leaving college altogether. Two long weeks after that birthday, he made an appointment at the campus career center and began a series of discussions with a counselor. After taking several interest inventories and completing some written exercises, Jason gradually came to understand that his talents lay in oral communication and persuasion. He interviewed several successful marketing graduates of the college and, for the first time, could see himself developing a career in professional marketing. Everything began to fall into place.*

How can simply finding the right career path make everything fall into place? Well, Jason is in the midst of the transition period called *independence,* and this career decision is the result of many factors, but it is only a first step in a long process. In the space of just a few years, his life has changed across three major dimensions: how he thinks (cognitive), how he feels (affective), and what he does (behavioral). **Independence** is *that time in which we are initiated into the adult world;* in just a few years, we become an equal of people we had heretofore seen as impossibly older.

Independence means that our living arrangements change; we usually move away from our families, both physically and psychologically. Finances change too, as we contribute more to our own support and are responsible for monitoring the business of life. Lifestyle also changes in this period. Jason's life had reflected all these changes since he came to college. He had begun working a part-time job to help with expenses because his younger sister was entering college. He moved out of the dormitory into his own apartment with two new friends, and he became serious about cycling. He even joined the cycling club on campus and made regular distance excursions into the local countryside.

A stunning difference in Jason's life is that his relationships have changed. His parents now give support and express concern but no longer make decisions for him. They are willing to listen but give fewer suggestions. All but one of his high school friends have drifted away, and his college friends are different in their values and behaviors. His college roommates and friends are ambitious and directed, and most are in long-term romantic relationships. Jason still goes out with his groups of friends, but he has had few serious relationships. He feels ready for such a relationship and has spent significant time contemplating the characteristics he wants in that person.

Jason is experiencing both affective and behavioral changes in his life that are appropriate and also characteristic of the independence period. However, the greatest changes have arisen in his thinking.

---

exercise 6.3

Your Self-Perceptions

Your views about yourself can influence your quality of life. Answer each of the following questions and then write at least two specific examples to support each of your answers. This exercise will help you identify some of your current self-perceptions and gain insight into areas that you can work toward as you make transitions from one stage in your life to the next.

1. Do you see yourself as having the potential to succeed in life?

_____ Yes _____ No _____ Sometimes

Examples:

2. Do you trust yourself?

_____ Yes _____ No _____ Sometimes

Examples:

3. Do you see yourself as an independent person?

_____ Yes _____ No _____ Sometimes

Examples:

4. Do you have the ability to be loved?

_____ Yes _____ No _____ Sometimes

Examples:

5. Do you have the capacity to give love?

_____ Yes _____ No _____ Sometimes

Examples:

6. Do you see yourself as confident?

_____ Yes _____ No _____ Sometimes

Examples:

7. Do you see yourself as caring and accepting?

_____ Yes _____ No _____ Sometimes

Examples:

8. Do others see you as a happy, positive person?

_____ Yes _____ No _____ Sometimes

Examples:

9. Do you see yourself as making a positive contribution to society?

_____ Yes _____ No _____ Sometimes

Examples:

10. Do you see yourself successfully making a transition from one stage of your life to the next?

_____ Yes _____ No _____ Sometimes

Examples:

---

exercise 6.4

How Others See You

Do you have misperceptions about how others view you? Do your friends really know your strengths and weaknesses? Could you learn anything about yourself from their perceptions? To learn the answers to these questions, ask two close friends whom you rely on and trust to give you honest feedback. Ask them to write a list of your top five strengths or best attributes and give specific examples of each. Then ask them to list five attributes they would like to see you improve and to provide specific examples of each. Remember to use the feedback for personal growth and insight and be sure to thank them for their help.

Perry's Theory of Cognitive and Moral Development

Our cognitive development makes a huge journey during the transition of independence. Although many theorists and researchers have attempted to explain how our minds develop during this period, no one better captured the flow of that change than William Perry (1970). Perry developed a classic model for intellectual development among college students. Although his theory has been adapted by others (Belenky, Clinchy, Goldberger, & Tarule, 1986), it remains a useful template to understand why we think and believe as we do. It is important to remember that Perry conducted all his investigation with Anglo male students. Although his work remains the dominant theory, Belenky and coauthors posit that some women progress through these ways of thinking differently. As we discuss Perry's theory, we allude to their ideas. In the next chapter, we look at how differing personality structures may interface with Perry's stages as much as gender.

Perry posited a journey of intellectual and moral development in the independence period through nine stages that can be grouped into four categories. For the purposes of this text, we look only at the categories, although you may wish to investigate the full theory in the classic text *Forms of Intellectual and Ethical Development in the College Years* (Perry, 1970). See Figure 6.1 for a student's perspective of Perry's stages of cognitive development.

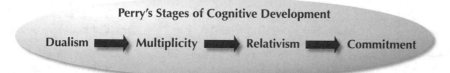

Perry's Stages of Cognitive Development

Dualism ➡ Multiplicity ➡ Relativism ➡ Commitment

Category 1—Dualism

People in the dualism stage believe there is a correct answer to every question. They view knowledge in terms of absolutes and try to conform all knowledge into being either right or wrong or good or bad. They depend on authorities (such as their college instructors) for such truths, and they resist thinking independently or making their own value decisions. As students they believe teachers should deliver knowledge to them. They view learning in terms of simply memorizing information and then selecting the correct answer for an exam. Difficulties arise for them when they witness authorities in disagreement.

When Jason was 16, he believed that there was a right and a wrong answer to everything, and his job was to find the authority who knew the right answer and learn it. Sometimes the authority was a peer, sometimes a teacher, sometimes his parents. He felt comfortable with questions that asked him to remember and understand, but he had two classes that required more considered opinion. He was uncomfortable in those classes primarily because he did not know what the teacher really wanted. Facts were his friends and ambiguities were stressful. He rarely questioned the dominant views of his peer group.

Category 2—Multiplicity

The movement to multiplicity means that students, for the first time, begin to view knowledge as being based more on opinion rather than certainty. They become more accepting when authorities disagree with each other or when an authority, at least temporarily, is in search of an answer. As students, they begin to view their opinions as being equal to others', and they sometimes fault their authorities (teachers) for not seeing the value in their answers.

By the time Jason entered college, he understood that there are conflicting answers to many serious questions. Although he still believed that there were *right* answers (such thinking often took the form that there was one perfect major for him or one perfect mate), he acknowledged that some problems seem not to have solutions and thus everyone has a right to his or her opinion. Jason still looked to authorities for the final answer, and he remained impatient with professors who resisted giving simplistic answers. He often expressed his opinion that they were just incompetent because they did not know the answers.

Multiple opportunities crowded Jason's life. In college, he was confronted with a myriad of choices about politics, religion, lifestyle, and ethics. Many of his professors did not seem interested in ritualized answers; instead, they promoted

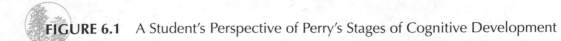

FIGURE 6.1   A Student's Perspective of Perry's Stages of Cognitive Development

	Dualism	**Multiplicity**	**Relativism**	**Commitment**
Knowledge perspective	I believe knowledge is either right or wrong, good or bad. Answers exist somewhere for every problem and authorities know them. Knowledge is quantitative.	When authorities do not know the answer, everyone has a right to their own opinion; none can be called wrong. Authorities are still searching for the answers.	I view knowledge in relation to context—everything is valid, but not always equal. Point of view is relevant. I evaluate knowledge based on evidence and logic. Knowledge is qualitative.	I make a commitment, an affirmation, or a decision. Major commitments include choosing a career, choosing religious and political affiliations, and choosing a mate.
Instructor	She is responsible for teaching me. She is the ultimate source of my learning.	He is the authority on the topic; he will provide the answers to difficult questions.	She provides guidance and many sources of learning. She facilitates discussion. She challenges me to create new questions.	He is interested in my commitment affirmation, or decision. He allows me to form my own opinion.
Goal of learning	Learning is mastered by memorizing. I memorize facts, dates, places, and events.	I comprehend the material. I do not just memorize it. I begin to see the importance of ideas.	I apply and analyze what I am learning. I consider differing points of view and grapple with difficult issues.	I synthesize and evaluate the information. I form an opinion and seek personal relevance.
Expectations	Please tell me what to learn. Stick to the syllabus. Will this information be on the test?	Help me understand how different pieces of information relate. You want me to search for the answers, but eventually you will tell me what is correct.	Do not give me answers; let me struggle to solve problems. There may be many correct answers.	My answer is correct as long as I can support it with evidence. I need to find personal relevance with what I am learning.
Method of testing	I prefer objective tests—true/false, multiple choice, matching.	I prefer objective and some subjective tests—short-answer and fill-in-the-blank questions.	I prefer subjective tests where I can support my answers through logic and evidence.	I prefer subjective tests that ask me to make some kind of commitment to a choice or an option.
Grades	If I get all the correct answers, then I will earn an A.	I hope my teacher allows for effort, especially if I understand the process of getting the correct answers.	My grades should reflect my ability to support my answers with sound reasoning, logic, and evidence.	I understand grades are important, but I learn for the sake of learning and expanding my knowledge.

inquiry and asked questions. He had to write essays and his grade was based on the quality of his argument. Like most freshmen, Jason struggled, thinking that the professors cared more about how much he could write rather than thoughtfully constructed responses to questions. By his sophomore year, Jason had made real progress in cognitive development. He was enjoying the freedom of exploring new ideas and positions. His religious beliefs came under scrutiny, as did his political views. He heard speakers and read authors who challenged the philosophy of his family, and gradually he began to relinquish his search for outside authority.

Category 3—Relativism

Students at the relativism level of cognitive development begin to question everything. The typical initial reaction of students as they enter relativism is that all opinions are equal, but many college assignments help students recognize that their opinions are evaluated by the quality of the supporting evidence they provide. Authorities are not asking for the one right answer but for students to have the ability to support an opinion (answer) with data and solid reasoning. Students begin to see knowledge as relative depending on the context or circumstance. They begin to enjoy the art of debating both sides of an issue, seeking personal relevance for each. Students search out their own truths.

Jason's twentieth birthday was a turning point. Although he had begun accepting responsibility for his behaviors several years prior, he now realized that his life was in his hands. He knew that the responsibility for choosing a major and a career was his, so while he investigated the options carefully, he took control of the process. He realized that his choice to major in business was just one step in a complex series of choices.

Relativism is the freedom to ask and attempt to answer any question. It is a delightful, exciting time for many and a terrifying time for others. For those who find it exhilarating, they relish trying on new ideas (as well as companions, hairstyles, and language). Relativism can be a playful time intellectually, but it is not intended as a permanent place. Rather, it is a time of exploration and daring, a time in which we challenge any and all assumptions.

Perry (1970) noted that cognitive growth to relativistic thinking was not always possible for every person. He presented three deflections to growth: retreat, escape, and temporizing.

Retreat. Retreat is a regression to earlier stages. It is fair to say that not everyone is enamored with relativism. For some people, the loss of absolutes, even temporarily, is unbearable. They run away in one of two ways. First, they may retreat back to the safety of dualism, sometimes even moving back home and trying to re-create a safer time with old friends and ideas. Second, they may choose an extreme version of retreating. Such extremes include joining groups that espouse rigid belief systems, whether military, political, or religious. Cults are the epitome of dualism in which one figure is the absolute authority.

Escape. In escape the student avoids commitment by settling in at the relativistic stage and rejects further movement. Typical of this stage is alienation and abandonment of responsibility by not making a commitment. Another common word that describes escape is *drifting*. Students caught in escape often passively delegate responsibility to fate. They drift into majors or weak relationships. They often drift out of college because nothing seizes their interest.

Temporizing. Perry (1970) defined temporizing as a postponement of movement for a full academic year. Sometimes people temporize; that is, they stay in relativism, treading water and refusing to move forward. They do not seriously explore career choices but, instead, take a variety of entertaining courses. Although they may work, they rarely seek jobs or internships that could give them useful experience in a journey toward a career. In other words, they stay in relativism but they do not use the opportunities that relativism provides for further growth.

An important characteristic of both escape and temporizing is avoidance. Avoidance is simple in our society; alcohol and other drugs provide an easy path, as do social or family overinvolvement. Some students work all the time, thereby avoiding the important questions that relativism initiates. Others overuse campus organizations and stay so busy that they cannot thoughtfully explore the questions that relativism raises.

Jason's twentieth birthday galvanized him into action. In many ways he had been drifting. Now he felt compelled to explore his many choices. He took the time and made the effort to understand himself and his deepest longings, his talents and abilities, his values and goals. These months were intense and full of powerful insights. He shared pieces of his journey with those people he trusted, and for the first time, he really listened to their responses and encouragement. He was almost ready for the fourth category of Perry's model—commitment.

---

exercise 6.5

Deflections to Cognitive Growth

Complete the following statements to determine which deflections you may have experienced with regard to making commitments:

I have retreated from making a commitment when I . . .

I have escaped from making a commitment when I . . .

I have temporized a commitment when I . . .

Category 4—Commitment

Relativism allows students to exercise reason as they look to alternatives; it allows them to examine themselves and their lives. However, reason alone does not move them to commitment. When they are ready to decide how and why they want to live their lives, then they are poised to commit to particular beliefs, values, relationships, principles, and work. According to Perry (1970),

> The word 'Commitments,' then, refers to affirmations: in all the plurality of the relativistic world—truths, relationships, purposes, activities, and cares, in all their contexts—one affirms what is one's own. As ongoing creative activities, Commitments require the courage of responsibility, and presuppose an acceptance of human limits, including the limits of reason. (p. 135)

Note that Perry (1970) uses a capital *C* when he talks about category 4. By that, he means that Commitments (choices) made after relativism are choices made after all the alternatives are examined. We can make commitments (lowercase *c*) at any time in our lives, but only the ones in category 4 follow the use of reason with numerous options. A powerful example is the startling difference between two 17-year-olds getting pregnant unintentionally and a couple in their thirties deliberately choosing parenthood. The two adolescents may make a thoughtful choice to become committed parents, but they have not had the time or the opportunity to explore what directions their lives might have taken without the pregnancy. They have a limited knowledge and experience base. No matter what action they choose, their lives are changed forever. Perry differentiates between a commitment and a Commitment. Although both are honorable and important, only the latter is a truly free choice.

Jason stands at the beginning of Commitments. The first stage of his professional life is his Commitment to the world of business. Marketing will require initiative, it will probably be more autonomous than collaborative, and there will be continual pressure to meet external goals. His reflections have led him to the conviction that he has the talent and interest to enjoy such a working life. Advanced courses and internships can help him narrow options and focus on a specific type of marketing. As he begins to take his business courses, an ethics course catches his attention.

Jason's father is a quiet and reserved man, unlike Jason's uncle, who is loud and aggressive. As Jason studies the principles of business ethics, he realizes that his father's business practices are built on solid ethical practices and have gained the respect of peers and customers. On the other hand, his uncle always has a new scheme, a new company, but he never stays anywhere long and has become an uncomfortable presence in the family. His uncle never follows through with promises, and Jason remembers many disappointments. Jason's father, Mike, owns a small accounting business, and Jason worked for him during high school. So many times, Mike's clients would tell Jason how much they trusted his father and that Mike always looked after them. Sometimes a new client would push Mike to bend the rules about a tax report, but Mike always held to his convictions, even if the client went to another company. Jason really took his father's behavior for granted; he always knew he could count on his father's word. In the ethics class, he begins to see that his father had made deliberate choices about how he wanted to be as an accountant, and Jason determines that he wants to live and work by the same ethical standards.

A theorist named Lawrence Kohlberg (1981) created a model for the development of moral reasoning, or the judgment of right and wrong. Such evolution fits within the view of life-span development, with specific types of moral reasoning congruent with specific stages of cognitive growth. By committing to a set of ethical business standards, Jason is making an important step toward the higher levels of moral reasoning, those that include abstract concepts of justice.

Jason's relationships with authorities have dramatically changed. Now he consults with people who have expertise and knowledge in a specific area and he pays close attention to what they offer him. However, he realizes that they do not have final answers or complete knowledge but that they are also grappling with relativistic knowledge. They may be more expert than he, but he no longer accepts their conclusions unconditionally. Jason is realizing that he is becoming his own authority; that is, he must determine his own beliefs, opinions, and actions.

Another realization for Jason is his Commitment to maintain the friendships he has. He has joined a campus business fraternity. Although he knows that most college friendships end, he is willing to work hard to maintain his relationship with his four closest college friends. Close, trusted friends have a high value for Jason, and he is determined to maintain such relationships.

Jason also knows that someday he wants a Committed relationship, but he has not yet found his partner. He dates and has had a few short romantic relationships, but he realizes that he feels no urgency. Partnership is a long-term goal, one that will come eventually.

• • • MEREDITH • • •
Jason's younger sister strives for independence

While Jason is dramatically changing during the midst of the independence transition, his younger sister Meredith is just entering college. Her changes are also startling, but they are occurring at the onset of the independence transition and, thus, the issues are different. Meredith has followed her elder brother to the same campus, but she plans to direct her college career very differently. She has long dreamed of a law career and began an intense drive to academic excellence while still in high school. At 17, she fell in love with Marcus, a fellow junior, and they are still in a committed relationship. He, too, is ambitious and received a scholarship to an out-of-state school. Financial concerns kept Meredith from attending that school, but they have promised to maintain their relationship even though they are hundreds of miles apart.

Meredith feels ready for college; she achieved good grades in high school and was responsible for her own behaviors. She understood the system and played by the rules. According to Perry's scheme, Meredith is still quite dualistic. She believes law is her only career option and Marcus her only mate. In high school, her friends resembled her; no one was different. College immediately challenges her simplistic views.

Meredith's roommate is a whirlwind of enthusiasm and energy. Within minutes of meeting, Janice describes herself and her family, her boyfriend, and her major. All are extremely different from Meredith's. Janice comes from a different religious background, her boyfriend is of a different ethnic group, her family is wealthy, and she is a theatre major. Janice's half of the room is already overflowing with clothes, posters, and sound. She is flamboyant in manner and appearance, exactly the kind of student Meredith avoided in high school.

The first class days are also shocking. Large classes, stern professors, intimidating syllabi, and piles of books! Overwhelmed at first, Meredith steps back and reflects how she can begin to control and understand this new environment. She quickly registers for a mentor (a senior woman) and explores the library for places to study. She is apprehensive but still feels confident that she can make this transition well.

Within a few weeks, Meredith settles in. There are some surprises. A required class in anthropology is fascinating, and she finds herself thinking about taking more courses in that discipline. Although Meredith is interested and attentive in her classes, she remains quiet, even when the professor asks for discussion. After all, she is there to learn; it is the professors who have the answers.

Meredith's behavior is typical for many women, who maintain silence in the classroom. Belenky et al. (1986) believe that many women at the dualism stage remain quiet because they do not believe they can know the "right" answers.

> *College life is more than academics, and Meredith is trying to build a new social life. Meredith has found many of Janice's friends to be intelligent and funny even though she thinks they are outrageous in the way they dress and act. She enjoys their company, but she is still lonely. She communicates with Marcus daily via the Internet and talks with her mother each week. Privately, she worries about the competition in her classes. Some students are clearly irresponsible, but there are many students who take academics seriously. She wonders, "Even though I am studying, will I make the grades I need?"*

Perry (1970) would describe Meredith's development as the beginning movements from dualism to multiplicity. Her worldview is becoming more complex, but she is still holding on to the absolute and rigid ideas of what her life is about. Leaving dualism is frightening, and most of us fight it. Dualism represents a way of concrete, predictable thinking that feels so safe, so organized. If we follow the rules, then we will be successful. After witnessing Jason's struggles, Meredith never questioned whether the rules and expectations taught by her family were good. She simply accepted them.

Now Meredith is confronted by alternate views. Her anthropology teacher challenges some traditional religious views; her history professor provides several interpretations of what Meredith had supposed were facts; her roommate's casual sexual behavior is unsettling; the blatant use of alcohol/drugs among some students is shocking. The combined result is that Meredith finds herself questioning her own beliefs. The walls of her dualistic views are being shaken, and she is grudgingly admitting other viewpoints.

Meredith's initial weeks as a freshman are exhilarating and daunting, but she believes that if she works harder than she did in high school she will make the high grades she wants. Some serious surprises await her, for college study is quite different from that common to high school. Meredith is not yet an expert learner; in fact, she still expects to simply follow a teacher's lead.

exercise 6.6

Matching Your Cognitive Level to a College Course

Your current developmental level of cognitive growth and the way a class is taught can sometimes be a challenge. Select a challenging course for which you are currently enrolled. Then answer the questions that follow. This exercise will help you assess your developmental level as well as the level a challenging course is being presented to you.

1. What cognitive level of development does your teacher exhibit? Using Perry's stages of cognitive development, analyze your teacher's cognitive level of development according to the following criteria:

   a. attitude/behaviors toward students (e.g., absolute authority, facilitator, colleague, friend)

   b. instructional methods used (e.g., lectures, class discussions, group work, presentations, research)

   c. types of assignments and activities (e.g., independent, collaborative, papers, case studies, group projects, simulations, laboratories)

   d. types of examinations (e.g., multiple choice, true/false, matching, short answer, essay, case studies, in-class exams, out-of-class exams)

   e. course policies (e.g., mandatory class attendance, allowance for some excused absences, no taking of attendance, penalty for turning in late assignments, allowance for makeup tests)

   f. teaching styles (e.g., teaches in absolutes, allows for opinions, encourages problem solving, allows for creativity)

2. What is your cognitive level of development for this class? Analyze your cognitive level according to the following criteria:

   a. attitude toward how your teacher interacts with you and the class

   b. comfort level with your teacher's instructional methods

   c. amount of extra readings and assignments you complete

   d. ability to successfully perform well on assignments

   e. ability to successfully complete and pass examinations

   f. comfort level with the course policies

3. If there is congruence between you and your teacher, how can this be useful toward your learning the material and completing the course? If there is incongruence, how can this hinder your learning?

TEACHER-DIRECTED VERSUS SELF-DIRECTED LEARNING

Expert learners control their academic learning and shape it to meet their goals. That behavior is strikingly different from that of students who only react to the demands of various courses and instructors. Unfortunately, students are accustomed to relinquishing control to teachers; in fact, they believe that teachers are responsible for setting the goals and providing the impetus for action. Such a viewpoint is the crux of teacher-directed learning.

Teacher-Directed Learners

Teacher-directed learners, like Meredith, *expect to learn by following the teacher's assignments and directions.* They rarely set their own learning goals; they rarely or never deviate from given guidelines. They are usually unclear about how specific activities will yield actual learning. They view the teacher as the source of the right answers, the authority. In other words, they are dualistic in their learning (Weinstein, 1988).

Dualistic students write down what the teacher presents, usually word for word. They dutifully look at the textbook assignment, and they often use rote memory (i.e., memory with only minimal understanding) to answer test questions. They wait for the teacher to make connections. Procrastination and boredom are frequent companions.

Passive is the most descriptive word for this stage. Whereas this attitude and these behaviors are frequently sufficient for high school, they are deadly in college. College professors rarely value teacher-directed learners; they expect students to become self-directed learners. However, professors usually do not state that directly to students; the primary indicator is poor grades.

Beginning college students often exert real effort in their courses, but usually they do so as dependent learners. When we try hard and use the behaviors that have worked well in the past, we become confused when the results are disappointing. It is common to hear students say, "I studied harder for that test than I have ever studied before, and I *failed* it! I don't know what to do." They are being called to become self-directed learners, but no professor uses that word. It is like a secret password to college success.

By the fifth week in Meredith's first semester, she was facing four major exams. There were huge amounts of reading that the professors expected to be completed outside of lectures. She struggled to keep up with the assigned readings and tried to take notes in her classes, but in spite of her best efforts, she began to fall behind. Not knowing what to expect from her first set of exams, she pushed herself to read and look over her notes. Taking the exams was relatively unpleasant because she found that she could not answer some of the questions. Frankly, she saw questions on material she did not recognize. Her grades were poor, primarily low Cs and high Ds. She was stunned and disappointed, and she did not tell anyone what had happened. After several days of reflection, she went to the campus learning center and asked for some help. Without consciously realizing it, Meredith had taken the first step in becoming a self-directed learner and in moving from dualism to multiplicity.

FIGURE 6.2 Teacher-Directed Versus Self-Directed Learners

Teacher-Directed Learners	Self-Directed Learners
Do not set their own learning goals	Set their own learning goals
Use few learning strategies	Use a variety of learning strategies
Are primarily motivated only by grades	Are motivated by the challenge of learning something new
Rarely do more than what is required	Learn well beyond what is required
Learn passively	Learn actively
Prefer to learn dualistically	Prefer to learn relativistically

Self-Directed Learners

To be a self-directed learner is to move to a new stage as a student. Jason, at the end of the independence transition, is in relativism. He is becoming a **self-directed learner**—*one who sets clear goals for the knowledge and skills one wants to acquire in a course.* He is better able to assess the demands of the learning situation, determine which strategies are appropriate, manage his behaviors, and evaluate the results. *Active* is the best descriptor for a self-directed learner. See Figure 6.2 for a comparison of teacher-directed and self-directed learners.

Jason is taking a political science course, and he has a first exam scheduled for week five in the semester. He is now a business major with a 2.6 GPA, taking four other courses this term and working a part-time job of 15 hours per week. The test will cover six chapters, class notes, and several outside readings. The test will have 40 multiple-choice questions (remembering and understanding levels), 10 identification questions (remembering and understanding levels), and a choice of 1 of 3 essay questions (analysis level). His semester goals for this course are to achieve a good understanding of the federal political process so that he will become an informed voter and to earn a B to help his GPA.

Jason has attended almost all the class sessions (and secured a copy of a friend's notes for the lecture the day he was ill). He has read and marked the textbook chapters and quickly skimmed the outside readings. A week before the test, he organizes his materials and writes down the major topics that will be on the test. He lists the items he believes might be the identification questions and poses several possible essay questions. During the next five days, he spends two hours reviewing notes and writing outline answers to the possible essay questions. He also verifies that he knows the answers for the identifications. Two days before the test, he goes to the scheduled review session led by the teaching assistant and then meets with several classmates who are as determined as he is to do well on this test. They quiz each other and compare predictions about the test content. The night before the exam he reviews his notes and the marked text, practice his answers to the identification items, and then writes a practice answer to the essay question he believes is most likely to occur on the test. He knows he performs best when he has had enough sleep, so he goes to bed early enough to get six hours of sleep, then catches a quick breakfast of coffee and bagels before using the last 15 minutes to review his class notes.

Jason is clearly at the stage of self-directed learning. He has clear goals; he knows his abilities and manages his study behaviors without procrastination, he adapts his study strategies to the task of test preparation. He realizes it is his responsibility to understand the content of the course material and then prepare for a test performance that will demand memory, understanding, and analysis. Although his teacher is the authority in the discipline, it is the student's job to make the connections between the various parts of the content.

Collegial Learning

Self-directed learning is not the final stage of learning. Down the road, late in the life of an undergraduate student (but essential for a graduate student) lies the stage of **collegial learning.** This is the stage of learning in which many professionals, including professors, remain for their careers. The primary characteristic is *the reliance on a collegial process in the search for knowledge and truth.* Graduate students and scholars usually create new concepts, techniques, and strategies, through research, discussion, and reflection. Collaborative learners are the authorities; they are the final arbiters of the content investigated. This type of learning correlates with the Commitment stage in Perry's (1970) schema.

Youth

[INDEPENDENCE]

Adulthood

[MIDLIFE]

Maturity

MIDLIFE

At the beginning of this chapter, we said that the two longest transition times were independence and midlife and that they are, in many ways, parallel experiences. Ideally, by the time people are in their midtwenties, they are making Commitments, to work, family, friends, faith, society. The next years in adulthood usually involve hard work in building families and careers, but they tend to be stable stages. Sometime when people are in their late thirties or forties, another transition begins. This time, the beginning is usually not tied to a specific chronological event such as going off to college. Instead, an increasing dissatisfaction and unease emerges. What was a complete life just the week before now seems limited or pale. Most people do not welcome this change; they tend to put more effort into the tasks of their lives. However, the dissatisfaction increases, and the old ways of thinking and being begin to disintegrate. This transition time is called **midlife,** and many writers follow Carl Jung's conviction that midlife is *the beginning of the second half of life, a time of exploration into the inner life, a journey toward integration and wholeness* (Brewi & Brennan, 1999).

What causes tension in many American families is that as daughters and sons move into the independence transition, their parents are moving into midlife. Jason and Meredith's parents are no exception.

• • • MIKE AND SARAH • • •
Jason and Meredith's parents

Mike's business is stable and he enjoys it, but his wife, Sarah, is increasingly worried about her job. She finished three semesters of college 20 years ago and then secured a job as a teller in a large bank. Although she has had a few small promotions and raises over the years, she is frustrated because she has been routinely bypassed for management positions. She has watched as banking has changed dramatically over the last 10 years; there have been many buyouts and layoffs and no one feels secure. She and Mike have had long conversations; they need her income with two children in college and one in high school. Additionally, Sarah's mother has recently fallen and broken a hip, so she has moved in with them. What if the bank is sold and Sarah is laid off? Because she has had to invest so much time in parenting, she has been willing to work at a repetitive, low-level job, but lately she has become restless and dissatisfied.

Sarah is moving into midlife transition from both internal and external forces. She is ready to have a more demanding and interesting work life, even though her parenting responsibilities are not over. However, she can see the end of active parenting; her youngest child, Justin, is 15. She is also concerned about the changing nature of banking because technology is replacing so many jobs. With trepidation, Sarah visits the local community college and inquires about enrolling in its night program. To her relief, she finds that many students at that college are older and the advisor seems unsurprised that she is considering finishing a degree.

During Christmas holidays, she sits with her children and tells them that she is planning to take two courses during spring term. Jason and Meredith are excited at the news of her plans, but their younger brother, Justin, becomes angry. He responds, "What about me? Who's going to watch after Grandma, since the caretaker leaves at five? Dad always works late, so who's going to cook dinner? It's not going to be me! That's not fair!"

With Mike's support, Sarah has made the decision to reenter school. Her restlessness and unease signal that she is beginning again the cycle that Perry described. She has spent 25 years honoring the commitments she made as a young woman; she will continue to honor those, but now she is ready to chart a new professional path for herself. In some important ways, she is reentering the cycle at the point of multiplicity. Her initial choice is to major in accounting, but she feels unsure about what she really wants to study and what type of professional job she wants. Two courses are a cautious beginning.

Sarah is adopting a gradual move into midlife, but many people do not have that opportunity to change gradually. Divorce, widowhood, empty nest, disability, layoffs, military retirement—all of these and more propel midlifers into rapid and unexpected changes. Sometimes depression or boredom motivates the change; sometimes the search for knowledge and self-fulfillment is the impetus. Whatever the cause, the result is almost always a second journey through multiplicity, relativism, and commitment.

This journey is often as puzzling to a midlifer as it is to someone in the independence transition. Many older students return to college with the expectation that they will learn new things, but they usually do not expect to experience dramatic internal changes in their beliefs, thoughts, and goals. Then they find themselves examining and discarding long-held convictions, adopting new visions, and becoming invigorated by a wealth of possibilities. Although many of these changes are exciting, they can also threaten the stability of relationships with family and friends. The student is changing, but those around her may resent the change.

By her second semester, Sarah is surprising herself. First, she often contributes to class discussion whereas in the past she was shy and quiet. Her behavior at home has also become more assertive, and both Mike and Justin have taken more responsibility for the household and Grandma. Sarah's grades are also excellent; she made the dean's honor roll her first semester. Although she gets tired juggling all the facets of her life, she is excited about what she is learning and how she is changing. More and more, she trusts her own judgment. Her hesitancy in many areas, including work, is falling away. Sarah's increasing ability to discern her own voice—that certainty of self based on conviction and experience—is a characteristic of relativism, especially of midlifers who are moving through it for the second time.

Belenky et al. (1986) posit that women search to discover their private and public voices in ways that differ from men's. Our experience is not that simple. With traditional-age college students, we find that many women are quiet in public discussion and are loath to speak forcefully in class. They tend to participate nonverbally. Other young women seem comfortable in the public arena and adept at class discussion. We find that both men and women at midlife search for their own voice. They seem to be equally assertive in class and determined to make what they are learning meaningful to them.

Autonomy

Autonomy is *psychological emancipation.* Corey & Corey (1993) give an expanded definition of an autonomous person as one who can "function without constant approval and reassurance, is sensitive to the needs of others, can effectively meet the demands of daily living, is willing to ask for help when it is needed, and can provide support to others" (p. 34).

In this chapter we have focused on two transition periods—independence and midlife—because they are the two most relevant periods for college students. In each, the process of cognitive and moral development posited by Perry (1970) leads to autonomy, that confident sense of self-determination, self-sufficiency, and self-reliance. Now we can see how many of the concepts we have presented in these chapters describe an individual's journey to autonomy. In Chapter 2 we discussed attribution theory, how we explain our successes and failures. Taking responsibility is the first step we make to claim control over our lives. An essential psychological task of the independence period is *to shift our perception of who or what controls us from outside of ourselves to within.* The classic term for that concept is **locus of control** (place of control). Do we believe that we control our behaviors or do others control them? If we have the generalized mind-set that we are in control and we are responsible, then that mind-set permeates every aspect of our lives.

The period of independence moves us to autonomy, which is the normal status of adulthood. The midlife transition, however, moves us to another sense of autonomy. In midlife, we have to explore carefully the limitations of autonomy. We begin to discover that we are not totally free, although sometimes we wish to be released from all our Commitments and obligations. Our actions can impact others in important ways, and we begin to realize that we have obligations to ourselves, our families, our local community, and the larger community of humankind. Sarah, Jason's mother, is just beginning that journey. She has much to discover about her values and beliefs, and she will be astonished by the power and ferocity of the midlife transition. She believes that she has made the decision to return to school only for economic purposes. Although that may be the initial reason, she soon finds that many of her comfortable ideas are being

BECOMING AUTONOMOUS

As you move toward autonomy you may find that . . .

- You are no longer controlled by guilt or by the promise of love from your parents;

- You have a desire to become both free and responsible;

- You begin to have a sense of identity and uniqueness;

- You become committed to some idea;

- You tend to blame yourself rather than others for your mistakes;

- While you like to consider the opinions of others, you begin to make your own decisions;

- You have a new concern to reach out to others and give of yourself to make society a better place; and

- You begin to discover a meaning and purpose for your life.

Source: Corey G., & Corey, M. S. (1993). *I Never Knew I Had a Choice* (p. 81). Pacific Grove, CA: Brooks/Cole.

challenged at every turn. These challenges are often unexpected and disconcerting, and Sarah will find herself questioning many things. As she changes, and she almost surely will, her family may or may not be encouraging. The college experience tends to accelerate the cognitive and moral process, whether for traditional college-age students or midlifers, but the outcomes will differ.

Jason is developing a strong sense of autonomy as he moves through the independence period. That self-direction will serve him well as he develops his professional and personal life in adulthood. Meredith has just begun her journey to self-direction, and Sarah has embarked on a path that should lead her to question many things she has heretofore simply accepted. She may question what role work and career will play in the next part of her life; she may explore the desire for more power in the workplace; she may begin a serious study of her spiritual beliefs; she may discover intense interests in other places and peoples; she may commit to new actions or beliefs.

You will notice that this discussion of autonomy is congruent with the expanded definitions of autonomous learning that form the foundation of this text. Learning to be successful in college can foster your growth toward autonomy, your psychological emancipation.

---

exercise 6.7

The Interview

This chapter has focused on major transitions and current developmental stages of growth. Now take the time to learn from someone who has gone through similar experiences. Interview someone from a different developmental stage from yours (preferably someone in a more advanced stage of development) and answer the following questions. Completing this exercise will help you look to another person for guidance and to learn from his or her life experience.

1. What is it about this person that you most admire?

2. How has this person handled major transitions in his or her life?

3. What would this person do over again if he or she could?

4. What is this person most proud of accomplishing?

5. What advice does this person have about meeting your next transition period?

CONCLUSION

The developmental life cycle provides us with an intellectual model to help us understand our own and others' thoughts, behaviors, and feelings. These changes erupt in us regardless of our own desires; it is as if we have time-release capsules inside us. Living each stage and each transition well frees us to lean into the next part of life with excitement and anticipation, rather than fear and dread.

SUMMARY

- One constant in human life is change.

- There are five dimensions present among humans: biological, social, ecological, spiritual, and psychological.

- Our movement through life occurs in alternating periods of change (transitions) and stability (stages).

- The six stages in the Life Cycle are prenatal, childhood, youth, adulthood, maturity, and old age.

- Movement through these different stages affects how we think (cognitive), how we feel (affective), and what we do (behavioral).

- The six transition periods in the Life Cycle are birth, puberty, independence, midlife, retirement, and death.

- The transition of independence is moving from youth to adulthood, and the transition of midlife is moving from adulthood to maturity.

- According to William Perry (1970), dualism, multiplicity, relativism, and commitment are the four categories of intellectual and moral development that adults experience as they move through the transition period of independence.

- Students in the dualistic stage see the world in terms of no uncertainty: knowledge is right or wrong, good or bad. They depend on authority figures to tell them how to think.

- Students in the multiplicity stage begin to view knowledge as being based more on opinion than certainty. Lack of answers is viewed as temporary.

- Students in the relativism stage evaluate knowledge based on the quality of evidence supporting it. They see knowledge from a contextual point of view, derived through one's experiences and values.

- Retreat is a deflection from making a commitment by regressing to an earlier stage.

- Escape is a deflection from making a commitment by settling in at the relativistic stage and rejecting further movement.

- Temporizing is a deflection from making a commitment by postponing it.

- Commitment is a major affirmation or choice made after several alternatives are examined.

- Perry uses a capital *C* when one makes a Commitment in relativism. Commitments made before relativism are distinguished by a lowercase *c*.

- Teacher-directed learners are passive in that they expect the teacher to set the learning goals and provide all the assignments and instruction. They rarely vary their learning strategies or self-evaluate their own progress.

- Self-directed learners are active in setting their own goals for the knowledge and skills they want to learn. They assess the demands of the learning situation, determine appropriate strategies, manage their behaviors, and evaluate results.

- Collegial learning is the reliance on a collegial process in the search for knowledge and truth by professionals.

- The midlife transition begins during the second half of life and is a time of exploration into the meaning of one's life.

- Moving through developmental stages leads to autonomy or a confident sense of self-determination, self-sufficiency, and self-reliance.

- Locus of control is the perception of whether we are controlled by external forces or internal forces.

KEY CONCEPTS

Autonomy

Collegial learning

Deflections: retreat, escape, temporizing

Independence

Locus of control

Midlife

Perry's theory of cognitive
   development: dualism,
   multiplicity, relativism,
   commitment
Self-directed learners

Teacher-directed learners
The Life Cycle
The Universal

GUIDED JOURNAL QUESTIONS

1. If you are a traditional-age college student, describe what it is like moving from the stage of *youth* to *adulthood* through the transition time of *independence.* Discuss two major turning points associated with this transition period. What struggles or major conflicts have you had to overcome as you move from one stage to the next? What struggles are yet unresolved?

    or

  If you are a nontraditional-age college student, describe what it is like moving from the stage of *adulthood* to *maturity* through the transition time of *midlife* or *maturity* to *old age* through the transition time of *retirement.* Discuss two major turning points associated with this transition. What struggles or major conflicts have you had to overcome as you move successfully from one stage to the next? What struggles are yet unresolved?

2. Who has been most instrumental in your life in helping you to make major transitions? Give specific examples of what the person did that was helpful to you.

3. What do you miss most about being in the stages of childhood and youth? What do you miss least about those stages of your life?

4. Do you wish to become more independent in your life? If so, how do you plan on accomplishing this goal? Do you have fears related to more independence? If you do not wish to become more independent, why not?

5. When you first began college how similar were your experiences to those of Meredith, Jason's younger sister?

6. To what degree to you believe you can live by your own set of values and standards and still be sensitive to the needs of other important people in your life?

7. How frustrated do you feel when there is no apparent answer to a question? How comfortable do you feel with "it depends"?

8. Which of the following statements best represents your current thinking? Support your answer by referencing Perry's theory of cognitive development.

   a. I want my college instructors to tell me the answers to my questions.

   b. I want my college instructors to guide me in finding answers to my questions.

   c. I want to find my own answers to my questions.

9. According to Perry's theory of cognitive development, what do you estimate your developmental stage to be? Use at least three examples of decisions/values that you have made that would support your analysis.

10. Can you be in more than one of Perry's stage at a time? For instance, reflect on your current stage in relation to your parents, your college teachers, your significant others, etc.

11. In which of your classes are you a teacher-directed learner? A self-directed learner? How do these different styles affect your current methods of learning?

12. What are your expectations for the transition of midlife? What might your career and family life be like?

13. If you are in the transition of midlife, is this a time of change or stagnation for you? In other words, do you feel productive or nonproductive? How fulfilling is your life?

14. What do you most hope to accomplish by the time you reach old age (or have you accomplished if you are in old age)? What worries do you have about growing old? What can you do at this time (or have you done) in your life to prepare for your retirement?

The Last Word

The transition period of independence was relatively easy for me, but midlife . . . now that's a different story!

—*Carol Dochen*

Exploring the Diversity of Individuality

I've just gotta be me.

One gift of human awareness is the awakening realization that each of us is a unique being. Yes, we share much with others of our species and our culture, but the uniqueness of "I" comes from the interaction of the qualities and abilities with which we were born, the circumstances of our lives, and the unique path we have taken through each developmental stage.

In Chapter 6, we examined some aspects of theories related to the universal and the culture that help us understand ourselves. In this chapter, we study concepts and theories that aid us in grasping how each of us is different from others. From the outset, however, it is important to note that a crucial difference about the value of the individual versus the group occurs between the Anglo cultures of Western Europe and the United States and the cultures of the rest of the world as well as specific subcultures within the United States.

exercise 7.1

SELF-ASSESSMENT: How I Am Different

Feeling at ease with oneself and being comfortable making one's own decisions are traits of a secure and confident individual in the mainstream American culture. With 5 being "Almost Always" and 1 being "Almost Never," assess your assumptions and feelings about your individualism. Rate each of the following statements honestly by circling the appropriate number. Completing this exercise will help you identify areas of concern or tension.

	Almost Always		Sometimes		Almost Never
1. I feel like I am my own person.	5	4	3	2	1
2. I prefer to set my own goals.	5	4	3	2	1
3. I set up personal challenges for myself.	5	4	3	2	1
4. I get along well with others.	5	4	3	2	1
5. I do not mind if my beliefs are different from others' beliefs.	5	4	3	2	1
6. I find value in spending time alone.	5	4	3	2	1
7. I respect myself for the hard decisions I have had to make.	5	4	3	2	1
8. I do not have to depend on others for my happiness.	5	4	3	2	1
9. Others find me self-assured and content with life.	5	4	3	2	1
10. I have special talents and abilities.	5	4	3	2	1
11. I have a strong will to do what is right.	5	4	3	2	1
12. I am rarely manipulated by others.	5	4	3	2	1

Add up the numbers circled. Your total score will be between 12 and 60. The higher your score, the more likely you feel confident about being your own person. For total scores below 36, write or reflect on items for which you have concerns. Also, consider talking with a trusted friend, a family member, a teacher, or an advisor.

INDIVIDUALITY

Two terms—individuality and individualism—sound similar but mean dramatically different ways of being. Let us look first at **individualism** because it is the more common term. "Individualism refers to one's self-concept, to the image of oneself as an individual unit whose motivations and behavior are aimed at individual goals, as opposed, for instance, to a member of a group whose behavior is directed toward smooth harmonious interpersonal relations" (Augsberger, 1986, p. 86). Many of the world's cultures do not support individualism; rather, they support the value of the group over the individual. Many American families from Latin, Asian, Native American, and Middle Eastern subcultures, as well as religious groups, value group centeredness over individualism.

American college students represent the entire range of beliefs about individualism versus group centeredness. An initial step in understanding ourselves is the realization of our position on the spectrum. Have we been raised to choose and pursue our own individual goals? Or raised to satisfy our desires within the context deemed best for the group (family) to which we belong? Or are we somewhere in between? How much do we agree or disagree with the values of our family/group?

As educators we have witnessed many of our students struggle with conflicts between their goals and the goals of their families:

My parents have always dreamed that I would become a doctor, but I am interested in psychology.

I have three exams next week, but my grandfather is ill. Do I go home or stay at school to study?

Should I take over the family business or pursue a different career path?

I have started attending my roommate's church, and my family makes fun of me.

I might want to work in America for a few years before I return to my home country, but I'm not sure if I would be allowed to.

My children complain that I don't have time for them anymore because all I ever do is study.

I am dating a person from another cultural group, and my family is really angry.

American community colleges and universities generally model the value of individualism by creating a competitive environment in which our success is determined by our ability to set and achieve our own goals. Even though specific courses may require collaborative work through group projects, the ultimate purpose of the institution is the education of the individual. Our transcripts belong only to us.

Individuality is the term we use in this text to describe "the development of differences within the personality" (Augsberger, 1986, p. 86). We believe this term is much more appropriate for students who are learning how to be successful in college because individuality occurs across the complete range of individualism/group centeredness. Thus, we are all capable of developing as individuals. Besides the obvious physical differences among us, we differ markedly in both cognitive and emotional attributes. Although there are numerous methods by which people explore their own individuality, we have chosen a simple three-part strategy that we hope will give you a clear self-portrait. Each part is a way of reflecting on ourselves, and we have labeled these concepts *talents, will,* and *preferences.*

These three characteristics—talent, will, preferences—combine to create our own learning style. **Learning style** is most often used as "a metaphor for thinking about individual differences" (Jonassen & Grabowski, 1993, p. 234). In the past few decades, many educators attempted to help students understand their own ways of learning. Self-report instruments, such as Kolb's *Learning Style Inventory* (1999) and Dunn, Dunn, and Price's *Learning Style Inventory* (1984), rely on student reflections. All try to measure a student's holistic approach to learning, but they have differing premises and use different measurements. We believe that you will be able to ascertain your unique learning style through reflections on your talents, your will, and your preferences.

TALENTS

Talents are *those abilities that come as a result of the interaction of our genes, our environment, our experience, and our effort.* We are all born with an astounding array of gifts, and we spend our lives enhancing those gifts or ignoring them. For many decades, our society has used the term *intelligence* to denote a specific set of two talents, linguistic and logical–mathematical (Gardner, 1995). These talents are useful in an academic environment, and educational achievement tests examine both areas. However, these two talents are only two of eight intelligences that educational psychologists use to categorize talents that are relevant to an academic setting (Gardner, 1983; Gardner, 2000). Our understanding of our talents across these eight dimensions of intelligence help us gain accurate self-knowledge, which can then help us understand ourselves as learners. A clear view of our own talents helps us make good decisions about work and how we can better lead our lives.

exercise 7.2

Animal School

We are unique individuals with our own special talents and gifts. To understand more about how we differ from each other, read the following fable and answer the accompanying questions:

FABLE OF THE ANIMAL SCHOOL
author unknown, as retold by Russ Hodges

Once upon a time, the animals decided they must do something heroic to meet the problems of a new world, so they organized a school. They adopted an activity curriculum consisting of running, climbing, swimming, and flying. To make it easier to administer, all the animals took all the subjects.

The duck was excellent in swimming (better, in fact, than her instructor) and made passing grades in flying, but she was very slow in running. She had to stay after school and drop swimming to practice running. This was kept up until her webbed feet were working badly and she was only average in swimming. But average was acceptable in school, so nobody worried about that except the duck.

The rabbit started at the top of the class in running, but she had a nervous breakdown because of so much makeup work in swimming. The squirrel was excellent in climbing until he developed frustration in the flying class because his teacher made him start from the ground up instead of from the treetop down. He also developed charley horses from overexertion and then got a C in climbing and a D in running.

The eagle was a problem child and was disciplined severely. In the climbing class, he beat all the others to the top of the tree but insisted on using his own way to get there.

At the end of the year, an abnormal eel that could swim exceedingly well and also run, climb, and fly a little had the highest average and was valedictorian.

The prairie dogs stayed out of school and fought the tax levy because the administration would not add digging and burrowing to the curriculum. They apprenticed their child to a badger and later joined the groundhogs and gophers to start a successful private school.

1. What lessons can you infer from this fable?
2. As a student, which animal can you most identify with? Explain.

Multiple Intelligences

Educational psychologists now use the term *multiple intelligences* from a theory by Howard Gardner to differentiate human talents into eight categories. Gardner first introduced his theory of seven multiple intelligences in 1983, when he wrote *Frames of Mind: The Theory of Multiple Intelligences.* His theory expands and challenges the more traditional view of intelligence, especially the use of standardized Intelligence Quotient (IQ) tests. IQ assessments typically measure a person's linguistic and mathematical aptitude and assign a number that represents the person's intelligence. Gardner felt that an individual's intelligence should not be measured in such a limited realm.

Gardner (1995) defines **intelligence** as "a biological and psychological potential that . . . [is] a consequence of the experiential, cultural, and motivational factors that affect a person" (p. 202). In other words, he believes intelligence emerges from both a biological and cultural basis. The biology of intelligence, for example, may be understood by the connections formed between brain cells as learning occurs. Most educational psychologists would agree that intelligence is biologically based. However, Gardner adds a new perspective by including culture as an influence. He believes all societies value different types of intelligences. The cultural value placed on a person's ability to acquire certain skills and perform certain tasks is the motivational factor that affects a person to gain mastery in certain skills.

Gardner believes that a person's intelligence will grow and change over time and that the different intelligences rarely operate independently; rather, they complement each other as a person develops skills and solves problems. The seven original intelligences are logical–mathematical, linguistic, musical, spatial, bodily–kinesthetic, interpersonal, and intrapersonal. In 1996, Gardner added an eighth intelligence that he termed naturalist (Gardner, 2000). Let us now examine each of these eight intelligences in detail.

GARDNER'S EIGHT MULTIPLE INTELLIGENCES

Logical–mathematical

Linguistic

Musical

Spatial

Bodily–kinesthetic

Interpersonal

Intrapersonal

Naturalist

1. **Logical–mathematical intelligence** is *the ability to calculate, quantify, consider propositions and hypotheses, and carry out complex mathematical operations.* It enables us to perceive relationships and connections and to use abstract, symbolic thought; sequential reasoning skills; and inductive and deductive thinking patterns. Logical intelligence is usually well developed in mathematicians, scientists, and detectives. Examples include solving mathematical problems as well as creating hypotheses based on observation and testing those hypotheses.

2.   **Linguistic intelligence** is *the ability to think in words and to use language to express and appreciate complex meanings.* Linguistic intelligence allows us to understand the order and meaning of words and to apply metalinguistic skills to reflect on our use of language. Linguistic intelligence is the most widely shared human competence and is evident in poets, novelists, journalists, and effective public speakers. Examples include easily understanding subtle and complex verbal arguments as well as writing clear and persuasive prose.

3.   **Musical intelligence** is *the capacity to discern pitch, rhythm, timbre, and tone.* This intelligence enables us to recognize, create, reproduce, and reflect on music, as demonstrated by composers, conductors, musicians, vocalists, and sensitive listeners. Interestingly, there is often an affective connection between music and the emotions. Mathematical and musical intelligences may share common thinking practices. Examples include performing instrumentally or vocally, creating musical compositions, and accurately critiquing musical works.

4.   **Spatial intelligence** is *the ability to think in three dimensions.* Core capacities include mental imagery, spatial reasoning, image manipulation, graphic and artistic skills, and an active imagination. Sailors, pilots, sculptors, painters, and architects all exhibit spatial intelligence. Examples include imagining a picture and creating three-dimensional models.

5.   **Bodily–kinesthetic intelligence** is *the capacity to manipulate objects and use a variety of physical skills.* This intelligence also involves a sense of timing and the perfection of skills through mind–body union. Athletes, dancers, surgeons, and craftspeople exhibit well-developed bodily–kinesthetic intelligence. Examples include excelling in a sport as well as engaging in needlework/arts and crafts.

6.   **Interpersonal intelligence** is *the ability to understand and interact effectively with others.* It involves effective verbal and nonverbal communication, the ability to note distinctions among others, sensitivity to the moods and temperaments of others, and the ability to entertain multiple perspectives. Teachers, social workers, actors, and politicians all exhibit interpersonal intelligence. Examples include maintaining healthy friendships and effectively interpreting nonverbal cues.

7.   **Intrapersonal intelligence** is *the capacity to understand oneself and one's thoughts and feelings and to use such knowledge in planning and directing one's life.* Intrapersonal intelligence involves not only an appreciation of the self, but also of the human condition. It is evident in psychologists, spiritual leaders, and philosophers. Examples include understanding reasons for your own behavior as well as creating goals that reflect your desires and values.

8.   **Naturalistic intelligence** is *the ability to recognize, identify, and classify patterns in nature such as plants and animals.* Individuals with this intelligence are keen observers of their environments. They are particularly interested in the

balance and relationship between man and nature. Farmers, hunters, ecologists, landscapers, meteorologists, biologists, and holistic healers share these traits. Examples include identifying flora and fauna that are edible as well as being aware of the subtle changes of stars during various seasons.

To learn how you can enhance each of your multiple intelligences, see Figure 7.1.

FIGURE 7.1   Enhancing Each of Your Multiple Intelligences

Intelligence	Activities to enhance each intelligence
Logical–mathematical Intelligence	Learn to use the scientific method. Ask more questions when learning. Learn deductive logic strategies (syllogisms, Venn diagrams). Learn to use inductive logic strategies (analogies). Think mathematically by creating more graphs and placing knowledge into common patterns. Work with numbers (averages, percentages, calculations, probability, formulas). Overpractice each type of math problem you are learning. Use T-notes and write out procedures used to solve problems—not just examples. Think of real-life examples when learning mathematical concepts.
Linguistic Intelligence	Learn to focus listening and concentration skills during lectures and classroom discussions. Practice public speaking at every opportunity (oral reports, answer questions, engage in classroom discussions). Build your vocabulary by learning Greek and Latin roots and reading often for pleasure. Improve your writing skills by taking classes that require research papers, essays, poetry, and essay exams. Use outlines to study lectures and textbook chapters.
Musical Intelligence	Listen and create various sounds, rhythms, and lyrics. Create rhythms and songs for the material you are learning. Learn to play a musical instrument. Learn to read musical notation. Learn music associated with periods of history.
Spatial Intelligence	Be attentive to nonverbal communication. Practice drawing. Organize information graphically (flow charts, outlines, matrices, concept maps). Highlight materials with color. Visualize material by using imagery (pictures in your mind). Draw pictures when taking notes to illustrate concepts. Learn by watching films, videos, and slide shows.
Bodily–kinesthetic Intelligence	Learn by using drama (role plays, simulations). Manipulate objects to learn (board games, puzzles, scientific equipment). Engage in physical activity while learning such as move from group to group or different locations while learning. Use computers (video games, touch screens, eye–hand coordination activities).

FIGURE 7.1   Enhancing Each of Your Multiple Intelligences (*Continued*)

Intelligence	Activities to enhance each intelligence
Interpersonal Intelligence	Work with others in class (collaborative learning activities, team projects). Attend study groups outside of class (supplemental instruction, peer tutoring, review sessions). Learn from service projects. Engage in multicultural experiences (interview others from different cultures, role-play events from diverse perspectives). Teach others after you learn the material. Debate others over class material.
Intrapersonal Intelligence	Acknowledge and express feelings as you learn. Learn more about yourself through self-assessment inventories. Understand your own ability to learn (use metacognitive strategy). Reflect and think about class material. Journal (write reflective answers to questions). Study by yourself in a quiet area. Meditate.
Naturalist Intelligence	Observe nature. Identify groups or species, recognizing flora and fauna. Interact with your physical surroundings. Work with plants and animals. Learn outdoors through field observations. Relate material you are learning to the environment when possible. Select research topics that relate to nature.

Source: Adapted from Campbell, L., Campbell B., & Dickinson, D. (1999). *Teaching and Learning Through Multiple Intelligences.* Boston: Allyn & Bacon.

exercise 7.3

Your Multiple Intelligences

Determining how you learn best is one way to assess your unique talents or multiple intelligences. Check only the statements that are most often true for you. Completing this exercise will help you identify areas of strengths (talents) and areas for future growth. The assessment is based on Howard Gardner's multiple intelligences theory.

I learn best when I

_____1. move around my physical surroundings.

_____2. am with another person or groups of people.

_____3. use three-dimensional thinking, visualizing, or conceptualizing.

_____ 4. use my physical skills and stay active.

_____ 5. use my artistic skills and imagination.

_____ 6. reflect and think about how what I am learning affects me.

_____ 7. incorporate sounds, rhythms, pitch, and tone.

_____ 8. use mathematical concepts or logical reasoning.

_____ 9. use my musical skills.

_____10. explore nature and the environment.

_____11. express myself using words.

_____12. assess my own feelings about the material.

_____13. verbalize the material to myself or others.

_____14. teach others and am sensitive to their needs.

_____15. recognize patterns and create classifications.

_____16. work with plants and animals.

Statements 8 and 15 correspond to logical–mathematical intelligence.

Statements 11 and 13 correspond to linguistic intelligence.

Statements 7 and 9 correspond to musical intelligence

Statements 3 and 5 correspond to spatial intelligence.

Statements 1 and 4 correspond to bodily–kinesthetic intelligence.

Statements 2 and 14 correspond to interpersonal intelligence.

Statements 6 and 12 correspond to intrapersonal intelligence

Statements 10 and 16 correspond to naturalist intelligence.

a. Based on the statements you checked, which multiple intelligences best describe you?

b. How do they affect your range of choices of majors and careers?

c. Are there any weaknesses you wish to strengthen? If so, how do you plan to strengthen them?

> ••• **JASON, MEREDITH, AND SARAH** •••
> ### *A family of college students*
>
> *Jason, Meredith, and Sarah, the family of college students described in Chapter 6, are good examples of three people from the same family who differ across the eight dimensions of intelligence. Whereas Jason is competent in logical–mathematical abilities and below average in spatial abilities, he excels in interpersonal abilities. His move from preengineering to business as a major makes good sense, and he was able to discern a better match for his talents because his intrapersonal abilities developed through counseling. His good bodily–kinesthetic abilities fuel his love for intramural sports, but he decides to enroll in a golf class to acquire a lifelong individual sport to enhance his future business career.*
>
> *Meredith has excellent linguistic and logical–mathematical abilities; poor musical, spatial, and bodily–kinesthetic abilities; and above average inter- and intrapersonal abilities. Her choice of prelaw as a possible major is appropriate, although she may want to strengthen her interpersonal skills through a minor in communication.*
>
> *Their mother, Sarah, has excellent logical–mathematical and good linguistic abilities, as evidenced by her competent work history and her first semester's grades. She plans to improve her linguistic abilities by taking advanced and technical writing courses. Although she enjoyed performing as a singer during high school and her early college years, she abandoned that interest when she had a family. In spite of juggling a demanding schedule of work, classes, and family, she decides to join the church choir, a hidden desire she has had for many years.*

Discerning your talents across all the dimensions of intelligence helps you make wise decisions in educational, vocational, and leisure activities as well as relationships. Thoughtful self-reflection may include data from school and test performances, but it should also include many other memories and opinions. It is important to remember that you can improve your abilities through study and practice. Ask yourself these questions:

What are my talents?

How do they affect my range of choices?

Are there any weaknesses I wish to strengthen?

If so, how do I plan to strengthen them?

WILL

Talent is not enough to accomplish goals. All of us witness people who *underachieve;* for example, they do not do the work to attain a goal, even though they have the talents. No place is this more obvious than in school. Students know they have the talent, they want to achieve the goal, their families and friends know they have the talent, but they lack the power to make themselves do what they want and intend to do. *The power of conscious control that we have over our own actions or emotions* is the definition of **will** appropriate to our purposes in this text. At one time or another, all of us have wished to have a stronger will so that we could more easily reach a desired goal. Whether we wish to quit smoking or study more, we know that we have to use our will to control both our actions and emotions in order to reach our goals. Philosophers have pondered the obvious differences among people for centuries. Interestingly, more than 2,500 years ago, Greek thinkers created the word *akrasia* to represent a deficiency of the will (Mischel, 1995).

While most thinkers have agreed that there are individual differences in strength of will, a much more serious debate occurs when we investigate whether we can change the strength of our will. In other words, can we increase our will and thus control our actions and emotions in ways that help us reach goals that are important to us? Or are we limited to a predetermined level of will with which we were born?

All of us have witnessed individuals who seem to exert enormous will in a specific arena of their talents. Athletes, artists, scientists, writers—there are many public and historical examples of people who devote most of their energy and passion to excellence in one endeavor. They develop a specific talent to the highest degree possible through the dedication of their will.

One phenomenon of twentieth-century America has been the self-help programs spawned by Alcoholics Anonymous (see Figure 7.2 for its 12-step program). Each week, millions of people attend 12-step programs in efforts to overcome addictions. The primary concept of these programs is that the individual admits to having insufficient will to abstain from a destructive behavior and relinquishes his or her life and will to a "Higher Power" in order to return to a sane existence.

Although there are many other aspects of 12-step groups, including the power of the support of other people, the core principle is the request that a Higher Power increase the person's will to abstain from the particular behavior. The principles of these self-help groups aid the individual in connecting to the spiritual sense of the divine, to the universal nature of humans, and to the culture as explicated in the group. For millions of people, 12-step principles and the groups that live them provide the pathway to a healthy life. For examples of 12-step programs, see Figure 7.3.

Currently, we have yet to discover a comprehensive, modern theory of will, so we choose to use a pragmatic approach based on our experiences in helping

FIGURE 7.2   The 12 Steps of Alcoholics Anonymous*

1. We admitted we were powerless over alcohol—that our lives had become unmanageable.

2. Came to believe that a Power greater than ourselves could restore us to sanity.

3. Make a decision to turn our will and our lives over to the care of God *as we understood Him.*

4. Made a searching and fearless moral inventory of ourselves.

5. Admitted to God, to ourselves, and to another human being the exact nature of our wrongs.

6. Were entirely ready to have God remove all these defects of character.

7. Humbly asked Him to remove our shortcomings.

8. Made a list of all persons we had harmed, and became willing to make amends to them all.

9. Made direct amends to such people wherever possible, except when to do so would injure them or others.

10. Continued to take personal inventory and when we were wrong promptly admitted it.

11. Sought through prayer and meditation to improve our conscious contact with God *as we understood Him,* praying only for knowledge of His will for us and the power to carry that out.

12. Having had a spiritual awakening as a result of these Steps, we tried to carry this message to alcoholics, and to practice these principles in all our affairs.

Other 12-step groups have adapted AAs 12 steps for their own use.

students. We frequently refer students with addictions to campus 12-step programs. As we have helped other students regulate their academic and personal behaviors, we have found that over time most students can increase the strength of their will. An important concept is to understand the difference between what we can directly will by our behaviors and what are the desired outcomes. We can will the first, but not the second. According to Kurtz and Ketcham (1992, p. 125),

We can directly will *knowledge* . . . but not *wisdom.*

We can directly will *pleasure* . . . but not *happiness.*

We can directly will *congratulations* . . . but not *admiration.*

We can directly will *reading/listening* . . . but not *understanding.*

We can directly will *going to bed* . . . but not *sleeping.*

We can directly will *meekness* . . . but not *humility.*

FIGURE 7.3   Examples of 12-Step Programs

Sample programs for individuals seeking help	Sample programs for family members
Alcoholics Anonymous	Al-Anon/Alateen—for family members and friends of alcoholics
Narcotics Anonymous	
Cocaine Anonymous	Adult Children of Alcoholics—for those affected by a loved one's drinking
Debtors Anonymous	
Marijuana Anonymous	Co-dependents Anonymous—for those who struggle with codependency in their relationship
Overeaters Anonymous	
Smokers Anonymous	Families Anonymous—for those affected by drug abuse or related behavioral problems of a relative or friend
Sex Addicts Anonymous	
Gamblers Anonymous	Nar-Anon Family Groups—for the loved ones who are concerned about the drug abuse of a family member
	Recovering Couples Anonymous—for couples to work on building a more solid relationship in recovery
	S-Anon International Family Groups—for families and friends of sexaholics

We can directly will *executing a play* . . . but not *winning a game.*

We can directly will *dryness* . . . but not *sobriety.*

Many people have secret doubts and fears that they do not have the will to accomplish their goals. Our culture is an intensely achievement-based culture, and competition starts early. Children are taught early that knowing the right answers, making the grade, winning the game matter. Intense criticism at home or in the family can lead children to be afraid to try something, to take a risk. Academic self-confidence is fragile for most of us, even if we are talented.

· · · JASON · · ·

As Jason has progressed to Perry's stage of Commitment, he is discovering that he is becoming more self-disciplined as he discerns what his values and goals are. In other words, he is more able to will his behavior and his feelings to match his goals. Jason is already feeling a sense of relief because he had been secretly anxious that he did not have the will to suc-

ceed in work, that he did not have the self-discipline and ability to initi-ate and complete appropriate behaviors in marketing. These interior doubts have been difficult for him because his parents and his sister ap-pear to have little difficulty in controlling their own behaviors.

Using specific strategies, students can increase the strength of their will (Mischel, 1995; Smart & Wegner, 1996). The technical term for such control is *self-regulation.* We explore both the theory and strategies of self-regulation deeply in Chapters 8–10, including an intensive discussion of the reasons for successes and failures. Self-regulation is a huge topic with strong implications for most college students. To prepare for that topic, spend some time reflecting about your will.

exercise 7.4

Your Will

Do you have conscious control over your own actions and emotions? This exercise will help you to seriously consider some questions as you strive for a deeper understanding of your will.

1. How often do you accomplish your intentions?

2. When you are confronted with a difficult task, do you persist or abandon it?

3. When you want something to occur, do you spend time dreaming about it or constructing strategies to achieve it?

4. How do you explain the differences in your levels of will in different areas of your life?

5. Describe any areas of your life that you feel are out of your control. What steps can you take to regain control?

6. How strong-willed are you?

PREFERENCES

A third reflective strategy to further our self-understanding is the use of a personality classification system. There have been many systems postulated over the centuries, from the Chinese ideas of yin/yang and personality traits attributed to our birth year to the Hindu ideas of spiritual personality types (reflective, emotional, active, experimental) to the Greek ideas of four humours (earth, air, fire, water) to Carl Jung's system of eight personality types to more recent versions (Jung, 1923; Jung, 1971). We say that men are from Mars, women from Venus; that we are Coke or Pepsi people; that our personalities are shaped by our birth date (astrology). In educational psychology, we categorize learners by their learning styles, a metaphor for thinking about individual differences (Jonassen & Grabowski, 1993).

All of the aforementioned examples represent just some of the myriad ways humans have tried to understand themselves and others close to them. As teachers, we have tried to help our students make sense of these systems and choose one or two as tools to help them ascertain their inclinations, their values, and their strengths. All of these systems share a common concept—**cognitive** (thinking) **and affective** (feeling) **preferences,** defined as *the way we prefer to use our minds and hearts.* In simple terms, these theories all postulate that much of the seeming variation in human behavior

> is not due to chance; it is in fact the logical result of a few basic, observable differences in mental functioning.
>
> These basic differences concern the way people *prefer* to use their minds, specifically, the way they perceive and the way they make judgments. *Perceiving* is here understood to include the processes of becoming aware of things, people, occurrences, and ideas. Judging includes the processes of coming to conclusions about what has been perceived. Together, perception and judgment, which make up a large portion of people's total mental activity, govern much of their outer behavior, because perception—by definition—determines what people see in a situation, and their judgment determines what they decide to do about it. Thus, it is reasonable that basic differences in perception or judgment should result in corresponding differences in behavior. (Myers & Myers, 1980, p. 1)

Jason, Meredith, and Sarah can benefit from a deeper understanding of their own preference, just as all of us can. Preferences form much of what we term *personality,* and careful reflection about our own preferences can help us set meaningful goals, discern the best circumstances of study and work, and create better relationships. There are thousands of books and hundreds of Internet sites devoted to preferences. Many educational psychologists create theories about the ways we learn by studying preferences of students.

In this section, we look at the primary theory of personality preferences, the *Myers-Briggs Type Indicator*® (MBTI), which is based on the work of the Swiss psychiatrist Carl Jung. Next we examine the concept of temperament as explicated by David Keirsey. Throughout this tour we pay special attention to those concepts that can help college students move toward academic and personal success.

---
exercise 7.5

Learning About Preferences

You have probably developed the viewpoint that certain learning strategies work better for you than others. To illustrate the concept of preference, follow the directions below.

a. Sign your name as you normally do on the line below:

_____

b. Now sign your name using your opposite hand:

_____

While you were probably able to use both hands to sign your name, your less preferred hand took more effort, time, and concentration. Learning preferences can be viewed the same way. You have come to depend on a few preferences to take in and process information.

c. Under what circumstances might you need to use your opposite hand to sign your name or even to write?

d. Under what circumstances might you need to more fully develop additional ways to take in and learn information and not simply rely on your preferred methods of learning?

Source: Idea for signature exercise from Ditiberio, J. K., & Hammer, A. L. *Introduction to Type in College.* © 1993 by Consulting Psychologists Press.

---
exercise 7.6

SELF-ASSESSMENT: Your Learning Preference

Assessing the way you learn best can be helpful information for a successful college experience. The following exercise may be useful as a beginning point in exploring your preferences.

Directions:

Read the two preferences in each row. In a **learning situation**—that is, when you are *listening* to a lecture, *reading* a book, *concentrating* on homework, *writing* a paper, or *preparing* for a test—which **one** of the two characteristics describes you *most of the time?* Put a "✓" in that circle.

SCALE I

Extraversion	*OR*	**Introversion**

○ I prefer action and variety.

○ I prefer quiet and time to consider things.

○ I prefer talking to people when doing mental work.

○ I prefer to do mental work privately before talking.

○ I often act quickly, sometimes with little reflection.

○ I prefer to understand something *before* trying it.

○ I prefer to see how others do a task and to see results.

○ I prefer to understand the *idea* of a task and to work alone or with just a few people.

○ I want to know what other people expect of me.

○ I prefer setting my own standards.

Total number of ✓'s for E_____   Total number of ✓'s for I_____

SCALE II

Sensing	*OR*	**Intuition**

○ I usually pay most attention to *experience* and what something *is*.

○ I usually pay most attention to the *meanings* of facts and how they *fit together.*

○ I prefer to use my *senses*—see, hear, say, touch, smell—to find out what is happening.

○ I prefer to use my *imagination* to come up with different ways and possibilities to do things.

○ I dislike new problems *unless* I've had prior experiences regarding how to solve them.

○ I like solving *new* problems. I dislike doing the same thing over and over.

○ I enjoy *using skills already learned* more than learning new skills.

○ I enjoy *learning new skills* more than practicing old skills.

○ I am *patient with details,* but impatient when the details become complicated.

○ I am *impatient with details* and don't mind complicated situations.

Total number of ✓'s for S_____   Total number of ✓'s for N_____

SCALE III

Thinking	*OR*	**Feeling**

○ I prefer to use *logic* when making decisions.

○ I prefer to use *personal feelings and values* when making decisions.

○ I expect to be treated with *justice and fairness.*

○ I expect praise and like to *please other people,* even in small matters.

○ I may neglect and hurt other people's feelings *without realizing it.*

○ I am usually very aware of *other people's feelings.*

○ I can get along with *little or no harmony* among people.

○ I feel unsettled by arguments and conflicts; I prefer *harmony* among people.

○ I tend to give more attention to *ideas or things,* rather than to human relationships.

○ I often can predict how others will *feel.*

Total number of ✓'s for T_____   Total number of ✓'s for F_____

SCALE IV

Judging	*OR*	Perceiving

○ I prefer to make a *plan* and to have things settled and decided ahead of time.

○ I prefer to stay *flexible* and avoid fixed plans.

○ I prefer to make things come out the way they *ought to be.*

○ I deal easily with *unplanned and unexpected* happenings.

○ I prefer to *finish* one project before starting another.

○ I prefer to start many projects, though I may have *trouble completing* all of them.

○ I usually have my *mind made up* and may decide things too quickly.

○ I usually am seeking *new information* and may decide things too slowly.

○ I live by *standards and schedules* that are not easily changed.

○ I live by *making changes* to deal with problems as they come along.

Total number of ✓'s for J_____   Total number of ✓'s for P_____

Scoring: For Scales I–IV, total the number of "✓'s" in each column. Write the totals next to each preference.

Preferences

Scale I:	_____ Extraversion (E)	*or*	_____ Introversion (I)
Scale II:	_____ Sensing (S)	*or*	_____ Intuition (N)
Scale III:	_____ Thinking (T)	*or*	_____ Feeling (F)
Scale IV:	_____ Judging (J)	*or*	_____ Perceiving (P)

Your dominant, clearer preference is the higher of the two numbers for each scale. Circle the term with the higher number for Scales I–IV; then write the four letters representing your "type" (for example, "ESFP" or "ISFJ"): _____

Consider these factors when using your four-letter type (Lipsky, 2004, p. 7):

1. The higher the number, the more dominant or clearer is the preference.

2. If the difference between the two numbers is slight—that is, only 1 point—then this measure is showing no clear-cut dominant type for you on that scale.

3. By completing this informal exercise, you are receiving an *approximate* measure of your learning preference.

Source: *People Types and Tiger Stripes,* 3rd edition, by Gordon D. Lawrence, Center for Applications of Psychological Type, Gainesville, FL, 1993. Used with permission. This exercise is *NOT* a type indicator, nor does it replicate the Myer-Briggs Type Indicator®, which is a validated instrument.

MYERS-BRIGGS TYPE INDICATOR®

The MBTI is a questionnaire that helps people understand their personalities through cataloging their preferences. It is widely used in American and international business as well as on American college campuses. Created by Isabel Myers and her mother, Kathryn Briggs, the MBTI is a set of forced-choice questions; that is, each question has two opposing answers. Several forms of this questionnaire exist, but it must be administered by a psychologist or someone especially trained in the field. Most college counseling centers administer this instrument, and your instructor may require or suggest that you take it. We strongly concur that the MBTI is a useful tool and believe that the rest of the information in this chapter will be more useful if you can receive your specific results. The forced-choice structure of the questionnaire works well because the MBTI is based on the Jungian premise that ways of perceiving and judging occur in opposing pairs.

Acquiring Information

As Jung points out in *Personality Types,* humankind is equipped with two distinct and sharply contrasting ways of perceiving. One means of perception is the familiar process of sensing, by which we become aware of things directly through our five senses. The other is the process of intuition, which is indirect perception by way of the unconscious, incorporating ideas or associations that the unconscious tacks on to perceptions coming from outside (Myers & Myers, 1980, p. 2).

All of us have both ways of perceiving, but all of us also developed early in life a preference for one way over the other. That preference is easy to observe in small children, and the preference grows in competence as a child will enjoy and use the preferred way over the nonpreferred way. Again, it is important to remember that we have both abilities, but repetitive practice allows the preferences to develop more fully.

Sensing. People who develop their preference of **sensing (S)** tend to pay attention to what they hear, see, feel, taste, and smell. Their senses tell them what is real, and this preference keeps them in the present moment. They trust their own experience, not the experience of others. Students who have this preference often read well for detail and can memorize facts that they can confirm by experience. They prefer clear, unambiguous assignments and instructions. They value practicality and rarely question the validity of the presented material. They strongly prefer material that is presented in sequential order. The sensing way of perceiving is especially useful in learning that requires an orderly memorization of specific information.

Intuition. People who develop their preference of **intuition (N)** tend to focus on ideas implied by the information; in other words, they like to go beyond the data and look at the relationships among ideas and the possibilities. They tend to disregard the present moment and feel comfortable thinking about the future. As students, they read for the ideas and often miss the specific facts; memorization is difficult because they are interested in the large view. The order or sequence of presentation is usually irrelevant to them. They value originality and usually create their own interpretations of material. Therefore, they want teachers to value and support their independent thinking. The intuitive way of perceiving is necessary in learning that is primarily conceptual and analytical.

Both ways of perceiving or gathering information are necessary for competency in college learning. Whichever is our preference, we must quickly learn to develop our nonpreference. If we have always relied on our senses to learn, then subjects and teachers whose focus is abstract and conceptual will challenge us. We will have to stretch.

• • • JASON • • •

Jason is a good example of someone with a preference for sensing. He lives and thinks in the present; he enjoys practical, concrete activities. Remember that he originally majored in engineering; even his final choice of a major, marketing, is a practical, specific activity. He is wisely choosing a work life that is congruent with his preference. However, to be successful in college and in his professional life, he is developing his intuitive capabilities in order to function well in business and marketing. He must understand trends and the nuances of the market and be able to analyze his customers' needs.

Now that Jason has discerned the major course of study most appropriate for him, he brings his sensing strengths to his work as a student. He can read for details easily and creates note cards that help him memorize factual information. His class notes reflect the concrete information the instructor is presenting, but he has trouble attending to the larger themes in the material. To compensate for this undeveloped preference for intuition, Jason uses three specific study strategies. First, as he reads the texts, he uses a prereading technique that helps him see the larger ideas in a text chapter before he reads for the details. Second, he has a study partner in each class that stresses ideas and concepts. He deliberately chooses partners who are strong in intuitive learning, so he can help them with the specifics and they can help him learn the concepts. Third, he uses a mapping technique that focuses on the ideas of larger sections of material, such as an entire chapter or several weeks of lecture notes.

• • • MEREDITH • • •

By contrast, Jason's sister Meredith has a strongly developed preference for intuition. She was academically successful in high school because she was self-disciplined, but her great strength as a learner will begin to flourish in college. She loves to read, and ideas and concepts seem so obvious to her that she has trouble understanding why other people have difficulty learning them. Although she was overwhelmed by the initial workload of college classes, Meredith is interested in the concepts in a variety of subject areas. Her attraction to differing ideas/theories will lead her to consider several majors and career choices. Law may remain a persistent theme for her, and she can explore the many types of careers within that arena. There are several undergraduate majors that are appropriate for law school, so Meredith has the time to explore fields that seem interesting to her.

Meredith's strength as an intuitive learner will serve her well in liberal arts courses that demand analytical and integrative learning skills. However, she will have to compensate for her tendency to overlook details and factual information. Note cards and memorization techniques will help her in science and math courses as well as social science classes. She will probably excel more on essay exams, rather than tests with multiple-choice or true/false questions. Therefore, her study techniques should focus on test-taking skills for objective tests.

Making Decisions

Thinking ←—————————————→ Feeling

As humans have two ways of perceiving, so too do we have "two distinct and sharply contrasting ways of coming to conclusions. One way is by the use of *thinking,* that is, by a logical process, aimed at an impersonal finding. The other is by *feeling,* that is, by appreciation—equally reasonable in its fashion—bestowing on things a personal, subjective value" (Myers & Myers, 1980, p. 3).

Thinking. Obviously, all of us make decisions by using both the **thinking (T)** function and the feeling function, but our preferences of one over the other develop from childhood. People who have the preference of thinking become good organizers of facts and ideas, and they are analytical and want decisions and the resulting consequences to be fair. People with this preference strive to be objective and detached; even if they have strong feelings, they trust their logical thinking over their feelings.

As students, thinkers learn by challenge; they debate with teachers, authors, other students. They value professors who state the rules of the course clearly and provide a forum for discussion. Students with a preference for thinking can listen calmly to ideas to which they disagree because they do not generally attend to either their own feelings or those of the speaker. They enjoy manipulating and analyzing ideas and theories, whether or not they consider those ideas and theories to be true.

Feeling. People with a preference for **feeling (F)** in making decisions tend toward a personal, rather than an impersonal, approach to learning and to life. They are adept in human relationships and value harmony, and they usually intensely dislike conflict. They are the peacemakers. Compassionate, empathetic, subjective—all are adjectives used to describe people with this preference. As learners, they succeed best when they are supported and appreciated. They want to engage with the content material personally, and they value faculty members who establish rapport with the class. Such students struggle if both the content and the instructors are perceived as cold and distant.

· · · MEREDITH · · ·

Meredith's and Jason's preferences represent the two ways of making decisions—feeling and thinking. Meredith has always been the peacemaker in the family, and her approach to life is personal. She wants to know her professors, and she gets excited about applying the ideas she studies to her understanding of herself and her world. She is struggling with the impersonal atmosphere in some of her classes, but she has learned to go and talk with her professors individually during their office hours. In her larger classes, she has sought a study partner to allay feelings of isolation. They face the challenges together by comparing notes and working problems.

· · · JASON · · ·

By contrast, Jason has a strong preference for thinking. His choice of marketing as a career field reflects his comfort with work that is primarily competitive rather than collaborative. Jason is deliberate in his planning to maintain relationships with friends; he has formed his professional ethical rules early by modeling them after his father's behaviors. Jason is comfortable studying material that is logical and practical.

The two ways of acquiring information and the two ways of making decisions have a profound impact on how we prefer to learn and whether learning situations are easy or difficult for us. Understanding our own preferences across these dimensions helps us use our strengths and compensate for our weaknesses. Another dimension of our personalities outlined in Jungian psychology is whether we direct our attention primarily to the inner world of our thoughts and feelings or the outer world of people and events. That dimension is termed *introversion/extraversion.*

Focus of Attention and Energy

Jung used the terms *introversion* and *extraversion* to differentiate between two opposing aspects of how we generate our energy and focus our attention. As we begin to look at this dimension, we must note that he did *not* mean that people with a preference for extraversion have good social skills and those with a preference for introversion are shy. He created specific meanings for these two terms in order that we might understand our own behaviors.

Introversion. "According to Jung's ideas, introverts are more interested in their own inner world, their concepts and ideas and feelings, than in the outer world of people and things" (Myers & Myers, 1980, p. 7). People with a preference for **introversion (I)** are reflective, often preferring to think before they speak. Even more often, they prefer to think and then write. "Reflection, introspection, and solitude . . . produce energy, focus, and attention for the introvert" (Kroeger & Thuesen, 1988, p. 36). Introverts relish time alone and require solitude to replenish their energy and activity level. Although they may have good social skills, they usually have only a few good friends whom they know deeply.

As learners, introverts value reading and learn best by pausing to think. They need quiet to concentrate and prefer to study individually rather than in groups. Often they believe they are unskilled in public speaking or other forms of verbal expression (Ditiberio & Hammer, 1993, p. 6). They can dislike classes that focus on discussion and group work but can enjoy clear lectures.

Extraversion. By contrast, people with a preference for **extraversion (E)** tend to focus on people and events in the outer world. They are energized by other people and have multiple interests and multiple relationships. Usually sociable and gregarious, they often speak before they think. Rather than reflect, they prefer to talk about ideas or projects as the method for thinking. As students, they enjoy class discussions and group study and usually report feeling competent in verbal and interpersonal skills (Ditiberio & Hammer, 1993, p. 6). Quiet does not help their study concentration; in fact, they prefer background sounds. Since writing is a solitary activity, they usually do not enjoy it as much as group projects.

• • • MEREDITH • • •

Meredith and Jason differ on this personality dimension. Meredith likes her private time and space. She had that at home during high school, so adjusting to life with an extraverted roommate is difficult; Meredith is sometimes fatigued by Janice's inexhaustible energy. Janice is willing to honor Meredith's privacy by spending time away and turning off the music while they are studying. Meredith is also learning to study in the library. Because they are willing to be candid about their differences, each compromises and learns to enjoy living with the other.

Although Meredith has a pleasant and easy manner, personally she finds her freshman year difficult. She does not feel close to anyone, and her boyfriend is at another college. Making friends comes slowly. She relies on weekly dinners with Jason to relax because she can express her feelings. Visits home on occasional weekends help her to connect to places and people with whom she feels comfortable.

• • • JASON • • •

Jason's extraverted nature is easy for all to see. His sociable and gregarious manner has served him well throughout school, and it will certainly contribute to his future career in marketing. He makes friends easily, but recently he has made a deliberate decision to maintain his college friendships. (An extravert has to decide this action deliberately; an introvert automatically does it.) When he feels tired, he goes out with his friends and recharges his energy through activity.

Lifestyle Orientation

The fourth difference in preference is "which function—information gathering or decision making—you most naturally use as you relate to the outer world, verbally and behaviorally" (Kroeger & Thuesen, 1988, p. 40).

Judging. If we prefer our lives to be planned and controlled and if we prefer to be decisive and deliberate, then we are using our decision-making (judging) function more easily and more often than our information-gathering (perceiving) function. That characteristic is called **judging (J).** Judgers like to make decisions quickly, rather than listen to new information, and they deplore indecisiveness. As students, judgers are organized. They plan in advance, usually work steadily toward a goal, and like to be in charge. They value faculty who are organized. Closure is emotionally satisfying to them.

Perceiving. If we value flexibility and spontaneity and are frequently uncomfortable with making and carrying out decisions, then we have a preference for **perceiving (P)** (information gathering). The great strength of perceivers is their continued willingness to be open to new information and circumstances. They are comfortable with spending the necessary time to learn everything they can learn. As students, perceivers work impulsively, and they like to solve problems spontaneously. They value faculty who are entertaining and inspiring.

No personality preference is more evident than whether we are judgers or perceivers. In families, the workplace, organizations, and so forth, judgers and perceivers can make each other crazy. Judgers feel compelled to always have an opinion, to plan, to schedule everything, whereas perceivers want to be spontaneous and easygoing. Conflicts are inevitable. However, each preference has its strengths, and we all have the capacity to improve our lives by deliberately exercising our nonpreference in this dimension, as in the other three. In other words, judgers can relinquish trying to control everything and learn to relax and play, and perceivers can push themselves to make appropriate and timely decisions.

Academic work is the outer world for students, and the preference for judging or perceiving can dominate how we handle the job of being a student. Both preferences have strengths and weaknesses, and it behooves us to pay close attention to how our particular preference helps us and hurts us in our academic pursuits. Jason and Meredith are no exceptions.

· · · JASON · · ·

Jason is clearly a perceiver, and it took him until his junior year in college to place his academic behaviors under control. Once he learned to set goals and monitor the management of his time, Jason began to make better grades. Jason is working hard to end his habit of procrastination of assignments through the use of self-regulation techniques. As he strives to develop his nonpreference for decisive academic behaviors (judging), he is also developing those habits that will serve him well in his career. Setting goals, managing time, making decisions—all are important professional behaviors.

• • •   MEREDITH   • • •

Meredith has been organized and decisive all of her life. Even as a freshman in college, she is comfortable with a time planner. Her biggest shock is how much she has underestimated the amount of time certain academic tasks would take, such as reading college textbooks. Within weeks of the semester's onset, she is anxious and frazzled by the sensation that she is not in control. College time management opens up more possibilities, even though she is stunned by the suggestion that she has to have time to play. As a judger, Meredith must plan for play, a concept completely foreign to a perceiver. As she moves through the first semester, Meredith gradually becomes cognizant of the collegiate workload and better able to accurately estimate how much time each academic task will take. She is learning to balance work and play within her college life.

The MBTI and other instruments help us determine our preferences, although they seem to be less reliable for older students. We frequently recommend that our older students use a questionnaire and an interview with a counselor to determine their preferences. *When all four preferences are determined,* the result is called a **type** or a **personality type.** See Figure 7.4 for descriptions of these types and preferences.

There are 16 types in the version of the Jungian system articulated by the MBTI (see Figure 7.5). As we work with individual students, the concept of type is the most powerful. There are numerous books and other resources that help students understand their own attitudes and behaviors through the lens of their type. We have listed many of those sources in the references at the end of the book.

WE RECOMMEND

If you have taken the MBTI, we recommend a small booklet written especially for college students titled *Introduction to Type in College* by Ditiberio & Hammer (1993), published by Consulting Psychologists Press.

FIGURE 7.4   Personality Type and Learning Preferences

Acquiring Information	**Sensing (S)** *Detailed*	• Are observant, factual, concrete; notice detail. • Value practical knowledge. • Prefer to move from concrete material to the abstract in small steps. • Learn best with clear directions and assignments; like hands-on experiences.
	Intuition (N) *Big picture*	• See the big picture; focus on the relationship of information. • Learn best through independent thinking and use of imagination and creativity. • Occasionally careless about details as they like to focus on the overall concept. • Like to study theories.
Making Decisions	**Thinking (T)** *Logical*	• Are logical, objective, fair, impartial, detached. • Find that logic guides learning; learn best by critiquing and debating. • Want a logical rationale for projects and assignments. • Enjoy studying cause-and-effect relationships.
	Feeling (F) *Value oriented*	• Find that personal values dominate decision making. • Learn best by relating to the material personally. • Have a strong need to like the teacher. • Are motivated by teacher's encouragement.
Focus of Attention and Energy	**Introversion (I)** *Time to reflect*	• Focus on their own inner world of ideas. • Learn best by reflecting and thinking. • Are willing to share ideas with advance notice. • Need time to think before making a decision or participating in a discussion.
	Extraversion (E) *Excitement and enthusiasm*	• Focus on the outer world of people and external events. • Learn best by doing and discussing. • Prefer collaborative group work. • Like to connect facts, theories, and concepts to their own experience.
Relating to the Outside World	**Judging (J)** *Planned and organized*	• Are planned, scheduled, organized, goal oriented. • Learn best by planning and organizing material. • Like organized instructions and assignments. • Find that completing a task or an assignment is very reinforcing.
	Perceiving (P) *Spontaneous and flexible*	• Are adaptable, open to change, flexible. • Learn best by being spontaneous; want faculty to be inspiring. • Find that completing tasks and assignments on time is difficult. • Prefer less structured learning environments.

Source: Compiled from Ditiberio & Hammer, 1993; Lawrence, 1997; Myers & Myers, 1980.

If the types were distributed equally throughout the population, each type would comprise 6.25%, but interestingly they are not distributed evenly. Estimates vary because they are drawn from different sample groups that have been tested. In 1962, Myers made the following estimates (Myers & McCaulley, 1985, p. 45):

About 75% of the population in the United States prefer E.

About 75% of the population in the United States prefer S.

About 60% of males in the United States prefer T.

About 65% of females in the United States prefer F.

About 55% to 60% of the population in the United States prefer J.

Just a few examples from the MBTI Databank show some extremes of distribution. In male traditional-age college students, the Databank shows ESTJ as 11+%. In the same population, INFJ is 3% and ENTP is 6+%. The highest and the lowest for non-traditional male college students are ISTJ 17+% and INFJ 2%. For female traditional-age college students, the Databank shows ESFJ as 16+%, ENFP as 12+%, INTJ 2%, ISTJ 6%. For non-traditional female college students, the Databank shows ESFJ 12+% and ESTP 2+% (Myers & McCaulley, 1985, pp. 46–48).

exercise 7.7

Matching Your Personality Type to Your Instructor's Type

Does your instructor's personality type influence your learning? This exercise will help you investigate that possibility.

1. Identify your personality type.

2. For each of your classes, try to determine the instructors' personality types (your best guesses) from the observations you have made thus far in each class.

3. Which instructors closely match your personality type? Do you have an easier time learning from these instructors?

4. How have you compensated for instructors with teaching styles very different from the way you prefer to learn?

TEMPERAMENT

Another way of using personality type that is especially popular in business and education is the grouping of the 16 types into four temperaments. This method works well within groups, either familial or professional. Realizing the temperaments of the other people with whom we live or work helps us understand and accept their behavior and thus frequently reduces conflict. We can of-

FIGURE 7.5   Shared Personality Characteristics Among Four
Temperaments

Temperament Percent of Population	Motto	Important Psychological Needs
Guardians (SJ) 38% ISFJ, ESFJ, ISTJ, ESTJ	*To serve is to be*	Membership/Belonging Responsibility/Duty
Artisans (SP) 38% ISFP, ESFP, ISTP, ESTP	*To do is to be*	Freedom/Action Excitation/Variation
Idealists (NF) 12% INFP, ENFP, INFJ, ENFJ	*To be is to do*	Identity/Self-actualization Meaning/Significance
Rationalists (NT) 12% INTP, ENTP, INTJ, ENTJ	*To know is to be*	Knowledge/Competence Willpower/Mastery

Source: Adaped from Fairhurst, A. M., & Fairhurst, L. L. (1995). *Effective Teaching, Effective Learning*. Palo Alto, CA: Davies-Black.

ten deduce someone's temperament by observation, which is useful for college students because they spend hundreds of hours listening to and observing their professors. Understanding a professor's probable temperament can help a student determine how best to work with that professor.

Although there are several differing groupings, we focus here on the most widely used version articulated by David Keirsey (1998). He uses the term **temperament** to denote *the shared personality characteristics of four types of people.* Temperament theory is based in *constitutional psychology,* an ancient system that categorizes people based on their observable behaviors (Fairhurst & Fairhurst, 1995). In brief, the four temperaments are Guardians, Artisans, Idealists, and Rationalists.

As evidenced in Figure 7.5, all four types of one temperament share two preferences. Guardians share the preferences of sensing and judging, whereas Artisans share sensing and perceiving. Rationalists share intuition and thinking, whereas Idealists share intuition and feeling. It is interesting that the distribution of temperaments and types is not equal; there are far more Guardians and Artisans in the general population than there are Idealists and Rationalists. In American colleges, however, there seem to be almost an equal number of all four temperaments among students (Porter, 1995).

Guardians

Guardians (SJ) comprise approximately 38 percent of the general population, 28 percent of college students, and 24 percent of college faculty (Porter, 1995).

Generally, guardians stress order and responsibility, value routines and traditions, and plan carefully. This is the most stable of all the temperaments; they are loyal and do not like surprises. They prefer rules to be consistently enforced.

As teachers. Guardians want students to become good citizens. They establish consistent rules and routines, use meticulous lesson plans, and often lecture. They provide students with thorough, fair, and well-supported feedback.

As students. Guardians tend to be serious and dutiful. They plan activities carefully and do not like to take risks. Often they do not like group work because they become angry at other students who are irresponsible (Fairhurst & Fairhurst, 1995).

Artisans

Artisans (SP) comprise approximately 38 percent of the general population, 21 percent of college students, and 5 percent of college faculty (Porter, 1995).

Artisans like freedom, spontaneity, and actions; in other words they are flexible and sometimes impulsive. Good problem solvers and troubleshooters, they can focus on an immediate issue and take action. Many become athletic or artistic performers.

As teachers. Artisans create choices and opportunities for students and incorporate a wide variety of activities, some rapid and some tranquil. They prefer projects to tests and frequently overlook rules and constraints.

As students. Artisans are spontaneous and can distrust authority. They resist rules and other constraints because they want to feel free, not under someone's control. Often they procrastinate as a form of rebellion. However, their great strength as students comes when they get excited, even passionate, about a subject. Then their energy is contagious (Fairhurst & Fairhurst, 1995).

Idealists

Idealists (NF) comprise approximately 12 percent of the general population, 25 percent of college students, and 11 percent of college faculty (Porter, 1995).

Idealists are usually optimistic and romantic and try to bring out the best in others. They encourage harmony and dislike conflict. Idealists are diplomatic, cooperative, sensitive, and enthusiastic.

As teachers. Idealists value their own unique identity, and they encourage their students to express themselves as individuals. They use praise rather than criticism. They favor instructional techniques such as group discussion, creative writing, and peer tutoring, and they are skilled at individualization. Good listeners, they can elicit the best from their students. Sometimes they are charismatic and inspiring. However, they often procrastinate in the ordinary tasks of teaching such as grading or class preparation and then are forced to innovate.

As students. Idealists tend to be creative, flexible, unconventional. They are often either the best student in class or the worst, although usually they desire praise and thus work best in situations in which their work is complimented. These students treasure including everyone in activities, and they like to help others achieve. As Idealists, they often enjoy group work, and they act as catalysts for others' achievements. Usually they are good writers, with a gift for description by metaphor (Fairhurst & Fairhurst, 1995).

Rationalists

> *Rationalists (NT) comprise approximately 12 percent of the general population, 28 percent of college students, and **60 percent of college faculty** (Porter, 1995).*

People with this temperament value knowledge and mastery; that is, they like to understand and control. They want to be competent at whatever they do. If they do feel incompetent, then they are highly self-critical. They are skeptical, verbal, logical, relentless.

As teachers. Rationalists give challenging assignments and expect answers that use logic and reason. They especially want their students to develop their intellectual abilities. They enjoy being experts in a discipline because they are usually deeply interested in the subject and want their students to also become expert. They may lack interpersonal skills and sensitivity when interacting with students. Frankly, many college teachers who are Rationalists care only about their subject and can be insensitive about the total workload of a student.

As students. Rationalists want to be intellectually competent; they like Socratic questioning, independent projects, and competition. They live in the world of ideas, and they intend to change that world by understanding it. They focus on the *big picture,* the main idea, rather than details, and they especially like unraveling complex systems. In groups, they tend to lead and they become impatient with members who learn or produce slowly. A primary characteristic is that Rationalists will question everything, including professors! They tend to be quick learners and critical thinkers, but others often see them as arrogant (Fairhurst & Fairhurst, 1995).

Temperaments provide a good method of understanding ourselves and our professors. We can use such insight wisely in our interactions in and out of the classroom. In the early weeks of a term, listen carefully to your professors and read the course syllabi. What are the values you discern? What temperament does each of your teachers exhibit in the classroom? All temperaments have advantages and disadvantages; however, understanding these concepts can help us communicate with others as well as understand ourselves.

Some of the most powerful uses of these concepts are in career counseling. Obviously, different preferences take us on different career paths. Your campus career center has numerous resources to help you explore the world of work through the concepts of temperament.

CONCLUSION

Talents, will, and preferences—these three components of ourselves shape our educational experiences and accomplishments. Each of us makes myriad decisions about how we will use these components. Do we pursue only those goals that seem easy to us or are we determined to achieve even in areas in which we are not gifted? Are we confident in our abilities or afraid that we will fail? College is the testing ground for many people. It is in college that we can choose majors and move toward careers, not jobs. It is in college that our personal lives can take a new direction. Understanding ourselves is a key to thoughtful choices.

SUMMARY

- Individualism is one's self-concept, the image of oneself as an individual unit whose motivations and behaviors are aimed at individual goals.

- Individuality is the development of differences within the personality. We can differ physically, cognitively, and emotionally.

- Talents are those abilities that come as a result of the interaction of our genes, our environment, our experience, and our effort.

- We can differentiate human talents into eight categories defined by Howard Gardner. These are logical–mathematical, linguistic, musical, spatial, bodily–kinesthetic, interpersonal, intrapersonal, and naturalist.

- These different multiple intelligences operate as a complement to each other. As individuals, we have a preference of one or more over others and tend to use those intelligences more often.

- Logical–mathematical intelligence is the ability to calculate, quantify, consider propositions and hypotheses, and carry out complex mathematical operations.

- Linguistic intelligence is the ability to think in words and to use language to express and appreciate complex meanings.

- Musical intelligence is the capacity to discern pitch, rhythm, timbre, and tone.

- Spatial intelligence is the ability to think in three dimensions.

- Bodily–kinesthetic intelligence is the capacity to manipulate objects and use a variety of physical skills.

- Interpersonal intelligence is the ability to understand and interact effectively with others.

- Intrapersonal intelligence is the capacity to understand oneself and one's thoughts and feelings and to use such knowledge in planning and directing one's life.

- Naturalistic intelligence is the ability to recognize, identify, and classify patterns in nature such as plants and animals.

- Will is the conscious control that we have over our own actions or emotions. The technical term for such control is *self-regulation*.

- As individuals, we have cognitive and affective preferences. Based on Carl Jung's theory, we can define these preferences as personality type. We differentiate preferences based on the way we acquire information, the way we make decisions, our focus of attention and energy, and the way we relate to the outside world. The MBTI is a means of assessing personality type.

- Sensing (S) or Intuition (N) is the way we prefer to acquire information.

- Thinking (T) or Feeling (F) is the way we prefer to make decisions.

- Introversion (I) or Extraversion (E) is the way we prefer to focus our attention and energy.

- Judging (J) or Perceiving (P) is our preference for how we relate to the outside world.

- Personality types can be grouped into four temperaments: Guardians, Artisans, Idealists, and Rationalists.

KEY CONCEPTS

Individualism

Individuality

Learning styles

Multiple intelligences:
  logical–mathematical, linguistic,
  musical, spatial, bodily–
  kinesthetic, interpersonal,
  intrapersonal, naturalist

Myers-Briggs Type Indicator (MBTI)

Personality type

Preferences: sensing (S) and
  intuition (N), thinking (T) and
  feeling (F), introversion (I) and
  extraversion (E), judging (J) and
  perceiving (P)

12-Step programs

Talents

Temperament: Guardians,
  Artisans, Idealists, Rationalists

Will

GUIDED JOURNAL QUESTIONS

1. To understand more about yourself is the realization of your position on the individualism versus group-centeredness spectrum:

   Where would you place yourself on this spectrum and why?

   Have you been raised to choose and pursue your own individual goals or to do what is best for the group (family) to which you belong?

2. Does your will sometimes interfere with your learning? If so, explain how. If not, explain how you have overcome this.

3. *Extraverts* are energized by being with other people; *Introverts* are energized by spending time alone. Which is most true of you and why?

4. *Sensors* value realism and common sense; *Intuitives* value imagination and innovation. Which is most true of you and why?

5. *Thinkers* value logic, justice, fairness, and one standard for all; *Feelers* value empathy and harmony and see the exception to the rule. Which is most true of you and why?

6. *Judgers* prefer knowing what they are getting into; *Perceivers* like adapting to new situations. Which is most true of you and why?

7. How are your multiple intelligences and personality type similar? How do they differ? Especially address learning approaches that are similar and different for each.

8. What are your strengths associated with your multiple intelligences and your personality type? What are your weaknesses associated with each?

9. What multiple intelligence would you like to develop more fully? Explain several strategies that you can implement for yourself. Complete the same exercise for a personality preference that you would like to strengthen.

10. Based on your evaluation of your multiple intelligences and personality type, list at least three possible career choices for you to consider. Why are these careers good possibilities for you?

11. Meredith and Jason exhibit the characteristics of two of the temperaments discussed in this chapter: Meredith is an Idealist (NF) and Jason an Artisan (SP). Look back over the descriptions of the four temperaments in this chapter. What temperament would you select for yourself and why?

The Last Word

Nothing has ever helped me understand myself and other people more than the concepts in this chapter—talents, will, and preferences.

—De Sellers

8

Establishing Direction in Your Life

The promised land.

I have a dream that my four little children will one day live in a nation where they will not be judged by the color of their skin but by the content of their character.
—*Martin Luther King, Jr.*

CHAPTER HIGHLIGHTS

- Fantasies, Dreams, and Goals
- Goals: Characteristics of Achievable Goals, Translating Goals into an Action Plan
- Self-Regulation: Academic Self-Regulation, Timeliness, Procrastination Issues and Remedies

What dreams do you have for your life? It is now time to turn those dreams into reality. Thus far, we have given you varied ways of reflecting so that you can develop the most accurate self-awareness possible. The insights you have achieved through the journal exercises and other assignments may have already engendered some changes in how you are living your life as a college student. The great traditions of psychology, education, spirituality, self-help, and theology stress that knowing ourselves well is the only feasible beginning to the construction of a healthy and productive life. With that foundation now in place, you can begin to look at the specific strategies available as you contemplate how you wish to shape your collegiate experience.

SELF-ASSESSMENT: Self-Regulation

Self-regulation is your ability to monitor and manage your behaviors, emotions, and feelings and make positive adjustments when necessary. With 5 being "Almost Always" and 1 being "Almost Never," assess your assumptions and feelings about your ability to self-regulate your life. Rate each of the following statements honestly by circling the appropriate number. Completing this exercise will help you identify areas of concern you may have with self-regulation.

	Almost Always		Sometimes		Almost Never
1. I set goals for myself.	5	4	3	2	1
2. I base many of my goals on my core values and beliefs.	5	4	3	2	1
3. I set goals that are achievable.	5	4	3	2	1
4. I am aware of when my feelings interfere with my actions.	5	4	3	2	1
5. I am aware of negative self-talk (negative thoughts that I say to myself that keep me from success).	5	4	3	2	1
6. I use positive self-talk to motivate myself.	5	4	3	2	1
7. I am able to manage my negative feelings in a constructive way.	5	4	3	2	1
8. I am able to delay having fun until after I finish studying.	5	4	3	2	1
9. I am able to spread out the work on a long assignment and not wait until the last minute to complete it.	5	4	3	2	1

10.	I have self-discipline.	5	4	3	2	1
11.	I like finishing assignments before the due date.	5	4	3	2	1
12.	I monitor my own progress in my classes regularly.	5	4	3	2	1

Add up the numbers circled. Your total score will be between 12 and 60. The higher your score, the more likely you feel confident about your ability to self-regulate. For total scores below 36, write or reflect on items for which you have concerns.

Also, consider talking with a trusted friend, a family member, a teacher, or an advisor.

FANTASIES, DREAMS, AND GOALS

When we were children, other people managed our lives. As we grew, we practiced managing ourselves, from tying our own shoelaces to doing chores without being told. In the long transition (*independence*) between adolescence and adulthood, we increasingly take responsibility for how we live and we begin to manage our own lives. *Midlife,* the other long transition period, often requires that we make major adaptations in how we manage our behaviors. Of all of life's tasks, managing our own behaviors seems to be the most difficult for many people. Beyond simplistic management of daily chores, living well or living toward our quality world means that we develop the flexibility to navigate the complexities of life. To do so, we must learn how to modify and maintain our own behaviors so as to reach our goals. That skill is called *self-regulation.* The appropriate foundation for self-regulation is competence in setting goals—goals that are congruent with our quality world. Thus, this chapter begins specific instruction about constructing achievable goals and then translating those goals into actions. After a formal definition of self-regulation, we present the concept of timeliness, a way to decrease procrastination. In the following two chapters, we present a simple model of self-regulation and use it to demonstrate how we can manage time and stress.

· · · CHRISTINA · · ·

She dreamed of a successful career as a clothing designer

Christina is a second-semester student from a small rural community. Even though her parents did not complete high school, since the third grade she dreamed of going to college. Those dreams started because her teacher knew that Christina liked to make clothes for her dolls and creative costumes for Halloween and encouraged her to imagine herself as a clothing designer. This teacher challenged Christina to work hard in school and gave special attention to her academic achievements. Christina held on to the ideas of achievement throughout middle school, and her parents grew increasingly proud of her schoolwork. All the typical distractions erupted during high school—boys, clubs, the Internet—but Christina persisted on a college prep track, even though many of her friends succumbed to easier roads. Christina envisioned herself designing clothes for music performers. A few teachers encouraged her, and the high school counselor reluctantly provided information about college scholarships. Christina and her parents drove to a nearby university for a Visitors' Day. It seemed overwhelming, but also exciting, and she could envision herself being a student there. None of her older siblings shared her ambitions, but her family supported her desire to go to college. Her dream became a specific goal, and she worked nights and weekends during her senior year to save money.

The first college semester was tough for Christina. Even though she had enrolled in two art classes, she found her courses in sociology and communications far more interesting. Her goal to get to college had been met, but now what? What kind of life did she wish to make there? What should be her major? What type of professional life did she want? Christina found herself in a dilemma. After years of having such a clear-cut goal, she felt as if she were drifting, not really sure about what she wanted or how to get there. One strong habit she had already developed was to search for help if she felt confused. So Christina made an appointment at the campus counseling center and began to investigate her future.

The first conversation tackled the difficult task of differentiating among fantasies, dreams, and goals. **Fantasies** *are ideas that cannot happen; they are fun to think about but they are not possible.* In our time, fantasies usually involve looking different or having talents we do not possess or acquiring fabulous riches. In our fantasies, we do not have to work for achievement. Everything magically appears.

On the other hand, **dreams** *are possible—sometimes probable and sometimes improbable—but they are possible.* When we begin to examine a dream or a wish, we begin to translate it into goals. A dream unexamined remains a dream forever. Christina had an early dream of going to college, and her teachers and parents helped her convert that wish into specific goals—good academic performance, college prep courses, college visits, scholarship applications. Christina came to believe in the feasibility of her wish; she believed her dream of attending college could happen. People around her helped her ask and answer the question: "Do I possess the necessary skills and talents, time, access to means, and opportunities?" (Gollwitzer, 1995, p. 289). Repeatedly she made decisions that moved her toward her goal. Along the way, she turned away from other roads, other possibilities. Each time she acted in a manner that supported her goal, she became more confident and believed in herself. In Chapter 2, we presented Branden's ideas of self-esteem. Each time we keep our promises to ourselves, we become more trustworthy to ourselves (Branden, 1994, p. 26). Thus, Christina's level of self-efficacy increased because she did what she had set for herself to do; she trusted that she would act in ways congruent with her goals. As she progressed through high school, she made "a transition from wishes and desires to binding goals, . . . accompanied by a feeling of determination" (Gollwitzer, 1995, p. 289). This stage is called goal-directed action, and we will discuss it soon.

For a moment, however, reflect on the concept of the quality world introduced in Chapter 1. The visions we have of our perfect world fuel not only our fantasies but our dreams as well. If our quality world is ethical and based on our deepest core values, then the dreams that emerge can be translated into goals that will help our life resemble our quality world.

Christina has accomplished her goal of attending college. Now she must discern what she wants to accomplish, why she wants those goals, and how to achieve them. As she works with a counselor, Christina realizes that she envisions herself in a professional job in which she interacts with others frequently. After studying the results of career inventories and the Myers-Briggs Type Indicator® (MBTI), she reflects on the importance that helping others has always been in her life. That core value has permeated her life and comes, at least in part, from the way her family has always helped others. As a Latina, she feels she has much to give others, because she understands the complexity of a bicultural world. Christina forms a clear and concrete goal to determine her major and future professional career within the next two semesters. She and her counselor create a list of specific interviews and readings as well as two exploratory courses for the next term.

Dreams Do Come True

Your dreams are possible. The first step is to think about possible changes you hope to make in your life—especially possibilities connected to your quality world. This exercise will help you begin this process.

What are five dreams that you hope will come true for you? For each, tell why you hope to reach these dreams.

1. _____

2. _____

3. _____

4. _____

5. _____

GOALS

As Christina has learned, goals set directions for our actions and our lives; they eliminate the aimless wandering through the days, not knowing what we want or why we are doing what we are doing. From our earliest days, we all have goals. Watch a baby intently reaching for an object or a toddler attempting to walk across a room or a young child struggling to read, and you will see determined effort to reach a specific goal.

Usually we have goals in many areas of our lives. Consider these areas as you begin the goal-setting process: education and training; career and job development; spiritual, religious, and character building; health and emotional development; physical and recreational; social, relationships, and family; financial; civic, service, and volunteerism. Here are sample goals for these areas:

- **Education/training:** *I will earn a master's degree in counseling education by my twenty-fifth birthday.*

- **Career/job development:** *I will be a school counselor by my twenty-sixth birthday.*

- **Spiritual/religious/character building:** *I will attend religious services once a week for the next three months.*

- **Health/emotional:** *I will lose 20 lb within the next six months.*

- **Physical/recreational:** *I will exercise by lifting weights and jogging at the student health club three days each week.*

- **Social/relationships/family:** *I will introduce myself to three new people each month during my first semester in college.*

- **Financial:** *I will save $25.00 a month for the next 12 months.*

- **Civic/service/volunteerism:** *I will volunteer at the humane society once a month for the next six months.*

Goals can be intermediate or final. Outcome goals are those goals that you set to achieve for a final product such as a final grade in a course or a certain GPA or graduation. Process goals are usually the strategies involved to reach an outcome goal, such as learning to use Cornell and T-notes. Often several process goals serve as reinforcements along the way to our reaching an outcome goal. Here are examples of outcome and process goals:

- **Outcome** (a final product such as a certain GPA): *I will earn a 3.5 GPA by the end of this semester.*

- **Process** (strategy to reach an outcome goal such as learning to use Cornell and T-notes): *I will attend the campus tutoring center to work on my statistics homework two days each week (for at least one hour each visit) for the entire semester.*

Setting goals that reflect our quality world and help us achieve the lives we want is an important skill that we can learn. In other words, we can study the principles of goal setting and apply those principles to our own lives. As you have reflected about your quality world, you have thought about the type of person you wish to become, the family and friends you wish to have, and the work you wish to do. Each of those is a lifetime desire. What are the long-term outcome goals that can lead to those desires? What constellation of process goals will lead you to that life you desire? Are your goals compatible with your ethics? These questions are not hypothetical, nor easily answered. They require careful scrutiny and thoughtful reflection.

Translating Goals into Behaviors

We recommend formulating your goals as actions (which are really behaviors). Behaviors are easily measured. You can easily measure an increase in the number of pages you read or a decrease in the amount of money you spend. We have found that decreasing or ending actions of obsessive behaviors such as smoking or overspending money is often a challenging goal to implement and obtain but also rewarding once it is met. Here are several ways that you can formulate your goals as behaviors:

- **Expand** (seek mastery or improvement with a behavior): *I will score a 75 on 18 holes of golf within six months.*

- **Reduce** (seek to cut back or to spend less time on a behavior): *I will spend only five hours a week playing computer games for the rest of this semester so that I will have more time for study.*

- **Maintain** (seek to keep the behavior at its current level): *I will continue to ride my bicycle three miles once a week in order to maintain my physical stamina.*

- **Innovate** (begin some new behavior): *I will take exploratory courses in two majors next term to search for a major.*

- **Problem solve** (institute action to resolve or prevent difficulty): *I will review the status of my checking account online each week to prevent overdrafts.*

Not only do goals differ across areas of our lives, but they also differ in their immediacy or their distance. Some goals are immediate (today!), some are short term (1 year or less), some are intermediate (between 1 and 10 years), and others are long term (10 years or more): Here are examples of each of these types of goals:

- **Long term** (10 years or more): *I will have traveled to all 50 states by my fiftieth birthday.*

- **Intermediate** (between 1 and 10 years): *I will be promoted to vice president of finance at my job within the next five years.*

- **Short term** (1 year or less): *I will take the graduate record exam so that I can apply to graduate school within the next three months.*

- **Immediate** (within hours or days): *I will review my history notes for one hour by 4 P.M. today.*

An assumption we must make in this text is that academic success in college is an appropriate goal for you, even though we realize that this may not be true for every reader. As you move through this chapter and the exercises, ruminate carefully about the purpose of attending college in your life. Can a college education help you reach your desires? Is this the right school? Is this the right time? Is this the right course of study?

exercise 8.3

Turn Your Dreams into Goals

Now that you have listed your dreams, begin to reflect on how those dreams are connected to your values—those life beliefs you hold in the highest regard that are the foundation of your quality world. For example, if your dream is to receive a college degree in psychology, you probably value education. Think about your other values especially as they relate to your dreams. This exercise will help you explore your values and how they relate to your dreams.

List your top values that you hope will enhance your quality world and place them in order of importance with 1 being the most important and 5 being the least important.

1. _____

2. _____

3. _____

4. _____

5. _____

Which values are connected to your list of dreams? Explain.

Now complete each of the following goal statements and answer the accompanying questions.

1. In 10 years I will . . .

Is this goal connected to a dream? ___ yes ___ no

Is this goal connected to one of your values? ___ yes ___ no

What area does this goal apply to (check all that apply)?

___ Education/Training   ___ Career/Job Development

___ Spiritual/Religious/   ___ Health/Emotional
     Character Building
                           ___ Social/Relationships/Family

___ Physical/Recreational   ___ Civic/Service/Volunteerism

___ Financial

2. In 3 years I will . . .

Is this goal connected to a dream? ___ yes ___ no

Is this goal connected to one of your values? ___ yes ___ no

What area does this goal apply to (check all that apply)?

    ___ Education/Training   ___ Career/Job Development

    ___ Spiritual/Religious/   ___ Health/Emotional
        Character Building

                        ___ Social/Relationships/Family

    ___ Physical/Recreational   ___ Civic/Service/Volunteerism

    ___ Financial

3. In 6 months I will . . .

Is this goal connected to a dream? ___ yes ___ no

Is this goal connected to one of your values? ___ yes ___ no

What area does this goal apply to (check all that apply)?

    ___ Education/Training   ___ Career/Job Development

    ___ Spiritual/Religious/   ___ Health/Emotional
        Character Building

                        ___ Social/Relationships/Family

    ___ Physical/Recreational   ___ Civic/Service/Volunteerism

    ___ Financial

4. By next week I will . . .

Is this goal connected to a dream? ___ yes ___ no

Is this goal connected to one of your values? ___ yes ___ no

What area does this goal apply to (check all that apply)?

    ___ Education/Training   ___ Career/Job Development

    ___ Spiritual/Religious/   ___ Health/Emotional
        Character Building

                        ___ Social/Relationships/Family

    ___ Physical/Recreational   ___ Civic/Service/Volunteerism

    ___ Financial

Characteristics of Achievable Goals

We cannot stress strongly enough the crucial importance of discerning your goals through the lens of your quality world and your ethical system. Covey, Merrill, and Merrill (1994) tell a story of a man who spent years climbing the ladder of success only to find at midlife that the ladder was leaning against the wrong wall. Often we have witnessed students doggedly pursuing a major even when they do not like it only to be miserable after graduation, or students choosing social behaviors that conflict with their own values. We often see students hurrying through school toward the earliest possible graduation date rather than taking enough time to explore a variety of options and experiences available in college.

Once you have discerned your goals, test them against four characteristics of achievable goals: believable, realistic, desirable, measurable (Nist & Holschuh, 2000, pp. 81–82). This strategy will help you determine whether you are conceptualizing your goals in ways that you can successfully accomplish.

Believable. The characteristic *believable* simply means that we are certain that we have the talent and the will to achieve the goal. We may draw upon our own feelings of self-efficacy (internal) or we may draw upon others' conviction that we have the necessary talent and the will (external). Christina drew upon both sources to trust that she could achieve her goal of attending college.

Realistic. Once we believe we have the talent and will to achieve a goal, the next step is to ascertain whether the goal is *realistic*. External validation (reality check) is the means to assess whether a goal is realistic. Christina checked the realism of her goal by investigating and visiting colleges, talking with the high school counselor, maintaining her GPA, and attaining an acceptable score on the required standardized entrance exams.

Desirable. The third characteristic, *desirable*, is simple—how much do we want this goal? In crass terms, just how much are we willing to sacrifice? Christina sacrificed much of her social life and free time by working nights and weekends to save money for college to achieve her goal. Sometimes the price tag is high, sometimes not, but the degree of desirability is a great determiner of our motivation.

Measurable. The final characteristic, *measurable*, allows us to know when we have achieved a goal. *I want to be a good student* is not measurable; *I want to graduate with honors,* that is, a GPA >3.5, is measurable. Christina's goal was measurable; she wanted to be accepted by and to attend a college.

Which Goals Are Achievable?

Measure each of your goals stated in Exercise 8.3 against the four achievable criteria—believable, realistic, desirable, and measurable—by checking all that apply for each goal. Then rewrite any goals that do not meet all four criteria to make them achievable. Completing this exercise will reinforce the concept of learning to write achievable goal statements.

10-year goal: ___ believable ___ realistic ___ desirable ___ measurable

3-year goal: ___ believable ___ realistic ___ desirable ___ measurable

6-month goal: ___ believable ___ realistic ___ desirable ___ measurable

Next week goal: ___ believable ___ realistic ___ desirable ___ measurable

Translating Goals into an Action Plan

Creating the most appropriate goals for ourselves is no guarantee that we will reach them. The easiest example is the New Year's resolutions that often last less than a week. How can we translate goals into actions—actions that will help us accomplish the very goals that have spawned them? The answer comes from cognitive behavioral psychology, a branch of psychology that investigates how human behavior changes deliberately. We use here a commonplace example to demonstrate how a student's goal of academic success in a freshman math class translates into the specific behaviors.

Tim is a geography major who wants to go to graduate school and earn a master's degree. He knows that he must make good grades to achieve that goal. This term he is taking a required class in college mathematics, and he is concerned because his high school math performance was weak. He knows he must make consistent, strategic effort in studying for this class if he is to achieve the B he has determined as his goal. He believes he can accomplish his goal (*believable*). Although his prior math performance was weak, he did complete high school math and pass the mathematics portion of a college entrance exam (*realistic*). He wants this goal and is willing to sacrifice procrastination to achieve it (*desirable*); and he has set a specific result, a semester grade of B (*measurable*).

Action statement. The first step in translating a goal into an action is to specifically create an action statement. Tim writes,

I will work on my math homework at least one hour each day, five days a week.

Tim has never before committed to study the same subject each day; thus, this behavior is a new or *innovative* action. It is important to note again that an action statement can *innovate, maintain, problem solve,* or *reduce/expand* our behaviors:

- **Innovate.** Depart from current routine or former habits and experiences such as beginning a new relationship, going to the library to study, taking exploratory courses in different disciplines, pursuing a leadership role in an organization, or initiating an exercise program.

- **Maintain.** Continue performance in some area at its current acceptable level. Examples include persisting in community service involvement, continuing good class attendance, and attending 12-step programs.

- **Problem solve.** Institute action to resolve the difficulty *or* take preventive action so that the problem is unlikely to occur. Examples include using mediation to resolve roommate disagreements, balancing a checkbook routinely, and keeping a calendar of assignments.

- **Reduce/expand.** Decrease or increase specific actions such as exercising, eating, studying, working, watching TV, smoking, being jealous, procrastinating, or displaying road rage (Lee, 1978, pp. 21–26).

Let us return to Tim's action statement:

I will work on my math homework at least one hour each day, five days a week, beginning the first week of school.

In this example, working on math homework is the specific behavior. The unit of measurement or amount of behavior to be accomplished is one hour per day, five days a week.

Strategies and activities. The second step is to identify when, where, and how long the activity will take place.

I plan to work on math homework in the math lab from 12:00–1:00 P.M., Monday through Friday, so I can get help when I have trouble.

Gather materials. Step three is to gather the materials, supplies, and resources needed to accomplish the action statement. Examples relevant to Tim's action statement are the location and schedule of the math lab, a textbook and workbook, a calculator, the syllabus, class notes, pencils, and the names of other students in the class.

Price tag. Step four is called the price tag. Since every goal has a price, Tim must state what he must give up to obtain his goal. These sacrifices will likely include time, energy, money, and even the postponement of other goals. For example, *I'll* *have to eat lunch after math lab; otherwise I'll get too sleepy while trying to do my math. I'll record my favorite show while I'm gone.*

Rewards and punishments. Step five is identifying how to use rewards (including what you say to yourself) and punishments to help meet action statements. For example, Tim might make the following promises to himself: *Each day I work at the math lab, I can go home and eat a good lunch while I watch the recording of my favorite show. Each day I do not work at the math lab, I will not watch my show or go to the student recreation center.*

Set specific time lines. Step six is to evaluate the action by setting specific deadlines (time lines). Tim creates the following time line: *I will begin my actions the first week of school, and I will evaluate my progress after three weeks by averaging all my homework grades and talking with my math tutor. After the first exam, I will reevaluate whether I need to increase or decrease my study time in the math lab.* Tim chooses to use his homework and test grades as the measure of his progress toward achieving his goal of a B in the course.

> ## TRANSLATING GOALS INTO AN ACTION PLAN
>
> 1. Create an action statement.
> 2. Identify strategies and activities.
> 3. Gather materials, supplies, and other resources.
> 4. Determine the price tag.
> 5. Identify how to use rewards and punishments.
> 6. Evaluate by setting specific time lines.

exercise 8.5

Putting Your Goals into Action

Take the extra step by putting your goals into an action plan. The time it may take to rework your goals into an action plan will certainly pay off in the end. Use some of the goals you have already written or create five to seven new goals—especially goals you can complete during this semester. Try to have several outcome as well as process goals. Then address each of the following directives as you put each of your goals into an action plan.

1. Create an action statement.
2. Identify the strategies and activities.
3. List the supplies, materials, and resources you will need.
4. Determine the price tag.
5. Identify rewards and punishments.
6. Evaluate with specific time lines.

SELF-REGULATION

The previous example of Tim's efforts to achieve his goal of a B in math illuminates the specificity and effort essential to the achievement of his goal. As humans, *our effort to monitor and regulate our own behaviors, cognitions (thinking), and emotions* is called **self-regulation,** that is, our ability to manipulate ourselves to reach specific goals. In psychology, such self-regulation is labeled internal locus (place) of control, as opposed to external locus of control, in which other people control or direct our behaviors. It is a normal desire to want to control our own behaviors; witness the three-year-old who insists on doing it (whatever it is) herself. Developing our self-regulation skills occurs throughout our lives. In our culture, most adolescents struggle with independence and responsibility, and they vacillate between dependence and independence in their academic lives as well as other areas for several years.

The college environment is an especially difficult one for many students, for it presupposes a high degree of internal locus of control, or self-regulation. Some students can regulate their own behaviors appropriately, but many students struggle with the simple tasks of going to class, doing assignments in a timely manner, maintaining their finances, and even doing their laundry. Especially for the students who rely heavily on their parents, the need for self-regulation can be intense.

Academic Self-Regulation

We can deliberately increase our self-regulation by consciously using strategies developed by cognitive behavioral psychologists. Although the strategies work for all sorts of behaviors, the remainder of this chapter and the next chapter stress their application in academic settings. Cognitive behavioral psychologists view every action through a triple lens: first, the observable behavior itself; second, the feelings of the person doing the behavior; and, third, the person's thoughts about the behavior. **Academic self-regulated learning** is *your ability to monitor and control your own behavior, thinking, and emotions as you acquire knowledge and skills during learning* (Zimmerman, 1989).

An example of this triple view would be the work we did with Jack, a sophomore communications major. Jack came to us because he was in danger of losing his scholarship. He had to maintain a 2.5 GPA, and he was perilously close to failing Spanish because he

SELF-REGULATED LEARNING

A good analogy of self-regulated learning is to think of a thermostat and how it monitors and regulates room temperature. The goal of the thermostat is the preset desired temperature.

"Self-regulated learning is your ability to monitor and control your own behavior, thinking, and emotions as you acquire knowledge and skills during learning" (Zimmerman, 1989).

Setting a goal is your "preset desired attempt at change."

routinely missed class at 8 A.M. The obvious behavior is that Jack would stay in bed rather than get up when his alarm sounded. He reported that when he heard his alarm, he would tell himself that he could sleep just a few more minutes (and he believed that!). Those were his thoughts, but he felt guilty and angry when he woke up at 9 A.M. With Jack, we looked at his behavior, his thoughts, and his feelings. Later in this chapter, we review how Jack was able to change his behavior through self-regulation.

exercise 8.6

Self-Regulation

What are the behaviors, thoughts, and feelings that interfere with your academic success? Becoming aware of these behaviors, thoughts, and feelings is the first step in learning to use self-regulated learning strategies.

List five academic behaviors that interfere with your academic success.

Sample: *I watch too much television.*

1.

2.

3.

4.

5.

List five academic thoughts that interfere with your academic success.

Sample: *Before I take an exam, I always think I m going to fail.*

1.

2.

3.

4.

5.

List five emotions (feelings) that interfere with your academic success.

Sample: *I have continual fear of not succeeding when I am in a math course.*

1.

2.

3.

4.

5.

Timeliness

Of all the ways in which college students want to change, one topic always tops the list. College students procrastinate, some more than others, but all do it. They do not do what they believe they need to do *when* they need to do it. Whether it is studying for a psychology test, paying bills, writing letters, beginning a research paper, or simply cleaning their room, they are experts at delaying, denying, rationalizing, avoiding. Some are perfectionists; others are afraid of success or failure. Some simply rebel at any authority figures, including professors. Sometimes they lack the academic skills necessary; sometimes they are bored or lazy. Whatever the reasons and however the procrastination is expressed, most students want to *accomplish their goals in a timely manner, without guilt or self-punishment.* We have labeled that skill **timeliness.**

> ### • • • LIZ AND MARCUS • • •
> ### *Struggling with timeliness*
>
> *Liz and Marcus have been dating for more than a semester. Their relationship is stable and enjoyable, for friendship is its foundation. They are both sophomores, she a sociology major and he an information systems major. Although both are able and ambitious students, they struggle with timeliness in their academic work, although their procrastination takes different forms and has different causes. Together, they come to the campus learning lab in search of help in overcoming procrastination.*
>
> *Marcus describes himself as a perfectionist; he prefers to do a job well, or not at all. He enjoys his two information systems classes and has easily met every project deadline. He is also current with his Western civilization course, but he admits the reason is that the professor gives weekly quizzes and frequent exams. The work that he routinely avoids is the reading for his world literature course and studying for the lecture portion of chemistry. When queried, Marcus describes his lack of interest in the literature readings. The readings are long and tedious for him; they are not contemporary writings and often they are in translation.*

Marcus is an introverted-sensing-thinking-judging type (ISTJ) on the MBTI (see the "Preferences" section in Chapter 7 to review your type). He prefers pragmatic, concrete, current writings. The readings in world literature seem abstract and distant to him. There is no daily work required, and a midterm and a final exam are the only tests. A long analytical research paper comparing two classic works is due toward the end of the term.

As Marcus reflects over his continued procrastination in reading for the literature class, he realizes that he prefers classes with frequent assignments and projects. Deadlines help motivate him. When he understands the specific expectations of a professor, his anxiety lessens. He also enjoys the sense of completion when he has done a project well. Marcus's insight is that his literature class is open ended; he is simply to read, deeply and with understanding. Then he is to think about what he read from an analytical viewpoint. The midterm and final exams are primarily essay. To Marcus, these instructions seem vague, and he is uncomfortable with the lack of structure. The research paper is even more formidable, because the professor expects each student to create a topic. How can Marcus do a perfect job if he does not really understand what the criteria are?

Marcus simply does not know where to begin. As he works with the learning specialist, he creates a study plan for literature that includes some rapid library or online research about each assigned reading, a realistic reading schedule, and a commitment to find a classmate who is willing to discuss the readings with him twice a week. He sets his goal of achieving a B in the course and creates his own structure by using the six-step model for translating goals into actions.

Chemistry is a different experience for Marcus. He likes the lab, but the lectures are dry and dull. The subject is demanding, and he realizes that he simply does not have enough time to do extremely well in this course because his information systems classes are so time demanding. With only one high school chemistry class, Marcus has little prior information, and the college lectures often seem confusing. He copies what the professor writes on the board or the PowerPoint slides, but he rarely reviews his notes or uses the textbook as a resource for clarification. One thing Marcus does, however, is punish himself verbally for not studying chemistry. He avoids and he punishes; neither is helpful.

Marcus's first task is to set a specific goal for this course. He struggles with setting a grade goal, for he is normally an ambitious student. Finally, after looking at his commitments this term, he decides that a C is a realistic and good enough grade under these circumstances. Accepting that goal is difficult, for Marcus does tend to be a perfectionist, but his re-alism prevails. Once the goal is set, Marcus will have little difficulty translating it into action. Even though he is an introvert, he decides to join a study group that meets immediately after the lecture. There he will com-pare his lecture notes with those of others, and the group will discuss the important concepts just presented. Later each day, he will work at least a few practice problems and create some vocabulary cards for technical terms and formulas. The specificity of the tasks matches his preferences.

Liz listens carefully as Marcus speaks with the learning specialist, but none of the situations seem to match her circumstances. When the specialist turns to her, she begins to quickly list all the obligations she faces with her membership in the sociology club and a campus min-istry as well as a Greek social organization. She is always tired be-cause she is missing sleep, and she exercises only irregularly. She checks her email several times a day and is never without her cell phone. She loves the excitement of being busy and loudly proclaims that she works better under pressure. Liz asserts that she can pull an all-nighter, and she enjoys the adrenaline rush of just barely meeting a deadline.

Liz is an extroverted-intuitive-thinking-perceiver (ENTP), and her preferences lead her to be interested in many fascinating activities, peo-ple, and ideas. She has a hard time focusing, and it is easy for her to be-come overwhelmed when she realizes how much work she has neglected and how many commitments she has made. It is typical for a person with these preferences to neglect his or her own health (Provost, 1988). The first step to timeliness for Liz is to realistically determine how much she can (and should) do as a college student with a full load of classes. That means learning to say no to many of the social and leadership opportu-nities that come her way. The next step is to take the time to sleep and exercise. A daily planner will help her organize the specific tasks for each day, and it will also show her when she can study for small amounts of time, especially during the day. Additionally, the planner will also help her plan each week, balancing academic, social, and per-sonal demands.

By far the largest issue for Liz is her enjoyment of the "magical feel-ing in being able to wait until the last minute, then work frantically, and end up with a decent grade" (Provost, 1988, p. 9). This strategy worked well for Liz in high school and helped her survive in her college freshman year, but as a sophomore, it is a deadly trait. It eliminates the possibility of excellence, and it delays the acquisition of professional work habits.

Procrastination Issues and Remedies

Timeliness is easy to define: *It is the accomplishment of our goals in a timely manner, without guilt or self-punishment.* In other words, it is knowing what we have decided to do and then choosing to do it. What stands in the way of that productive behavior is *when we deliberately choose not to do the necessary action to reach a goal in a timely way,* that is when we **procrastinate.** "Whether procrastination is a problem or not depends on the degree of impact the procrastination has on an individual's life" (Provost, 1988, p. 3). This behavior often has complex emotional roots, and it can greatly damage our self-esteem.

Many factors can increase the likelihood that we will procrastinate on academic tasks. Some of the most obvious are the high school experience of waiting until the last minute and still being academically successful, distractions that are interesting and entertaining, the juggling of too many demands, rebellion, perfectionism, and lack of interest.

If procrastination is damaging your ability to reach your goals, then the following sections may help you determine why you procrastinate and how you can decrease procrastination and increase timeliness in academic behaviors.

Strategy 1: Become Aware of Your Personality Type

As we have demonstrated in the example of Liz and Marcus, timeliness (and its evil twin, procrastination) varies dramatically across personality type. Most of us struggle toward timeliness much of our lives, but we believe that there are two specific cognitive methods of combating our tendencies toward procrastination. An awareness of our personality type can give us insight into the type of tasks that we are likely to avoid so that we can initiate useful actions to counter our inbred tendencies.

People with preferences **ENTP** and **ENFP**

- have difficulty focusing due to interests in so many different things.
- overcommit and overinvolve in social, personal, and academic arenas, so they delay beginning tasks until the last minute.
- neglect health issues, especially sleep and regular exercise.
- enjoy the adrenaline rush of last-minute completion.

Remedy. Practice setting realistic goals and priorities in relation to time available. Use Sunday evenings to review the upcoming week to prevent overlooking assignments, appointments, etc.

People with preferences **INFP** and **INTP**

- often delay the writing/production phase of large papers and projects because they have trouble ending the idea/research phase.

- experience a painful gap between their ideal performance and practical limitations of time and resources, creating a perfectionistic attitude.

- often criticize themselves intensively for procrastinating and use this criticism as motivation.

- become deeply interested in one subject or project and ignore all other assignments.

Remedy. On large projects, set intermediate completion goals and rewards. If there is a "writing block," use prewriting techniques to start writing. Talk with a counselor about changing perfectionistic expectations.

People with preferences **ESFP** and **ESTP**

- thrive on immediate activities and interactions with others, rather than studying (delayed rewards).

- find inactive, unexciting tasks boring.

Remedy. Reflect on long-term goals and feelings about those goals; then translate long-term goals into practical actions and use concrete reward systems for completing even the smallest tasks.

People with preferences **ISFP** and **ISTP**

- avoid academic work to engage in immediate, more enjoyable activities.

Remedy. Identify strongest motivators; then set a study schedule with specific rewards for completing each task.

People with preferences **ISTJ** and **ISFJ**

- look organized but often collect too much data.

- have an "all or nothing" attitude; they often avoid jobs that cannot be done perfectly.

- may become discouraged and avoid the task altogether.

Remedy. Try to see the "big picture" of assignments and test preparation by looking for main ideas and patterns of thought. Accept that there is not enough time to do everything perfectly, and deliberately choose a realistic, acceptable level of desired performance.

People with preferences **INFJ** and **INTJ**

- appear organized, but tension can exist between the enticement of many ideas and the desire to complete assignments.
- may become angry and impatient with themselves, producing secondary obstacles to completing tasks.
- also harbor perfectionistic tendencies, which leads to difficulty in starting tasks.

Remedy. Understand the innate tension between the desire to continue discovering and the desire to complete the task. Organize ideas to determine a starting place, confront negative self-talk, and maintain focus on producing a "good enough" product.

People with preferences **ESTJ** and **ENTJ**

- may avoid tasks that provoke feelings of incompetence or powerlessness.
- may avoid tasks perceived as uninteresting or useless.
- procrastinate, which fosters intense self-criticism.

Remedy. Begin a task quickly, if only for a few minutes (break the ice). Write specific tasks for each day and use verbal rewards. Talk with a counselor about strong or recurring feelings of incompetence or anxiety.

People with preferences **ESFJ** and **ENFJ**

- exhibit high standards of promptness, rarely procrastinating unless in situational difficulties, usually concerning a relationship.

Remedy. Speak or write about the conflict with trusted others to clarify feelings; then try to resolve the conflict.

Strategy 2: Change Irrational Thinking to Rational Thinking

We can become aware of the irrational thinking that fosters so much avoidance behavior and deliberately change our internal dialog (self-talk) in order to slowly change our belief system. If we listen carefully and hear exactly what we are saying, then an analysis of that awareness can help us change our self-talk into messages that will promote timeliness. Here is a simple example: *I can't learn this subject. I've never been able to understand this stuff.* (This type of self-talk promotes procrastination; it is based on fear of failure, feelings of incompetence, lack of self-efficacy.) We can then change that statement to *If I get help and I make a concerted effort, I can learn this subject.* (This self-talk promotes timeliness.) Here is another example of transformed self-talk. We can change the statement, *If I do too well, more will be expected of me* (based on fear of maintaining performance level or fear of success), to *I don't have to do everything at this level; I can choose (control) what I excel in.* A common set of unhelpful self-talk statements is *Why should I have to learn this? I don't like the teacher. This subject bores me. My parents are making me be here.* All are probably based on rebellion or anger at others who are trying to control the speaker. The simplest transformation is *This is what I want; I have chosen to be here; I will consciously choose appropriate behaviors to reach my goals.* Another common statement students frequently make is *I'll study later, after . . . [the movie, the party, the meeting].* Such statements are almost always unrealistic; we are lying to ourselves if we believe that we will sit down and study after a social activity. Remember that it is imperative that we keep our promises to ourselves in order to trust ourselves. A far more realistic and helpful self-statement is *I'll study for [x amount of time] and complete these specific tasks before I go out.*

SOME CAUSES OF PROCRASTINATION AND EXAMPLES OF THE RESULTING IRRATIONAL THINKING

- Fear of Success—*If I succeed then others will expect more and more of me.*

- Fear of Failure—*Since I failed before I will fail again.*

- Rebellion/Anger—*This will hurt them much more than it will hurt me.*

- Lack of Self-Efficacy—*I can't do it; I am not good enough.*

- Unrealistic Goals—*I can push myself to do more and more.*

- Low Frustration Level—*I am no good at this and will never succeed.*

- Disorganization—*I'll find it when I need it.*

- Perfectionism—*I have to make everything perfect.*

- Lack of Rewards—*I need others to motivate me.*

- Inappropriate Commitments—*I can do it all.*

---

exercise 8.7

Procrastination Survey

We often procrastinate due to irrational beliefs. However, once we become aware of those beliefs, we can begin to make positive changes toward timeliness. Complete this exercise to assess your procrastination tendencies.

Read each irrational belief and the accompanying question and check the appropriate response. For any answer for which you checked "yes" or "sometimes," examine the irrational belief and change the statement to a rational one. Here is an example:

Irrational belief: *Since I failed before I will fail again.*

Rational belief: *Just because I failed before does not mean I will fail this time.*

If I succeed then others will expect more and more of me.

1. Do you ever feel too discouraged to work on a project because if you succeed someone might ask you to do more?

____ Yes ____ No ____ Sometimes

Rational belief:

Since I failed before I will fail again.

2. Have you ever felt too discouraged to work on a project because of a previous negative experience with a similar activity?

____ Yes ____ No ____ Sometimes

Rational belief:

This will hurt them much more than it will hurt me.

3. Do you sometimes quit working on an important task just to "get even" with someone?

____ Yes ____ No ____ Sometimes

Rational belief:

I can't do it; I am not good enough.

4. Do you continually question your ability or skill level?

____ Yes ____ No ____ Sometimes

Rational belief:

I can push myself to do more and more.

5. Do you try to do too many projects at one time?

____ Yes ____ No ____ Sometimes

Rational belief:

I am no good at this and will never succeed.

6. Do you often give up trying to understand an assignment?

____ Yes ____ No ____ Sometimes

Rational belief:

I'll find it when I need it.

7. Does a lack of planning or time management interfere with your ability to complete projects?

   _____ Yes _____ No _____ Sometimes

   Rational belief:

I have to make everything perfect.

8. Do you feel compelled to keep working and working on a task even though you know you could stop and receive a good grade?

   _____ Yes _____ No _____ Sometimes

   Rational belief:

I need others to motivate me.

9. Do you usually need reinforcements from others (praise, material goods, money) to motivate you to complete a task?

   _____ Yes _____ No _____ Sometimes

   Rational belief:

I can do it all.

10. Do you tend to overschedule yourself and take on too much?

    _____ Yes _____ No _____ Sometimes

    Rational belief:

Strategy 3: Change Negative Self-Talk to Positive Self-Talk

Transforming self-talk is a primary strategy of self-regulation of any behavior. Such transformation has the title *cognitive restructuring,* a type of psychological counseling called Rational Emotive Behavior Therapy, pioneered by Albert Ellis (Ellis & Harper, 1975). When we become aware of what we say to ourselves and thoughtfully analyze those statements, we have the ability to discern whether those statements are logical, reasonable, and rational. If they are not, then we can change them. Interestingly, our feelings often follow our thoughts, as well as generate them. Thus, transforming our self-talk can have long-term effects on our beliefs about our abilities and our worth.

Negative Self-Talk	Positive Self-Talk
I'll finish the assignment after the party.	*I'll finish the assignment now so that I can go to the party and not feel guilty.*
This stuff is so boring; I just can't learn it.	*I need to pass this course, and I am smart enough to learn the material.*
This material is too hard for me. I'll never understand it.	*This material is tough. I can learn it if I find some help from a tutor or the teacher.*

Strategy 4: Try Study Starts

If you have difficulty starting to study (but once you start, you keep going), then try a technique called *study starts*. A study start occurs when we promise to do at least 10 minutes of study before a certain time of day. For example, *I will start reading the assigned chapter in history by 5 P.M. this afternoon and spend at least 10 minutes on the task.* A study start breaks the impasse, the logjam, and once we have started, the likelihood is that we will continue. Some students contract with themselves to do a study start before 1 P.M. and another by 5 P.M.

Additional Suggestions

If you have difficulty completing long projects,

- Set a specific date, time, and location to start. *(I will go to the library Wednesday after lunch.)*

- Talk yourself into starting by planning an immediate reward afterward. *(When I finish working in the library, I'll treat myself to an hour at the recreation center.)*

- Break the task into small, concrete parts. *(I'll list all the parts of a paper— potential topics, focused topic, thesis statement or idea, outline of points to cover, support for each point, etc.)*

- Choose one part and commit to working on it for 5–10 minutes only; then reassess whether to continue working or quit. *(I'll just brainstorm and write down ideas for my paper; then I'll decide whether to start my outline or come back tomorrow.)*

If you can start a project but have difficulty persisting to completion, then try these suggestions:

- Use self-talk to encourage/motivate yourself. *(I can finish this assignment on time if I stick to my schedule.)*

- Set interim due dates for each part with tentative rewards for each one. *(I'll put a calendar on my wall and list each due date. For each part I complete, I'll go to my favorite place to eat.)*

- Choose a partner who is working on the same or similar assignment and encourage each other to reach your goals. *(We'll meet at the library at 2 P.M. and find sources together.)*

- Maintain a system of rewards throughout the project. *(I've been making real progress, and I cannot quit now. So I'll be careful to keep giving myself rewards for each and every step.)*

We have been using examples about studying and completing projects, but many other behaviors impact academic performance. Remember Jack, the student who was not routinely going to his Spanish class? His procrastination was simple; he was not getting out of bed in time to go to class. First, we confronted Jack about the self-deception in his self-talk as he pressed the snooze button, and we recommended two immediate changes—moving the clock across the room so he has to get up to turn it off and changing his self-talk to be more realistic, such as *I have to go to Spanish if I want to keep my scholarship!* Next, we suggested that he reward himself for getting up, and he chose that he would stop at the student union on the way to class and buy coffee. Then Jack admitted that he often watched TV until the early morning hours, so he was not getting enough sleep. The next part of his self-regulation was to go to sleep before midnight the night before his early classes. As Jack brought his class attendance under control, his feelings turned from guilt to confidence. His thoughts, feelings, and behavior became positive and congruent and contributed to the completion of his goals.

CONCLUSION

Formulating goals that rest on the foundation of our values allows us to direct our time and attention so as to realize our dreams. Independence and midlife are critical times in our lives when selecting wise goals is especially important because these goals are destined to drive our efforts for many years.

Pintrich (1995) strongly validates the triple view of behavior, affect (feeling), and cognition (thought) as the entry point to self-regulation when he states that academic self-regulation is "the active, goal-directed, self-control of behavior, motivation [and affect], and cognition for academic tasks by an individual student" (p. 5). In other words, we can actively control our behavior through access to resources, that is, time, study environment, peers, teachers. We can control and change our motivational beliefs such as self-efficacy and emotions and affect (such as anxiety) to improve our learning. We can control cognitive strategies for learning, including self-talk, and we can use our self-understanding to recognize our own preferences and strategies especially helpful to counter procrastination.

SUMMARY

- Fantasies are ideas that cannot happen because we do not work to achieve them.

- Dreams are possible.

- Goals set direction for our actions and our lives.

- Goal areas include education and training, career and job development; spiritual religious, and character building; health and emotional; physical and recreational; social, relationships, and family; financial; and civic, service, and volunteerism.

- Goal options include expanding, reducing, maintaining, innovating, or problem-solving a behavior.

- Outcome goals are those goals that you set to achieve a final product such as a final grade in a course or a certain GPA. Process goals are the strategies involved to reach an outcome goal.

- Some goals are immediate (today!), some are short term (1 year or less), some are intermediate (between 1 and 10 years), and others are long term (10 years or more).

- To achieve a goal it should be believable, realistic, desirable, and measurable.

- To set a goal action plan, create an action statement, identify strategies and activities, gather materials, determine the price tag, identify how to use rewards and punishments, and evaluate by setting specific time lines.

- Self-regulation is your ability to monitor your own behavior, thinking, and emotions to adjust to fit the demands of the situation.

- Academic self-regulated learning is your ability to monitor and control your own behavior, thinking, and emotions as you acquire knowledge and skills during learning.

- Timeliness is the accomplishment of one's goals in a timely manner, without guilt or self-punishment. Procrastination stands in the way of timeliness.

- Procrastination is when we deliberately choose not to do the necessary action to reach a goal in a timely way.

- Remedies for procrastination include becoming aware of your personality type, becoming aware of irrational thinking, becoming aware of negative self-talk, and trying study starts.

KEY CONCEPTS

Academic self-regulation

Achievable goals: believable, realistic, desirable, measurable

Dreams

Fantasies

Goal action plan

Goal areas

Goal dimensions: outcome and process

Goal lengths: immediate, short term, intermediate, long term

Goal options: expand, reduce, maintain, innovate, problem solve

Goals

Procrastination remedies

Self-regulation

Timeliness

GUIDED JOURNAL QUESTIONS

1. Discuss the dreams that you had for yourself when you were very young. Now discuss your current dreams. How are they the same, and how have they changed?

2. Discuss three core values that guide your quality world. How have you come to hold these values? How have you incorporated these values into your life?

3. What goals have you previously set for yourself that have been achieved? What strategies did you implement for your success?

4. What goals have you set for yourself that you have not been able to achieve? Discuss the reasons why you have been unsuccessful.

5. When you set an achievable goal you must make it believable. A believable goal means we have the talent and the will to achieve it. What does having "the will" to achieve a goal mean to you?

6. Every goal has a price tag (a sacrifice you must make to achieve a goal). Usually this means that you must give up something pleasurable to engage in something less pleasurable. What current price tags (sacrifices) are you having to make as you try to achieve several of your goals?

7. To use self-regulated learning, you need to set goals and self-monitor your progress in each class. Set an academic goal for each of your classes (either process or outcome). How you will monitor your progress?

8. We learned in this chapter that we can self-regulate our behaviors, thinking, and emotions. In what ways can you self-regulate your behaviors, your thinking, and your emotions?

9. What suggestions (other than the ones you read from the text) do you have for Marcus and Liz to help them improve their timeliness and avoid procrastination?

10. Of the three likely causes of procrastination (personality characteristics, irrational beliefs, and negative self-talk), which one do you struggle with the most? Explain.

The Last Word

My fantasy growing up was to be world famous. As I grew older, I dreamed of leaving this world in a better place than I found it.

—*Russ Hodges*

9

Making Behaviors Work for You

Walking the academic tightrope.

In this chapter, we explore three primary self-regulatory methods for managing our lives so that we are more likely to live a balanced and fulfilled life. These methods are key behaviors, use of time, and self-change. The following chapter presents some powerful methods for stress management. As in all other parts of our lives, our ability to use these methods wisely develops over time. We believe that there are four basic stages of self-regulation through which we move as we develop.

We begin this chapter with a concept explaining the peak experiences of human endeavor—a concept entitled flow. Humans long for those experiences and hope to create them in daily lives. Our own reflections and teaching experience have convinced us that competent self-regulation increases the likelihood that flow will occur.

SELF-ASSESSMENT: Balancing My Life

The challenge of any college student is to balance his or her life between hard work and pleasure. You have heard it said before, "Attending college can be the very best time of your life." With 5 being "Almost Always" and 1 being "Almost Never," assess your ability to effectively manage your life. Rate each of the following statements honestly by circling the appropriate number. Completing this exercise will help you identify areas of concern you may have about your ability to cope and change.

	Almost Always		Sometimes		Almost Never
1. My life flows well without much difficulty.	5	4	3	2	1
2. When my life becomes too chaotic, I quickly build in structure to help myself.	5	4	3	2	1
3. Having flexibility in my daily schedule works well for me.	5	4	3	2	1
4. I prioritize my daily tasks effectively.	5	4	3	2	1
5. I resist temptation "to play" when I have important work to complete.	5	4	3	2	1
6. I spend an appropriate amount of time organizing and planning.	5	4	3	2	1
7. I recognize important changes I need to make in my behavior.	5	4	3	2	1
8. I make important changes in my behavior when necessary.	5	4	3	2	1
9. I change my behavior without being forced by others.	5	4	3	2	1

10. I reward myself for a job well done.	5	4	3	2	1
11. I punish myself when I break a commitment to myself.	5	4	3	2	1
12. I balance work and pleasure effectively.	5	4	3	2	1

Add up the numbers circled. Your total score will be between 12 and 60. The higher your score, the more likely you feel confident about your ability to balance your time and cope with difficulties. For total scores below 36, write or reflect on items for which you have concerns. Also, consider talking with a trusted friend, a family member, a teacher, or an advisor.

FLOW

Most of us can describe experiences in which our efforts were so engrossing and enjoyable that we realized later that we were in as "positive a state as it is possible to feel" (Csikszentmihalyi, 1999, p. 825). At those times, we are so imbedded in the moment that we are not even aware we are happy; it is only after the fact that we have a sense of what has happened. Csikszentmihalyi (1999) labels such experiences as flow or autotelic. He writes of a famous lyricist and former poet laureate of the United States who describes his flow experience, writing, in the following way:

> You lose your sense of time, you're completely enraptured, you are completely caught up in what you're doing, and you are sort of swayed by the possibilities you see in this work. . . . The idea is to be so, so saturated with it that there's no future or past, it's just an extended present in which you are . . . making meaning. (Csikszentmihalyi, 1996, p.121)

Of course, we would all want our work to allow "the full expression of what is best in us, something we experience as rewarding and enjoyable" (Gardner, Csikszentmihalyi, & Damon, 2001, p. 9). Goal setting, self-regulation, and learning strategies are the tools that can help us have more flow experiences in our lives and especially in our work. We have chosen to share these ideas with you because we believe that study and learning is your work as a student and that you can experience these activities as flow experiences. For those of you who have found academics boring most of the time or only slightly bearable because of the potential rewards, our contention that study and learning can be deeply rewarding, both intellectually and emotionally, might seem silly. However, that is exactly what we contend, and we ask that you be willing to listen to the arguments in this and subsequent chapters with an open mind. After all, if we are right, then academics could become an entirely different experience for you. If we are wrong, then you have only lost a few minutes of reading.

In thousands of interviews, across age, culture, gender, and job, eight characteristics were mentioned repeatedly to describe such an enjoyable experience:

1. We have clear goals every step of the way.

2. We receive immediate feedback to our actions.

3. Our skills and the challenges we face are in good balance.

4. Our action and awareness are merged; we are not mentally separate from what we are doing.

5. We are totally focused on the task without distractions.

6. We are too involved to be concerned with failure (self-efficacy).

7. We are too involved to be self-conscious.

8. Our sense of the quantity of time passing is distorted.

If these conditions exist, then we enjoy the experience for its own sake; that is, the experience is autotelic (Csikszentmihalyi, 1996). "We feel 100 percent alive when we are so committed to the task at hand that we lose track of time, of our interests—even of our own existence" (Gardner et al., 2001, p. 5).

Clearly, flow is a desired state and far more possible than many cynics would allow. In this chapter, we weave some new ideas about self-regulation together with the beginning concepts we presented in Chapter 8. Together they form an extraordinary set of tools you can use to manage your life well. The first new idea is the vision that our ability to regulate our own behavior develops over time, in four definitive stages.

STAGES OF SELF-REGULATORY ABILITY

We gradually develop self-regulatory ability from early childhood, and we are heavily influenced by our families and our school experiences. The habits of academic self-regulation coalesce in elementary school, but puberty and adolescence strain those habits. By the time students arrive in college, their self-regulatory abilities are extremely varied. Some students easily slip into the demands of college life whereas others struggle.

The stages of self-regulatory ability are chaos, stability, flexibility, and mastery, but our progression through these stages is complicated. It is possible, even likely, to live simultaneously in several stages in differing areas of our lives. For example, a student might have personal tasks such as budgeting and exercise under control through a rigid set of rules but she often delays writing papers or studying for tests.

Stage 1: Chaos

Most of us have experienced academic chaos at some time in our lives—those times when we lose track of assignments and due dates or we are so far behind that we cannot even decide where to begin. Occasionally, students even stop going to class without consulting their teacher or any campus office. Sometimes, such chaos is triggered by troubled personal relationships, economic or family crises, depression, or major illness. Addictions of any kind also plunge a person into chaos. We know we are in chaos when our behaviors are routinely, even outrageously, inconsistent with our goals.

Climbing out of the pit of academic chaos is difficult, but possible. Usually a first step is to talk with a campus adviser or teacher in order to outline the dimensions of the chaos. List the areas in which you have some control and those areas that are most frighteningly out of control. What information do you need and where can you find it? Set some specific tasks about finding that information in a timely way.

If the chaos is the result of personal problems, then those problems must be ameliorated before academic order can be restored. Speaking with a campus counselor or your pastor is a sensible first step. Family emergencies or financial problems may necessarily supersede academics, and you may find it necessary to withdraw for the remainder of the term. Addictions are best helped by combining individual counseling and 12-step groups, such as Alcoholics Anonymous, Narcotics Anonymous, or Gamblers Anonymous.

If the chaos is solely academic, some obvious strategies are to find the syllabus for each course and reread all the requirements; then go to each professor during office hours to ascertain what your status in that course is. Discern whether each course is salvageable after your consultation with the professor. If it is not, then withdraw immediately. If it is salvageable, then make a clear and concise list of the priority tasks and set due dates for each one. Sometimes a professor is willing to negotiate your reentry into a course and even give you some extended due dates.

Stage 2: Stability

The logical path from chaos to stability is to consciously set and follow rules. To avoid the chaos that can engulf beginning freshmen, they often need to set the absolute rule of class attendance: to attend every class, without exception.

Another example of an academic behavior that can move students out of chaos is to maintain a master calendar daily with all assignments and due dates written down. Setting aside a certain time and place for daily study, without exception, also helps students move toward stability. Fear is often a strong motivator in this process, because students in chaos are usually miserable and confused.

The rigidity of such rules is comforting to many students and provides a structure lacking in the collegiate atmosphere. Once stability becomes our normal academic demeanor, we have school tasks under basic control. We know what is required in every course, we have set goals, our behaviors are sufficient to achieve our goals, and we begin to build confidence in our ability to follow the rules we have set.

Stage 3: Flexibility

As our confidence grows, we begin to trust that we have the self-control to carry out the necessary behaviors to reach our academic goals. We realize that we can adjust our behaviors to the circumstances and that we can still achieve our goals. In other words, we become more flexible. Part of the flexibility stage is the conscious experimentation with the rules from the earlier stage of stability. How absolute do the rules have to be? When can you break the rules or suspend them without damage to your achievements? For example, if you had set Tuesday evenings as a primary study time for history and one Monday your good friend calls and says he will be in your town on Tuesday and wants to take you to dinner, you will want to be with him. What happens to the study time? If you are at the flexibility stage, you will simply reschedule that time for earlier on Tuesday or later in the week and know that you will accomplish the necessary study in a timely way. Gradually, rules become principles, and we have the experience to judge each situation. In this stage, confidence fosters calm, and we tend to be less anxious. Our achievement of this stage is a powerful source of academic self-esteem.

Stage 4: Mastery

The last stage, mastery, occurs when the principles and the adjustments take place automatically, unconsciously. We have internalized useful habits. Managing our behaviors seems easy, and we can trust ourselves to manage the elements of our daily lives to foster the quality of our experiences. A good vision of a master student is an expert surfer who rides the waves with seeming ease. It takes effort and attention for that surfer to adapt to all the changes in the environment. A master student does the same. She accommodates the changes in work schedules, the demands of everyday problems, the vicissitudes of life. It is in the last two stages, flexibility and mastery, that academic flow experiences are likely to occur.

Possible Regression

An important realization about this concept of the stages of self-regulatory ability is that new and challenging environments can force us to regress to an earlier stage. For example, many high school students reach the flexibility stage when they are juniors and seniors. However, under the challenges of entering college, they may regress to chaos or the rigid rules of stability. The same sort of regression can happen to college graduates who enter their first professional job. We can usually regain our normal stage through the conscious adoption of earlier techniques.

---

exercise 9.2

Your Self-Regulatory Ability

Your awareness of the different stages of self-regulatory ability and how they apply to your life is critical to your academic success as a college student. Answer each of the following questions. This exercise will help you analyze your current stage of self-regulatory ability and its impact on your life as a college student.

1. Which stage do you think best describes your current stage of academic self-regulatory ability?

   _____ Chaos _____ Stability _____ Flexibility _____Mastery

2. Why did you choose this stage? Give three concrete examples to support your choice.

3. How does being in this stage help or hinder your academic success as a college student?

4. If you are currently in the stage of mastery, what three things can you do to ensure that you do not regress to a previous stage? If you are currently in the stage of chaos, stability, or flexibility, what three things can you do to reach the next level of self-regulatory ability?

PROCESS OF IMPROVING SELF-REGULATION

As we gradually pull our behaviors under control, we can use a simple process of realizing that we need to change, targeting the specific behavior to change, strategizing how we can change it, paying attention to the new behavior, and being responsible for our actions. Each time we do this process successfully, our confidence in our own abilities increases, as does our self-esteem. Conversely, if we fail, our confidence can plummet.

Why Do I Want to Change?

Usually the first hint that we need to attend to a behavior is the nagging feeling that we are not accomplishing what we wish to accomplish. Sometimes it is a painful slap in the face by a low test score or a friend's negative comment. Whatever the initiating event, when we choose to look realistically at our goals and determine whether they are congruent with our ethical standards and then examine our behaviors, we are preparing to change.

What Do I Need to Change?

A clear understanding of the discrepancy between how we are acting and how we should act points to the behavior that needs to change. When we select that target behavior and state it as a goal, we can apply to it the four characteristics of achievable goals (believable, realistic, desirable, measurable).

How Will I Change the Desired Behavior?

The key question is, *What can I do to increase the likelihood that I will do the desired behavior?* There are numerous strategies that we can employ to help us reach our behavior: translating goals into actions, implementing self-talk, visualizing, monitoring, triggering events, evaluating results of our actions, enlisting social support. Later in this chapter, you will have the opportunity to design and implement a self-change project.

How Will I Monitor What Is Happening?

Once we have chosen the specific behavior changes we intend to make, then our job is to focus on the new behaviors and persist in our efforts to reach them. Throughout we must regularly verify exactly what we are doing (reality check). To do this verification, we must be aware of what we are doing. In other words, we must be present to ourselves. This skill comes with practice and continual, gentle reminders to ourselves about what we are doing at any particular moment. Self-talk is especially helpful in learning this skill.

An important factor in self-regulation is our willingness to hold ourselves accountable for our new behaviors. The simplest way to assume this accountability is to verbally promise ourselves that we will do a certain behavior by a certain time. However, we can increase the power of such a promise by writing it down and then checking it off when it is done. An even more powerful method is to announce to a roommate, a friend, a family member, or someone else with whom we feel comfortable that we will do the new behavior. This type of public accountability can be especially effective for extroverts.

KEY ROUTINES

Although our days are full of hundreds of behaviors, some conscious and some unconscious, just a handful of those behaviors have the capacity to influence all the others. Those few powerful behaviors are key routines. A primary method of strengthening our self-regulation is to identify and implement our key routines, those five or six behaviors that keep us from chaos and move us toward mastery. Key routines can be simple—getting enough sleep, balancing the checkbook—or complex—maintaining a detailed calendar, creating and maintaining healthy relationships. Interestingly, key routines vary from one person to another. What is powerful for you may not work well for your friend.

The variability of key routines is evident when we work with students. Two of our students come to mind: Todd, a second-semester freshman, and Cecilia, a single mother who has returned to college after a 15-year absence. Although both are full-time students and academically capable, neither was prepared for the regression into chaos that they had experienced the prior semester. Both started the spring term with good intentions, but they were worried, so they came to consult with us. Both had already discerned that they needed to change so that they could be academically successful. Thus, they had already begun the process of improving their self-regulation.

• • • **TODD** • • •
A student experiencing chaos

Todd is a freshman—he lives on campus and belongs to several organizations. He works 15 hours each week in a campus office, takes five courses, has numerous friends, and dates regularly. He is a casual, laid-back guy who managed high school reasonably well. The changes inherent in living in a dorm and the free-form lifestyle available to freshmen caught him by surprise. He reports that he simply does not feel in control of anything, and he feels worried and guilty most of the time. Upon discussion, we discern that Todd was at the flexibility stage in high school, but he has regressed to a somewhat chaotic stage now. He is still attending and barely passing most classes, and alcohol/drugs are not interfering with his life. He does not have any major financial, family, or emotional problems.

After discussion and reflection, Todd chooses to focus on four key routines: sleeping, attending class, scheduling, and exercising regularly. Like many freshmen living on campus, regular sleep is hard to accomplish. The dorm is active 24/7. Todd often delays studying until late in the evening, then goes online, and finally goes to sleep around 2 A.M.

Even if he makes his nine o'clock class the next day, he is usually tired. He sets the target behavior that he will go to sleep by midnight before any class day. To do so, he has to begin studying by 8 P.M.

Attending every class is another key routine Todd chooses. Like many freshmen, Todd took most of his excused absences early in the term. Now, he realizes that he needs to go to every class. College teachers simply do not repeat what is in the book; they give new information in every lecture. Todd resolves to keep a checklist of all his classes and mark his attendance. Each week that he achieves perfect attendance, he will reward himself with a movie.

Of all the key routines Todd has chosen, scheduling is a new skill. College competency simply demands that students learn to schedule, plan, and keep a written or electronic record of activities and obligations. We spend several sessions with Todd to help him create the scheduling system that will function for him. He has to learn to implement it throughout each day, and that effort is intense. He learns that he prefers an academic calendar with space for each day's activities. On Sunday evenings, he will spend 30 minutes previewing the coming week—classes, assignments, organizational commitments, and social times. He will then quickly scan the next few weeks to determine when the exams and major papers are due and whether he has to begin such large projects soon. The specific times he works on scheduling are target behaviors.

The fourth key routine Todd chooses is to exercise regularly. He already goes to the campus gym sporadically to work out. He decides that he will also run for 30 minutes three days a week before class and then come back to the dorm to get ready.

We ask Todd to check his four key routines against the criteria we learned for setting achievable goals: believable, realistic, desirable, and measurable. He quickly sketches the following graph.

Todd's Key Routines

	Believable	Realistic	Desirable	Measurable
Sleeping	√	√	√	√
Attending Class	√	√	√	√
Scheduling	√	√	√	√
Exercising	√	X	√	√

After reviewing his plan, Todd realizes that he has scheduled his primary exercise early in the morning, a time with which he is already struggling. His choice is unrealistic. Reluctantly he goes back to his weekly schedule and chooses Tuesday, Thursday, and Saturday afternoons as the times he commits to exercise. He already knows that the best exercise for him is a 45-minute workout on machines followed by a 30-minute run at the track. He rightly expects that such exercise will quickly increase his energy and reduce his stress.

Todd works with us throughout the semester by regular appointments. We review his performance on his selected routines and then plan for the next several weeks. He struggles with the new routine of scheduling but gradually learns to rely on his academic calendar and his new habits. At spring break, he goes home and shows his mother what he is doing about scheduling. His mother, a corporate manager, laughs and pulls out her electronic scheduler, saying, "I couldn't do my work without this; it's a lifesaver. You are developing an important skill."

• • • CECILIA • • •
A single parent attending college

Cecilia is a 32-year-old single parent with two children, ages 8 and 6. She works part-time and takes four courses at the downtown campus of a community college. Although she has some help with child care from her relatives, she carries the main responsibility for herself and her children. Cecilia is highly motivated to succeed in school; she wants to complete her degree, and she has a few credits from her time in college 15 years ago. This term she is experiencing the shock of the workload of parenting, working, and studying. She comes to the learning center for help in managing this new life. She reports that mornings are chaotic and she is exhausted and stressed by the time she arrives at class. Her children resist getting up and getting dressed. However, she is in control of her academic work.

After discussion, Cecilia realizes that although she is stable in her academic work, her family routines have digressed to chaos. Her goal is to have pleasant and less stressful mornings. She chooses several target behaviors that should ease the confusion and stress of the mornings.

The night before a school day, Cecilia will supervise the children's packing of their backpacks; lay out their school clothes; and assemble any necessary notes, money, or supplies. She will pack their lunches and put them in the refrigerator. Then she will set the table for breakfast. The next morning she will arise 15 minutes early and dress before she wakes the children. Notice the specificity of these target behaviors. Each is designed to increase the efficiency and calm of school mornings, and each meets the criteria of believable, realistic, desirable, and measurable. Within just a week, Cecilia reports that this routine has become habitual, and she is much more able to concentrate in class.

Making Key Routines Automatic

A part of the mastery stage is the automatic execution of key routines, in other words, making our key routines habitual. When a behavior becomes a habit, we no longer consciously consider doing it or not doing it; we just do it. Whether it is going to class or paying the bills on time, doing habitual behaviors is usually not stressful. We do not have to make the same decision over and over again.

Moving from chaos to habitual key routines requires our accepting responsibility for our actions. As we discussed in Chapter 2, accepting responsibility is the essential first step in academic transformation. Next comes the design of several rigid rules about certain tasks, such as Todd has chosen for class attendance. Keeping a written record of our performance of those tasks, plus reinforcing our accomplishment, helps us to hold ourselves accountable.

The movement from chaos to stability to flexibility and eventually to mastery takes time and practice. As you develop your ability to control (self-regulate) your behavior, you will realize which of your rules must be firm and which can be flexible. You will also learn to adapt your routines to your goals, for your goals may change in the process. For example, as you progress through college, your ambitions may become more specific. Thus, your goals will change, and your key routines also. College is the training ground and the practice place for a well-managed life.

exercise 9.3

Key Routines

Often you may find that life is controlling you as opposed to you controlling your life. How often do you feel out of control? This exercise will help you strengthen your self-regulation by establishing key routines to create stability out of chaos.

1. In which areas of your life are you experiencing chaos?

2. For what part of the chaos can you claim responsibility? In other words, what is your contribution to the chaos in your life?

3. What key routines can you immediately establish to help you stabilize your life?

4. What rules can you implement to support your key routines?

5. How honestly committed are you to these rules?

6. What positive reinforcements can you provide for yourself to support and maintain your key routines?

Implement two or three key routines and corresponding rules for a period of two weeks. Then write a one-page evaluation of your progress. If you are not experiencing success, rethink the project, consult with your instructor, make changes, and try again.

EFFECTIVE USE OF TIME

Time is the great equalizer. Whether you are smart or dumb, ugly or beautiful, you have the same 168 hours each week that everyone else has. How you spend that valuable commodity determines the quality of your life, just as surely as if you walked into a store and ordered it.

You have probably already noticed that time passes more quickly for you than it once did. Those endless hours and days of childhood slip away by adolescence, and adulthood brings an ever-increasing acceleration. Whether you are 18 and just beginning college or 26 and managing a full-time job while going to college or 45 and returning to a campus after a long absence, you may fall prey to the conviction that you have enough time to do everything, enough time to forgo planning. A dangerous self-deception. One of the purposes of college is to determine which people can control their time in order to meet their goals. College graduates with professional jobs structure their own time and often the tasks as well. A hidden requirement for success in college and in the professional world is the desire and the ability to use time wisely. Such a skill is not instantly conferred on graduation, but it is slowly and painfully constructed throughout the college years.

Time management is one of those phrases that many people respond to emotionally. Either it engenders guilt because we feel we never complete what we *should,* or it creates panic because we do not want to feel trapped in a prison of schedules. How to find the path to balance, the place of reaching our goals in a way that is nurturing to our spirit, is the subject of hundreds of books and seminars every year. Many topics already mentioned in this text can help you find that place of balance, and we hope the following information will also help you adopt a wise use of your time, a balance between structure and freedom.

Driving and Resisting Forces

In the battlefield of time use, two forces repeatedly fight each other. Driving forces are those ambitions that we have to achieve and to acquire. The desires we feel arise from deep within us. Some examples are our vision of our quality world, our identity of who we are and what we want to be, our purpose or where we want to go in life, our priorities, our integrity or honor, our accomplishments, and our balance of wants and shoulds. Ideally, an important aspect of our driving forces is self-care (e.g., those activities such as exercise, rest, play, time with people we love, meditation, prayer). Make no mistake, such activities help us renew ourselves so we can fulfill our vision of our quality world, a world of health and balance.

Standing opposed to the driving forces are resisting forces—an array of impediments, circumstances, and mind-sets that hamper, and sometimes stop, our efforts to achieve. Merrill (1987) names some of these resisting forces: too many things to do, fatigue, conflicting wants/shoulds, not enough time or money, demands/expectations of others or lack of cooperation from others, lack of purpose and goals, unclear values and confused priorities, and lack of organization. To these we can add low self-esteem and life crises. Good time use techniques diminish the effect of these resisting forces because they strengthen our drives and our coping abilities. Clarity about the circumstances that are our particular opponents helps us design the time plan that will enable us to reach our goals.

exercise 9.4

Identifying Driving and Resisting Forces

Effective use of time means having the drive (internal motivation) to continue even when difficulties arise. When we ignore our priorities and spend time on less important things, our lives get off track. This exercise is designed to provide you with an opportunity to assess the impact of current driving and resisting forces in your life.

1. How much does each of the following driving forces positively affect how you spend your time? Rate your responses on a scale of 1 to 3, with 1 being hardly ever, 2 being sometimes, and 3 being most of the time.

   _____ Your vision of your quality world

   _____ Your identity of who you are and what you want to be

   _____ Your purpose or where you want to go in life

   _____ Your priorities

   _____ Your integrity or honor

   _____ Your accomplishments

   _____ Your self-care

   _____ Your balance of wants and shoulds

2. What does your total score mean to you?

3. What changes, if any, should you make at this point?

4. How much does each of the following resisting forces negatively affect how you spend your time? Rate your responses on a scale of 1 to 3, with 1 being hardly ever, 2 being sometimes, and 3 being most of the time.

   _____ Too many things to do

   _____ Fatigue

   _____ Conflicting wants/shoulds

   _____ Not enough time or money

   _____ Demands/expectations of others or lack of cooperation from others

   _____ Lack of purpose and goals

   _____ Unclear values and confused priorities

   _____ Lack of organization

   _____ Low self-esteem

   _____ Life crises

5. What does your total score mean to you?

6. What changes, if any, should you make at this point?

Productive versus Counterproductive Use of Time

How we spend our time determines the quality of our lives (Merrill, 1987). That expenditure of time can be roughly divided into two categories: productive and counterproductive. If we have considered what we want our lives to be as well as who we want to be, then our goals should flow from those considerations. When we act in ways that support and further our goals, whether they are academic, occupational, personal, social, spiritual, physical, or artistic, then we are using time productively. Since most of us are ambitious, we may have so many goals that we have to prioritize, and it becomes seductively easy to focus on those activities that seem time urgent or immediately rewarding, such as tests, social activities, and family needs. Thus, we may delay, or forgo, the activities that give us long-term benefit, such as rest, exercise, play, or those activities that maintain a balanced life, such as doing laundry, paying bills, shopping for groceries. Renewal activities also include finding the major that truly fits, planning/organizing, building relationships, meaningful work, flow experiences, meditation.

The concept of counterproductive time is only too familiar for most of us. Some obvious examples are working extra shifts during the semester and missing class/study time, taking a long weekend before several tests or finals, vegging in front of the TV, overindulging in computer games, alcohol/drugs, and parties. We usually realize when we are using time counterproductively because we feel guilty. It may not be possible to completely eliminate counterproductive use of time, but it is extremely important to limit it so it does not interfere with the quality of our lives. Self-regulation helps us maintain that limit through awareness, accountability, and action.

Crises interfere with our best intentions because they require an enormous amount of time. Preventable crises include bank overdrafts, bad hangovers, car breakdowns due to poor maintenance, sleeping through your alarm and missing a test, not saving your computer document before printing and then losing it all. Doing what needs to be done in a timely way is the best defense against preventable crises. Another type of crisis, however, is not preventable. Whether it is a serious illness, accident, divorce, death—these and other catastrophic events can disrupt our lives and our academic work. As students, it is important to contact the campus Dean of Students office or the Counseling Center immediately for help in negotiating the best means of completing your academic work for the term.

Living well means that we strive to live productively as much as we can. Organizing and managing our time well means that we increase the amount of time spent productively. This task is difficult because the resisting forces mentioned above tend to push us toward wasting time. The uneasy feeling we get when we know we are not taking care of ourselves mentally, physically, emotionally, and spiritually is the clear indication we are not living in ways congruent with our goals.

Monitoring Your Time

Monitoring your time can be a powerful tool to help you become more successful with self-regulation. This exercise will take you one full week to complete
and it is in two parts. Completing this exercise will help you see trends in your
time usage so that you can make appropriate adjustments.

PART I: TIME MONITOR

Keep track of how you spend your time for a week by completing the Weekly Time
Monitor. At least three times a day, take a few minutes to update the time monitor
to ensure accuracy in recording (it is all too easy to *overestimate* the amount of
time you study and to *underestimate* how long you spend doing everything else!).
A blank copy of this form is provided at the end of this chapter.

Weekly Time Monitor							
	Mon	Tues	Wed	Thurs	Fri	Sat	Sun
6:00–7:00							
7:00–8:00							
8:00–9:00							
9:00–10:00							
10:00–11:00							
11:00–12:00							
12:00–1:00							
1:00–2:00							
2:00–3:00							
3:00–4:00							
4:00–5:00							
5:00–6:00							
6:00–7:00							
7:00–8:00							
8:00–9:00							
9:00–10:00							
10:00–11:00							
11:00–12:00							
12:00–1:00							
1:00–2:00							
2:00–3:00							
3:00–4:00							
4:00–5:00							
5:00–6:00							

Once you have recorded how you spend your time for seven days, add up the number of hours you spent in each of the following categories (note: there are 168 hours in one week):

_____ Sleep	_____ Personal hygiene
_____ Class	_____ Meetings
_____ Study	_____ Spiritual
_____ Meals	_____ Television
_____ Family	_____ Computer/games
_____ Work	_____ Social
_____ Commute	_____ Other: _____
_____ Exercise	_____ Other: _____

PART II: USE OF TIME

Once you have analyzed your completed time monitor, place your week's activities into the three boxes below. Estimate how much of your time was spent in each of the three categories (how many hours)? Then estimate the percentage of total time you spent in each category for the week (_____% of 168 hours).

Productive	Counterproductive	Crises

What changes, if any, would you like to accomplish in your use of time?

Underlying Assumptions for Time Management

Many time management systems have appeared in the past 50 years. They exist in paper format, personal digital assistants (PDAs), day planners, computer programs. However different they may appear on the surface, all share the same assumptions. Whatever format you choose, be aware of the following assumptions.

Assumption #1. Time management systems start with vision and goals. We have spoken in this text about our quality world and the goals that can emerge from our vision of how and who we want to be. Discerning our goals and checking them by the criteria of belief, realism, desire, and measurement allow us to build a strong foundation for effective time management.

Assumption #2. We are the managers, not the slaves, of our time. Although some of our time each day is fixed, such as work, class, and commuting time, we do control most of the rest of our time. We actively choose what we do and when we do it. Some simple examples are when we get up and when we go to bed; when and how long we eat; when we run errands or do household chores; when and how long we study, play, vegetate, etc.

Assumption #3. We focus on clear and truthful prioritization of tasks. What has the most importance? It is normal to have pressing tasks in several areas of your life, especially if you are working at a job outside of school and/or you have children. Whether you make a list or write the tasks on a series of Post-it notes, it is imperative that you decide the level of importance of each task. Once you have decided the priority and labeled or numbered the items, then you can ask the question posed in Assumption #4.

Assumption #4. We ask ourselves, What is the best use of my time right now? (Lakein, 1973, p. 96). Holding this question in the back of our minds helps us realize when we are procrastinating, when we are overwhelmed, when we are confronted by a crisis that interrupts our time plan. Sometimes the best use of our time is to help a friend, or to take a nap; sometimes it is to study the subject we like least because the test is tomorrow. *What is the best use of my time right now?* puts the questions of priorities and flexibility forefront in your thinking.

Creating the Right Plan

"Planning is bringing the future into the present so that you can do something about it now" (Lakein, 1973, p. 25). However, our plan has to be the right plan for us or it will not work. To create the right plan, we have to answer the following questions:

What are my goals? When we determine to use time wisely, it is crucial to look at the goals we have in every facet of our lives—personal, academic, social, occupational, family, athletic, spiritual. They comprise what we value. The right plan encompasses the goals from all areas of our lives.

As emphasized in the previous chapter, our list of goals needs to be achievable; for example, I will make a GPA of 3.0 on the 13 hours I am taking this semester or I will complete a career search so that I will choose my major by January or I will meet at least three new people each week or I will spend at least an hour each school night helping my son with his math homework. Obviously, those goals need to be your goals, not someone else's. If we write our goals down and put them where we can see them frequently, they will help our motivation.

What are my priorities among those goals? Covey (1989) promotes first things first as a mantra for good time use. In simple terms, that means paying bills before watching TV, studying before going to the movie, spending time with your significant other before hanging out with friends, getting to work early, etc. A good time/task plan helps us set and meet priorities.

What support, supplies, and circumstances do I need to accomplish those goals? A good time/task plan will help you get to a needed tutoring or study session on time; it will allocate study time during the day; it will help you manage the numerous errands, phone calls, and mail to manage your life and your family.

What will be the cost to accomplish those goals—the price tag? A good plan helps us be honest about what we have to give up to accomplish our goals. We may have to relinquish watching sports on television or time with extended family or pleasure reading. It may mean quick meals rather than elaborate dinners. It may mean less PTA or church work. It may mean using breaks and holidays to catch up on studying.

How can I establish a time plan that will work for me? We believe that most people fall into two categories of feelings about using time. Either we need the sense of safety that structure provides *or* we need the sense of freedom that structure inhibits. Roughly, these two categories correlate with two preferences mentioned in Chapter 7. People who enjoy structure are usually Js (Judging) and those who enjoy freedom are Ps (Perceiving). In simplistic terms, people with a preference for structure/safety usually are comfortable with time-use planning. In fact, sometimes they spend much of their time planning and do not complete the tasks. By contrast, people with a preference for freedom often fight the idea of planning, thinking erroneously that a time-use plan is a jail.

In reality, both types of people need a good time plan, but they need different types of time plans. However, both need time plans that include a list of goals, a semester calendar, a to-do list, and a weekly planner. In Chapter 3, we recommended constructing an academic calendar listing all your academic commitments. Now we are adding several more pieces to that original concept to give you a complete system. Such a system combines all the facets of your life in one place.

To-Do List

A to-do list is a simple and highly effective daily strategy. You may write it in a daily planner, on a notepad, or on a Post-it note. It is a list of the tasks that should be completed during the next day or week; these tasks are separate from the normally scheduled times of class, work, meals, and sleep. A to-do list is always changing as you check off those things you have completed and add new tasks. Sometimes you may have enough tasks that you will need to prioritize by marking some as As (top priority), Bs, etc.

Daily or Weekly Planner

Using a daily or weekly planner is a good way to integrate your goals, academic calendar, to-do list, and specific schedule for the week all in one place. We recommend that you use 15–20 minutes on Sunday afternoon or evening to schedule the next week in your planner, noting any specific conflicts. Here are some guidelines for keeping a weekly planner:

- Transfer academic commitments, such as classes, labs, tutoring, study groups, from your academic calendar. Note any due dates for tests or projects that are upcoming in the next two weeks.

- Mark study times, allocating one to three hours per class hour, depending on the difficulty of the class for you. It is more productive to do one- or two-hour study sessions than marathon sessions of five or more hours.

- Set realistic goals for studying; for example, estimate how much time you think you will need and then add another 50 percent.

- Set specific starting and stopping times or beginning and ending points for accomplishing academic tasks.

- Mark the hours you are at work, including drive time.

- List social or family plans, including dates, parties, and meetings.

- If you have regularly scheduled exercise and/or meditation time, enter it on the planner.

- Plan for some downtime; such personal time is necessary for rest and refreshment.

- Make sure you have some time each day that is not allocated. This time is what you will need to handle the unexpected crises of work, children, car repairs, etc.

- Reflect on how much time you have allocated for renewal activities.

Technology Aids

Laptops, PDAs, electronic address books, and microrecorders are some of the hardware tools available now, and scheduling software is common on most desktops. All cost money and time in learning how to use and maintain them. As your life becomes more complex, especially if you are comfortable with technology, you may find that electronic scheduling is helpful. However, "even the best tool is no substitute for vision, judgment, creativity, character, or competence" (Covey, Merrill, & Merrill, 1994, p. 327).

Personality Type and Time

Just as our temperaments affect procrastination, they also affect how we relate to time management and academic tasks.

Introversion. Introverts prefer to study alone; it is easy for them to put a Do Not Disturb sign on the door; they can say no to friends and family; they do not allow voice mail or email messages to interrupt their study. Introverts have a talent for protecting themselves so they can work, but they sometimes avoid study groups.

Extraversion. Extroverts often prefer being with other people, so it is more difficult for them to isolate themselves to study. They tend to answer the phone or allow distractions to interrupt their study. Extroverts often have a talent for multitasking.

Perceiving. People with a preference for perceiving (freedom) have a talent for adapting to the moment and believing that things will work out, resist the idea that we should control time, tend to start projects at the last minute, and work well under pressure. They often disregard their schedule and prefer working for immediate gratification. Studying, except last-minute cramming, rarely has immediate gratification, so academic timeliness is often difficult. They prefer to play first, then work.

Judging. People with a preference for judging (structure) need a detailed schedule to function well; they prefer to work first, then play. They either want to be in control or want someone else to be in control. They do not like being caught unprepared at the last minute. They tend to use waiting time (before class or waiting in line) productively, get things ready the night before, and are aware of when their best study times are. They often study the most difficult courses first and then use studying their favorite course as a reward. They are often comfortable working for delayed gratification, rather than immediate.

BALANCING OUR LIVES

The challenge of modern life, either as a college student or a working professional, is to manage the time we have so that we reach our goal of a quality life—a quality life that incorporates what we want to achieve both personally and professionally. It is not an easy task for anyone to navigate the balance between doing what we should do for long-term goals (delayed gratification) and doing what we want to do right now (immediate gratification). Obviously, we benefit if we use vision rooted in our quality world, develop both long-term and short-term goals based on that vision, and manage our daily lives in a thoughtful manner.

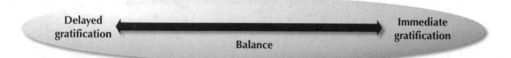

"Balancing is the discipline that gives us flexibility. Extraordinary flexibility is required for successful living in all spheres of activity" (Peck, 1978, p. 64). Sometimes a good method for developing balance is to look at the characteristics of people who are our opposite in relation to the structure/freedom preference. What can we learn from those who are so different from us? If we prefer structure, we may need to learn to incorporate more play into our lives (but we are almost sure to schedule it!). If we prefer freedom, we may need to use a planner for schoolwork and personal tasks (even though it may be a struggle initially).

Let us now look at some specific examples of students who can move toward greater balance in their lives:

> Maria is an international student who has come to the United States to study computer science. She is so determined to succeed that she studies every moment that she is not working at her campus job. She has made few friends and seems anxious and worried.
> **Remedy:** Maria realizes that she will benefit from joining at least one campus organization and giving herself one hour a day to listen to music and relax.

> Jim is a single parent with an eight-year-old daughter. He works 25 hours a week and carries four courses. His day is nonstop from 6 A.M. to 9 P.M., as he juggles caring for his child, doing schoolwork, and working at his job. He feels exhausted and worries that he is on an endless treadmill.
> **Remedy:** Jim begins to examine the resources in his extended family and the community for child care to allow him some time to himself, for both study and recreation.

Kimberly is enjoying every aspect of college. She loves living on campus, and her room is always full of friends. The television is usually on as well as instant messaging on her computer. She has good intentions about exercising and study, but often finds herself at the end of the day with few tasks accomplished. **Remedy:** Kimberly realizes that she cannot study in her room because it has far too many distractions. Her first priority becomes studying enough to maintain her scholarship, so she schedules study time at the library immediately after her afternoon classes. She finds a quiet study carrel, away from the elevators and walkways. She completes her studies before she goes back to the dorm. After a few weeks, she feels that her study behaviors are stable, so she schedules two workout sessions each week in the campus gym.

David is a junior who lives off campus. He enrolls in at least 16 hours each term and is vice president of the student government association. He also participates in a professional organization for his major. He feels anxious most of the time because there are so many details to remember. Most important, he never feels that he is doing anything well. **Remedy:** David begins to use a planner to help him remember the multitude of tasks. However, he also reevaluates his goals and makes some important changes. He turns down the offer of a leadership role in the professional organization, preferring just to participate as a member. He schedules time to play his guitar several times a week; it is an activity that he used to enjoy. He decides to take a break during the summer and work rather than take extra courses to graduate early.

Balance leads to inner harmony: "It is the selection of appropriate and realistic goals congruent with inner values. It is the resolution of wants and shoulds. It is the balance of work, family, community and personal priorities" (Merrill, 1987, p. 41).

exercise 9.6

Balancing Your Life

Balancing your life is like learning to walk on a circus tightrope, high up in the air. It takes plenty of practice and patience. How well have you mastered your balancing act as a student? This exercise will help you focus on your ability to balance your life.

1. How well are you balancing the various areas of your life?

    _____ Well   _____ Somewhat   _____ Poorly

2. If you answered "Well," what recent decisions have helped you improve or maintain balance?

3. If you answered "Poorly" or "Somewhat," what three decisions or changes could you make to improve your balance?

A HOLISTIC APPROACH TO CHANGING BEHAVIORS

All of us have tried to change our behaviors, thoughts, and feelings from time to time. Sometimes the beginning of a new semester motivates us to change how much we study, or sometimes we use New Year's Day as the reason for launching a diet. We have all used those magic words *willpower* and *discipline.* We all want to be able to change what we do, feel, or think without effort or guilt, but creating positive change requires commitment, attention, and persistence.

We draw from the field of behavioral psychology in a deliberate attempt to help you change specific behaviors using the knowledge and techniques culled from years of psychological experiments. There are many ways to change behaviors, thoughts, and feelings; however, one technique that has proven successful with our students is the implementation of a behavioral self-change project. Working to change a behavior first often leads to subsequent changes in thoughts and feelings. Although we can sometimes change behaviors because we are frightened or because there are powerful rewards involved, our good intentions can weaken over time, and our old behaviors creep back. Self-change increases our chances of reaching our behavioral goals because it is based on what we know about how people learn and change.

If you decide to try a self-change project, you must commit to a minimum period of four weeks. Although you may wish to focus on changing an academic behavior, we encourage you to think of other possibilities such as exercise, eating habits, smoking, money management, TV watching, computer use, and assertiveness. If you value yourself and wish to create a more desirable future, plan well, follow through thoroughly, and monitor your progress regularly so that you can achieve your goal. Remember, you have the power to make positive changes in your life. The following steps will assist you in completing a self-change program; blank forms are provided at the end of the chapter.

Step 1: Formulate a Target Behavior

Choosing a goal is the first step. Say, for example, your goal is to lose 15 pounds. Now translate your goal into a target behavior by identifying specific behaviors you can engage in to reach your goal. To lose weight, your target behavior could be to restrict your caloric intake to 1,000 calories each day *or* to eliminate all in-between-meal snacks *or* to run three miles a day *or* a combination of diet and exercise. If your goal is to increase your GPA, your target behavior could be to increase the amount of daily study time to two hours each day *or* to get tutoring in specific subjects three times a week *or* to complete all homework the day it is assigned. Your target behavior must be achievable (believable, realistic, desirable, and measurable), just like the action statements you created when you were learning to set goals in the previous chapter.

Step 2: Collect Baseline Data

Once you have selected a target behavior, you will conduct a seven-day observation period. Observe the behavior as it naturally occurs. Do not consciously try to change the behavior, although it may change slightly due to your increased awareness. We call this step collecting baseline data, and you will need to keep a record of how often, when, and where your behavior occurs as well as some of the thoughts and feelings you associate with the behavior.

To lose those 15 pounds over the next month, count how many calories you consume each day *or* measure how much exercise you get *or* analyze the types of food you eat and when and where you eat them. What are you thinking and how are you feeling as you observe and engage in this behavior?

If your target behavior is to quit smoking, count the average number of cigarettes you smoke each day. Are there certain periods of time when you tend to smoke more often or less often? What types of activities cause you to crave a cigarette? How tense do you become between cigarettes? This information will be useful when you move to the third step, so record it in a daily journal or behavior-tracking log. (See Figure 9.1 for a sample behavior-tracking form. A blank one is provided at the end of the chapter.) We also encourage you to graph your behavioral observations; pictures often say more than words.

FIGURE 9.1   Sample Behavior-Tracking Form

Date	Time	Count	Behavior	Feelings	Self-Talk	Consequences
2/16	4–5 P.M.	I hour	Completing homework; finished rough draft of English essay	Relaxed, motivated to finish	"If I get this done before dinner, I'll have time to read biology this evening."	Relieved, ready to turn rough draft in the next day for a completion grade
2/18	—	0 hours	Completing homework; was supposed to finish math but went to party instead	Had fun at the party but felt guilty all night for not doing math assignment	"I'll try to finish it when I get home or get up early."	Failed pop quiz in math the next morning

Another important part of collecting baseline data is to research your target behavior at your campus library. Find at least three good sources that can help you design your self-change project, and photocopy articles and relevant parts of book sources to keep as references.

Step 3: Design a Contract

The next step of the project is to design a self-change contract. (See Figure 9.2 for a sample self-change contract and Figure 9.3 for a sample four-week graph for a self-change project. A blank contract and graph are provided at the end of the chapter.) The contract is a detailed description of how you plan to achieve the target behavior. Because you will create a contract with yourself to change the target behavior, the most important part of the contract is your honor. You are promising to follow the terms of the contract, that is, impose the artificial consequences. The promise is to yourself, not your teacher, classmates, or family members (although their active support or sabotage can certainly affect your success). Honor lies at the heart of self-change. You may gradually shape your behavior by setting different levels of behavior for each of the weeks you attempt the contract.

Your contract will include self-imposed reinforcements (rewards) to administer as you experience success as well as a few self-imposed punishments when you are unsuccessful. Often natural consequences (positive and negative, immediate and delayed) that immediately follow behaviors do not reinforce the right things strongly or quickly enough. For example, smokers get immediate relief from nicotine cravings (positive natural consequences), but the serious health problems caused by smoking are usually delayed (negative natural consequences). Successful behavior change requires that you apply strong, immediate positive (or negative) consequences after you engage in (or fail to engage in) your target behavior.

Psychologists term these consequences reinforcements and punishments. **Reinforcement** is *a consequence that follows a behavior and increases the likelihood that the behavior will increase in frequency.* For example, the natural consequences of exercise are usually increased energy and better health (immediate and delayed), but regular exercise is one of the more difficult behaviors for people to maintain. An artificial consequence you can self-impose after each exercise session is listening to your favorite music or watching television for 30 minutes. Implementing **punishments,** which are *consequences that follow a behavior and decrease the frequency of the behavior from occurring,* is also effective in helping you achieve your target behavior. For example, the natural consequences of not studying are usually poor grades (immediate and/or delayed). An artificial consequence you can self-impose when you do not study is to deny yourself the use of your cell phone or

FIGURE 9.2 Sample Self-Change Contract

Self-Change Contract

My overall goal for this self-change project is:
  To quit smoking cigarettes forever!

The target behavior I want to initiate, increase, maintain, decrease, or stop is:
  Stop smoking by the end of next month.

During the project, I will make the following *specific changes* (environmental, social, personal) to support my target behavior:
  I will leave my cigarettes in the car, carry gum/mints/toothpicks in my backpack, sit in nonsmoking sections of restaurants, and hang out with more of my nonsmoking friends.

During the project, I will replace negative self-talk about my behavior with positive self-talk such as the following:

| Change | *I <u>have</u> to have a cigarette after dinner.* | to | *I've made it all day without a cigarette, and I'm not going to give in now. I'll just chew another stick of gum.* |

During the project, I will apply the following reinforcements and punishments to support my target behavior:

Each day I succeed in following the conditions of my contract, I will:
  Allow myself 30 minutes to listen to music or rent a video for the evening or take a walk with a friend.

Each day I fail to follow the conditions of my contract, I will:
  Wash and fold all of my laundry or lose one night of television/computer time or handwrite a letter to one of my relatives.

During the project, I will enlist the help of other people in the following ways to support my target behavior:
  I'll ask my friends not to smoke around me or let me bum cigarettes or to walk with me or to watch videos with me on the days I fulfill my contract.

Darvin Jones
Student

Beth Ruelos
Project Partner(s)

Russ Hodges
Instructor

2/25/05
Date

2/25/05
Date

2/25/05
Date

FIGURE 9.3   Sample Four-Week Graph for a Self-Change Project

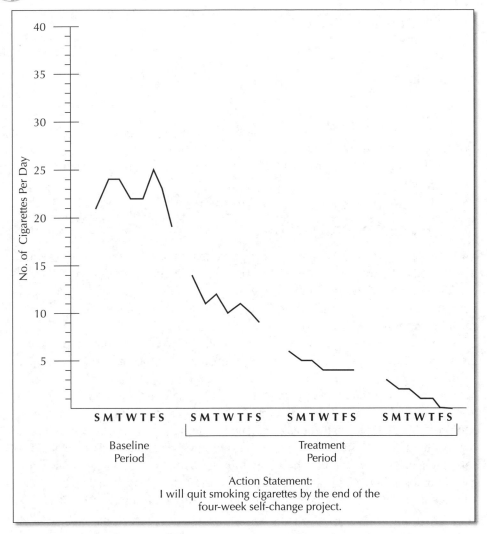

computer for a day. Here are some examples of consequences (reinforcements and punishments) our students often use:

Reinforcements

Spending time with friends	Listening to music
Reading a favorite book	Surfing the Internet
Going to the movies	Spending time outdoors
Eating favorite foods	Shopping
Taking an entire afternoon off for yourself	

Punishments

Putting money in a jar and giving it all to charity

Not allowing yourself daily pleasures (email, phone calls, favorite TV shows/electronic games)

Cleaning house

Washing cars, clothes, or pets

Taking the stairs instead of elevators

Not allowing yourself dessert, soda, or pizza

A powerful part of this project is collaborating with a partner. Seek out the help of at least one other student in class who is supportive and willing to help you design your contract and provide you with consistent moral support during the treatment phase.

Step 4: Implement Treatment

The fourth step is your attempt to change your target behavior during the next three weeks, the treatment phase of the project. During treatment, you will follow the conditions outlined in your contract to try to change your target behavior and continue to update your daily journal or behavior-tracking log and self-change graph.

You may have to adjust your contract conditions because your target behavior is too challenging (e.g., studying four hours a day) or too easy (e.g., exercising 15 minutes a day). Ineffective reinforcements and punishments will also need to be changed. As noted earlier, an essential part of the treatment phase is your involvement with your self-change partner. You are expected to listen attentively and provide constructive feedback and encouragement to your partner; she or he is expected to do the same for you. If you find that you are not experiencing success in changing your target behavior within the first week, do not give up. Modify your contract conditions, reinforcements, and punishments, and seek additional social support from your friends, family, instructor, and self-change partner.

Step 5: Evaluate the Project

The final step is to evaluate the design and implementation of your entire project. Your evaluation should contain an analysis of your target behavior, baseline data collection results, contract design, and treatment-phase results. Focus on what worked and what did not work, and provide concrete reasons for the success/lack of success of your project. During the treatment phase, you may have achieved all, part, or none of your goal, so you should address the appropriateness of your target behavior goal and your future plans regarding further change. Do you plan to maintain the target behavior? Abandon it? Adjust it? Maintaining or continuing to change the target behavior will not happen by accident; it must be carefully planned. Continuing to monitor your behavior, especially when you begin to gradually withdraw the artificial consequences, is crucial to maintaining your behavior successfully.

As you study and struggle with the self-change project, you can gain mastery over one of the mysteries of being human—our ability to determine and direct our own lives. When we care enough about ourselves to believe that our own lives and efforts are important, then we care about managing our behaviors.

---

exercise 9.7

Self-Change Project

Experience the gratitude of personal growth. Creating balance in your life means attempting to better yourself when possible, but this is not always easy. Attempting a self-change project is a big commitment, in both time (four weeks) and effort. You will identify a target behavior, spend one week collecting baseline data, and spend three weeks in a treatment phase. You will track and reflect on your progress, making changes along the way. Self-honesty and integrity are paramount. All of the forms you need to complete a self-change project are located at the end of this chapter. Successfully completing this project will provide you with a real sense of accomplishment as you make a positive change in your life.

STEP 1: FORMULATE A TARGET BEHAVIOR

To formulate a target behavior, address each of the following:

a. What are some changes I need to make for a more positive future?

b. Why do I want to make these changes?

c. What specific behavior do I wish to change?

d. How will I attempt to change this target behavior?

e. How will I monitor what is happening? In other words, what will I count or measure each day?

f. At what times or in which situations does my target behavior occur more frequently? Less frequently?

g. What self-talk am I using that causes this behavior to occur or not occur?

h. What specific behaviors can I identify that will help me reach my target behavior goal?

STEP 2: COLLECT BASELINE DATA

Keep track of your baseline data for a week on the behavior-tracking form and graph provided for you at the end of this chapter. Locate at least three library resources with information about changing your behavior.

Once you complete your baseline data collection, answer the following questions:

a. What were the results of my baseline data collection?

b. Did any of my observations surprise me? If so, which ones?

c. What were some of my recurring thoughts and feelings during this week?

d. What were some self-talk trends I noticed?

e. How did my library resources help me understand more about my behavior?

f. Now that the baseline period is over, has my target behavior goal changed? If so, explain.

STEP 3: DESIGN A CONTRACT

Using the contract form provided at the end of this chapter, design and complete a self-change project contract. Be sure that you, your partner, and your instructor each sign the contract. Be thoughtful of the reinforcements and punishments you implement, and make sure they are strong enough to support your efforts to change your target behavior.

Before you begin to fill out your contract, answer each of the following questions:

a. What things are likely to get in the way of my accomplishing this project?

b. How might I sabotage or resist the process of pursuing this project?

c. How committed am I to completing this project?

d. How will I demonstrate that commitment in my actions?

e. What are some abilities, strengths, and skills I already have that I can use?

f. Who are some people who would support me in pursuing this project?

g. What other resources (information, tools, techniques) can help me?

h. What types of reinforcements am I willing to work for? Examples include spending time with friends, going to the movies, shopping, and taking unscheduled free time.

i. What types of punishments would I implement for not honoring my contract conditions? Examples include putting money in a jar and giving it all to charity, riding the bus instead of driving, and not allowing time with friends on the weekend.

STEP 4: IMPLEMENT TREATMENT

During the weeks of treatment, you will follow and carefully monitor all aspects of the contract just like you did when you collected baseline data. Continue to update your behavior-tracking form and graph.

After each week of treatment, answer the following questions:

a. What was the outcome of my project during this week of treatment?

b. What were some of my recurring thoughts and feelings as I engaged in the target behavior?

c. What were some self-talk trends I noticed?

d. What things are likely to get in the way of my accomplishing this project?

e. How helpful was my social support (partner, friends, family, instructor)? How can I make better use of my social support?

f. How committed am I to completing this project?

g. Which reinforcements and punishments are working and why? Which reinforcements and punishments need to be changed and why?

h. What can I change immediately to make this project more successful?

STEP 5: EVALUATE YOUR PROGRAM

Using your graph, behavior-tracking form, and answers to the previous questions in this exercise, evaluate your success (or lack of success) with this project by answering the following questions:

a. How well did I accomplish my target behavior, and how do I feel about my results?

b. What did I do that was helpful, and how can I build on that strength?

c. What did I do that was not helpful, and what did I learn?

d. What happened that was surprising or unexpected?

e. What did I learn most from my baseline data collection?

f. What changes could I have made to the design of my contract?

g. What changes could I have made to my reinforcements and punishments?

h. How could I have better used my partner (social support)?

i. Do I plan to maintain my target behavior? If so, how? If not, why?

CONCLUSION

Within this chapter, we have continued to explore the inner world of self-regulation using the concepts of flow, stages of self-regulatory abilities, key routines, effective use of time, balancing, and self-change. All are practical concepts, and all can help us strengthen our behaviors so that we are more likely to reach our goals.

SUMMARY

- Flow is the state of being where one is completely caught up in what he or she is doing, with no sense of time or duration of the activity that is occurring. Another term for flow is *autotelic*.

- Goal setting, self-regulation, and learning strategies are the tools that can help us have more flow experiences in our lives and especially in our work.

- Eight characteristics describe a flow experience: clear goals for every step, immediate feedback, skills and challenges in good balance, merged action and awareness, total focus, lack of concern with failure (self-efficacy), lack of self-consciousness, and a distorted sense of quantity of time passing.

- The stages of self-regulatory ability are chaos, stability, flexibility, and mastery. It is possible to live in more than one stage at the same time, and new and challenging environments can force us to regress to an earlier stage.

- We can improve our self-regulation by realizing that we need to change, targeting the specific behavior to change, strategizing how we can change it, paying attention to the new behavior, and being responsible for our actions.

- There are a handful of behaviors that have the capacity to influence all the others, and they are termed *key routines*. It is the turning of key routines into habitual behaviors that is important to one's movement from chaos to mastery.

- Time management, the hidden requirement for success in college and in the professional world, is the desire and ability to use time wisely. It is being able to ask, and appropriately answer, the question, *What is the best use of my time right now?*

- Driving forces are those ambitions we have to achieve and to acquire. Resisting forces are an array of impediments, circumstances, and mindsets that hamper, and sometimes stop, our efforts to achieve.

- Living well results from productive actions based on our goals.

- Four assumptions that we must make for proper time management are time management systems start with vision and goals; we are the managers, not the slaves, of our time; we focus on clear and truthful prioritization of tasks; and we ask ourselves, *What is the best use of my time right now?*

- To create the right plan to guide one's use of time, there are a number of questions one needs to answer in order to clearly identify goals, the prioritization among the goals, and the supports and costs associated with each goal.

- Creating a to-do list, using a daily or weekly planner, using technology aids, and understanding our personality type all aid in time management.

- Balancing is the selection of appropriate and realistic goals congruent with inner values. It is making choices along a continuum of delayed and immediate gratification.

- Creating self-change requires commitment, attention, and persistence.

- The five steps in implementing a self-change project are formulating a target behavior, collecting baseline data, designing a contract, implementing treatment, and evaluating the project.

KEY CONCEPTS

Balancing

Effective use of time (driving and resisting forces, productive/ counterproductive, time management, the right plan, to-do list, daily/weekly planner, technology aids, personality)

Flow

Key routines

Process of improving self-regulation

Self-change (target behavior, baseline data, contract, treatment, evaluation of project, reinforcement, punishment)

Stages of self-regulatory abilities: chaos, structure, flexibility, mastery

GUIDED JOURNAL QUESTIONS

1. Describe an academic situation in which you experienced learning as *flow* (as defined in this chapter).

2. Think of a time in your life when you successfully charted a path from chaos to structure, structure to flexibility, or flexibility to mastery. How did you accomplish this? Give examples.

3. What is the one thing you would like to change most about your life? Explain. What stands in the way of your making this change? What benefits will you experience? When would you like to begin this change?

4. How well are you able to use reinforcements to shape or change your behaviors? In what situations have you used them successfully? How well are you able to punish yourself? What punishments have you tried and how successful were they?

5. What other key routines (besides the ones mentioned in the text) could you suggest for Todd to help him out of chaos? What key routines do you need to implement for yourself and why?

6. What methods do you currently use to manage your time? How well are these methods working? How many hours per week do you study? When do you complete the majority of your studying? When are your most efficient times to study (when you are learning at your peak)? Explain.

7. What is the relationship between your personality type and your ability to manage your time?

8. Analyze your self-discipline for college by answering the following: How difficult or easy is it for you to delay gratification? Accept responsibility? Balance between immediate and delayed gratification? Explain and use examples for each.

The Last Word

Having a strong preference for "judging," self-regulation comes naturally to me. Years ago, I came to realize it was an asset for anyone juggling the roles of student, parent, and employee simultaneously!

—*Carol Dochen*

Weekly Time Monitor							
	Mon	Tues	Wed	Thurs	Fri	Sat	Sun
6:00–7:00							
7:00–8:00							
8:00–9:00							
9:00–10:00							
10:00–11:00							
11:00–12:00							
12:00–1:00							
1:00–2:00							
2:00–3:00							
3:00–4:00							
4:00–5:00							
5:00–6:00							
6:00–7:00							
7:00–8:00							
8:00–9:00							
9:00–10:00							
10:00–11:00							
11:00–12:00							
12:00–1:00							
1:00–2:00							
2:00–3:00							
3:00–4:00							
4:00–5:00							
5:00–6:00							

Behavior-Tracking Form

Date	Time	Count	Behavior	Feelings	Self-Talk	Consequences

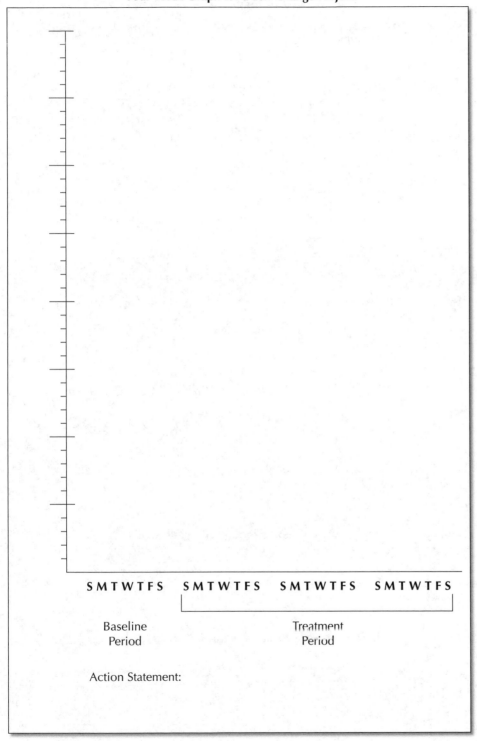

S M T W T F S   S M T W T F S   S M T W T F S   S M T W T F S

Baseline
Period

Treatment
Period

Action Statement:

Self-Change Contract

My overall goal for this self-change project is:

The target behavior I want to initiate, increase, maintain, decrease, or stop is:

During the project, I will make the following *specific changes* (environmental, social, personal) to support my target behavior:

During the project, I will replace negative self-talk about my behavior with positive self-talk such as the following:

During the project, I will apply the following reinforcements and punishments to support my target behavior:

Each day I succeed in following the conditions of my contract, I will:

Each day I fail to follow the conditions of my contract, I will:

During the project, I will enlist the help of other people in the following ways to support my target behavior:

_____   _____
Student   Date

_____   _____
Project Partner(s)   Date

_____   _____
Instructor   Date

10

Appropriate Stress Reduction Techniques

AAUUUGH *%^$# &!@
(I feel much better now.)

W*hy does everyone seem so tense and worried? I thought college was supposed to be fun.* You may have asked this same question after the first few weeks in the term. College is supposed to be exciting and fun as well as productive, but the first semester can leave you with feelings of exhilaration, terror, and a myriad of other emotions. You may feel tired, lonely, excited, homesick, apprehensive, or a combination of all these emotions and more.

If you are entering or reentering college, the first semester is a crucial passage time. Even if you are commuting, most of your life is undergoing enormous change. You are in a new environment that makes unfamiliar expectations and demands, and you are with new people who may or may not be like you. If you have moved away from your family home for the first time, you probably have a roommate, share a common bath, and eat in a dining hall. If you have left your job to return to school, you may be carrying a backpack instead of a briefcase. If your children are now in school, you may be packing your own school lunch as well as theirs. In all of these scenarios, there is enormous change. Although change is wonderful and scary, times of intense change are stressful times. Even if you have dreamed of going to college for years and now your dreams have come true, this much change is stressful.

College students are particularly vulnerable to stress. "Indeed, students as a whole represent one of the most stress-prone groups in American society" (Rowh, 1989, p. 4). Almost one-third of college freshmen report feeling "frequently overwhelmed" about all they have to do. Twice as many women (40 percent) report feeling stressed as men (20 percent) (University of California, Los Angeles, Higher Education Research Institute, 1999).

The focus of this chapter is the application of self-regulation strategies to manage stress as well as the reduction of some specific academic anxieties regarding test taking, mathematics, speeches, and writing.

---

exercise 10.1

SELF-ASSESSMENT: Stress

Your thoughts and actions can either reduce or add stress to your life. As a college student, your ability to cope during stressful events is paramount to ensure your success. With 5 being "Almost Always" and 1 being "Almost Never," assess your coping skills. Rate each of the following statements honestly by circling the appropriate number. Completing this exercise will help you identify areas of concern you may have with your ability to cope with stress.

	Almost Always		Sometimes		Almost Never
1. I let go of negative thoughts and worries at the end of the day.	5	4	3	2	1
2. I forgive others even when I feel wronged.	5	4	3	2	1
3. When I get angry I express it appropriately.	5	4	3	2	1
4. I have a high tolerance for frustration and discomfort.	5	4	3	2	1
5. I use positive self-talk during stressful situations.	5	4	3	2	1
6. I use my feelings of tension as an indicator that I need to do something to eliminate anxiety.	5	4	3	2	1

7. I experience an appropriate amount of stress during tests.	5	4	3	2	1
8. I avoid obsessing over poor performance on assignments or tests.	5	4	3	2	1
9. I take responsibility when I do something wrong or inappropriate.	5	4	3	2	1
10. I use relaxation techniques during stressful events.	5	4	3	2	1
11. I manage my time so as not to overschedule myself.	5	4	3	2	1
12. When I have conflict with another person, I resolve it appropriately.	5	4	3	2	1

Add up the numbers circled. Your total score will be between 12 and 60. The higher your score, the more likely you feel confident about your ability to cope with stressful events. For total scores below 36, write or reflect on items for which you have concerns. Also, consider talking with a trusted friend, a family member, a teacher, or an advisor.

DEFINITION AND EFFECTS OF STRESS

Stress is *the wear and tear that our bodies, minds, and feelings experience as we perceive and respond to everyday life.* It ranges from the negative extreme of actual physical danger to the exhilaration of falling in love or achieving some long-desired success. In between, day-to-day living confronts even the most well-managed life with a continual stream of potentially stressful experiences. Not all stress is bad. In fact, stress is not only desirable but also essential to life (Davis, Eshelman, & McKay, 2000).

All aspects of being human are affected by stress: physical, mental, and emotional. Stress can be acute and short-lived or it can be chronic and debilitating. Moderate levels of stress can improve our performance and enhance the quality of our lives. We feel energized and excited, our concentration improves,

FIGURE 10.1   Some Effects of Acute and Chronic Stress

	Acute (Short Term)	*Chronic (Long Term)*
Physical Symptoms	Cold, sweaty hands and feet, headaches, backaches, nausea, stomach knots, dizziness, rapid heart beat	Muscle strain, tension, stomach upset, gut or bowel problems, elevated heart rate and blood pressure
Psychological Symptoms	Worry, irritability, negative self-talk	Depression, specific fears or anxieties, anger

and we learn to set priorities and make wise choices. Thus, some stress keeps us alert and productive, but too much stress, especially over an extended period of time, can ruin our physical health, our ability to concentrate and create, and our relationships. Stress, both good and bad, is cumulative. For college students, that means that stress resulting from family events, academic pressures, finances, relationships, and jobs combines to create physical, mental, and emotional effects within us. If the cumulative stress we feel is too great, quite negative effects occur. Figure 10.1 shows some of the probable negative effects of too much stress.

We develop our individual coping strategies to manage stress throughout our life span, and in this chapter, we look at the particular stressors of college life and the self-regulation strategies that work well for many students. Throughout your reading of the chapter, reflect about the stressors in your life and how well (or poorly) you manage them.

exercise 10.2

Physical and Psychological Symptoms

Stress can affect your mind as well as your body. From the following list, check the physical and psychological symptoms you experience as a result of stress:

Physical

_____   Frequent sweating

_____   Frequent dizziness

_____   Inability to sleep

_____ Breathing difficulties

_____ Nausea

_____ Stomach knots

_____ High blood pressure

_____ Elevated heart rate

_____ Upset stomach

_____ Tension headaches

_____ Neck or back pain

_____ Skin problems

_____ Frequent illness such as colds

_____ Gut or bowel problems

_____ Ulcers

Psychological

_____ Constant worry

_____ Bad moods

_____ Negative self-talk

_____ Inability to focus attention

_____ Preoccupation with specific concerns

_____ Inability to concentrate

_____ Thoughts of inadequacy

_____ Irrational beliefs

_____ Depression

Consider talking with a trusted friend, a family member, a teacher, an advisor, or a physician if you have concerns about your responses to this exercise.

STRESSORS OF COLLEGE LIFE

Most experiences of stress flow from the following sources: our personal circumstances, our thoughts, our bodies, and our environment (Davis et al., 2000). College students live within a complex structure of circumstances

based on interpersonal relationships—boyfriends or girlfriends, family, friends, professors, roommates. Parents moving to another location or divorcing can be devastating to a student. Financial pressures; grade expectations from self, parents, or organizations; homesickness (a result of change); loss of a loved one; lack of personal connection to college teachers; loss of former identity; and peer group all contribute to college students' stress. For traditional-age students, the onslaught of personal responsibility for laundry, car, bills, food, etc. is frequently overwhelming. The families of nontraditional students can either support or sabotage the student's return to college. For many students, poverty is an increasing reality, and poverty spawns many stressors.

Our thoughts are both a powerful source of stress and an equally powerful antidote to it. Our view of our own competence (self-esteem) and our self-talk create an attitude toward the stressful events in our lives. Our beliefs about success and failure also contribute heavily. Worry is the classic symptom that our thoughts are increasing stress, rather than decreasing it. There are classic examples of thoughts that spin out of control and create extreme reactions such as anxieties about tests, math, speeches, or writing. Such intense reactions are described later in this chapter along with the appropriate self-regulation strategies.

How we manage our bodies greatly contributes to the stress we feel. If we deprive ourselves of sleep, eat large quantities of junk food, use alcohol or other drugs, or rarely exercise, then we are much more likely to suffer negative results of stress. Illness and injuries, and the recovery, are also stressful. The normal evolutionary times—adolescence, pregnancy, and menopause—are also stressful physically and emotionally.

Our environment is the fourth source of stress. From the simple weather, geography, and pollens to the physical landscape of our campus, everyone has some challenges. We may have moved to another state or culture. Whether we live in apartments, dormitories, or houses, we may have changed our physical location, and adjustment can be difficult. Sharing small spaces with roommates can be challenging if we have had our own private space before. College classrooms are another specific environmental stressor. Immense lecture halls, small seminar rooms, and scholarly libraries can be intimidating.

exercise 10.3

Stressful Life Events

Past research has linked significant changes in a person's life to physical illness (Holmes & Rahe, 1967). This exercise will help you recognize possible causes of stress.

Check those negative events that you have experienced during the past year:

_____   Death of a family member or friend

_____   Divorce, separation, or breakup

_____   Arrest or sentencing to jail or prison

_____   Personal injury or illness

_____   Trouble with an employer or fired from a job

_____   Unwanted pregnancy

_____   Sexual difficulties

_____   Life-threatening catastrophe (fire, earthquake, automobile accident, etc.)

_____   Other _____

_____   Other _____

Even positive events can cause stress. Check those positive events that you have experienced during the past year:

_____   Retirement

_____   Marriage

_____   Pregnancy

_____   Promotion at work

_____   Beginning or ending college

_____   Beginning a new job

_____   Holidays

_____   Vacation

_____   Personal achievements

_____   Other _____

What conclusions do you draw from completing this exercise?

STRESS REACTION MODEL

Stress reactions vary dramatically across the population. What one person perceives as fearful and distressful, another may optimistically view as a challenge. Our perceptions of events are unique; they are based on our own life histories, our values, and our expectations. Our perceptions determine how we will initially react. Stress management techniques are those self-regulation strategies that can modify our reaction to a stressful event as well as decrease the negative effects. Because excessive stress is so prevalent in our culture and exacts such a high price on our health and happiness, hundreds of programs, books, and articles purport to give instant answers to stress reduction.

> ### • • • MARIA • • •
> #### *Just out of the military and beginning college*
>
> *Maria is a 25-year-old freshman who has just completed four years in the military. She is ambitious about making outstanding grades because she wishes to go to veterinary school. She chose this college because it has excellent science departments and a good record of preparing students for medical, dental, and veterinary schools. Maria was competitive in high school athletics and also in her work in the military. The lack of discipline she sees around her is confusing; her professors are not giving the explicit assignments that she had in the military; she feels alone in a sea of 18-year-olds. Although she has much experience in motivating herself, Maria has had headaches and muscle tension for the first time in her life. She also has nagging feelings of sadness and depression.*

Because Maria does not feel nervous and she is not aware of worrying, she does not see her physical symptoms and sad feelings as effects of stress. Yet she is likely suffering from stress in ways different than she has ever experienced before. As we begin our work with Maria, we introduce her to the model in Figure 10.2. Note that this model begins with the person. All of us have habits, physical and psychological, that affect how we will react to a stressful event. Physical conditioning, self-talk, confidence, fear—all are examples of such habits. The stressful event can be overt, an event observable by others, or covert, a psychological event within our minds. Each of us responds to a stressful event in a unique way, and that perception, like the habits mentioned earlier, has a distinct effect on our reaction. We choose one of three reactions to a stressful event: fight, flight, or manage. Obviously, we recommend the third reaction as preferable, and much of the rest of

 **FIGURE 10.2**   Stress Reaction Model

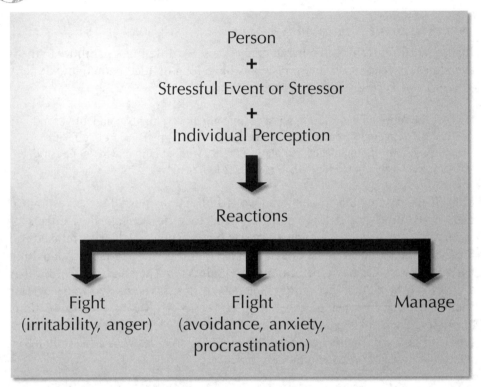

this chapter focuses on strategies to increase the likelihood that you will choose it in stressful circumstances.

Person

Maria instantly recognizes that the desired outcome is choosing to **manage,** that is, to *choose the appropriate manner to deal with the event with the least wear and tear on us.* To begin, each of us has a wide range of habits that contribute to how we will respond to stressful events. Some habits are clearly harmful, but there are also **defenders,** *habits that increase the likelihood that our reaction will be to manage, not to flee or to fight.* Maria has many defenders. She is self-disciplined in her habits and used to working hard. She has clear and explicit goals and a good academic plan. Although her family and high school friends are important to her, she has been apart from them for several years, so she is not homesick. Many of these self-regulated habits have already been presented in this text, including clear goals and planning, time management, timeliness, and ethical awareness. Others include regular exercise, healthy nutrition, assertiveness, and money management. A network of good and supportive friends and family is an important defender. The more we incorporate these strategies into our lives, the greater their effect will be.

Three areas of psychological research are especially relevant to this discussion of the individual differences within each person: Type A and Type B personalities, stress-hardy individuals, and gender differences.

Type A vs. Type B Personality

Just as we differ from each other in many ways, we differ in our abilities to manage stress. Psychologists and physicians have long divided people into Type A (driven) and Type B (laid back) personalities:

> A Type A person has a strong sense of time urgency, is highly competitive, and is easily angered when he doesn't get his way. . . . Type B's don't suffer from chronic time urgency. They can play and relax without guilt and are not hostile or excessively competitive. (Davis et al., 2000, p. 9)

Many Type As are perfectionists and workaholics; they push themselves to produce more in a shorter time, and they tend to suffer the physical effects of chronic stress. By contrast, Type Bs tend to be team players; they are relaxed and forgiving, rather than critical or cynical (see Figure 10.3). Maria starts laughing when she reads these two definitions and claims that she and her older brother are the only type As in her family. She has always driven herself to excel. Her friends even accuse her of scheduling recreation. If we look at those traits through the lens of temperament (see Chapter 7), then we can say that there seems to be a correlation between Type A and Judging as well as a similar correlation between Type B and Perceiving.

FIGURE 10.3   Examples of Type A and B Personality Types

Type A individuals tend to ...	Type B individuals tend to ...
Become irritated having to wait	Be patient
Like being in control	Follow others and not lead
Be more aggressive than passive	Be more passive than aggressive
Fidget	Be still
Be nervous and anxious	Be calm and collected
Be fast paced	Be slow paced

Recent research is revealing that a critical factor for Type As seems to be the generalized hostility that many of them exhibit. The hostility is more harmful to the person than ambition or striving to achieve (Center for Social Epidemiology, 2004). After learning this, Maria becomes quietly reflective and then begins to talk about her brother. She says that he is angry all the time; everything is someone else's fault. She always wanted to be ambitious like him, but she just cannot get angry and blame other people. She cannot even tell most people how she feels. She just keeps everything inside.

Stress-Hardy Individuals

Another insight from research is that some individuals seem *stress hardy;* they have a dispositional resilience to the effects of stress. These people have specific psychological characteristics:

- **Stress-hardy people seek challenge rather than seek security.** "They view stressors as challenges and chances for new opportunities and personal growth rather than as threats" (Davis et al., 2000, p. 9).

- **Stress-hardy people feel capable rather than helpless.** "They feel in control of their life circumstances, and they perceive that they have the resources to make choices and influence events around them" (Davis et al., 2000, p. 9).

- **Stress-hardy people choose connection rather than alienation.** "They also have a sense of commitment to their homes, families, and work that makes it easier for them to be involved with other people and in other activities" (Davis et al., 2000, p. 9). They see their lives as worthwhile.

Maria gives herself high scores on the first two but admits that she is a real *loner* and rarely joins others in activities or organizations. She also states that she feels somewhat uncomfortable in school because she does not really know how to prepare for her college tests. Her discomfort causes her to feel less capable than when she was in high school. We give Maria several specific suggestions: first, talk with her teachers about assignments and test preparation to reduce her sense of confusion; second, go to the campus learning center and look at materials on college test preparation; third, find serious study partners for the courses about which she is concerned. It is stressful to feel alone in a new situation, so we hope that she will begin to make some connections with her teachers and fellow students. Additionally, we urge her to consider joining one campus organization as another means of connection. Although some of us may automatically have the psychological characteristics of stress hardiness, all of us can strengthen them. The benefits include greater life satisfaction, reduced depression, and increased physical health.

Gender Differences

A provocative arena of research in the last decade is the deliberate investigation of gender differences in response to stress. Most of the early research on stress was conducted in predominantly male populations, so Taylor et al. (2000, 2002) began to study women and concluded that "females are more likely to mobilize social support, especially from other females, in times of stress. They seek it out more, they receive more support, and they are more satisfied with the support they receive" (p. 418). The initial and subsequent research by Taylor and other researchers has yielded the model of *tend and befriend,* a descriptive explanation of why and how women help other women cope with stressful experiences. Yet women often let go of friendships with other women when they get too busy with family and work (Apter & Josselson, 1998). Because women can be such a source of strength and nurture for each other, it is important to maintain those relationships in stressful times. Maria has isolated herself from other people, and her family and long-term friends are far away. We encourage her to stay in close contact with that established support through telephone and email.

What is the implication from this research for men? Many American males do not share with other men the most potentially stressful circumstances of their lives, such as failing relationships, work troubles, fear of unemployment, financial woes, sexual functioning, and addiction issues. Yet sharing with a trusted other person can relieve some of the stress and increase mental clarity. With a clearer mind, we can often find strategies to cope with the stressor. Some males find a trusted counselor or mentor; some choose a good female friend in whom to confide.

---

exercise 10.4

Relaxation Response

One powerful habit or defender is the **relaxation response,** "the inborn capacity of the body to enter a special state characterized by lowered heart rate, decreased rate of breathing, lowered blood pressure, slower brain waves, and an overall reduction of the speed of metabolism" (Benson, 1984, pp. 4–5). The Relaxation Response is "a bodily reaction brought on by relaxational and meditative techniques that anyone can employ to strip away destructive inner stresses" (Benson, 1984, p. 24). Benson (1975, 1984) has explored the effects of the relaxation response through more than 20 years of meticulous medical research. Practiced regularly, the Relaxation Response is an extraordinarily powerful defender, for it gives the serenity and focus to avoid the fight-or-flight reactions and choose the *manage* reaction.

Are you stressed with no solution in sight? Find a quiet room to practice relaxing using this famous technique. Completing this exercise should help you lower your blood pressure and heart rate and alleviate stress. Here, in Benson's words, are the directions:

. . . two essential steps to eliciting the relaxation response are:

1. Repetition of a word, sound, phrase, prayer, or muscular activity.
2. Passively disregarding everyday thoughts that inevitably come to mind and returning to your repetition.

This is the generic technique . . .

1. Pick a focus word, short phrase, or prayer that is firmly rooted in your belief system.
2. Sit quietly in a comfortable position.
3. Close your eyes.
4. Relax your muscles, progressing from your feet to your calves, thighs, abdomen, shoulders, head, and neck.
5. Breathe slowly and naturally, and as you do, say your focus word, sound, phrase or prayer silently to yourself as you exhale.
6. Assume a passive attitude. Don't worry about how well you're doing. When other thoughts come to mind, simply say to yourself, "oh well," and gently return to your repetition.
7. Continue for ten to twenty minutes.
8. Do not stand immediately. Continue sitting quietly for a minute or so, allowing other thoughts to return. Then open your eyes and sit for another minute before rising.
9. Practice the technique once or twice daily. Good times to do so are before breakfast and before dinner. (Benson, 1975, pp. xxi–xxii)

Remember that *defenders* are habits that increase the likelihood that our reaction will be to manage, not to flee or to fight. Defenders are long-term strategies that yield powerful lifetime results. College students vary dramatically in how many of these strategies they have mastered and regularly use. What seems difficult for many students, of both traditional and nontraditional ages, is maintaining these good habits in the midst of the upheaval of entering collegiate life. As you have seen in this text, we strongly advocate the acquisition and maintenance of these behaviors as effective self-regulation methods.

Maria chooses not to practice the relaxation response because she wants some immediate solutions for the effects of stress; however, she is intrigued with the concept and puts it aside for later consideration. She has maintained a rigorous workout schedule since leaving the military, but because she now realizes she is vulnerable to injury and muscle strain (both responses to stress), she decides to moderate her schedule slightly.

The Stressful Event

A stressful event can be an external event such as a test, a confrontation with a friend, a visit home, or a financial setback. Remembering a painful or unpleasant experience is an example of an internal event, as are self-statements about expectations or beliefs. For example, a student may say to himself, *I feel like a real loser sitting at this table by myself; everyone else is surrounded by friends.* Another might say, *I know I'm going to mess up when I have to make my presentation in class on Friday.* An event is stressful only if we perceive it as stressful.

An important skill in managing stress is the accurate recognition of a truly stressful event. If we perceive that a particular event is genuinely stressful (e.g., a parent or grandparent is diagnosed with cancer, all three of our children come down with the flu simultaneously, our backpack with all our class notes is stolen), then we can marshal our forces. One key is to use self-talk helpfully as we plan to respond to the event: *As I support my family member, whom can I ask to support me? Who in my extended family can stay with the children while I'm in class? I'll call my teachers and ask for their help; maybe they can tell me the names of some good students who would let me copy their notes.* On the other hand, sometimes we perceive something as stressful that is only moderately taxing or disappointing. It is easy to exaggerate our feelings by using extreme, unhelpful self-talk: *I'll never pass that philosophy essay test because I just can't write! Everyone else has a date this Saturday night! I'm just too old to handle school; it's been too long.*

The stressful event in Maria's life is her first college semester. The challenge is new, and initially she did not understand that she would need support to handle so much change so fast. This experience is common for many first-semester students, regardless of age and prior experience. Older students often expect that they should be able to handle everything with little or no trouble, yet few do.

Individual Perception

Again and again in this chapter, we return to the realization that our perceptions are unique, grounded in our talent, preferences, and experiences. Whether or how we react to any event is determined by how we perceive it. Tests can be a challenge or a terror. Meeting new people can be exhilarating or painful. The adventure of doing something new can bring dread or delight. Much of stress management is understanding our own perceptions and, if necessary, changing them.

The Reaction: Fight, Flight, or Manage

Maria's reaction to the event of college is both psychological and physical. She has feelings of sadness and depression in spite of her desire to be in college and succeed there. Feeling uncomfortable and disturbingly incompetent fosters her depressive reaction. Her headaches and sore muscles, in spite of her excellent physical condition, are another sign of her body's reaction to her perception of this first semester.

We react to a stressful event in one of three ways: fight, flight, or manage. The fight-or-flight response has been studied for almost a hundred years, beginning with Walter Cannon, a physiologist at Harvard. The **fight-or-flight response** is "a series of biochemical changes that prepare you to deal with threat or danger" (Davis et al., 2000, p. 2). Although still useful in some physical circumstances, generally it is unhelpful in modern life. Our fight-or-flight responses are not always obvious. Sometimes we get irritable or angry (a fight response) as a reaction to a stressful event. Road rage is an extreme example. Far more likely is that we will be grumpy with or critical of our families or roommates and then feel guilty about our behavior. The flight response has less obvious outcomes. We may try to avoid situations in which we feel fear. Such avoidance can become a specific anxiety or phobia. A common example is social anxiety, in which people may avoid going to any type of gathering. Academic examples of flight responses are procrastination on assignments and a variety of anxieties regarding tests, math, speeches, and writing.

Maria wants to manage her collegiate experience in such a way that she meets her goals and is happy. One of her best strategies is simply to ask for help, to talk with another person about her feelings. She does not run away from her feelings and she does not blame herself or others. Instead, she thoughtfully analyzes the situation and her reactions and then is willing to try new strategies. She chooses to keep a journal of her feelings by recording her own internal dialog. Gradually her depressed feelings ebb as she begins to pass her tests through serious studying, and her body no longer hurts because she is resting more. Most important, she begins to make friends with whom she can share her feelings. Several visits home to her supportive family also bolster her spirits. By the end of the term, she is cheerful and confident.

Maria is successful in managing her stress because she has set clear goals, she monitors her actions, and she has the psychological strength or will to persist in helpful behaviors. She is willing to work diligently to solve this problem. One of the primary causes of self-regulation failure is underregulation, which "occurs because people lack stable, clear, consistent standards, because they fail to monitor their actions, or because they lack the strength to override the responses they wish to control" (Baumeister & Heatherton, 1996, p. 13).

STRATEGIES FOR MANAGING STRESS

As we said earlier, managing stress means that we use the strategies and the actions that will solve the issue and leave the least wear and tear on us. Let us use the four sources of stress—our personal circumstances, bodies, environment, and thoughts—as a method of organizing some useful strategies.

In terms of our personal circumstances, a basic goal is to keep our core relationships healthy. Who are the people who care about us and whom do we care about? Keeping connected by visits that encourage closeness (that ubiquitous term *quality time*) and by telephone and electronic media help maintain healthy relationships. Honesty, assertiveness, and compromise are assets in any relationship. As a college student, if you manage your time and your money so that you always have something extra for the unexpected demand, then that demand will not be so stressful, and you can remain calm. Build a supportive system of people on campus; some possibilities include your roommate, hall director, adviser, mentor, counselor, and teacher. Join an organization and get to know the sponsor and the upperclassmen.

Strategies to protect our bodies are also important. Regular aerobic exercise, good nutrition, enough sleep, and vitamins all contribute to an increased self-awareness of our bodies and to becoming more stress hardy. The excessive use of alcohol, nicotine, and other drugs takes a toll on us. Counseling support groups help control these behaviors, as can Alcoholics Anonymous, Overeaters Anonymous, and Narcotics Anonymous.

We respond to our physical environment in subtle ways. Our first suggestion to students is to make where they live their home and their sanctuary, even if it is just half of a small room. Post pictures and mementos that bring good memories. Set up a quiet place to study (not your bed!) that has all the tools you need. Wear the right clothes, especially as the weather changes, and go to the doctor if you are ill. Regular physical checkups help too.

Our thoughts can be a source of stress, but they can also be a powerful tool for managing stressful reactions. Increasing our self-awareness of our beliefs and cognitive processes, changing our self-talk, participating in group or individual counseling, and using mental techniques to reduce phobic responses are examples of cognitive stress management strategies. The following sections explicate two cognitive stress management strategies: refuting irrational ideas and breaking the worry cycle.

• • • ROY • • •
A first-semester freshman who worries and worries

Roy is a beginning freshman who has entered a college in a state 1,000 miles away from his home. He is excited to finally be in college, but within a few weeks, he reports that he is not sleeping well, has gained weight, and has trouble concentrating on his studies. What surprises him the most is that he is almost constantly worrying. He worries about the girl he left at home, he worries about his academic performance, and he worries that he will not fit in on campus even though he had a large circle of friends in high school.

Refuting Irrational Ideas

When Roy comes to talk with us, his self-talk pours out of him. By listening to our self-talk, we realize what we are thinking and believing, so we ask him to write down all the things he is saying to himself. If what we are saying is irrational—*It is horrible when things are not the way I want them to be; I must be competent in everything I do; I need someone to decide for me; Everybody has to like me*—then we greatly increase the likelihood that our stress level will rise. Irrational beliefs not only lead to inappropriate stress; they can also lead to feelings of low self-esteem and depression. The easiest way to recognize irrational beliefs is to examine our self-talk for catastrophic and/or absolute words. Catastrophic words and ideas include *terrible, awful, all over, I'll get fired,* and *she'll leave me.* Absolute words include *should, must, never,* and *always.*

Roy's self-statements are classically catastrophic and absolute: *Why did I think I could succeed here? Everyone else is so much smarter than I am. Julie is going to find some other guy; she won't wait for me. She won't want to be with a failure.* We have the ability to change our self-talk (cognitive restructuring) to statements that are rational, such as *Things are the way they are, and I can handle that; I will try hard to do the best I can do, but I am not perfect; I am a competent person and can learn to make my own decisions.* If we are aware of what we say and strive to say and believe rational or logical statements, then our stress responses will be much lower.

Here is the five-step process Davis et al. (2000) recommends for changing unhelpful self-talk into helpful self-talk:

1. Describe the event that has triggered your stressed response.

2. Write down your self-talk and mark any irrational statements.

3. Write down your feelings during your response.

4. Challenge the irrational statements that you identified by replacing the catastrophic/absolute thinking with logical thinking.

5. Replace any irrational self-talk with rational self-talk.

Roy reluctantly agrees to try this exercise, so he chooses an event that had happened the night before. He had tried to call Julie, and there was no answer. He immediately said to himself, She saw my number and doesn't want to talk to me. I bet she's with someone else. *He felt low and dispirited and wanted to be home, not where he was at school. To challenge his irrational statements, we ask him some simple questions:* Has Julie always been honest with him about her feelings? Is she an ethical person who has always honored their relationship? Does she turn off her phone sometimes to study or to be with friends? *Soon, Roy begins to see that there are many rational explanations for Julie's not answering his call, and he quickly changes his statements. He decides to call and talk with her that evening. Roy has many irrational beliefs imbedded in his self-statements, so this initial exercise is a good beginning for him.*

exercise 10.5

Changing Negative Self-Talk

How frequently do you experience negative self-talk? Probably more often than you imagine. Completing this exercise will help you to become aware of your irrational beliefs.

1. Keep a log of all your negative self-talk for one day. Write down both the trigger and your stressed response.

2. Select one or two examples from your log and complete Davis's steps to change your irrational beliefs to rational beliefs.

   - Describe the event that has triggered your stressed response.

   - Write down your self-talk and mark any irrational statements.

   - Write down your feelings during your response.

   - Challenge the irrational statements that you identified by replacing the catastrophic/absolute thinking with logical thinking.

   - Replace any irrational self-talk with rational self-talk.

Breaking the Worry Cycle

When we feel distressed, troubled, or uneasy, we are worrying. Worry can be healthy when it leads to problem solving such as *I'm uneasy about that history test next week. I wonder if I can find a study group. I'd better make the time to go to the test review session.* When worry does not lead to productive solutions, it is unhealthy. You have a serious problem with worry if you

- are chronically anxious about future dangers or threats,

- consistently make negative predictions about the future,

- often overestimate the probability or seriousness of bad things happening,

- can't stop repeating the same worries over and over,

- escape worry by distracting yourself or avoiding certain situations, and/or

- find it difficult to use worry constructively to produce solutions to problems. (McKay, Davis, Fanning, 1997 in Davis et al., 2000, p. 135)

Roy agrees that he has a serious problem with worry because almost all of the listed statements are true about him. Copeland (1998) recommends the following strategy to turn worry into problem solving:

- Describe in detail one worrisome situation.

- Make a list of possible solutions, that is, actions you can take to improve the situation.

- Choose the actions you can do right now (the others may be useful later).

- Make a contract with yourself to do up to three of those actions and set a date for completion.

- Evaluate your progress and set a new contract for other behaviors. (Davis et al., 2000, pp. 137–138)

> *Roy chooses his concern about making a good life on campus as the focus of his exercise. The specific situation he chooses is that the past Friday night several guys who live on his floor went out to shoot pool and no one invited him.* Why didn't they include me? That hurts, especially since we usually eat dinner together in the dining hall. *As Roy describes this situation and his own internal dialog, he begins to speculate about what really happened. He admits that he was studying in his room with the door closed and his headphones on, and his roommate had*

gone out of town for the weekend. Maybe the guys didn't even know I was there. If they had knocked on the door, I wouldn't have heard them. How can I make sure this doesn't happen again this weekend? *Roy makes a list of possible solutions: ask a couple of the guys on the floor on Thursday what their plans are for the weekend, check the campus and local newspapers for Friday events, and invite his roommate to go to a movie. Roy decides to try the first two and then perhaps include his roommate. He promises himself that he will do the first two behaviors by Thursday night at 10 P.M. and come back to see us with an evaluation of the results.*

exercise 10.6

Worry No More

If you are like most college students, you have probably worried about an exam or assignment. You may have worried about your performance or the consequences of doing poorly. You may have also experienced feelings of inadequacy. Think back to your most recent academic worrisome situation and follow Copeland's (1998) steps below. Completing this exercise will provide you a model to help you turn worry into problem solving.

- Describe in detail one recent worrisome situation.

- Make a list of possible solutions, that is actions you can take to improve the situation.

- Choose the actions you can do right now (the others may be useful later).

- Make a contract with yourself to do up to three of those actions and set a date for completion.

- Evaluate your progress and set a new contract for other behaviors.

OVERCOMING SPECIFIC ACADEMIC ANXIETIES

The fear response to a stressful event ranges on a continuum from a low level of anxiety (feeling mild physical symptoms and a desire to avoid the event) to a crippling level of phobic response in which a person cannot perform at all. People often think of airplanes, elevators, high places, snakes, etc. when they think of phobias. However, there are four common academic anxieties: speech anxiety, test anxiety, math anxiety, and writing anxiety. Overcoming such an intense anxiety is serious business. What follows is a brief overview of the cognitive strategies used to subdue such a response. If you are mildly or moderately anxious in an academic situation, you can utilize these strategies; if you are intensely anxious in one or more of these situations, we recommend that you work with a counselor at your campus counseling center. Remember that you can learn how to *manage* rather than suffer the painful road of anxiety.

· · · TODD · · ·
He is afraid to enroll in a required speech communication class

Todd is a senior who has avoided taking speech communication since entering college. He is a competent student but has always been terrified of public speaking. Now his department has mandated that he enroll in the freshman speech course, and he knows he must pass it to graduate. He has even had fantasies of leaving college, running away. When he had to take a short speech course in high school, he discovered that he felt nauseous, had trouble breathing, and usually forgot most of what he had planned to say.

Todd is anxious, not just mildly nervous, but so anxious that he has extreme physical symptoms and cognitive interferences that inhibit his performance.

Four primary sources of academic anxiety are your academic reputation with others (what opinions other people will have if you perform poorly), your own opinion of your abilities and competence, your concerns about actualizing your goals, and your uneasiness about being unprepared (Divine & Kylen, 1982). What frequently happens to many students is happening to Todd. The memory of his poor prior performance increases his anxiety level, so there is an increasing spiral of intensity about his responses. In this state, his emotions interfere with his ability to think clearly and rationally. His ability to attend and concentrate suffer; he feels intimidated and defensive. Thus, the cycle continues, and he wants to escape such negative emotions. He is even willing to fantasize about leaving college, just to achieve a sense of relief. "Brain-body misbehavior causes havoc" (Divine & Kylen, 1982, p. 74).

The purpose of anxiety reduction principles is to reduce or modify a fear response so as to be able to

PRIMARY SOURCES OF ACADEMIC ANXIETY

- The opinions of others
- Your own opinions
- Your fear of not achieving your goals
- Your feelings of being unprepared

perform competently. Performance anxiety, sometimes called stage fright, is a learned response. The fact that we learn to be anxious is actually good news because that means we can learn how to be calm. There are some common themes in the strategies to overcome these specific academic anxieties: appropriate content preparation, rehearsal, rational self-talk, physical self-care, and good use of time.

Speech Anxiety

Many students have similar feelings to Todd's. It is the *public* in public speaking that can intimidate so many people. Most of us have had little experience in public speaking through our high school years, yet it is a crucial professional skill. Increasingly, college faculty are requiring public presentation of projects as required components of advanced courses in differing majors. If you become nervous about making a formal presentation in class, the following strategies can help:

BEFORE THE EVENT:

- Finish appropriate, timely, comprehensive content preparation.
- Use rational and helpful self-talk.
- Practice or rehearse your performance.
- Get enough sleep, exercise, and good nutrition.

DURING THE EVENT:

- Make careful and deliberate use of your time.
- If you feel yourself becoming tense, refocus on the task using appropriate self-talk and breathe deeply.
- Use rational and helpful self-talk throughout.

OTHER SUGGESTIONS:

- Adapt your vocabulary and examples to your audience.
- Grab the audience's attention by using an audiovisual aid (pass out any handouts at the end).
- Make eye contact with individuals.
- Speak loudly enough for people in the back row to hear.
- Use accurate information.
- Place a watch on the lectern to monitor your use of time.
- Deliver an effective, structured, and upbeat conclusion (a short summary of your main points will help the listener). (Rowh, 1989)

As we begin working with Todd, he is horrified by our first sugges-tion—we strongly recommend that he quickly volunteer to make the first speech. He is registered for the course and is attending class. The first speeches begin in two weeks. Everything inside Todd wants to delay his speech as long as possible (actually, his feelings want to delay it for-ever). However, going first has several benefits, including less time for anxiety and increased pressure to prepare (Rowh, 1989). As he begins to prepare, Todd uses many of the strategies he is learning in class, in-cluding selecting and narrowing a topic. As he researches his topic, he realizes that he will know more about it than anyone else in class (ra-tional and helpful self-talk). After completing his outline and notes, he practices his speech three times to himself, then twice before a mirror. Several of his friends volunteer to be an audience, and one even has a videocamera, so Todd gets lots of feedback. As a final practice, he goes to the classroom when there is no scheduled class and gives his speech standing in the front of the room. Using helpful self-talk, he exercises the night before and gets a few hours of sleep. After the speech, he reports that he made a C+ and that his feelings of relief are immense. He tells us how he had to stop several times and refocus with a deep breath and the statement I am doing okay; I can do this.

Test Anxiety

The most common academic anxiety is test anxiety. How many times have you lost points on a test when you knew the material? How many times have you raced through a test and turned it in without checking your answers because you just wanted to get it over with and escape? How many times have you worried more about a test than studied for it? A little anxiety can help motivate us and focus us on the task, but too much anxiety simply destroys performance.

exercise 10.7

Test Anxiety Survey

Test anxiety is a frequent experience for college students. Look at the following checklist. How many of these characteristics describe you? Completing this ex-ercise will provide an assessment of your test anxiety.

_____ You feel that tests are more of a threat than a challenge.

_____ You have a lot of worrisome or negative thoughts about what might happen if you do poorly.

_____ You have physical reactions (such as butterflies in the stomach, sweaty palms, altered heart or breathing rate) when you are about to take a test.

_____ You have trouble keeping your mind on the test items or remembering ideas you learned recently.

_____ You worry about other people scoring higher than you on the test.

_____ Your worries about tests have not decreased as you have matured (Divine & Kylen, 1982, pp. 60–61).

If you suffer from test anxiety, is your response generalized to all tests or is it specific to one course or subject? Your answer to that question is important. If it is specific anxiety about one course, then the strategies in this chapter can help you manage stress and increase performance. If you have been severely anxious in all testing situations for more than two years, then we strongly recommend that you work with a counselor on more powerful techniques such as progressive relaxation, cognitive desensitization, and thought stopping.

Many of the self-regulation techniques such as goal setting, timeliness, and key behaviors that we have described in these chapters can decrease test anxiety. Additional strategies stem from the following model to overcome test anxiety:

BEFORE THE TEST:

- Finish appropriate, timely, comprehensive content preparation, including all homework. In simple terms, read, study, and work with a study group. Go to any review sessions and be sure to go to class the week before the test.

- Use rational and helpful self-talk, such as *I have prepared sufficiently and I will answer the questions carefully.* Use the techniques for changing irrational self-talk and worry statements.

- Practice or rehearse your performance by answering practice questions.

- Get enough sleep, exercise, and good nutrition. Even if you study late the night before, get at least two to three hours of sleep.

THE DAY OF THE TEST:

- Grab the psychological edge by going to class on time with *all* the required materials.

- Be sure to take a watch so you can set specific time goals so you will have enough time at the end of the test to check your answers.

- Do not participate in the pretest fearful conversations that the other students are having.

- If you have a choice of where you sit during the test, sit away from friends and toward the sides or back of the room to minimize distractions when people finish early.

DURING THE TEST:

- Make careful and deliberate use of your time. Look over the test and allocate how much time you intend to spend on each section.

- If you feel yourself becoming tense or distracted, refocus on the question saying, *What is this question asking?* and breathe deeply.

- Use rational and helpful self-talk throughout. It is tempting to use *catastrophizing* and *awfulizing* statements; instead, deliberately use rational and calming statements.

Math and Writing Anxiety

Our abilities to solve math problems and to write college papers are procedural knowledge skills. Usually students who have math or writing anxiety have developed these responses over many years. An important initial step is to determine your level of competence in procedural knowledge skills. In other words, what is your competence when you are not anxious? Most campus learning centers have diagnostic tests to help you discern your skill level. If you are deficient in these skills, pursuing the appropriate remediation is imperative. You may need to learn these skills at the high school level before attempting a college-level class. Remedial courses or labs, computer tutorials, and individual tutoring are available through community colleges or local libraries. As you master each level, you will discover that your anxiety is lessening.

Many college students, however, have good procedural knowledge skills but freeze on the math test or in-class writing assignment. If that is your circumstance, review the following strategies:

BEFORE THE CLASS:

- Complete appropriate, timely, comprehensive content preparation, including all homework. Work with a tutor to clarify areas you find confusing and then attend study group and test reviews.

- Use rational and helpful self-talk. *I've practiced and gone to the test review. My tutor gave me some shortcuts that should really help.*

- Practice or rehearse your performance. For math, rework your homework problems and any additional problems available. Practice explaining to yourself how to do the problems. For in-class writing assignments, write possible questions and then outline your answer. Write thesis statements for each possible question.

- Get enough sleep, exercise, and good nutrition.

DURING THE EVENT:

- Make careful and deliberate use of your time. For math, immediately write the formulas down. Then plan how you will allocate your time on the various parts of the test. For the essay, quickly write down any key names, dates, etc. to organize into an outline later.

- If you feel yourself becoming tense, refocus on the task using appropriate self-talk and breathe deeply. Refocus by saying, *Okay, what is this question asking and what do I know about it?*

- Use rational and helpful self-talk throughout. *These first few questions look just like the ones in the test review last night. I'm going to be fine.*

CONCLUSION

In this and the previous two chapters, we have given you a powerful and complex set of self-regulation strategies that can help you structure and maintain not only your college life, but your professional and personal life beyond your college years. We hope that again and again you will return to these principles and adapt them to your current circumstances.

SUMMARY

- College students are particularly vulnerable to stress, for times of intense change are stressful times.

- Stress is the wear and tear that our bodies, minds, and feelings experience as we perceive and respond to the demands of everyday life.

- Moderate levels of stress can help energize and excite us, thereby improving our performance. However, too much stress over an extended period of time can ruin our physical and mental health.

- Stress can be acute and short-lived, or it can be chronic and debilitating.

- Most experiences of stress flow from the following sources: our personal circumstances, our thoughts, our bodies, and our environment.

- The stress reaction model is a combination of the person, the stressful event, and the individual perception that we have about ourselves. From these, we react to stress in one of three ways: fight, flight, or manage.

- Managing stress means choosing the appropriate manner to deal with the stressful event with the least wear and tear on us.

- Defenders are habits that increase the likelihood that our reaction will be to manage, not to flee or to fight.

- Three areas of psychological research relevant to individual differences are Type A and Type B personalities, stress-hardy individuals, and gender differences.

- The Relaxation Response is a physical reaction brought on by relaxational and meditative techniques.

- Two cognitive stress management strategies are refuting irrational ideas and breaking the worry cycle.

- Four common academic anxieties occur in the areas of math, speech, writing, and testing.

- Common themes in the strategies to overcome specific academic anxieties include appropriate content preparation, rehearsal, rational self-talk, physical self-care, and good use of time.

KEY CONCEPTS

Academic anxieties: speech, test, math, writing

Breaking the worry cycle

Defenders

Fight, Flight, or Manage

Gender differences

Refuting irrational ideas

Relaxation Response

Self-regulation strategies

Stress

Stress-hardy individuals

Stress reaction model: person, stressful event or stressors, individual perception, reactions (fight, flight, or manage)

Stressful event

Stressors of college life

Type A and B personalities

GUIDED JOURNAL QUESTIONS

1. Within the last few months, how often have you become upset, really nervous, or stressed? What were the main causes? How did you react? Are you still experiencing these feelings? Explain.

2. What do you tend to worry about most often? Do you consider your worry to be unhealthy? What types of self-talk do you say to yourself when you worry? Explain.

3. What physical and psychological stress symptoms do you have? What are the primary causes (personal circumstances, your thoughts, your body, or your environment)? Explain.

4. Thinking specifically of your academic life and the courses you are currently taking, which ones cause you the most stress? Why? Do you suffer from any of the following anxieties: speech, test, math, or writing? If yes, explain.

5. What major changes have you experienced in the past year or two? Describe the stress associated with those changes.

6. Are you primarily a Type A or Type B person in your academic endeavors? List several examples to support your choice. What do you think are the particular strengths and weaknesses of your characteristics? How content are you with this designation? Explain.

7. Do you tend to manage your stress or do you tend to fight or flee? Explain. When you do effectively manage your stress, what methods do you use? What methods might you consider now adopting (after having read the chapter) when you have the tendency to fight or flee from stress?

8. Describe an experience when stress actually improved your performance. Why do you think it helped you perform at a higher level?

The Last Word

I've always liked to live on the edge—not physically, but intellectually. The edge is lots of fun, but quite stressful, so I've learned to pull back from that edge a little, and life is sweeter.

—De Sellers

11

Neural Development, Attending, and Understanding

My, what nice frontal lobes you have.

We have been learning all our lives, so in some ways it seems peculiar to become self-conscious about this process we have been doing for so long. However, academic learning is different from other kinds of learning. The intention of academic learning is that we demonstrate our understanding and use of new information through a stylized set of performances: quizzes, tests, papers, reports, projects, presentations. Our performances then receive an evaluation in the form of a grade by experts (teachers). The recently renewed practice of internships follows the same model, with the evaluation done by supervisors in the field. One premise behind this elaborate evaluative system is that if we demonstrate competent performance, then we have *learned* the material and we will be able to use it in the future, that is, in our professional, personal, and civic lives. The second premise is that in the process of learning and performing, we will learn how to think analytically and evaluatively.

Thus, academic learning is inextricably tied to a specific kind of performance. It is neither a casual nor happenstance process. The first task of any of us as

291

students is to determine the specific academic expectations of a teacher: what is to be learned and how will that learning be demonstrated? The second task is to determine what we bring to this learning situation: what skills and content do we already possess? The third task is to determine how we need to acquire the information and how we should practice performing it. All these tasks require accurate and conscientious reflection.

---

exercise 11.1

SELF-ASSESSMENT: Learning and Memory

Your memory is your most important survival tool for college. As information increases each year, you are expected to learn more in your college experience than others before you. With 5 being "Almost Always" and 1 being "Almost Never," assess your learning and memory abilities. Rate each of the following statements honestly by circling the appropriate number. Completing this exercise will help you identify areas of concern you may have about your ability to learn and remember effectively.

	Almost Always		Sometimes		Almost Never
1. I remember names, dates, and places (facts).	5	4	3	2	1
2. I learn by connecting new learning to old learning.	5	4	3	2	1
3. I predict what level of learning (taxonomy) I need to accomplish for each class.	5	4	3	2	1
4. I practice repeating a skill or concept over and over as a regular part of my study repertoire.	5	4	3	2	1
5. I use varying methods when learning (read it, write it, say it out loud, explain it, etc.).	5	4	3	2	1
6. I have good attention and concentration while learning from lectures.	5	4	3	2	1

7. I have good attention and concentration while learning from textbook chapters.	5	4	3	2	1
8. I summarize what I learned at the end of a lecture.	5	4	3	2	1
9. I summarize what I learned after I read a textbook chapter.	5	4	3	2	1
10. I have good memory recall on exams on lecture material.	5	4	3	2	1
11. I have good memory recall on exams on textbook material.	5	4	3	2	1
12. I am motivated to learn on my own (for my own curiosity and satisfaction).	5	4	3	2	1

Add up the numbers circled. Your total score will be between 12 and 60. The higher your score, the more likely you will feel confident about your memory and learning abilities. For total scores below 36, write or reflect on items for which you have concerns. Also, consider talking with a trusted friend, a family member, a teacher, or an advisor.

DEFINING ACADEMIC PERFORMANCE

We come to college for many reasons, but the primary focus is that we will learn, that is, get an education, and thus become a different person. Many of you will go on to complete programs and graduate. If you choose to achieve a baccalaureate degree, you should differ dramatically from the person you were when you entered college. As a graduate you should have

- a specific set of declarative knowledge (theories, principles, concepts, data) and procedural knowledge (skills) in your major and minor fields.

- an increased ability to learn independently.

- the ability to reason, problem solve, and think critically about a wide range of subjects.

- a recognition of the primary principles necessary to understand our culture, including history, government, philosophy, literature, science, and the arts.

- a system of personal ethics.

Colleges and universities use several methods to ascertain that you have these characteristics before graduation. The most common are required courses and exams. **Academic performance** is *the demonstration of our understanding and use of new information through a stylized set of performances: quizzes, tests, papers, reports, projects, presentations.* Assessment can be done by an instructor, a peer, an outside expert, instructor evaluation of participation, objective tests, essay tests, projects, presentations, performances, creative works, papers, portfolios, field work, group process, student critiques, student reflections, reports, journals, etc. Institutions are recognizing that collaborative projects and internships are also important to professional development. Most of these formal processes are graded, but many opportunities are never directly graded, such as leadership/participation in student organizations, volunteer service, attendance at campus lectures, and performances. A few campuses are now using portfolios, an intensive method of monitoring each student's progress toward graduation. Portfolios are collections of student work. Students and their instructors choose papers, projects, and tests that represent the best academic work of a year. Some schools ask students to add to their portfolio each year. Even if your school does not require portfolios, you may wish to create one just for yourself, especially for work you complete in your major and minor fields.

Grades

Grades are the primary means of ascertaining whether you have met (grades A, B, C) or have not met (grades D, F) the criteria for graduation. College grading is much different from high school; instructors have a great deal of autonomy. Whether it is an essay test or an English theme or a group project, experienced teachers know quickly what grade is deserved. Even multiple-choice tests are designed to reflect particular levels of mastery. A major responsibility of faculty is to determine what are the appropriate standards for each field. What follows are descriptions of commonly held standards for college grades. Read these carefully, because they are the criteria most of your instructors use each time they grade your work.

A-level work standards. Consistent mastery of the subject matter, including key concepts and vocabulary, and frequent, insightful questions about the material; commitment to careful and accurate critical thinking using appropriate premises and language from the subject field.

B-level work standards. Competent mastery of the subject matter, including key concepts and vocabulary, but little insight; reasoning ability is competent, but rarely creative.

C-level work standards. Inconsistent competence with the subject matter and unclear reasoning; some knowledge and use of basic concepts and principles.

D-level work standards. Poor understanding, primarily rote memory, of basic concepts and vocabulary; unclear and illogical reasoning.

F-level work standards. Little or inaccurate comprehension of the basic concepts of the subject; incompetent reasoning and poor intellectual performance (Paul & Elder, 2001, pp. 173–175).

We realize that some instructors and some institutions have lower standards than the ones that we have articulated. However, we believe that these standards are a fair representation of American higher education.

---

exercise 11.2

Grading Your Teachers

What are the attributes of an A teacher? How do these differ from a B or C teacher? Do any of your teachers deserve the grade of D or F? This exercise will help you compare the criteria for earning good grades as a student with the criteria of being a good teacher.

1. Grade each of your current teachers and explain how and why they earned the grades you assigned.
2. What similarities exist between the criteria for grade-level standards for students versus those you created for your teachers?

PREDICTING ACADEMIC PERFORMANCE

How can we perform competently, or even brilliantly, if we do not know the criteria? The answer is that we cannot; yet many students enter the learning and studying process without serious and accurate prediction of what they need to understand and how they must perform that understanding. Prediction is an interesting business because we are rarely 100 percent accurate in any area, and academics is no different. As we stated in Chapter 3, the course syllabus is the first opportunity that the instructor has to state intentions and expectations.

Syllabi contain the structural requirements of a course: what type of performances and the relative importance of each. Equally important are the qualitative criteria (the standards) the instructor will use in evaluating each performance, but these are rarely stated overtly in the syllabus. If our expectations of how we will be evaluated are accurate, then our learning and study can be focused and efficient. How can we discern what our instructors value? In the following sections, we discuss some things you can do and questions you should ask yourself each time you receive an assignment for a test, project, paper, or speech.

What Is the Content?

The question, What is the content? encourages you to look at the scope of the material to be covered on the test. The syllabus is the first place to look, for often teachers will carefully explain the content covered in each assignment.

For a test. Make a list of all the major topics covered in the syllabus and the lectures. Are there additional topics in assigned readings? Has your instructor grouped or organized them? Has your instructor prepared a study sheet as a handout or on the Internet? Can you organize them logically? Which are the most important? The least important? Make a set of note cards or a list of all the technical terms and definitions.

For a project. What is the tangible outcome or product (e.g., written paper, oral presentation, multimedia, artwork, computer application, performance)? What is the purpose or question that the project should address? What are the limits imposed by the assignment? If the assignment is written as a handout or on the Internet, read it carefully and mark all the key words.

For a paper or speech. What is the thesis? Is it the appropriate scope (narrow/broad) for the length of the paper or speech? What source materials are needed? If the assignment is written as a handout or on the Internet, read it carefully and mark all the key words.

What Is the Level of Learning Needed?

One of the most powerful learning strategies is to study a subject at the level of learning you will be asked to perform. If you can accurately predict the level of a test, project, paper, or speech, then design your study so that you practice performing at that level. For example, if the content of a literature test involves comparing/contrasting two novels, then you can organize your study accordingly and practice writing short paragraphs comparing and contrasting the plots, characters, settings, significance, etc. The box on the following page is a reminder of the revised Bloom's Taxonomy, or the level of learning.

For a test. Keep in mind that objective questions start at the remembering level but generally range through understanding to application; short-answer questions start at the remembering level but usually require understanding; procedural classes such as economics and accounting require the application level for most questions; and essay questions tend to require the higher levels of the taxonomy—analysis, evaluation, and creation. Will sample test questions be available on the instructor's website, in textbook study guides, at review sessions, or in campus libraries? Some instructors are direct about the level of performance they expect; others use more subtle hints in offhand comments, such as *You need to be able to show me you understand these concepts* or *You'll have to give concrete examples of these principles.*

> **THE REVISED BLOOM'S TAXONOMY OF EDUCATIONAL OBJECTIVES**
>
> Create
>
> Evaluate
>
> Analyze
>
> Apply
>
> Understand
>
> Remember

For a project. The level of learning is crucial. Should your project simply demonstrate that you understand a concept or should it demonstrate that you can apply it, analyze it, evaluate it, or create something new? Consider talking with your instructor individually to determine whether you clearly understand the level required. If the project is to be done by a group, make sure the entire group has agreed on the level to be demonstrated.

For a paper or speech. Remember that you will be functioning at the creation level assuming that you will use analysis and evaluation to produce your work. How will you use your sources to produce an original work?

Prediction is a collegiate skill that develops slowly. The more careful you are in paying attention to these issues and then deliberately designing your learning and study strategies according to your predictions, the more successful you are likely to be. For example, if you are preparing for an essay test in introductory philosophy, and the instructor tells you that 25 percent of the test will be definitions and 75 percent will be three essay questions, you know that you need to master the content at the analytical level. So you might predict some questions and try to answer them or form a study group that discusses and debates the major points covered in the lectures.

---

exercise 11.3

Predicting Exam Questions

Predicting and creating sample test questions are valuable methods to assist your learning. Select a declarative knowledge–based course for which you are currently studying for an upcoming exam and answer the following questions. Completing this exercise will assist you in using prediction to prepare for an exam.

- Will you be tested by multiple choice, true/false, matching, fill-in-the-blank, short answer, essay, or a combination of several of these testing modes?
- What do you predict will be the highest level of learning that you will be expected to master?
- What are 5 to 10 sample questions at the appropriate learning level that reflect the predicted testing mode?

THREE APPROACHES TO ACADEMIC LEARNING

The premise of academic performance is that we will demonstrate our understanding of the information we have learned. Teachers and students often fail to communicate accurately on this point. Students sometimes determine that the only performance level needed is simple memorization, a recitation of data without any broader understanding. This level of learning, *remembering* from the taxonomy, is the ability to recognize or recall an idea, a fact, or an occurrence in a form similar to the original presentation. Although important as an initial step in academic learning, simple memorization is extremely limited.

Surface Learning

When we approach learning from the viewpoint that we simply have to answer so many questions to pass the test to meet the requirement and thus stay out of trouble, "learning then becomes a balancing act between avoiding failure and

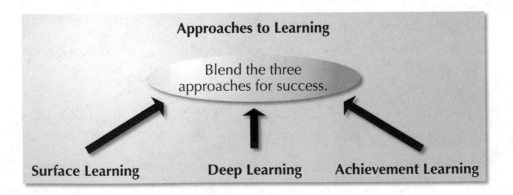

not working too hard" (Entwistle, 1990, p. 685). **Surface learning** describes an approach to academic learning in which *students are motivated by extrinsic or outside rewards, not their own desire to learn about the subject.* Students who engage in surface learning

- believe that the material being studied is boring, useless, or irrelevant.
- see assignments as demands rather than opportunities.
- focus on the literal aspects of the information rather than its meaning or significance.
- rely on rote memorization to prepare for performance.
- avoid making personal connections to the material or its implications.
- worry about failure.
- resent the time necessary for studying (adapted from Entwistle, 1990).

Both cynicism and anxiety foster surface learning (Entwistle, 1990) because both tend to push us toward using only memorization instead of learning the material at the other levels of the taxonomy—understanding, application, analysis, evaluation, and creation. Time pressures and our thoughts about assessment measures can increase our anxiety and lead us away from meaningful learning.

Deep Learning

Deep learning is dramatically different from surface learning in that *students are motivated to learn deeply to satisfy their own curiosity.* Students who engage in deep learning

- believe the material being studied is interesting and potentially useful.
- see assignments as opportunities.
- focus on the underlying meaning of the material.
- relate their understanding to their prior knowledge by reading and discussion.
- think about the information and create hypotheses about how it relates to other topics and subjects.
- find learning emotionally satisfying (adapted from Entwistle, 1990).

Sometimes students who want to learn deeply respond well to the collegiate atmosphere, and other times they become cynical and depressed if they feel no one, including teachers, shares their values. To be successful in school, they have to learn to meet practical deadlines and occasionally settle for less than the perfect outcomes they desire. The most important choice for such students is the choice of department and instructors. A major adviser who shares their philosophy is also helpful.

Achievement Learning

A third type of learning seems to be occurring more frequently in recent decades. **Achievement learning** occurs when *students are motivated by the ego enhancement that comes as a result of high grades and academic awards.* Students who engage in achievement learning

- see high grades as important.
- are competitive in academic settings.
- meet formal academic requirements carefully, such as time, length, and topic.
- use time strategically.
- value their self-discipline and systematic learning habits.
- concentrate on learning the material that the teacher views as important and avoid other material that might not help their grade.
- like highly structured courses and need little interaction with teachers.
- enjoy the external attention of success and the internal feelings of self-accomplishment. (Entwistle, 1990, p. 686)

Students who view learning as a vehicle for achievement often choose this road early in life, even in primary school. They pragmatically use both surface and deep learning to meet their ego needs.

These three extreme models of learning highlight a major dilemma in American higher education. Many collegiate faculty passionately believe in the deep-learning approach; it is the way they prefer to learn and it is usually the way they study within their own field. They often want their students to learn in the same way. Deep learning is an idealistic model, and it works for a few people all of the time and for many of us some of the time. Learning that way can be exhilarating; it is the flow experience that we talked about earlier. However, we may be so entranced by the intellectual journey that we do not pay attention to the specifics we are required to meet.

Deep learning in every course does not seem to be a practical choice for many students, especially those who struggle with balancing work schedules, organizational commitments, or family responsibilities. The shortcomings of surface learning are only too obvious. Although we may pass a quiz based on surface learning, we have little or no permanent learning. Essentially, we walk away from the learning experience with nothing but a grade. Achievement learning does give us permanent and usable knowledge, but it allows little room for creative intellectual exploration and for experiencing the intrinsic joy of learning. The choices we make in the type of learning we do in college matter. College is a serious and expensive business. How can we blend all three types of learning to create the right path for each of us?

· · · **SUSAN** · · ·

A mom in her thirties with two children

Susan is an energetic woman in her thirties who is married with two elementary school age children. She reentered college this year to complete a degree in environmental studies and is taking four courses: Physical Geography, Political Science, Calculus, and Environmental Sociology. Susan is highly motivated to do well in school because she wants to pursue a graduate degree, and her early years in college yielded mediocre grades. Her family encourages her, but her husband has to work overtime frequently, and one of her children is struggling in school. Occasionally, her mother comes over to watch the children, but that usually happens only once a week. Susan is a competent student, but she has to work hard for her grades. She feels she is continually juggling demands from many different sources.

Susan attends every class and is well prepared, and she often asks questions in class. She has reviewed her note-taking strategies and increased the quality of her notes by using some of the techniques mentioned in Chapter 3. Her attending skills are good, through both intent and practice. In working with Susan, we shared with her the grading standards and the three modes of learning: surface, deep, and achievement. She knew instantly that her primary mode is achievement, but she also believes she is ready to learn in a deep manner as well. She is motivated to make good grades, not only for her own need to achieve but also because her family is sacrificing for her to return to school. Her target GPA for this term is a B average (3.0). As an older student, she believes this is her last chance to prepare for a professional career.

We asked Susan to reflect on her course load this term and determine what mode of learning would best suit each course. Here is a summary of her reflections:

Physical Geography

This course is important to my major; they call it a foundational course, and my adviser told me that I need to master this material because it will be used in numerous junior- and senior-level courses. The material is complex and technical, with long vocabulary lists. I know I will have to do a lot of memorization just to learn the terminology, but I will also have to understand how to use all those terms and concepts. My learning mode in this course must be achievement. I will have to find ways to relate the material to other things I already know. Maybe I can find a study group for this course; talking about the subject should help me learn it better. It is important that I make a strong B in this course.

Political Science

Well, this course is required for everyone. Most of the students will be freshmen and sophomores. I've heard it's a large lecture course with mostly multiple-choice tests. I haven't been that interested in civics or history or courses like that, but maybe some of the information on elections will be okay. Frankly, I'll do what I have to do, but my learning mode will be surface, unless I get interested in some topic. I'll try for a B but will take a C if I have to. If I have extra study time, I won't put it into this course.

Calculus

As long as I work consistently in math, I can be competent on the tests. This course is required for my major, and it is important because some of my advanced courses and the graduate courses I plan to take require that level of mathematical skill. I'll never be a mathematician and I don't get really excited by math, but I can do this work. My learning mode in this course will be achievement, and I will make a B.

Environmental Sociology

This is the course I am most excited about because it is close to what I want to do with my major. Of course, my learning will be deep in this course; in fact, I am already reading ahead in the text, and I checked out some fascinating sources on the Internet. It is important to me to make an A in this course. I'm going to join the department club so I can hear all the speakers they're bringing to campus this term.

To reach her goals, Susan will use a variety of learning modes. She will adapt her classroom and study strategies as well as how she manages time to reach her goals. Several weeks later, Susan returned to talk about the first round of upcoming tests in her courses.

> *I'm excited about being back in school, but it's tougher than I expected. My first test is in calculus, and I'm sure that we will be tested at the application level. Our teacher told us that memorizing the problems would not be enough, that the test problems would be combinations of homework problems. I've been trying to explain my way through each type of problem, and that strategy is working.*
>
> *Political science is what I expected. It's a large lecture class, so the test will be objective. The teaching assistant told us to know identifications and vocabulary, so I've made lots of study notes, and I have been practicing memorizing that information.*
>
> *Environmental sociology is everything I hoped for. The professor is great! I'm understanding everything, and I ask a lot of questions in class. I'm really confident, even though the first test is all essay. I think the test will be at the analytical level with some remembering of terms, etc. It seems easy to analyze in this course; I'm always coming up with questions.*

We asked about physical geography and there was a long silence.

> *Well, I'm trying, but the material is confusing. I memorize as much as I can. Maybe I'll be all right. The test is objective and will probably be at the level of remembering with some questions at the level of understanding.*

Susan left to catch the campus bus before we had a chance to explore that difficulty in physical geography.

---

exercise 11.4

Your Approach to Learning

How often do you use surface, deep, and achievement learning? Just as we asked Susan to reflect on her courses, reflect on your courses this term and determine what mode of learning you are using for each and why. This exercise will help you evaluate appropriate learning modes for your courses.

HOW OUR BRAINS LEARN

In Chapter 7, we discussed the concepts of multiple intelligence—that each of us has a variety of intelligences—linguistic, logical–mathematical, spatial, interpersonal, bodily–kinesthetic, to mention just a few. Much of that work emerged from educational and psychological research. Until recent years, how our brains learn (the physiological process) has been only hypothesis. Now, modern technology illuminates many of our learning processes. We are discovering that our brains have inborn characteristics that include

- motivation to learn.
- imagination and creativity.
- problem-solving ability.
- tendency to seek patterns.
- logic and reason. (Smilkstein, 2003, p. 71)

Psychological Research: Brain Learning Theory

Did you know that human brains are getting larger over time? Your great-grandparents' brain weighed about four pounds less than yours! Each and every second of your life, several billion bits of information pass through your brain at speeds up to 250 miles per hour (Benesh, Arbuckle, Robbins, & D'Arcanjelo, 1988). As we learn more about the brain, we learn more about how to learn. Educational psychologists are combining knowledge and theory with biologists to give us new insights into how our minds grow, change, and learn.

We have about 100 billion *neurons* (brain nerve cells) in our brain. Each neuron has a body and from that body grow fibers called *dendrites.* Each neuron also has one long fiber called the *axon,* which also has more fibers called *teledendrites* or processes. At the end of each of these is a synaptic terminal filled with chemicals called *neurotransmitters. Synaptic terminals* allow dendrites and neurons to communicate with each other.

Learning is *the growing of dendrites* (see Figure 11.1). As we learn, neurons connect with each other into networks. "Neural networks can be inconceivably complex and numerous. Again, any one of a person's 100 billion neurons could be connected to as many as 10,000 other neurons" (Smilkstein, 2003, pp. 58–59).

FIGURE 11.1   Learning: The Growing of Dendrites

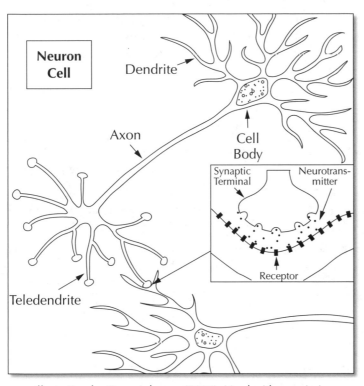

Illustration by Drew Johnson (2004). Used with permission.

The brain is in a constant state of change. When we practice those connections (by study and repetition), the neural network as a whole can learn (grow) and adapt. Such capability is labeled **plasticity;** in other words, "learning organizes and reorganizes the brain continually (Bransford, Brown, & Cocking, 1999, p. 103)" (Smilkstein, 2003, p. 78). Neural networks are being intensely studied by biologists, psychologists, philosophers, engineers, and computer scientists because such human network functioning is often superior to computer functions, especially when the data used are messy, incomplete, and inconsistent (King's College London, 2003).

exercise 11.5

Make a Fist

One of the first steps in enhancing your memory is to have some understanding of how your brain learns. This exercise will help you visualize a nerve cell and the growing of dendrites.

Make a fist with your right hand. Your fist represents one neuron (brain cell). Now slowly begin to extend each finger. Each finger represents a dendrite (remember that one neuron can connect to as many as 10,000 other neurons). Now make a fist with your other hand and slowly begin to extend each finger. Finally, make one finger from your left hand touch a finger on your right hand. When one finger touches another, you have now represented two nerve cells connecting (a dendrite connecting to another dendrite). Your two fingers (dendrites) touching each other represent making a strong connection of learning to a network of neurons.

- An "enriched" learning environment facilitates the growth of dendrites and an "impoverished" environment inhibits growth. Describe how you envision an enriched learning environment compared with an impoverished learning environment.

- What suggestions do you have for your current instructors to create a more enriched learning environment to facilitate dendrite growth?

- How can you enhance your own learning (create an enriched environment) to facilitate your growth of dendrites?

Theoretical Models

Four theoretical models developed over the past 40 years attempt to explain how we learn. In 1968, stage theory proposed that learning is sequential—that we process and store information in three stages from sensory memory to short-term memory to long-term memory. In the early 1970s, the concept of levels of processing expanded stage theory. This theory proposed that the more intensely and creatively we process and understand information, the better our ability to remember. Later, in the 1980s, psychologists hypothesized that our brains had so many networks that information could be processed simultaneously by several different networks in different parts of the memory system. This concept, called parallel-distributed processing, added to the complexity of how we think about learning. An extension of this model was the connectionistic model, in which duplicate information is thought to be stored in various parts of the brain. Increasingly, researchers believe that emotions affect our learning (Huitt, 2003).

In recent years, theorists have begun to refer to stage theory as the dual-store memory model because they believe that information is stored in the short-term as well as the long-term memory (Ormrod, 1999). Another important conceptual change is the renaming of short-term memory to working memory. "Working memory is that component of memory in which the active processing of information takes place. . . . Many theorists portray working memory as playing a *central executive* role, in essence controlling and monitoring an individual's overall memory processes (Baddeley, 1986; Barkley, 1996; Cowan, 1995, Haberlandt, 1997)" (Ormrod, 1999, p. 188). In simple terms, the **working memory** is *the part of the process where we think and understand.*

In this chapter, we will present a simplified model of learning and emphasize the roles of attending and understanding. In the next chapter, we will focus on memory theory with emphasis on the dual-store model and the practical applications for test preparation and test taking as well as other types of academic performance.

Connecting Psychological and Theoretical Research

In many ways, we are just beginning to know how our brains learn. Existing theoretical explanations of how we learn include physiological (dendrites, etc.), human information processing (sensory register, working memory, and long-term memory), constructivism (individualized construction of meaning), and contextual (the influence of social and physical circumstances) (Ormrod, 1999).

Some important principles for academic learning emerge from both the physical and theoretical research. As you study this chapter and the next, concentrate on how these principles can work for you in your life as a student. Making the connections between theory/research and practical applications empowers you to become an autonomous learner.

We learn by connecting new learning to old learning. In practical terms, that means whenever we hear a lecture or read a text, we must make the effort to connect new information to what we already know. The effort we make to remember what we already know activates those neural networks and makes new learning more powerful. Clearly, understanding the material is essential to build good networks. Rote memorization does not build connected and meaningful networks (Smilkstein, 2003).

STRATEGIES:

- Before a lecture class, briefly review the notes from the class before.

- Before reading a textbook chapter, preview the textbook and begin to reflect on what you already know about the material.

- Continually search for meaning by thinking about how the new information is similar to what you already know.

If we experience and practice new information, then the appropriate dendrites, synapses, and neural networks grow. The larger the network, the more we can remember and use that knowledge. Such effort also increases the likelihood that we will build parallel networks and parallel storage for this information, thereby increasing our chances of remembering the new information (Smilkstein, 2003).

STRATEGIES:

- Diligently practice. The more you practice, the more reliable your understanding and memory are.

- Allow for mistakes. Mistakes are a normal part of learning. Accurate and powerful learning takes time because the dendrites and neural connections must form.

The more ways we input and practice material, the larger the networks become. In other words, if we recite aloud, write items down, explain to someone else, or create colorful study aids, the networks will be larger and more reliable. If we use multiple ways of learning, then both the number and the variety of networks grow (Smilkstein, 2003).

STRATEGIES:

- Each time you are learning a concept or skill, find at least three or more ways to practice the material.

- Once you have learned the information, teach it to someone else. If you can teach the material to others effectively, then you have proper comprehension of the material.

If we use the information regularly, we will retain the networks. Conversely, if we do not use it, dendrites and neural connections die (Smilkstein, 2003). What we know and remember is stored physically in our brains, and we have to maintain it by practice, much as we have to maintain our muscles. The cruel fact is, use it or lose it.

STRATEGIES:

- Do not wait until right before an exam to begin to study. Reviewing and practicing material regularly is the key. We recommend that you review new material at least within the first 24 hours of receiving the information.

- Create an end-of-the-week review and practice schedule, and review all the notes (from your classes, assignments, textbook) for that week and previous weeks. Make it a weekly ritual.

Our emotions affect our learning, thinking, and remembering. Self-confidence and interest help; self-doubt and fear hurt. It is hoped that your classroom environment is emotionally comfortable. We now know that learning is enhanced by challenge and inhibited by threat (Smilkstein, 2003). However, some stress is important to optimize learning. Stress levels vary for each of us, so we must ask ourselves, How much stress is too much? Your best instructors create a challenging, yet engaging, environment.

STRATEGIES:

- Use positive self-talk when you begin to become overstressed in class.

- Quickly set up a meeting with your instructor if you begin to fear the class environment. Be honest with your feelings. Remember that fear may cause us to fight or flee.

- Remember that some stress is necessary to optimize learning. Recognize it as being helpful for your memory.

Susan pondered this new information and gave the following reflection:

All this information makes real sense to me. In my major courses, Physical Geography and Environmental Sociology, I don't have much prior academic knowledge since these are my first courses, but I have kept current about environmental issues for several years. I will have to work hard to create and master a body of knowledge, especially the technical vocabulary. If I make note cards and practice them every day, I can build those networks. I'll have to find some other students interested in this major so I can discuss the ideas because my husband is not interested and our children are too young. I will need to talk about the concepts frequently if I want to really understand and remember them. Math just takes practice; I'll do my homework the day of class and then do some extra problems if I have trouble. I like the idea that my emotions can help my learning. While I am not so interested in Political Science, I am interested in learning, and I am much more self-confident than I was years ago. I must take care to have a positive attitude about that course.

A DESCRIPTIVE MODEL OF ACADEMIC LEARNING

Current psychological concepts about academic learning are complicated and often confusing. On one hand, each of us has a lifetime of experience in learning; on the other hand, how we learn seems mysterious. The development of computers in the twentieth century helped us grasp some basic facts about learning, but the same computer technology also illuminates just how different

FIGURE 11.2   The Dual-Store Model

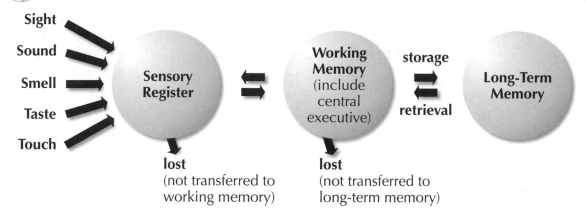

our brains are from the fastest computers. Because the theories and the research undergirding them are so complex, we have created a relatively simple model that integrates the primary principles of each theory for use in this text.

When we reflect on our own learning, some basic elements become clear. What follows is our description of what we believe is the academic learning process; the description is based on our reflection, current psychological and neuropsychological research and theory, and common sense. The primary structural model we use is the dual-store of memory (see Figure 11.2) that posits three components of memory: a sensory register, a short-term or working memory, and a long-term memory (Ormrod, 1999).

Moving from the Environment to the Sensory Register

Academic learning becomes possible when our *sensory register* (sight, sound, touch, smell, taste) grabs a signal from our environment. A signal may be the teacher's voice in a lecture, the print from a textbook, a graph written on the board, the image from a picture. At that moment, two other parts of our brain are active. First, that part of our consciousness called the *central executive* in the working memory is directing our sensory register to attend to the signal. Our sensory register intentionally grabs a signal; this act is called attending.

Second, our long-term memory, including declarative, procedural, and metacognitive knowledge, is immediately available. We not only have the ability to recognize or read the language used, but we also have the ability to know if the information (signal) is familiar or unfamiliar. So, from the very first moment, many parts of our brain are operational. Part of being a successful learner is being able and willing to attend to the signal. During our waking hours, we are always paying attention (our minds are constantly consumed with thoughts), but we may not be paying attention to the right signal, especially during academic learning. If we deliberately intend to learn, we increase the likelihood that we will learn. Our ability to attend to academic signals varies, but we can increase that ability by specific concentration strategies.

Moving from the Sensory Register to Working Memory

Once our sensory register has grabbed the signal, it comes to our conscious mind. The part of our conscious mind that thinks is called the *working memory*. Our central executive brings the new information (signal) to the working memory and activates the relevant neural networks in the long-term memory so that they are easily accessible. Our working memory is extremely limited. Some researchers insist that it is only a few seconds, but others believe it lasts a few minutes. Whichever is correct, we know that it is extremely limited, and that to hold on to information we must repeat it, write it down, or talk about it. Our working memory is also extremely limited in capacity and primarily auditory. It is here in the working memory that we understand new information. It is here in the working memory that we think. As soon as we understand something or create a new idea or connection, then our central executive function decides whether it is important to remember it. If we understand the information correctly, then we can store it in the appropriate neural networks. If we do not understand it, then we cannot connect it to the appropriate networks in our long-term memory.

Storing/Retrieving Information from Working Memory into Long-Term Memory

Storage is a deliberate act, and there are many methods especially suited for collegiate learning. A crucial part of storing is the practice of retrieving the information. So we store and retrieve, store and retrieve, each time building the dendrites and the neural networks. Most information in the long-term memory, especially that related to academic learning, is stored semantically, that is, by meaning. For example, all the information about a topic is stored as connected neural networks. Ideally, our retrieval process becomes automatic and easy because we have built rich and varied networks. When we are asked to perform that information or use it in a new way, we are able to do it quickly and accurately.

STRATEGIES FOR IMPROVING ATTENDING AND UNDERSTANDING

The following sections highlight the most powerful strategies for enhancing attending and understanding. The next chapter focuses on storage/retrieval. As you read these strategies, reflect about your own learning strengths and weaknesses. Which strategies already work for you? Which look promising?

Attending

We are bombarded with innumerable signals each day from our environment. As students, we are also bombarded by hours of lecture, hundreds of pages of print, and many classroom discussions. We can only learn academic information if we attend to it. Here are the ways that successful students manage their academic attention:

- Make the deliberate intention to pay attention and to learn the information, rather than daydream. If you drift away, gently bring yourself back to the task of attending. Research supports that intentional learning is more successful (Ormrod, 1999).

- Get enough sleep and exercise so that your body will support attending.

- Just before a lecture, look back over the notes you took before. When you are reading, quickly look back at the preceding chapter. In other words, activate the appropriate neural networks from your long-term memory.

- Use more intense strategies if the material is difficult or boring to you. For example, sit at the front of the room or sit at a desk or table to study. Ask questions as you read. Or explain the material to someone. Be active in the learning process.

- Avoid distractions. If sitting next to friends disrupts your learning, move. Clear your desk or study table of anything that promotes daydreaming. Go to the library and study in a place separated from noise or movement.

- Take notes during presentations, even discussions, and mark print while reading. Doing such an activity helps to hold your attention to the task.

- Use retrieval cues as you learn new information (e.g., reminding yourself of how something you are learning is similar to something else, or providing context for the material). Create your own cues while you are learning. The cues act as hooks to help you remember. The cues will help you locate the stored memories.

Some of us are primarily visual learners; that is, we learn best by seeing pictures, charts, graphs, and words. Some of us are primarily auditory learners; that is, we learn best by hearing information and explanations (Smilkstein, 2003). It is important to recognize our strengths, but also to compensate for our weaknesses. As college learners, we do not have to passively accept a learning environment. Instead, we can get information in other modes that accommodate our learning strengths.

Understanding

Understanding is the core skill of collegiate learning. In ideal circumstances, it is easy to understand data or concepts when we attend to them, but some circumstances are not ideal and we have great difficulty. The greatest temptation is to just memorize and hope to pass the test. However, memorization without understanding means we do not use meaning to store the information in the appropriate neural networks, so even if we remember it long enough for a test, we will not be able to use that information later. There are three cardinal rules for understanding collegiate material.

Rule #1. Continually search for meaning as you attend to new information. The search for meaning occurs through patterning. Your brain needs to find and connect the new information to something similar. **Comprehension monitoring** means *the continual awareness we have of our own understanding as we learn something new.* All of us routinely monitor our understanding of conversations and instructions and ask people to repeat what they have said. When we study academic material, it is important that we are aware when we do not understand so that we can take action immediately. Such monitoring of academic learning is not as easy as monitoring in our daily lives, especially if we have created a habit of not expecting to understand tough academic material.

Rule #2. Make sure you really understand the material. The most powerful method of determining whether you are comprehending a particular set of material is to engage in a miniperformance. In other words, test yourself before you face a teacher's test. The first step of understanding is translation—changing from one form of representation to another. For example, can you translate details into concepts *or* concepts into details; can you paraphrase (put into your own words)? The best method is oral; translate out loud, to your study partner, your roommate, the wall, if necessary. What can you say without consulting your lecture notes or the text? If you cannot say much, if you simply repeat or recite the message, or if what you say does not really make sense, then you are not comprehending at a level necessary for college.

If you have already developed good comprehension monitoring when you are learning, celebrate that skill. If you have not, then consider frequently stopping and checking how much you understand. Doing so will slow your studying temporarily, but it is the only way to improve this skill. Use study questions from the text to help you monitor. Turn the topics from the lecture into questions. Acquire the habit of question/answer as you study your notes (the Cornell system helps with this technique) or print material.

Most college teachers presume that your abilities in comprehension monitoring and understanding are competent. Frankly, many do not recognize comprehension problems and believe that students who are having trouble are simply not trying. Comprehending collegiate material requires intent, skill, effort, and determination. It is routine in college to read and reread, to ask for help, and to struggle with difficult and complex material.

As we presented in Chapter 4, understanding has three steps: translate/paraphrase, explain/interpret, and predict/infer/see connections. In all cases, understanding is active; we have to do something with the information. In practical terms, the first step is to review your notes or the print material. Does seeing it again help your comprehension? If not, what other sources could help? A conference with the instructor? A tutor? A study group? A fellow student? Other print explanations in the library or on the Internet?

Rule #3. Do whatever you have to do (but no more) to understand the material. (The realization that you do not really understand the material calls this principle into play.) Such work is hard and takes effort and time. If we have the attitude of a surface learner in a difficult course, we may struggle with how much time and effort is required. Although this book and others say that two study hours for every class hour is a reasonable ratio, you may find that you have to study four or five hours for every class hour in a difficult subject just to be able to understand.

Susan confronts these three principles early in her first semester. As stated earlier, her attending skills are good, and she comprehends the material in her political science and environmental sociology classes. After the first round of tests, Susan returns to discuss the results:

> *I can comprehend math if I attend every class, do my homework promptly, and go to the math lab for help when I am confused. I made a 79 on the first test; that's okay, not great, but okay. I knew I'd ace the environmental sociology test, and I did. A 92! My daughter made me a cake to celebrate. I predicted well about the political science test; I'm really glad I listened to the teaching assistant. That test was mostly at the remembering level, and I made an 84. I have a problem: I am really scared about Physical Geography. I knew the material would be complex and technical, but I had no idea it would be so tough. I tried to find a study group, but without success, given my tight schedule. Even though I am reading the text before going to class and making note cards, I think I understand less than half of what I am reading. The lecture helps somewhat, but my teacher speaks very rapidly and will not allow questions. I made a 57 on the first test; I've never made a grade that low. This is already the fifth week in the term, and there is no improvement!*

Susan is wise to be concerned, for if she continues to struggle, her chances of passing this course are small. Sitting with her, we brainstormed several strategies for this difficult situation:

- If the instructor is using a Web-based course management system, then access any of the features the teacher is using, such as lecture outlines, live chat, or a message board. Susan can use these aids from home.

- Search the Internet for the topics she is having difficulty understanding.

- Ask a reference librarian for help in finding other explanations of problematic topics.

- Ask the instructor to recommend as a tutor an advanced student who successfully completed this course.

- Schedule an appointment with her instructor to discuss her comprehension difficulties with the subject, her grade status in the course, and how long she should persist before withdrawing from the course.

CONCLUSION

Performance is the lens through which we recommend looking at academic learning. Knowing what we need to perform, how we need to perform it, and how it will be evaluated—all these direct our learning/study strategies to be efficient and effective. Understanding how we learn and our own learning strengths and weaknesses also helps us determine how much time and effort will be necessary to reach our goals.

In this chapter, we examined numerous aspects of academic learning, and we explored the first two steps of the model of academic learning: attending and understanding. The next two steps, storage and retrieval, are the initial subject in Chapter 12, after which we will discuss test preparation, test taking, and critical thinking.

SUMMARY

- Academic learning requires us to demonstrate our understanding and use of new information through a stylized set of performances that receive an evaluation in the form of a grade by an expert.

- As students, we need to determine the specific academic expectations of the teacher, what we bring in content and skills to the learning situation, and how we need to acquire the information and practice performing it.

- Outcomes of participation in college are knowledge in major and minor fields of study; the ability to learn independently, reason, problem solve, and think critically; a greater understanding of the culture; and a system of personal ethics.

- A major responsibility of each faculty member is to determine what are the appropriate standards for the content field.

- Predicting academic performance is based on appropriate responses to a set of questions that ask: What is the content? What is the level of learning needed?

- There are three different approaches to academic learning: surface learning, deep learning, and achievement learning.

- The brain has 100 billion neurons (brain nerve cells). Each neuron has the ability to grow fibers called dendrites. Dendrites and neurons can communicate with each other through synaptic terminals and create neural networks.

- Learning is the growing of dendrites.

- The brain is constantly changing. The term *plasticity* represents that learning organizes and reorganizes the brain.

- We learn by connecting new learning to old learning, when we experience and practice new information, when we input and practice material often, when we use the information regularly, and when our emotions are appropriate and connected to learning.

- A simple model of learning has four stages: attending, understanding, storage, and retrieval.

- Attending is when the sensory register grabs information from the environment. We can only learn academic information if we attend to it. Ways that can enhance attending are paying attention in class, getting enough sleep and exercise, reviewing notes before class sessions, accommodating for difficult or boring classes by sitting in the front of the class, avoiding distractions, taking good notes, and using retrieval cues.

- Understanding is the core skill in collegiate learning. To understand means that we are able to translate the material into our own words, explain and interpret the information, and predict or infer connections.

- Three principles that help understanding are monitoring your comprehension, testing your understanding, and doing what is necessary to learn.

KEY CONCEPTS

Academic performance

Achievement learning

Attending

Bloom's Taxonomy, Revised

Central executive

Comprehension monitoring

Deep learning

Dendrites

Environment

Grades

Learning

Long-term memory

Neural networks

Neurons

Neurotransmitters

Plasticity

Predicting academic performance

Sensory register

Surface learning

Synaptic terminals

Teledendrites

Understanding

Working memory

GUIDED JOURNAL QUESTIONS

1. How would you describe your ability to learn effectively? Provide examples.

2. How has the expectation of what it takes to make an A in college changed from when you were in high school? Which of your classes do you find the most difficult to make at least a B in this semester? Explain.

3. Describe an incident when you received a lower grade than you expected or felt you deserved (from high school or college). Did you talk to the instructor about the grade? What did you learn from the experience?

4. How fairly do exams assess your academic performance in various subjects? What other methods of assessment do you prefer?

5. Typically, what type of performance is more difficult for you: an exam, an individual project, a group project, a paper, or a speech? Explain.

6. From an emotional standpoint, what does it mean to have a safe learning environment? Describe a situation in which you tried to learn but stress or fear inhibited your learning.

7. Think of a recent example when you simply wanted to learn by using a surface approach to learning. What method did you use? What was the

outcome? Now describe a recent example when you engaged in a deep approach to learning. What method did you use? What was the outcome?

8. What are the positive and negative consequences for a student whose only motivation to do well in college is grades and academic work (achievement learning)?

The Last Word

Why is it that my strongest memories are those that I am most wanting to forget?

—*Russ Hodges*

12

Storing, Retrieving, and Achieving Maximum Performance

Lights, camera, action!

Academic transformation is about becoming an expert learner. As an expert learner, you can be successful in college and beyond, staying current in your professional field. However, another aspect of our minds is our ability to think, and that ability is different from expert learning. We all think spontaneously, but we do not all think critically. There are levels of thinking ability (not intelligence) that range from the unreflective thinker to the master thinker. No guarantee exists that you will become a critical thinker in college; in fact, many graduates are not critical thinkers. Becoming a critical thinker means that you can routinely use higher-order thinking skills based on reason and evidence, not only in your study but also in your life. Effective study strategies help develop such skills, especially when you study as a deep learner. An important aspect of critical thinking is the constant ethical concern of being fair:

Fair-mindedness entails a consciousness of the need to treat all viewpoints alike, without reference to one's own feeling or selfish interests, or the feelings or

319

selfish interests of one's friends, community, or nation. It implies adherence to intellectual standards (such as accuracy and sound logic), uninfluenced by one's own advantage or the advantage of one's group. (Paul & Elder, 2001, p. 5)

Becoming fair-minded is challenging because it is so much easier to be the opposite, selfish and shortsighted. To become fair-minded, we must be intellectually humble, courageous, empathetic, honest, perseverant, confident in our reasoning ability, and autonomous (Paul & Elder, 2001). College is a wonderful opportunity to develop these traits if we take the initiative.

It is easy to let the academic performance demands of tests, papers, and projects limit what we learn and become. Our contention in this chapter is that because you will spend many hours studying to pass tests and assignments, you might as well seize this opportunity and study to develop your critical thinking skills at the same time. If you do, you increase the likelihood that you will be able to bring your thoughts, emotions, and actions together to reach your life goals and experience fulfillment and a sense of well-being (Paul & Elder, 2001).

Frame your study by thoughtful questions and deliberately push yourself to analyze, apply, and evaluate the information fairly. Search out the assignments and the instructors that will help you develop advanced thinking skills. If becoming a critical, fair-minded thinker is an important goal for you, then you can accomplish it through your undergraduate study.

---

exercise 12.1

SELF-ASSESSMENT: Learning Strategies

Successful students use many strategies to help them learn. Selecting the best strategy for the right task comes with experience. Remember, too, that no one strategy works for everyone. With 5 being "Almost Always" and 1 being "Almost Never," assess your use of learning strategies. Rate each of the following statements honestly by circling the appropriate number. Completing this exercise will help you become a more efficient and reflective learner.

	Almost Always		Sometimes		Almost Never
1. I engage in active learning strategies (more than simply reading my textbooks and reviewing my notes).	5	4	3	2	1
2. I regularly condense material to help me learn.	5	4	3	2	1

3. I create summary sheets for my lecture notes and textbook material.	5	4	3	2	1
4. I use mnemonics (memory tricks) when memorizing lists or concepts.	5	4	3	2	1
5. I create note cards to help me memorize material.	5	4	3	2	1
6. I use color, pictures, diagrams, and graphics to help me learn material.	5	4	3	2	1
7. I synthesize my lecture and textbook notes by creating one- to two-page summary sheets.	5	4	3	2	1
8. I create note cards to help me comprehend and analyze material.	5	4	3	2	1
9. I create maps (visual representations to show relationships between concepts) to help me analyze material.	5	4	3	2	1
10. I create graphic organizers (matrices, tree diagrams, hierarchies) to help me learn material.	5	4	3	2	1
11. I create sample test questions and answers to help me learn material.	5	4	3	2	1
12. I reflect and think about the material I am learning to help me derive meaning.	5	4	3	2	1
13. To reinforce my learning, I try to teach the material to others.	5	4	3	2	1

Add up the numbers circled. Your total score will be between 13 and 65. The higher your score, the more likely you feel confident about your memory and learning abilities. For total scores below 39, write or reflect on items for which you have concerns. Also, consider talking with a trusted friend, a family member, a teacher, or an advisor.

THE ROLE OF THINKING IN STUDY

When we think, we make sense of what is going on; that is, we create meaning. In academic learning, we attempt to make sense of a content field, such as history, biology, philosophy, or economics. Each subject that we study represents a distinctive way of thinking about a particular set of questions, and those questions result in the basic concepts of that field. Those concepts provide the underlying unity in the field. Some examples are as follows:

- *mathematics* as the development of a language for quantification

- *algebra* as arithmetic with unknowns

- *sociology* as the study of how the life of humans is shaped by the groups in which they are members

- *physics* as the study of mass and energy and the interrelations between the two

- *philosophy* as the study of ultimate questions and their reasoned answers

- *biochemistry* as the study of the chemistry of life at the molecular level (Paul & Elder, 2001, p. 149)

If we can understand the basic concepts in a field, then we have a much better chance of creating meaningful learning in our daily study. Here are some beginning questions to help you determine such concepts:

- What is the main goal of studying this subject?

- What are people in this field trying to accomplish?

- What kinds of questions do they ask? What kinds of problems do they try to solve?

- What sort of information or data do they gather?

- How do they go about gathering information in ways that are distinctive to this field?

- What is the most basic idea, concept, or theory in this field?

- How should studying this field affect my view of the world?

- How are the products of this field used in everyday life? (Paul & Elder, 2001, p. 152)

Sometimes a good place to find the basic concepts and the logic of a subject is in a good encyclopedia or on the Internet. Your text may also have some introductory material that is useful. Having a clear grasp of the concepts and logic of each course provides you a mental framework in which to direct your learning. That mental framework also helps you understand and remember the material.

All academic subjects are the product of thinking. Thinking creates content. Thinking expresses, organizes, maintains, and expands content. Thinking analyzes and evaluates content. Thinking restructures and transforms content. Whenever you study, you can choose the level of thinking you want and need to use. The deeper your level of thinking, the deeper your level of learning. The fastest way to deepen your learning is to ask questions about the content:

- What is my purpose in studying this content? Will I be a surface, a deep, or an achievement learner for this course?

- What are my instructor's expectations for my learning this content?

- What are the questions/problems of the content to be considered?

- What concepts are important to those questions/problems?

- What information do I need to explore those questions/problems?

- How can I relate this information to daily life?

Your thinking ability is the cornerstone of your capacity to learn in college, and it will vary from subject to subject. Sometimes you will intuitively ask the questions that lead your study; other times you will need to be much more deliberative and find other sources to help you.

HOW WE LEARN THROUGH STORAGE AND RETRIEVAL

In the last chapter, we delved into the mysteries of academic learning and examined the first two stages of the cycle: attending and understanding. Because our brains process information in a nonlinear way, the stages become blurred once we move from theory to practice. For example, if we understand new information by using the steps of translation/paraphrase, explain/interpret, and predict/infer/see connections, we have begun the stage of storage because we are connecting that information to neural networks through meaning. Whenever we do that, we are laying the foundation for reliable retrieval from our long-term memory.

The realization that we will be expected to perform determines much of the academic learning process, and such realization is good, for students are inundated by so much information in each course that it is impossible to learn everything. Professors shape and narrow the content by their lectures and the required readings/problems. Students have to go much further as they look at the content and begin to organize what they need to remember, what they need to understand, what they need to apply, etc. The level of learning (the revised Bloom's Taxonomy); the student's approach to learning (surface, deep, achievement); the mode of performance; the awareness of the student's own learning strengths and weaknesses; the competing demands of other courses, work, and family—all contribute to the storage and retrieval practices chosen for study.

What and how and why we remember has fascinated psychologists for decades, and there exists a wealth of conflicting theory and research. Currently, the dominant theories are dual-store, levels-of-processing, and activation. **Dual-store theory** hypothesizes that *our memory functions as three components: sensory register, the working memory, and long-term memory.* Figure 12.1 depicts the dual-store model from Chapter 11.

All memory theories, including these, are metaphors; that is, they attempt to explain how our memory works by models because we really do not yet know exactly how we remember. Scientists are just beginning to be able to study the brains of living persons through new technology. For the purposes of this text on academic learning, we use the dual-store theory as the primary structure, but we occasionally highlight particular helpful insights from other theories.

FIGURE 12.1 The Dual-Store Model

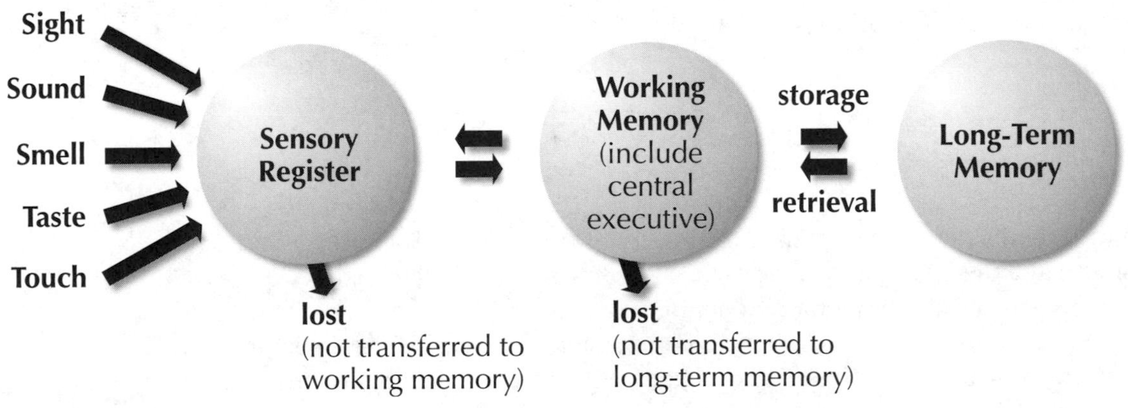

Sensory Register

In the dual-store model, the sensory register is believed to have unlimited capacity for all the environmental information that we are capable of sensing, and that information is held for a few moments in the form in which we sensed it (visual: less than 1 second, auditory: 2–4 seconds . . .). In those moments, we have neither understood nor interpreted the information. In academic learning, we must attend to the information that we are trying to learn so that we can move it to our working memory. At the same time, we are discarding all the other information as if it were junk mail. The most important aspect of attention for academic learning is that usually we "cannot attend to or otherwise learn from two complex situations at the same time" (Ormrod, 1999, p. 187), so we must purposefully attend to the academic information if we are to learn it. Research has shown that we pay greater attention to information if the size or intensity is exaggerated; if it is unusual or incongruous; if it has emotional or personal significance (Ormrod, 1999). Academic information usually does not come to us in these forms, but we can incorporate these characteristics in our study strategies to help us remember.

Working Memory

The information goes from the sensory register to the working memory, where it is held for less than 20 seconds. Interestingly, research indicates "that much of the information stored in working memory is stored in an *auditory* form, particularly when the information is language based" (Ormrod, 1999, p. 189). The capacity of our working memory is amazingly small. Miller (1956) explains that the capacity is the magical number seven plus or minus two (7 ± 2); in other words, we can hold about seven items of information in our working memory at one time. Those seven items of information are usually chunks of information, not individual letters or numbers. Five to nine items seem sufficient, even in difficult academic learning, and expert students easily combine pieces of information (chunking) into larger and larger chunks.

Central Executive

An interesting part of the dual-store model is the concept of the central executive, whose functions include controlling the flow of information from the sensory register, processing it for storage in the long-term memory, and retrieving it from that same long-term memory. The central executive concept interests educational psychologists because that part of the learning process is what study strategies (metacognitive knowledge) improve. This model also suggests that there are automatic auditory and visual systems that help maintain the information while the central executive function is working (LeFrançois, 2000). Along the way, this central executive system is also thinking (comprehending, selecting, comparing, creating). Such a workload is amazing, yet we do it continually.

WHY WE SOMETIMES FORGET

Certain types of forgetting occur in the working memory. Because the capacity of the working memory is short, information may simply disappear (decay) before it is processed and deliberately stored in the long-term memory. Additionally, the working memory has an extremely limited capacity, so old information may be displaced by new information. Another kind of forgetting is when previous learning may interfere with the acquisition of new information (LeFrançois, 2000). Memory theorists refer to these three explanations of forgetting as decay, displacement, and interference, respectively. Failure to store and retrieve information accurately also contributes to forgetting.

An important contribution from the **levels-of-processing** theorists Craik and Lockhart (1972) is the concept that *how thoroughly (deeply) we process information determines whether we retain it or forget it.* Effective learning strategies seek to intensify and deepen the processing of information so that there is a greater guarantee that it will be stored in the long-term memory in such a way that it can be retrieved. Meaning is the great key for this strategy, for if we understand the information and deliberately process it by translating, explaining, or inferring, then we have practiced retaining it and intensified its power.

Think of an air-traffic controller who is controlling departing and arriving aircraft, weather information, security information, and numerous other data systems. Like the air-traffic controller, the central executive naturally organizes information that comes to it (chunking), but it can also learn to organize academic information using specific methods to facilitate and enhance retrieval. These methods include mapping, outlining, graphic organizers, elaborations, memory systems, note cards, matrices, flow charts, time lines, and networks. Knowing which ones to use and when to use them effectively depends on your metacognitive knowledge (e.g., personal preferences, content, expected level and type of performance, prior knowledge and skills, and goals). Later in this chapter you will have the opportunity to learn and practice many of these methods.

Long-Term Memory

Long-term memory differs dramatically from working memory. First, long-term memory seems to have an infinite capacity and indefinite duration. Age, disease, and injury can cause dendrites and neural networks to die, but for most of us, the duration and stability of our long-term memory is quite remarkable. Information stored in our long-term memory becomes knowledge, and that knowledge has several important characteristics. Second, long-term memory is usually constructed knowledge; that is, our working memory selects, organizes, and manipulates the information before storing. Third, pieces of knowledge are usually stored with related pieces of knowledge in neural networks; that is, the organization of our long-term memory is primarily based on meaning (Ormrod, 1999). We have billions of pieces of knowledge already stored, primarily in **schemas,** *neural networks grouped by meaning.* The more we know, the more we can learn because we have created more networks. These principles are especially important in academic learning as we strive to become expert learners. See Figure 12.2 to learn more about the characteristics of the dual-store model.

Procedural knowledge (how to do something) is stored in networks as implicit memories, but often once we have thoroughly mastered a particular process, we will remember how to do the process but struggle to verbalize each step. Even academic learning that is procedural will eventually become automatic, almost unconscious, after extensive practice (e.g., certain math or accounting functions). Declarative knowledge is stored in networks as explicit memories. One type of declarative knowledge is our *personal experiences,* called **episodic memory,** and the other is **semantic memory,** *stable knowledge about the world, rules, and principles that can be verbalized* (LeFrançois, 2000).

The last type of forgetting is when we cannot retrieve the information that is stored in our long-term memory. Whereas personal experiences are so powerful that we remember them readily without any intent or practice, academic learning rarely has that impact. Deep processing and deliberate practice create the multiplicity of neural networks that support retrieval. The more modalities

FIGURE 12.2   Characteristics of the Dual-Store Model

	Sensory Registers	*Working Memory*	*Long-Term Memory*
Capacity	Unlimited	Extremely limited (7 ± 2)	Infinite
Duration	Fleeting (1–4 seconds)	Extremely short (<20 seconds)	Indefinite
Storage mode	Same as signal	Auditory	Meaning

Source: Ormrod, J. E. (1999). *Human Learning.* Upper Saddle River, NJ: Merrill/ Prentice Hall.

FIGURE 12.3   How to Minimize Forgetting

	Cause	*Remedy*
Failure to retrieve	Unreliable pathway of association between new information and prior knowledge.	Connect new information to prior knowledge and practice.
Failure to store	Timely, powerful retrieval exercises are lacking.	Use spaced and frequent practice to build reliable retrieval.
Decay	Information disappears from working memory before storage.	Deliberately choose and store important information.
Displacement	New information replaces old information in the working memory.	Link *new* information to old and practice both.
Interference	Prior information in long-term memory interferes with storage of new information.	Link *old* information to new and practice both.

Sources: Adapted from LeFrancois, 2000; Ormrod, 1998.

(e.g., auditory, visual, verbal, symbolic) we use in practice, the more powerful the practice will be. When we practice remembering, our working memory is accessing our long-term memory, finding the information, and pulling it to conscious thought. That cycle is the retrieval cycle, one we must do again and again in order to perform the information reliably. See Figure 12.3 for the causes of and remedies for forgetting.

BUILDING DENDRITES BY USING A VARIETY OF METHODS TO STORE AND RETRIEVE

The stark reality of collegiate learning is that there is far more information in any one course than we can reasonably learn, much less remember. From the first lecture to the last moments before a test, our primary learning strategy is to understand the material so that we can determine what parts we need to carefully store and retrieve in order to perform adequately both in the course and beyond. In other words, every time we write something down from the lecture or mark the text, we are continually sifting through the information and selecting what we believe is important. Freshmen are often shocked that college teachers are far less directive than their high school teachers were. The reason is simple: one of the skills college students are expected to master as undergraduates is the skill of determining what is more important for a specific purpose and what is less important for that same purpose.

As we move from understanding to deliberate storage/retrieval practice for performance, we process the course information over and over again. We select the content that we believe is important, we organize or elaborate that information, and we practice it until we are ready for performance. From summarizations to note cards to graphic organizers to matrices, we use methods of selection/elaboration/practice. Common sense dictates that the more time we spend on the material, the more thoroughly (deeply) we will learn it. A similar premise that was used for understanding—*Do what you have to do to learn the material*—applies here: *Do what you have to do to accurately remember or understand or apply or analyze. . . the material.*

METHODS OF INCREASING THE RELIABLE RETRIEVAL OF ACADEMIC LEARNING

- **Intention:** Make the deliberate intention to remember particular information for a specific purpose.

- **Effort:** Put energy and intensity into retrieval practice.

- **Structure:** Carefully choose the appropriate structure to store and retrieve the information.

- **Multiple modalities:** Use the modalities that work best for you and for the material.

- **Meaningful connections:** Connect what you are learning with prior knowledge, information from other courses, and personal experience.

- **Practice:** Do this again and again and again.

Learning strategies take time. Pick the most effective, but also the most efficient, techniques for your needs.

The accuracy of what we choose to store and retrieve is crucial. If we are careless or sloppy in our understanding or with the memory devices we use, then we will store and retrieve inaccurate or incomplete information. Such an outcome can be disastrous on a test, and replacing the inaccurate memory with an accurate one is much harder than simply learning the information correctly the first time.

SIMPLE TECHNIQUES TO AID MEMORY AND RETRIEVAL

In this section, we intersperse some email correspondence between students and StrongGrad, an expert learner, with technical information about some simple memory and retrieval strategies. As you look at all the examples, we recommend that you experiment with the different formats for material you are currently studying. The examples move from the simple to the complex, from the lowest level of learning, *remembering,* to the upper level, *analysis.*

How can I remember all of these dates for history?

StrongGrad: *Write all of them down in chronological order and create a time line. Label each event and star the three most important. Start by practicing those three in order several times, and then begin to add the in-between dates. If you're really creative, make up a story about the most important dates. For example, the Magna Carta was signed in 1215, and a story would be to envision all the nobles and the king coming to lunch at 12:15 at your favorite restaurant. Sometimes dates already are associated with something familiar, such as an address, phone number, the grade you were in and the corresponding year, movie title.*

How can I learn foreign language vocabulary?

StrongGrad: *Practice . . . practice . . . practice. Simple note cards are your best investment. You can make them or buy boxes of them. The word is on one side and the meaning on the other. Start by looking at the meaning and re-calling the word before you look at it. Then flip the cards and look at the word and try to recall the meaning. Use the word in a sentence. Scramble the or-der of the cards regularly (you do not want to remember them in sequence).*

Practice retrieval often but in short pieces of time. This timing is called spaced practice and works well for permanent retrieval. Even though you may forget some of the words between practices, over time your retrieval will become reliable and automatic, necessary to move forward in foreign language study.

Should I use the same techniques for scientific/technical vocabulary as for foreign language vocabulary?

StrongGrad: *Not necessarily. When you first begin to study a discipline, the vocabulary seems foreign, and simple note cards sometimes help. Often you'll be expected to label the various parts of a diagram, chart, or picture. When you predict that sort of test question, it is important to practice the in-formation in the same way in which you will be tested. So much of scien-tific/technical vocabulary requires sequential or associative memory performance that mnemonic devices (memory tricks) are helpful.*

Mnemonics. **Mnemonics** are "memory 'tricks' . . . devices that facilitate the learning and recall of many . . . forms of difficult material" (Ormrod, 1999, p. 298). We use jingles, rhymes, acronyms, key words, and created words/sen-tences. Here are a few examples:

Cows Often Sit Down Carefully; Perhaps Their Joints Creak? Persistent Early Oiling Might Prevent Permanent Rheumatism—the first letter of each word is the first letter of the geological time periods in chronological order: Cambrian, Ordovician, Silurian . . . Triassic, Jurassic . . .

C̲an I̲ntelligent K̲aren S̲olve S̲ome F̲oreign M̲afia O̲perations?—the Krebs cycle in order: Citric acid, Isocitric, Ketoglutaric . . .

You can use mnemonic devices for any academic subject. Here are a few more examples:

FOIL—ordered steps for multiplying a binomial (First, Outer, Inner, Last)

HOMES—the Great Lakes (Huron, Ontario, Michigan, Erie, Superior)

i before *e* except after *c* . . . (spelling rule)

N̲ick P̲refers L̲ettuce Y̲ellow T̲omatoes S̲ardines and H̲am on W̲ednesday—the royal houses of England in order (Norman, Plantagenet, Lancaster, York, Tudor, Stuart, Hanover, and Windsor)

How can I remember . . .

Formulas or theorems?

Steps in a procedure, in economics and accounting courses?

The characteristics of a concept with the name of the concept?

Identifications and label them accurately?

StrongGrad: *I know school requires memorizing a lot of stuff that seems like busywork, but all those details are important and are going to show up on a test sometime—you can count on that. My advice is make a game out of it, preferably a portable game with note cards so you can carry them with you and practice at those in-between times. Now you can get note cards in almost any color; my favorites are the neon ones that practically glow in the dark and keep me awake.*

We have already talked about using note cards for foreign language and some scientific/technical vocabulary. However, note cards are much more diverse.

MAKING MNEMONICS MORE POWERFUL AND ACCURATE

- **Thoroughly learn and practice mnemonic devices in order to be effective.**   If you remember a mnemonic device incorrectly, then chaos happens, and you will not be able to perform the information accurately.

- **Practice linking the mnemonic device to the information you are trying to retrieve.**   This is crucial; remembering the device without remembering what it represents is useless.

- **Whenever possible, make meaningful connections.**   The more information is linked and practiced by meaning, the more likely the information will be stored in neural networks based on meaning, and that type of memory is more permanent.

- **Practice items in sequence if the sequence is necessary for accurate content; scramble items for practice if there is no logical sequence.**

- **Use exaggerated visuals (size, color, humor, action) to strengthen the retrieval process.**

- **The mnemonics that we create are usually more powerful than those we get from other sources.**   However, we found thousands of websites devoted to academic mnemonics, especially in the scientific/medical/ health professions fields. In these fields, the need for mnemonic devices is so large that using other sources is time efficient. Here are just a few of our favorites:

www.medicalmnemonics.com

www.eudesign.com/mnems/ _mnframe.htm

http://users.frii.com/geomanda/ mnemonics.html

The next section includes examples of myriad other uses, and we are confident that you will discover many more. Remember that cards are also available in sizes other than three by five inches, and those bigger sizes can accommodate larger and more complex chunks of information.

Multiple Ways to Use Note Cards

Creating more complex note cards takes time, and students are frequently resistant to spending the time because they have not experienced the benefit of more sophisticated memory systems. However, memory theory explains that if we take the time to create the cards, we are selecting and storing the information in neural networks through multiple modalities (seeing, saying, writing), so the storage is much more powerful than simply looking at an item in the text or in notes. When we make such a strong connection through storage, then retrieval becomes much easier. Cornell notes and T-notes also are powerful retrieval practice systems, and one of the more difficult tasks for students is choosing what information to practice through their notes and what information to lift out and put on note cards.

The note card examples in Figure 12.4 are arranged from simple to complex, using the first four levels of learning. Your ability to accurately predict not only the content, but also the level of learning that you will be expected to perform, dictates the complexity and sophistication of the cards you produce. You can choose to use color coding, that is, use a different color card or ink for different topics etc. Again, creating your own cards infuses this retrieval process with power.

FIGURE 12.4   Examples of Note Cards Ranging from Simple to Complex

Remember: Identification note card
Person, event, circumstance   Data and their importance

Nelson R. Mandela

Born: July 18, 1918; near Umtata
Aspired to become a lawyer
Joined African Nat'l Congress 1942
Formed ANC youth league 1944
Apartheid created 1948 when Nat'l Party
    won elections
ANC campaign—Defiance of Unjust Laws 1952
Nat'l Party outlawed ANC 1960
Sentenced to life in prison 1961
Freed from prison Feb. 11, 1990
Won Nobel Peace Prize 1993
Elected president of S. Africa on April 27, 1994

FIGURE 12.4   Examples of Note Cards *(Continued)*

Remember: Simple diagram note card

Name of diagram

Arthropod body plan

Labeled diagram

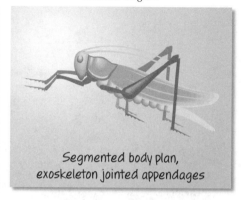

Segmented body plan,
exoskeleton jointed appendages

Remember: Formula note card

Name of formula/theorem

Pythagorean theorem

Formula and definition

$a^2 + b^2 = c^2$
The sum of the squares of the
sides (legs) of a right triangle
is equal to the square of the
hypotenuse.

Understand: Concept note card

Concept

Utilitarianism

Parts, components

• Theory of ethics—idea that the ultimate goal
  of any moral action is the achievement of
  the greatest good for the greatest number
• Should be the aim of all legislation
• Opposed to idea that one person's
  conscience determines good/evil since
  good/evil aren't determined by an individual
  alone
• Outlined by Wm. Paley in <u>Principles of moral
  and political philosophy</u> (1785) & by Jeremy
  Bentham in <u>Introduction to the principles of
  morals and legislation</u> (1789)

(Continued)

FIGURE 12.4 Examples of Note Cards *(Continued)*

**Understand: Example note card
(declarative knowledge)**

Data

Definition and example

Proportional
representation

Electoral system meant to produce a
legislative body where # of seats a party
holds is proportional to # of votes received
in most recent election
• 1st used in Denmark in 1855
• Used in early/mid 20th century in several
US cities (NY & Cincinnati) that hoped to
prevent machine politics & ensure minority
representation
• Now used in many European democracies

**Understand: Example note card
(procedural knowledge)**

Procedure

Steps of the procedure

Do Loop
(Process for advancing
numerical value)

1. <u>Do While</u> (condition is true)
2. (process statements)
3. <u>Loop</u>
Note: Avoid infinite loops
    Remember indents

- -

Ex: Prints #'s 0–9
  Dim n as integer
  n = 0
  Do while n < 10
    picBox. Print n
    n = n + 1
  Loop

Application: Practicing a problem note card

Problem

Solution

Completing the Square
Problem:
$x^2 + 4x + 3 = 0$

1. Subtract 3 from both sides.
   $x^2 + 4x = -3$
2. Divide the coefficient of x by 2
   and to both sides.

   $x^2 + 4x + \left(\frac{4}{2}\right)^2 = -3 + \left(\frac{4}{2}\right)^2$

3. Factor
   $(x + 2)^2 = 1$ A perfect square

FIGURE 12.4   Examples of Note Cards *(Continued)*

Analyze: Predict essay test question note card

Hypothesized essay question

What ways do American literature consist of a dialog between Puritanism and Transcendentalism?

Main points

1. The way they see the relationship between the individual and the community
2. How they relate to nature
3. The role and definition of religion in each school
4. The concept of America in each school
5. The difference between each school's concept of Fate

Analyze: Simple comparison/contrast note card

Name

The Ear

Anatomical divisions and functions

2 x 2 or 2 x 3 matrix

Anatomical division	Function
Outer ear (auricle & EAM)	Protection resonance transmission
Middle ear (drum & ossicles)	Impedance matching
Inner ear (vestibular system & cochlea)	Transduction of mechanical & hydrodynamic energy into neural impulses

ADVANCED TECHNIQUES

The simple techniques that we have suggested will help you learn concepts, formulas, steps in procedures, diagrams, and so forth, but successful performance on college tests usually requires more advanced techniques than you had to use in high school for several reasons. First, there is much more material, and teachers cover only part of it in class. Second, tests are less frequent, sometimes only twice a term. The first test usually occurs a month or later into the semester. Third, although some instructors give summary or study sheets, most do not. The combined effect of these differences results in placing the burden of study on students.

One advantage of using advanced techniques to organize and elaborate your own study material is that you are forced to select and process the information more deeply, thereby increasing the likelihood that you will understand and store the material by meaning. A second advantage is that the time you spend on these study techniques increases the likelihood that you will learn them deeply. A disadvantage is that organizing and elaborating take time and cannot be done at the last moment. However, once you have completed the task, you can cram during the last 48 hours.

What follows are myriad examples of complex and powerful study strategies. Look carefully at the examples and determine which types could help you learn in your current courses.

Summarization Techniques

Lecture notes. Review and create a summary sheet of the major concepts and simultaneously create note cards and mnemonic devices for remembering important data. Do not include items you already know and retrieve well.

Text readings. Read the chapter summaries and then go through and look at your text markings. List the major concepts and data that you need to remember for the test, and create note cards for important data that you need to practice to be able to remember. Again, exclude items you already know and retrieve well. Read the chapter summary again.

Last-ditch summary. Create a one- to two-page summary or review sheet (or up to four, five-by-seven-inch cards) of the major concepts, theorems, formulas, etc. from all your sources. These are the items (words and structures) that you have now memorized as your retrieval clues for the content to be covered on the test. Practice retrieving the test content by looking at each item and explaining or describing it. Practice the last thing before going to sleep, the first thing the morning of the test, and again just before the test.

Visual or Graphic Organizers

Linear arrays. When information to be learned has an internal linear structure, either as steps in a procedure or as occurrences in time, using that structure as the retrieval device is especially powerful. Use either a horizontal or vertical line and mark the major parts of the process or the historical events (see Figures 12.5 and 12.6). Then add in as much detail as necessary, using different colors or shapes if that is helpful. A time line is a simple linear array, but time lines can be expanded to incorporate much more data if you wish. The linear structure is a helpful memory tool.

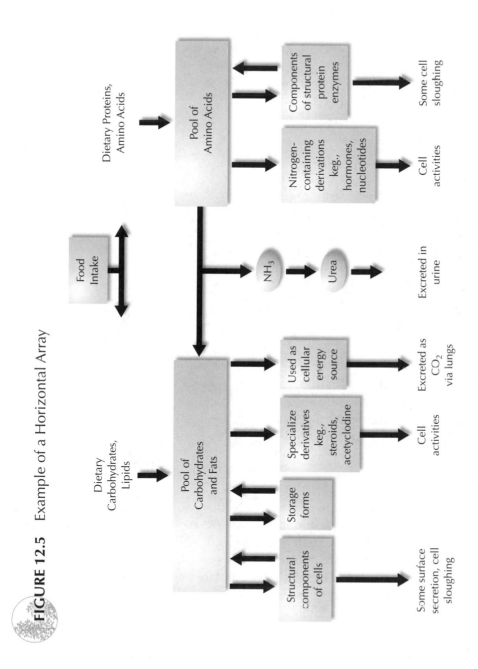

FIGURE 12.5 Example of a Horizontal Array

337

FIGURE 12.6   Example of a Vertical Array

American Revolution Time Line

1761 — Writs of Assistants
1763 — Navigation Acts
1764 — Sugar Act
1765 — Stamp Act
1765 — Quartering Act
1765 — Stamp Act Congress
1766 — Declaratory Act
1767 — Townsend Acts
1767 — Quartering Act
1770 — Boston Massacre
1772 — Gaspie Incident
1773 — Boston Tea Party
1774 — Intolerable Acts
1775 — Battle of Lexington & Concord
1775 — Battle of Bunker Hill
1776 — Ratification of Declaration of Independence
1776 — Battle of Trinton
1776 — Battle of Prinston
1777 — Battle of Saratoga
1780 — Battle of Yorktown
1783 — Treaty of Paris

A more complicated linear array is a hierarchy or *tree structure,* a visual way of organizing or grouping information around class inclusion rules, that is, when items are a part of one group (Halpern, 1997) (see Figures 12.7 and 12.8). Biology, geology, and other fields contain much information that is best represented by hierarchies. Drawing the hierarchy and labeling it is an effective memory storage/retrieval practice. Using color or size to designate certain levels of the hierarchy helps you to remember the structure.

Yet another type of linear array is a flow chart, "a diagram showing the progress of work through a sequence of operations" (Guralnik, 1986, p. 537) (see Figure 12.9). It is usually shown as a series of steps or events in graphic shapes such as rectangles and triangles. This type of graphic organizer is useful for math, accounting, economics, computer science, etc. It is also useful to design the process necessary for completing a project or paper.

FIGURE 12.7 Example of a Hierarchy

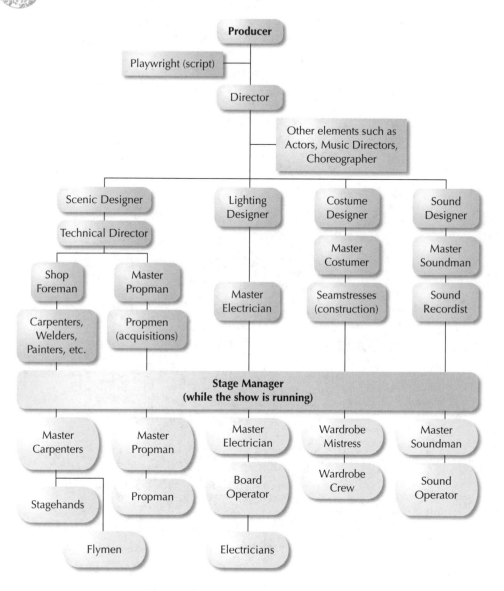

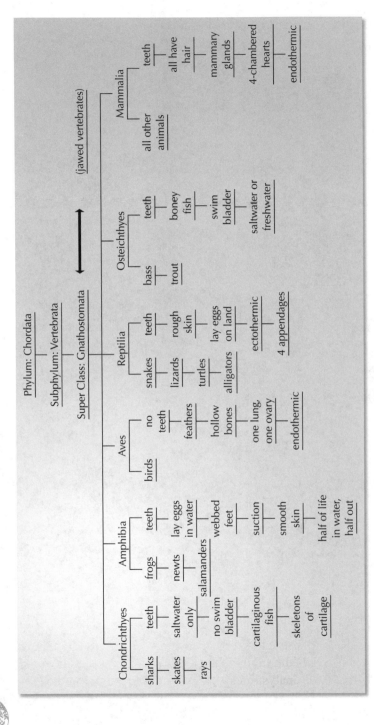

FIGURE 12.8 Example of a Tree Structure

FIGURE 12.9   Example of a Flow Chart

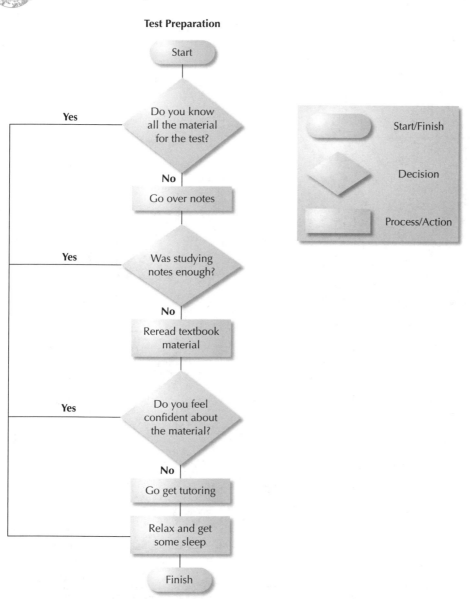

Test Preparation

Matrices. Often instructors expect students to demonstrate that they understand the differences and the similarities among complex sets of information. This level of performance is analysis, and a primary metacognitive strategy to master material at this level is the comparison/contrast matrix, a larger version of the note card matrix introduced earlier in this chapter (see Figures 12.10 and 12.11). This type of matrix is a grid with several related topics along one side. The purpose of the

FIGURE 12.10 Example of a Matrix Comparing/Contrasting Authors

Authors	Major Themes of Work(s)	Influences on Works	Poem(s)/Story	Main Idea of Poem(s)/Story	Other Famous Work(s)	Critics' Comments (of their time)
Sylvia Plath	• Horror • Death	• Father died of cancer when she was 10 • Pushed by mother to do well	1. "Daddy" 2. "Lady Lazarus"	1. Father died of cancer, guilt 2. Celebrating suicide attempts—ref. in both to Holocaust	*The Bell Jar*	Poems were "the longest suicide note ever written"
Walt Whitman	• Sexuality • Ecstatic perception of man and nature	• Natural talent for journalism • Emerson, friend	1. "When I Heard the Learn'd Astronomer" 2. "The Dalliance of the Eagles"	1. Rejection of astronomer's perception of nature 2. Power of sexual drive, celebration of life force	Nine editions of *Leaves of Grass* "One's-Self I Sing"	"poetry of barbarism," "mixture of Yankee transcendentalism and NY rowdyism"
Emily Dickinson	• Calvinism = to look inwardly • Coldness of the world • Love, death, nature, immortality, beauty	• Emotional crisis brought on by lost love of a married man • Shakespeare, Keats, the Brownings	1. "I Heard a Fly Buzz—When I Died—" 2. "Because I Could Not Stop for Death—"	1. Disbelief in afterlife/immortality 2. Belief in immortality, death-gracious gentleman caller	*The Poems of Emily Dickinson*	"farrago of illiterate and uneducated sentiment"
Nathaniel Hawthorne	• Concern with American past • Human isolation and seclusion	• Life in Salem, Puritanism	"Young Goodman Brown"	Evil is the nature of every human being (abstract meaning)	*The Scarlet Letter*	Wrote with "all the fascination of a genius and all the charm of a highly polished style"
Edgar Allan Poe	• World of perversity, disorder • Fascinated by the bizarre	• Depression • Psychologically crippling childhood • Unsuccessful suicide	"Cask of Amontillado"	Conditions of revenge, death bed confession, obsessed with murder that he got away with	"The Raven" "The Tell-Tale Heart"	"demonic" "egotistic villain with scarcely any virtue"
Herman Melville	• Confrontation of innocence and evil • World filled with lost innocence and betrayed hope	• Sea life • Adventures while traveling	"Bartleby, the Scrivener"	Bartleby is a greater person than the narrator, who thinks otherwise	*Moby Dick*	A man who could "neither believe nor be comfortable in his disbelief"
Robert Lowell	• Revelation of self • Instability of life through death, sin, and guilt	• Poet John Crowe Ransom • Convicted of draft evasion	1. "Skunk Hour" 2. "For the Union Dead"	1. Mentally ill narrator spying on lovers 2. Condemning lack of public service, contrasting with history	*Life Studies* (book of poems)	Poems were "trivia" and "organized jotting"

FIGURE 12.11   Example of a Matrix Comparing/Contrasting Types of Music

	Medieval	**Renaissance**	**Baroque**	**Classic**	**Romantic**
Melody	Conjunct, stepwise, & smooth	Smooth, parts are melodic	Hymn tunes, overlapping	Refined, courtly short phrases	Folk–nature, patriotic
Harmony		Nonfunctional	Functional, tonic-dominant	Predictable, short phrases	Rich, thick, dramatic
Rhythm	Subtle, no downbeats or strong beats	Subtle	Bar lines & downbeats	Clear and concise, shows form	Folk–dance, irregular
Timbre	Single vocal line	Multiple vocal or instrumental lines	Orchestra, organ, and harpsichord	Vocal	Exotic colors, extremes, orchestra
Mood	Church chant	Meditative	Stately, courtly	Elegant, floppish	Emotionalism, dramatic, violent
Texture	(single voice) Monophony	Polyphony	Clear, refined	Extremes	Clear and unusual, dodecaphony
Composers	Associated with Pope Gregory	Palestrina, Des Pres	Bach, Handel	Mozart, Haydn	Chopin, Verdi, & Wagner

matrix is to compare those topics across several dimensions (represented along the other side). Filling in the cells allows students to condense large amounts of information into one organizer. Empty cells indicate either that there is missing material that needs to be researched and added or that a relationship does not actually exist, in which case the cells remain blank. Creating a matrix is a powerful storage tool, and afterward it can be used for study practice. Again, color or exaggerated size helps emphasize certain points. A useful method of studying by a matrix is to ask questions (turn the dimensions into questions) and answer them.

Mapping. Maps are visual attempts to represent the relationships among various concepts and data. They can be simple drawings created in a few minutes (e.g., types of geographical regions) or extraordinarily elaborate designs that take hours to create (e.g., drawing the relationships of the content of five medical chapters) (Hyerle, 2000). Effective maps often utilize color, drawings, size, and shapes that aid retrieval. Two frequently used types of maps are concept maps (or clusters) and networks.

Concept maps allow you to group related information into two- or three-level drawings. You can use the bubble format or the spider format. Again, the use of color, size, and exaggeration helps make the map more memorable (see Figures 12.12 and 12.13).

Networks are the most complex and the most powerful types of maps. They require the most time to produce and should only be used when the content is especially complex and the expected performance level is analysis or above. Networks build on concept maps but have an extra step. All the links between the items are labeled: part, example, leads to, type, definition analogy, characteristic, evidence (Halpern, 2000) (see Figure 12.14). Since you have to determine the

FIGURE 12.12   Example of a Concept Map Using the Bubble Format

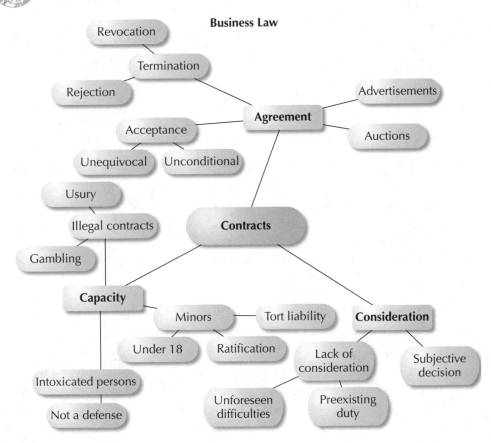

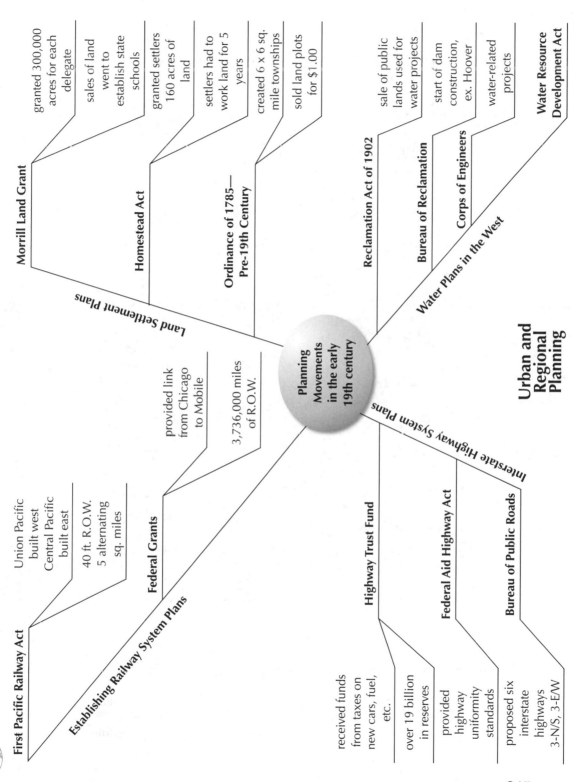

FIGURE 12.13 Example of a Concept Map Using the Spider Format

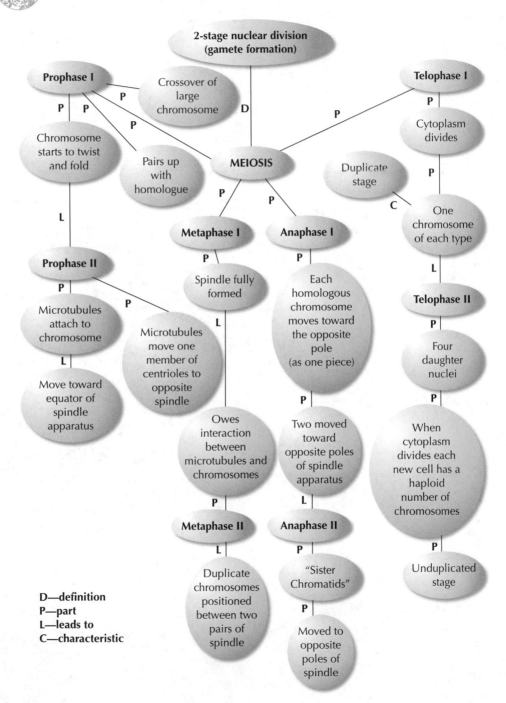

FIGURE 12.14   Example of a Process Network Detailing Meiosis

purpose of each link (and sometimes create labels to identify relationships), you must understand the deep structure of the content. Such deep processing creates powerful storage and retrieval of the information.

TEST PREPARATION STRATEGIES

In this section, StrongGrad provides answers to students' questions about what they need to do to prepare for tests.

How do I choose and organize the content material for a test?

StrongGrad   *Start early enough to really do the job. Three to four days before a test, write a list of all the content to be covered and the expected level of learning you will need to perform it. Do you have all the lecture notes? If not, get copies of any lectures you missed. Get all the handouts or material from the instructor's website. The most important question to ask is "Have I done the initial learning of this material—read the required materials, gone to class, used other required sources?" If the answer is no, then get started!*

The initial learning of any material takes time, especially if it is procedural knowledge, and such learning is most efficient when anxiety is low. However, re-learning material that is already familiar but not readily retrievable is usually much faster, and even moderate anxiety does not interfere. The marker for many experienced students is 48 hours before the test. By that marker, most students feel some anxiety, but if what they have to do is simply relearn the material and practice storing/retrieving to prepare for the test, then they can usually do that efficiently.

How do I select the most important items to study?

StrongGrad   *List all the content for the test; then look for all the clues about what will actually be on the test. What has the instructor or the teaching assistant emphasized? What will be the structure of the test—objective, short answer, essay? What is on any handouts or the instructor's website? Does the study manual or CD of your text have practice questions? What does the instructor say on the last day before the test? What is the focus of the review session (be sure to go!)? Talk to students who have had this course and instructor before. If you have exams from earlier in the term, use them to get an idea of what type of items your instructor tends to choose.*

There is so much information! How can I do this?

StrongGrad   *Hold on now—don't let the amount of information intimidate you! You have to get in front of it and organize it. Remember 7 ± 2; organizing helps us chunk the material so that we can remember it. You have to do this in four or five courses, so organization is your best weapon.*

exercise 12.2

Using a Test Prep

The purpose of this exercise is to help you differentiate between preparing to study and actually studying for an upcoming test as well as to create an organized study plan. Completing this exercise will give you an opportunity to apply many of the techniques discussed previously while you prepare for your test.

1. Select material that you are currently preparing to study for a major test.

2. Test date: _____

3. Complete the following chart:

Specific material test will cover	Incompleted Tasks		Completed Tasks	
	Test material	Time needed to complete	Test material	Time needed to review
Textbook chapters:				
Outside readings:				
Class notes:				
Other resources:				

4. Next to each of the following types of questions write the number of them that will be on the test:

_____ True/false   _____ Fill-in-the-blank

_____ Multiple choice   _____ Short answer

_____ Matching   _____ Essay

5. What is the time limit for completing the test? _____

6. Identify and list all major topics covered on the test:

_____

_____

_____

_____

_____

_____

7. Select one or more of the following simple techniques to practice memory and retrieval of the test material:

   a. Create 10–20 note cards using at least three of the following note card formats:

Vocabulary	Example
Identification	Concept
Formula	Practice problem
Simple diagram	Comparison/contrast

   b. Make time lines and/or stories to associate dates, names, events, etc.

   c. Create mnemonics using at least two of the following types:

Jingles	Key words
Rhymes	Created words
Acronyms	Created sentences

8. Select one or more of the following activities to help you learn the test material at a deeper level:

   a. Summarization—Create a one- to two-page summary sheet of information from the lecture or readings.

   b. Visual or graphic organizers—Create two organizers using more than one of the following formats:

Matrix	Spider concept map
Hierarchy	Network
Bubble concept map	

9. Predicted test questions—Create questions and answers based on the type of test you expect:

   10–15 Multiple choice and true/false

   Matching and fill-in-the-blank if appropriate

   5–7 Short answer

   3–5 Essay

What do I do when I have two tests in one day?

StrongGrad: *If these are declarative knowledge courses, then use color coding and different learning techniques so you can keep the content distinctly* *different in your mind. Study the material for the second test first; then study the material for the first test before you go to sleep. The next morning, review the material for the first test and take it. Then review the material for the second test and take it.*

If one test is declarative knowledge and the other procedural knowledge, practice the procedural knowledge first until you reach mastery level. Then study for the declarative knowledge course. The night before the tests, practice the procedures again. End your study that night with the material for the first test.

If both tests are procedural, start very early to master the procedures you will need to perform on the test. The night before the test, practice for one test, then take a 30-minute break, and then practice for the second test.

How do I stay awake when I study?

StrongGrad: *Keep it safe and legal; you know what I mean. Use active study techniques—with friends in a study group, reciting aloud, spacing study with some quick exercise breaks or some fast household chores. Stand up and walk around as you rehearse. Music may help some of you, but for others it is a distraction. Study in the library or another place without the distractions of telephones, family, friends, etc. During finals, you might put the television away in the closet. Study before your family or roommates wake up or after they go to bed. Get some sleep each night (all-nighters tend to destroy test performance). Use snacks, healthy if possible. Fresh air, opening a window or walking outside, can help.*

Do I need to study differently for objective, short-answer, and essay tests?

StrongGrad: *Absolutely. Objective tests require much more specific recognition and recall, so using various types of note cards and graphic organizers can help. Collegiate-level multiple-choice questions usually require you to select the best answer (many of the alternatives may be correct) or they may require you to function at the application level, such as mathematics, economics, accounting. Try to think like your teacher—what kind of questions would you write for this test?*

Short-answer tests often require that you demonstrate that you understand a concept or an important fact. Sheer memory is not enough; you have to be able to explain the material. Practice by explaining concepts, identifications, or definitions to yourself, your dog, anyone who will listen.

Essay tests require a very different type of preparation. To prepare well, you will need to study at the analysis level. Once you have learned the major concepts, write practice questions comparing/contrasting two or more of the concepts *or* tracing the development of an idea or historical event *or* analyzing the cause/effect relationships between several topics *or* considering the significance of certain occurrences. After you create some study questions, practice writing a thesis statement and a list of major points that you would want to make in your answer. Thinking about the material at this level of analysis is a powerful preparation strategy for essay tests.

TEST-TAKING STRATEGIES

This section provides test-taking strategies suggested by StrongGrad as well as some of our own.

Enough about preparation. I need some help on taking a test. What do you suggest?

StrongGrad: *Learning how to play the game and becoming an effective collegiate test taker are major goals of your first year in school. The first rule is simple: Nothing helps more than really knowing the material. If you learn the content and practice it at the appropriate level of learning, then the rest is just technique and common sense.*

Here are some strategies for making the most of your test-taking experience:

Before the Test

- Make sure you have all the supplies you need, as well as a watch.

- Arrive 5–10 minutes early.

- Do not hang out with other students who tend to catastrophize or psych each other out about what might be on the test.

- Sit away from your friends if they make you nervous or tend to finish earlier than you.

- Use positive self-talk and breathe deeply to relax.

At the Beginning of the Test

- Write down formulas, theorems, or processes you will need.

- Look over the entire test, noting how much each part of the test is worth. Mentally decide which parts you want to answer first and how much time you will allocate to each section. (You might want to start with the section that seems easiest to you.)

- Read and underline key words in the test directions. Be sure to note if the directions say to answer only some but not all of the questions (common on essay tests).

During the Test

- If you begin to feel nervous or blank out on a question, stop, take a deep breath, and say to yourself, *I prepared for this test, and I can answer these questions. I will move on and come back to this question later.* Take another deep breath and read the next question, paying close attention to monitor your self-talk as you progress through the test.

Objective Questions (Multiple Choice, True/False, Matching)

- Read every question carefully. On multiple-choice questions, try to answer the question before you look at the options. If that does not work, read each option and cross out those that are incorrect, ones that are too similar to distinguish between (unless there is an option such as "a and c" or "all of the above"), and those that are grammatically incorrect. Also examine options that are complete opposites of all the others; they are often correct.

- When you are confused by a multiple-choice question, read the stem and each option as a true/false question. This allows you to focus on each piece of information separately before trying to look at the question and options as a whole.

- Attempt to answer each question, but mark any that you are unsure of so you can return to them before the end of the test. Often you will find clues to the answer later on in the test.

- On true/false questions, look for absolute terms such as *all, always, never, none.* Such words are rarely found in correct answers, except in science courses such as physics and chemistry. Questions containing words such as *usually, frequently, rarely,* and *seldom,* especially in social science courses, allow for exceptions and are more likely to be true.

- If you can think of an exception to any part of a true/false question, then it is false. Be careful not to make assumptions or read anything that is not explicitly stated into a question.

- Beware of negatives because they change the meaning of the sentence. Circle the negative (*no, not, cannot, dis-, il-, im-, non-, un-*) and get the meaning of the statement without the negative. Then reread the statement with the negative. Remember that two negatives in one sentence cancel each other out.

- Determine the relationship between columns on matching questions and then start with the column with the longest items.

Subjective Questions (Identification, Short Answer, Essay)

- Remember that identification questions require these specific elements: when, what or who, where, and significance (importance or impact).

- On a short-answer question, define/describe the term or concept, cite a source, and give an example.

- Because many essay questions are quite long and involve several imbedded questions, be sure to read the entire question and briefly outline your answer to each part.

- Determine whether the essay questions are really statements, not questions. If this is the case, turn the statement into a question, identify limiting or directional words (these include *analyze, compare, contrast, define, describe, diagram, discuss, enumerate, evaluate, explain, identify, illustrate, interpret, justify, list, outline, prove, state, summarize, support*), outline your answer, answer the question in the first paragraph, give examples and details in the body, and provide a *big-picture* conclusion.

At the End of the Test

- Take the last 10 minutes of the test time to review your work.

- For any unanswered multiple-choice questions, look at the items you are still considering. Reread the question and choose the one that sounds as if it completes the stem the best (at least you have a 25 percent chance or better of getting it right).

- For any unanswered true/false questions, if the items contain unfamiliar terminology or facts, mark the statement false. If you are still unsure, pick true because it is harder to write a false statement that is not too obvious.

- Do not change answers unless you have remembered something or learned something from the test that contradicts the option you selected previously.

- Reread any essay questions and answers and correct any grammatical or logical errors. Check to see that you have included all the relevant information. If you run out of time, outline the rest of your response.

Analysis of Performance

The purpose of a test is to see how much you know, not merely to achieve a grade. Making mistakes, or even failing a test, is human. Rather than ignoring mistakes, examine them and learn from them as you learn from mistakes on the job and in your relationships. Working through your mistakes will help you avoid repeating them again on another test—or outside school life. (Carter, Bishop, & Kravits, 2002, p. 338)

When a test is returned to you, examine it carefully to see where your strengths were (and celebrate your successes!). Then look at your errors—were they careless or content errors? Content errors occur when we misunderstand a concept or do not remember factual information. Perhaps you never learned the concept or information in the first place. When you receive a graded paper or project, read the comments carefully. If the comments are few or confusing, make an appointment with your instructor to discuss how you can improve your work.

exercise 12.3

Analysis of Preparation and Performance

You can learn to enhance your performance by analyzing and reflecting on the results of a recent test, paper, or project. This exercise is designed to assist you with that process.

PREDICTIONS

1. How difficult did you think this test/paper/project was going to be?

2. What grade did you think you would receive before and after? Explain any difference.

PREPARATION

3. How much time did you spend?

4. What methods did you use?

5. How well did you learn?

PERFORMANCE

6. How well did you follow directions?

7. How well did you read the questions or assignment?

8. How well did you manage your time?

9. What effect did stress (positive or negative, anger or anxiety or excitement) have on your performance?

EVALUATION

10. Were you surprised about your grade? Why or why not?

11. Why do you think you made that grade?

NEXT TIME

12. How will you prepare differently for your next performance?

OTHER KINDS OF PERFORMANCE

This section discusses strategies suggested by StrongGrad and by us for doing papers and projects on an individual basis and as a group. It also addresses how we can learn from our mistakes.

What strategies help when I have a paper or a project to do?

StrongGrad   *Much of this stuff applies. Start early and pay close attention to the assignment. If it's a paper, carefully narrow your topic and create an outline or a concept map. Then write a thesis statement. If it's a research paper or project, be sure that your sources are academically credible and easy to document (especially if you get the information from the Internet). Start the actual writing process a week before the assignment is due and try to have the rough draft complete 48 hours before the due date. Be sure to print a copy, so if you have computer problems you'll still have something to work with. Then let the paper or project sit for a day before you edit it. Ask a friend to read it for logical consistency. Make your final copy the day before it is due, and make sure to use the required format and binding; you don't want to lose points for poor presentation.*

If the project is a group project, make sure the group meets quickly and exchanges email addresses, phone numbers, and schedules. Who emerges as the leader? The first meeting is crucial, for it is then that the project thesis, the time line, and the individual assignments are decided. Successful groups share the workload and act respectfully toward each other. Make sure you know exactly what you are to do and when it will be due. Consult with the instructor if you have questions. Then do your part well and quickly. If someone in your group is not doing his or her work, then all the rest of the group should go and talk to the instructor. Use your influence with the group to ensure that the project is presented in a professional manner appropriate to the field.

Groups can be great or terrible. When should I use a study group?

StrongGrad   *If you have done all the initial learning and need clarification on some topics or you want to predict and practice for the test, a motivated study group can be great. The benefits include increased motivation and deeper learning because practicing with other students means you can learn from what they know and you can teach what you know. Both ways of learning are powerful and will help you master the material.*

A regular study group, especially for a difficult course, can work well if you rotate leadership, set meeting goals, combine your study resources, and share the workload. It helps to have students of differing levels of ability within the group as well. The cardinal rule is study, not socialize; that is, stay on task.

I hate getting tests and papers back because I get so angry with myself when I have missed something I knew. What should I do?

StrongGrad   *It's easy to punish yourself, but frankly the smart thing to do is learn from your mistakes, just like good athletes do the day after the competition. Give yourself two minutes to experience all the feelings, good and bad, when you get the grade back. Then clear your mind of those feelings and take a hard look at how you did. Complete Exercise 12.3 to analyze your performance and improve it.*

Challenging Answers or Grades

If you wish to challenge any answer or grade, do so respectfully. If your teacher does not welcome challenges in the classroom, make an appointment for a private discussion.

CONCLUSION

All your academic performances are merely rehearsals for your professional life. Tests and papers and projects matter, and the grades matter, but the ultimate purpose is to help you attain the thinking and performance skills expected of a college graduate. The material in this chapter, and the entire book, is intended for your use throughout your collegiate career. You will not use all these techniques in any one semester, but you might need them all before you complete college.

We believe that we learn best, and perform best, when we evaluate our own performance in relation to our goals and our values. The cycle is continuous, throughout school and life.

SUMMARY

- Fair-mindedness entails a consciousness of the need to treat all viewpoints alike and without bias.

- When we think we create meaning. In academic learning, we attempt to make sense of a content field. All academic subjects are the product of thinking, which expresses, organizes, maintains, and expands content.

- The fastest way to deepen your learning is to ask questions about the content.

- The factors that contribute to the storage and retrieval process are the level of learning; the approach to learning; the mode of performance; the awareness of one's own learning strengths and weaknesses; and the competing demands of other courses, work, and family.

- Dual-store theory hypothesizes that our memory functions as three components: sensory register, the working memory, and long-term memory.

- The sensory register has unlimited capacity, and information from our environment is held very briefly (visual: <1 second; auditory: 2–4 seconds). Unimportant information is discarded because the brain can only attend to one complex situation at a time.

- Working memory holds information for less than 20 seconds. Most of the information is stored in auditory form (language based). The capacity of our working memory is 7 ± 2 items of information at one time.

- The central executive controls the flow of information from the sensory register, processes it for storage in the long-term memory, and retrieves it from the same long-term memory.

- Levels-of-processing theory posits that how thoroughly (deeply) we process information determines whether we retain it or forget it.

- Long-term memory has infinite capacity and indefinite duration. Long-term memory is usually constructed knowledge whereby our working memory selects, organizes, and manipulates the information before storing it in related neural networks based on meaning.

- Forgetting is caused by decay, displacement, interference, and insufficient practice.

- We must purposefully attend to academic information if we are to learn it, and the use of learning strategies is helpful to our retention of the material.

- As we move from understanding to deliberate storage and retrieval, we process information over and over again. We select content that we believe is important, we organize or elaborate on that information, and we practice it until we are ready for performance.

- Simple techniques to aid memory are the use of time lines, the creation of stories, the creation of simple note cards, and the use of mnemonics.

- Mnemonics are memory tricks that facilitate learning and recall and include jingles, rhymes, acronyms, key words, and created words or sentences. Mnemonics are more effective if they are thoroughly learned and practiced, linked to the correct information, meaningful, practiced in sequence, exaggerated, and individually created.

- Note cards can be created for formulas, examples, concepts, identification, diagrams, possible essay questions, comparison and contrasting, and practice problems.

- More advanced techniques for learning include creating summary sheets, linear arrays, matrices, and maps.

- Successful students study differently for objective, short-answer, and essay exams.

- Students should use effective test-taking strategies before, at the beginning, during, and at the end of an exam. They should also use past exams as a learning tool.

- Group work provides special challenges. Members should share the workload and act respectfully toward each other. Study groups work well if leadership is rotated, goals for meetings are set, and study resources are combined.

KEY CONCEPTS

Analysis of performance

Central executive

Creating a story

Dual-store theory

Episodic memory

Fair-mindedness

Forgetting

Levels-of-processing theory

Long-term memory

Mnemonics: jingles, rhymes, acronyms, keywords, created words/sentences

Note cards: formula, example, concept, test questions, identification, simple diagram, comparison/contrast

Schemas

Semantic memory

Sensory register

Storage and retrieval

Strategies for group study and projects

Strategies for individual papers or projects

Strategies for objective and subjective tests

Summarization techniques: lecture notes, text readings, last-ditch summary

Test preparation

Thinking

Time lines

Understanding basic concepts

Using associations for dates

Visual or graphic organizers: linear arrays, matrices, mapping (concept, bubble, spider, network)

Working memory

GUIDED JOURNAL QUESTIONS

1. Select one academic discipline or field that you are currently interested in studying (your major or a possible major), and answer the following questions:

   - What is the main goal of studying this academic discipline?

   - What are people in this field trying to accomplish?

   - What kinds of questions do they ask? What kinds of problems do they try to solve?

- What sort of information or data do they gather?

- How do they gather information in ways that are distinctive to this field?

- What is the most basic idea, concept, or theory in this field?

- How should studying this field affect my view of the world?

- How are the products of this field used in everyday life?

2. What are some of the most effective storage and retrieval techniques you use to learn declarative knowledge? Procedural knowledge? Explain.

3. Think about a time when you had trouble learning and retaining academic information. Which of the forgetting concepts addressed in this chapter help explain your experience?

4. Of the many learning strategies discussed in this chapter, which methods appeal to you the most? Why? Which ones do not appeal to you? Which ones will you adopt this semester and for which courses?

5. What actions have you normally taken when an exam or other graded performance has been returned to you? After having read about the benefits of analyzing performance, what changes will you make to improve your future academic performance? Explain.

6. Can you think of a recent learning experience when you used or could have used mnemonics to aid your memory? Simple note cards? Complex note cards? Explain.

7. Can you think of a recent learning experience when you used or could have used summarization techniques? Visual or graphic organizers? Explain.

8. Which do you prefer—objective or subjective test questions? Why?

9. Which test-taking strategies do you currently use? After having read this chapter, which new ones do you plan on trying in the future?

10. Compare and contrast a past group learning experience (study group or project) that worked well for you with one that did not. What could you have changed to salvage the unsuccessful experience?

The Last Word

Of all the techniques in this chapter, visual and graphic organizers (especially matrices) are second nature to me now. I even use them at work—just ask my colleagues!

—Carol Dochen

Postscript

> **The Seven Characteristic Competencies of Becoming an Autonomous Learner**
>
> 1. Autonomous learners have a healthy view of themselves and their academic abilities.
>
> 2. Autonomous learners are ethical.
>
> 3. Autonomous learners set realistic and appropriate goals for academic achievement.
>
> 4. Autonomous learners understand their own learning strengths and weaknesses.
>
> 5. Autonomous learners use effective learning strategies and adapt those strategies to new situations.
>
> 6. Autonomous learners manage their behaviors to reach their goals.
>
> 7. Autonomous learners use appropriate resources.

The transformation into an expert learner is neither easy nor ever completed. The seven principles of becoming an autonomous learner will serve you well in your academic, personal, and professional lives. You will, periodically, reexamine yourself through reflection and evaluate your academic abilities. Reflection and evaluation of your personal and, later, your professional lives will help you reap the benefits of a full life. But, remember, the healthy acceptance of what you discover allows you to face challenges confidently and helps you to move forward.

As you move forward, have the courage to move with integrity based on the ethics and fair-mindedness we hope you have come to see as an important part of your life. It is crucial to put into practice each day what you truly believe to be the right way to live. Whether it is in your academic, personal, social, or professional life, lead by example.

Always set realistic goals and expectations. When setting goals, try to achieve balance in all facets of your life. We live increasingly complex lives. To ensure that you live life to the fullest, set these goals based on an honest evaluation of your strengths and weaknesses. It is through an accurate self-assessment that you may choose the best path for you.

Knowing your strengths and weaknesses will help you to select the most appropriate strategies for learning and for life. As an autonomous learner, you will be able to adapt these strategies to fit an ever-changing environment, be it in the classroom or the boardroom. However, circumstances change and it is easy to let your actions hinder or even destroy your academic, personal, or professional achievements. You have the power to sustain your progress by maintaining behaviors that keep you on track and modifying those that slow your progress.

Finally, when you find you need help, always seek out the appropriate resources. If you break your leg, you do not want to be rushed to the dentist's office. If you are having difficulty with an essay for your English class, chances are a math tutor would not be your best alternative for help. As an autonomous learner, you know where to seek and whom to ask for assistance.

On this journey we have come full circle. All of the skills that we discussed throughout the text are adaptable to almost any facet of your life. We hope you will employ them not only in an academic setting, but in all the roles you will play in your life.

De Sellers
Carol Dochen
Russ Hodges

References

Anderson, L. W., & Krathwohl, D. R. (Eds.). (2001). *A taxonomy for learning, teaching, and assessing.* New York: Longman.

Apter, T., & Josselson, R. (1998). *Best friends: The pleasures and perils of girl's and women's friendships.* New York: Three Rivers Press.

Armbruster, B. B. (2000). Taking notes from lectures. In R. F. Flippo & D. C. Caverly (Eds.), *Handbook of college reading and study strategy research* (pp. 175–199). Mahwah, NJ: Lawrence Erlbaum.

Astin, A. W. (1993). *What matters in college?* San Francisco: Jossey-Bass.

Atkinson, J. W., & Feather, N. T. (1966). *A theory of achievement motivation.* New York: Wiley.

Augsburger, D. W. (1986). *Pastoral counseling across cultures.* Philadelphia: The Westminster Press.

Baddeley, A. D. (1986). *Working memory.* Oxford, UK: Clarendon Press.

Bandura, A. (1986). *Social foundations of thought and action: A social cognitive theory.* Englewood Cliffs, NJ: Prentice Hall.

Banks, J. A. (1993a). Multicultural education: Characteristics and goals. In J. Banks & C. M. Banks (Eds.), *Multicultural education: Issues and perspectives* (2nd ed.) (pp. 2–26). Boston: Allyn & Bacon.

Barkley, R. A. (1996). Linkages between attention and executive functions. In G. R. Lyon & N. A. Krasnegor (Eds.), *Attention, memory, and executive function.* Baltimore: Paul H. Brookes.

Baumeister, R. F., & Heatherton, T. F. (1996). Self-regulation failure: An overview. *Psychological Inquiry, 7*(1), 1–15.

Belenky, M. F., Clinchy, B. M., Goldberger, N. R., & Tarule, J. M. (1986). *Women's ways of knowing.* New York: Basic Books.

Benesh, B., Arbuckle, M., Robbins, P., & D'Arcangelo, M. (1998). *The brain and learning: Facilitator guide.* Alexandria, VA: Association of Supervision and Curriculum Development.

Benson, H. (1975). *The relaxation response.* New York: Quill.

Benson, H. (1984). *Beyond the relaxation response.* New York: Berkley Books.

Bloom, B. S. (1956). *Taxonomy of educational objectives.* New York: Longman.

Branden, N. (1994). *The six pillars of self-esteem.* New York: Bantam.

Bransford, J. D., Brown, A. L., & Cocking, R. R. (Eds.). (1999). *How people learn.* Washington, DC: National Academy Press.

Brewi, J., & Brennan, A. (1999). *Mid-life spirituality and Jungian archetypes.* York Beach, ME: Nicolas-Hays.

Campbell, L, Campbell, B., & Dickinson, D. (1999). *Teaching and learning through multiple intelligences.* Boston: Allyn & Bacon.

Carter, C., Bishop, J., & Kravits, S. L. (2002). *Keys to college studying.* Upper Saddle River, NJ: Prentice Hall.

Caverly, D. C., & Peterson, C. L. (2000). Technology and college reading. In R. F. Flippo & D. C. Caverly (Eds.), *Handbook of college reading and study strategy research* (pp. 175–199). Mahwah, NJ: Lawrence Erlbaum.

Center for Social Epidemiology. (2004). Job stress network: Type A behavior. Retrieved February 17, 2004, from http://workhealth.org/risk/rfbtypea.html.

Copeland, M. E. (1998). *The worry control workbook.* Oakland, CA: New Harbinger Publications.

Corey, G., & Corey, M. S. (1993). *I never knew I had a choice.* Pacific Grove, CA: Brooks/Cole.

Covey, S. R. (1989). *The 7 habits of highly effective people.* New York: Simon & Schuster.

Covey, S. R., Merrill, A. R., & Merrill, R. R. (1994). *First things first.* New York: Fireside.

Covington, M. V. (1984). The motive for self-worth. In R. Ames & C. Ames (Eds.), *Research on motivation in education: Vol. 1. Student motivation.* Orlando, FL: Academic Press.

Cowan, N. (1995). *Attention and memory: An integrated framework.* New York: Oxford University Press.

Craik, F. I. M., & Lockhart, R. S. (1972). Levels of processing: A framework for memory research. *Journal of Verbal Learning and Verbal Behavior, 11,* 671–684.

Csikszentmihalyi, M. (1996). *Creativity: Flow and the psychology of discovery and invention.* New York: HarperCollins.

Csikszentmihalyi, M. (1999). If we are so rich, why aren't we happy? *American Psychologist 54*(10), 821–827.

Davis, A., & Clark, E. G. (1996). *Study skills: T-notes and others.* Metamora, IL: Davis and Clark Publishing.

Davis, M., Eshelman, E. R., & McKay, M. (2000). *The relaxation & stress reduction workbook.* Oakland, CA: New Harbinger Publications.

Deci, E. L. (1975). *Intrinsic motivation.* New York: Plenum Press.

Dembo, M. H. (2000). *Motivation and learning strategies for college success.* Mahwah, NJ: Lawrence Erlbaum.

Ditiberio, J. K., & Hammer, A. L. (1993). *Introduction to type in college.* Palo Alto, CA: Consulting Psychologists Press.

Divine, J. H., & Kylen, D. W. (1982). *How to beat test anxiety & score higher on the SAT & all other exams.* New York: Barron's Educational Series.

Dochen, C. W. (1993). *The effects of the targeted academic groupings learning community on retention and academic performance of university freshmen.* Unpublished doctoral dissertation, University of Texas, Austin.

Dunn, R., Dunn, K., & Price, G. E. (1984). *Learning style inventory.* Lawrence, KS: Price Systems.

Ellis, A., & Harper, R. A. (1975). *A new guide to rational living.* Englewood Cliffs, NJ: Prentice Hall.

Entwistle, N. (1990). Teaching and the quality of learning in higher education. In N. Entwistle (Ed.), *Handbook of educational ideas and practices* (pp. 669–693). London: Routledge.

Erikson, E. (1963). *Childhood and society* (2nd ed.). New York: Norton.

Erikson, E. (1982). *The life cycle completed.* New York: Norton.

Fairhurst, A. M., & Fairhurst, L. L. (1995). *Effective teaching, effective learning.* Palo Alto, CA: Davies-Black.

Gagné, R. M. (1985). *The conditions of learning and theory of instruction* (4th ed.). New York: Holt, Rinehart & Winston.

Gardner, H. (1983). *Frames of mind: The theory of multiple intelligence.* New York: Basic Books.

Gardner, H. (1995). Reflections on multiple intelligences: Myths & messages. *Phi Delta Kappan, 77,* 200–210.

Gardner, H. (2000). *Intelligence reframed: Multiple intelligences for the 21st century.* New York: Basic Books.

Gardner, H., Csikszentmihalyi, M., & Damon, W. (2001). *Good work: When excellence and ethics meet.* New York: Basic Books.

Glaser, R., & Chi, M. T. H. (1988). Overview. In M. T. H. Chi, R. Glaser, & M. J. Farr (Eds.), *The nature of expertise* (pp. xv–xxviii). Hillsdale, NJ: Lawrence Erlbaum.

Glasser, W. (1998). *Choice theory.* New York: HarperCollins.

Gollwitzer, P. M. (1995). The volitional benefits of planning. In P. M. Gollwitzer & J. A. Bargh (Eds.), *Psychology of action* (pp. 287–312). New York: Guilford Press.

Guralnik, D. B. (Ed.). (1986). *Webster's new world dictionary* (2nd ed.). New York: Prentice Hall.

Haberlandt, K. (1997). *Cognitive psychology* (2nd ed.). Needham Heights, MA: Allyn & Bacon.

Halpern, D. F. (1997). *Critical thinking across the curriculum.* Mahwah, NJ: Lawrence Erlbaum.

Halpern, D. F. (2000). *Thought and knowledge: An introduction to critical thinking.* Mahwah, NJ: Lawrence Erlbaum.

Holmes, T. H., & Rahe, R. H. (1967). The social readjustment rating scale. *Journal of Psychosomatic Research, 11*(2), 213–218.

Hosinski, T. E. (1992). Epistemology. In D. W. Musser & J. L. Price (Eds.), *A new handbook of Christian theology* (pp. 150–156). Nashville: Abingdon Press.

Huitt, W. (2003, February). The information processing approach. Retrieved November 21, 2003, from http://chiron.valdosta.edu/whuitt/col/cogsys/infoproc.html.

Hyerle, D. (2000). *A field guide to using visual tools.* Alexandria, VA: Association for Supervision and Curriculum Development.

Jonassen, D. H., & Grabowski, B. L. (1993). *Handbook of individual differences, learning, and instruction.* Hillsdale, NJ: Lawrence Erlbaum.

Jung, C. G. (1923). *Psychological types.* New York: Harcourt Brace.

Jung, C. G. (1971). *Psychological types. Bollingen Series XX. The Collected Works of C. G. Jung* (Vol. 6). Princeton, NJ: Princeton University Press.

Karabenick, S. A., & Knapp, J. R. (1991). Relationship of academic help seeking to the use of learning strategies and other instrumental achievement behavior in college students. *Journal of Educational Psychology, 83*(2), 221–230.

Keirsey, D. (1998). *Please understand me II.* Del Mar, CA: Prometheus Nemesis Book Company.

King's College London. (2003). MSc in information processing and neural networks. Retrieved November 21, 2003, from www.mth.kcl.ac.uk/ipnn/subject/.

Kohlberg, L. (1981). *The philosophy of moral development.* New York: Harper & Row.

Kolb, D. A. (1999). *Learning style inventory.* Boston: Hay/McBer Training Resources Group.

Kroeger, O., & Thuesen, J. M. (1988). *Type talk.* New York: Dell.

Kurtz, E., & Ketcham, K. (1992). *The spirituality of imperfection.* New York: Bantam Books.

Lakein, A. (1973). *How to get control of your time and your life.* New York: Signet.

Lawrence, G. D. (1993). *People types and tiger stripes* (3rd ed.). Gainesville, FL: Center for Applications of Psychological Type.

Lawrence, G. D. (1997). *Looking at type and learning styles.* Gainesville, FL: Center for Applications of Psychological Type.

Lee, W. (1978). *Formulating and reaching goals.* Champaign, IL: Research Press.

LeFrançois, G. R. (2000). *Theories of human learning.* Belmont, CA: Wadsworth/Thomson Learning.

Lipsky, S. (2004). *College study: The essential ingredients.* Upper Saddle River, NJ: Pearson/Prentice Hall.

McClelland, D. C. (1961). *The achieving society.* Princeton, NJ: Van Nostrand.

McKay, M., Davis, M., & Fanning, P. (1997). *Thoughts and feelings.* Oakland, CA: New Harbinger Publications.

McMillan, J. H., & Forsyth, D. H. (1991). What theories of motivation say about why learners learn. In R. J. Menges & M. D. Svinicki (Eds.), *College teaching: From theory to practice* (pp. 39–52). San Francisco: Jossey-Bass.

Merrill, A. R. (1987). *Connections: Quadrant II time management.* Salt Lake City, UT: Publishers Press.

Miller, G. A. (1956). The magical number seven, plus or minus two: Some limits on our capacity for processing information. *Psychological Review, 63,* 81–97.

Mischel, W. (1995). From good intentions to willpower. In P. M. Gollwitzer & J. A. Bargh (Eds.), *Psychology of action* (pp. 196–218). New York: Guilford Press.

Myers, I. B., & McCaulley, M. H. (1985). *Manual: A guide to the development and use of the Myers-Briggs Type Indicator.* Palo Alto, CA: Consulting Psychologists Press.

Myers, I. B., & Myers, P. B. (1980). *Gifts differing.* Palo Alto, CA: Davies-Black Publishing.

National Center for Education Statistics. Retention rates by type of institution and by enrollment status for 1998. Retrieved October 1, 2003, from http://nces.ed.gov/.

Nelson-Le Gall, S. (1985). Help-seeking behavior in learning. In E. W. Gordon (Ed.), *Review of research in education* (pp. 55–90). Washington, DC: American Educational Research Association.

Newman, B. M., & Newman, P. R. (1995). *Development through life: A psychosocial approach.* Pacific Grove, CA: Brooks/Cole.

Nist, S. L., & Holschuh, J. (2000). *Active learning.* Boston: Allyn & Bacon.

Ormrod, J. E. (1998). *Educational psychology: Developing learners.* Upper Saddle River, NJ: Merrill/Prentice Hall.

Ormrod, J. E. (1999). *Human learning.* Upper Saddle River, NJ: Merrill/Prentice Hall.

Pauk, W. (1997). *How to study in college.* Boston: Houghton Mifflin.

Paul, R., & Elder, L. (2001). *Critical thinking: Tools for taking charge of your learning and your life.* Upper Saddle River, NJ: Prentice Hall.

Peck, M. S. (1978). *The road less traveled.* New York: Simon & Schuster.

Perry, W. G. (1970). *Forms of intellectual and ethical development in the college years.* New York: Holt, Rinehart and Winston.

Pintrich, P. R. (1995). Understanding self-regulated learning. In P. R. Pintrich (Ed.), *New directions for teaching and learning* (pp. 3–12). San Francisco: Jossey-Bass.

Porter, D. B. (1995, October 26). *Total quality and educational enlightenment.* Lecture presented for the University Lecture Series, Southwest Texas State University, San Marcos.

Provost, J. A. (1988). *Procrastination: Using psychological type concepts to help students.* Gainesville, FL: Center for Applications of Psychological Type.

Rowh, M. (1989). *Coping with stress in college.* New York: The College Board.

Schunk, D. H. (2000). *Learning theories: An educational perspective.* Upper Saddle River, NJ: Prentice Hall.

Slavin, R. E. (2003). *Educational psychology: Theory and practice.* Boston: Allyn & Bacon.

Smart, L., & Wegner, D. M. (1996). Strength of will. *Psychology Inquiry, 7*(1), 79–83.

Smilkstein, R. (2003). *We're born to learn.* Thousand Oaks, CA: Corwin Press.

Taylor, S. E., Klein, L. C., Lewis, B. P., Gruenewald, T. L., Gurung, R. A. R., & Updegraff, J. A. (2000). Biobehavioral responses to stress in females: Tend-and-befriend, not fight-or-flight. *Psychological Review, 107*(3), 411–429.

Taylor, S. E., Lewis, B. P., Gruenewald, T. L., Gurung, R. A. R., Updegraff, J. A., & Klein, L. C. (2002). Sex differences in biobehavioral responses to threat: Reply to Geary and Flinn (2002). *Psychological Review, 109*(4), 751–753.

Tieger, P. D., & Barron-Tieger, B. (1992). *Do what you are.* New York: Little, Brown.

Tinto, V. (1987). *Leaving college.* Chicago: The University of Chicago Press.

University of California, Los Angeles, Higher Education Research Institute. (1999). The American freshman: National norms for fall 1999—Record numbers of the nation's freshmen feel high degree of stress, UCLA study finds. Retrieved August 28, 2003, from www.gseis.ucla.edu/heri/norms_pr_99.html.

VanderStoep, S. W., & Pintrich, P. R. (2003). *Learning to learn: The skill and will of college success.* Upper Saddle River, NJ: Prentice Hall.

Weiner, B. (1980). *Human motivation.* New York: Holt, Rinehart & Winston.

Weiner, B. (1986). *An attribution theory of motivation and emotion.* New York: Academic Press.

Weinstein, C. E. (1988, Fall). Executive control process in learning: Why knowing about how to learn is not enough. *National Association for Developmental Education, 12,* 1–3.

Winograd, K., & Moore, G. S. (2003). *You can learn online.* Boston: McGraw-Hill.

Woolfolk, A. E. (1998). *Educational psychology* (7th ed.). Boston: Allyn & Bacon.

Woolfolk, A. E. (2004). *Educational psychology* (9th ed.). Boston: Allyn & Bacon.

Zimmerman, B. J. (1989). A social cognitive view of self-regulated academic learning. *Journal of Educational Psychology, 81,* 329–339.

Index